ISLAMIC EDUCATION IN AFRICA

ISLAMIC EDUCATION IN AFRICA

Writing Boards **and *Blackboards***

Edited by **ROBERT LAUNAY**

Indiana University Press   Bloomington and Indianapolis

This book is a publication of

Indiana University Press
Office of Scholarly Publishing
Herman B Wells Library 350
1320 East 10th Street
Bloomington, Indiana 47405 USA

iupress.indiana.edu

© 2016 by Indiana University Press

All rights reserved

No part of this book may be reproduced or utilized in any form or by any means, electronic or mechanical, including photocopying and recording, or by any information storage and retrieval system, without permission in writing from the publisher. The Association of American University Presses' Resolution on Permissions constitutes the only exception to this prohibition.

The paper used in this publication meets the minimum requirements of the American National Standard for Information Sciences—Permanence of Paper for Printed Library Materials, ANSI Z39.48-1992.

Manufactured in the United States of America

Library of Congress Cataloging-in-Publication Data

Names: Launay, Robert, 1949- editor.
Title: Islamic education in Africa : writing boards
   and blackboards / edited by
   Robert Launay.
Description: Bloomington ; Indianapolis : Indiana University Press, 2016. |
   Includes bibliographical references and index.
Identifiers: LCCN 2016030077 (print) | LCCN 2016030765 (ebook) |
   ISBN 9780253022707 (cloth : alk. paper) | ISBN 9780253023025 (pbk. : alk.
   paper) | ISBN 9780253023186 (ebook)
Subjects: LCSH: Islamic religious education—Africa,
   Sub-Saharan—History. |
   Islamic education—Africa, Sub-Saharan—History. |
   Muslims—Education—Africa, Sub-Saharan—History. |
   Education—Africa,
   Sub-Saharan. | Africa, Sub-Saharan—Colonial influence.
Classification: LCC BP43.A357 I85 2016 (print) |
   LCC BP43.A357 (ebook) |
   DDC 297.770967—dc23
LC record available at https://lccn.loc.gov/2016030077

1 2 3 4 5 21 20 19 18 17 16

In memory of my mentors

   Ivor Wilks (1928–2014)
   John Hunwick (1936–2015)
   Jack Goody (1919–2015)

   I have attempted to follow timidly in their footsteps

CONTENTS

Preface — ix

1 Introduction: Writing Boards and Blackboards — 1
   Robert Launay

The Classical Paradigm

2 Styles of Islamic Education: Perspectives from Mali, Guinea, and The Gambia — 29
   Tal Tamari

3 Orality and the Transmission of Qur'anic Knowledge in Mauritania — 61
   Corinne Fortier

4 Islamic Education and the Intellectual Pedigree of Al-Hajj Umar Falke — 79
   Muhammad Sani Umar

Institutional Transformations

5 Divergent Patterns of Islamic Education in Northern Mozambique: Qur'anic Schools of Angoche — 95
   Liazzat J. K. Bonate

6 Colonial Control, Nigerian Agency, Arab Outreach, and Islamic Education in Northern Nigeria, 1900–1966 — 119
   Alex Thurston

7 Muslim Scholars, Organic Intellectuals, and the Development of Islamic Education in Zanzibar in the Twentieth Century — 137
   Roman Loimeier

8 The New Muslim Public School in the Democratic Republic of Congo — 149
   Ashley E. Leinweber

Innovations and Experiments

9   The al-Azhar School Network: A Murid
    Experiment in Islamic Modernism   173
    Cheikh Anta Babou

10 Mwalim Bi Swafiya Muhashamy-Said: A Pioneer of the
    Integrated (Madrasa) Curriculum in Kenya and Beyond   195
    Ousseina D. Alidou

11 Changes in Islamic Knowledge Practices in
    Twentieth-Century Kenya   212
    Rüdiger Seesemann

12 Walking to the *Makaranta*: Production, Circulation, and
    Transmission of Islamic Learning in Urban Niger   234
    Abdoulaye Sounaye

Plural Possibilities?

13 How (Not) to Read the Qur'an? Logics of Islamic
    Education in Senegal and Côte d'Ivoire   255
    Robert Launay and Rudolph T. Ware III

14 New Muslim Public Figures in West Africa   268
    Benjamin F. Soares

15 Collapsed Pluralities: Islamic Education, Learning, and
    Creativity in Niger   285
    Noah Butler

Contributors   307
Index   309

PREFACE

In 2009, at the annual meetings of the African Studies Association in New Orleans, there were no fewer than three panels devoted to discussions of Islamic education in Africa, past and present: One was chaired by Leonardo Villalon, one by Cheikh Anta Babou Mbacke, and one by me. Until relatively recently, despite pioneering studies by Renaud Santerre, Stefan Reichmuth, and Louis Brenner, the subject had suffered relative neglect. Louis Brenner's work, in particular, has been a constant source of inspiration. The coincidence of these three panels, separately organized at the same time, conclusively demonstrates that this neglect is at an end and that at last Islamic education in Africa is receiving the serious scholarly attention it always deserved. Participants in these three panels, as well as various members of the audience, were invited to submit chapters to this volume, and fortunately many of them accepted with alacrity. I would like to thank all the participants in these various panels as well as their audience for their assistance and invaluable comments.

I have attempted, admittedly with only limited success, to cover the terrain as broadly as possible, with chapters discussing different forms of Islamic education as well as situated in countries with differing colonial histories. Even so, I am aware that francophone West Africa, not coincidentally the site of my own research, is overrepresented. This overrepresentation partly reflects biases in the scholarly literature, although I must accept much of the responsibility.

My colleagues at Northwestern, especially in the Institute for the Study of Islamic Thought in Africa, have been a continual source of support and inspiration. Jessica Winegar's comments have been especially helpful. Without them, this book would never have been possible. I would like to thank Christy Simonian Bean, who helped me edit the text. I am deeply indebted to Dee Mortenson's support and above all her patience, not to mention the patience of the contributors, for waiting for me to finish a project long overdue. I am grateful to Éditions Karthala in Paris for allowing me to publish a translation of Rudolph Ware III and my article, "Comment (Ne Pas) Lire le Coran: Logiques de l'Enseignement Religieux au Sénégal et en Côte d'Ivoire." The suggestions of the two anonymous readers of the first version of this book were immensely helpful.

Last but not least, I offer this volume as a tribute to my mentors: Jack Goody, Ivor Wilks, and John Hunwick. I have tried, as best as I can, to follow in the footsteps of giants in the field.

ISLAMIC EDUCATION IN AFRICA

1.
INTRODUCTION: WRITING BOARDS AND BLACKBOARDS

Robert Launay

WRITING BOARDS AND blackboards are emblematic of two radically different styles of education. Writing boards typify the centuries-old classical system of Qur'anic education. They are rectangular wooden planks on which a teacher or student writes a text, usually a passage from the Qur'an, in homemade black ink. The student then learns to recite, and sometimes memorize, the text in question. Blackboards, a nineteenth-century invention that marked the expansion of mass education in Europe and the United States, came to embody colonial institutions of education: state secular schools, of course, but also mission schools that proliferated in British, but also in Belgian and Portuguese, colonies. More recently, they have also been taken up by Muslim reformers who actively seek to "modernize" Islamic education.

The essays in this volume represent an attempt to take these different systems of education on their own terms and in historical context and to present a wide coverage of the continent—East, West, and, if to a lesser extent, Central and Southern; anglophone, francophone, and lusophone—to highlight critical similarities as well as differences. Indeed, the comparative dimensions of the subject have received relatively little attention. Bringing together the chapters in this volume constitutes a first step toward delineating the contours of the problem and of suggesting avenues for a more comprehensively comparative treatment. One of the aims of this volume is to call for a reevaluation of classical Islamic education in Africa in an attempt to understand it in its own right and on its own terms.[1]

Three important theoretical considerations underpin the collection of essays and can help to place them in a broader context. The rest of this introduction will develop these considerations in greater detail. First, writing boards and blackboards do not simply symbolize two different systems of education, but in a deeper sense literally embody them materially. Each of these supports called for different postures, different attitudes, and different behaviors, which served to inscribe different disciplinary projects on the bodies of pupils. These projects, in turn, correspond to different epistemic regimes, taken-for-granted ways of understanding the world and the word. Most if not all readers of this text take the *episteme* of the modern school system for granted. For this very reason, understanding the *episteme* of classical Islamic education on its own terms requires an effort of the theoretical imagination.

Second, as Comaroff and Comaroff (1991) and Mitchell (1988) among others have noted, the modern school system epitomized by blackboards was an intrinsic component of the colonization of Africa, in some cases even before or in the absence of direct imperial domination. This assertion comes as no surprise. However, analyses of colonial education, to the extent that they have tended to focus on one regime or another, have curiously underemphasized the very real differences between British, French, and indeed Belgian and Portuguese education in Africa, and most specifically the extent to which different colonial regimes relied on or alternatively avoided mission schools. It may seem counterintuitive to suggest that the involvement of missionaries in colonial schooling had an important impact on the attitudes of colonial administrations toward Islamic education—an impact that has often persisted after the independence of former African colonies. However, the British reliance on missionaries from multiple, and often rival, denominations opened a space for religious education in British colonies that did not exist in French, Belgian, or Portuguese territories.

Third, the centrality of mission schooling in the elaboration of different colonial policies toward Islamic education points to the importance of considering the constantly shifting field of educational alternatives, Islamic and otherwise, as a structured field. This is particularly relevant today, when neoliberal policies of structural adjustment have obliged African governments to scale down radically the public sector, and in particular public education. Brenner's (2001) pioneering account of the growth of madrasas in Mali correctly links their success to the deterioration of Malian public education without explaining the causes of their failure. As a result of this failure, parents and pupils in Mali (and elsewhere) are reduced to shopping among educational alternatives in what appears, at least superficially, to be a free market. They are obliged to weigh the costs (sometimes very literally) against the benefits of different kinds of Islamic and secular educations. The unintended consequences of this shift include the reinforcement of educational stratification by class in an African context, but also the opening of new spaces for and new forms of Islamic leadership and Islamic education—especially, though hardly exclusively, for women.

I have avoided the temptation to title this volume "*from* writing boards *to* blackboards." Obviously, in terms of a historical sequence, such a characterization is accurate.[2] Writing boards were used in Africa before blackboards were invented, much less before they were introduced in African classrooms. Unfortunately, it is all too easy to provide a teleological slant to a chronological sequence of events, to suggest that writing boards are backwards and outdated and that their replacement by blackboards is not only inevitable but, more important, represents a pedagogical advance. This was certainly the attitude of colonial educators and administrators, for whom schools were a fundamental instrument for inculcating the values and the virtues of "civilization." For the same reason, I have deliberately avoided labeling classical education as "traditional," though I have no objection to calling colonial systems of education "modern." In the first place, to label the classical mode of education as traditional implies that it is in some sense fundamentally African, a manifestation of a syncretic (and mythical) *Islam noir*, which deviated from a putatively pure Middle Eastern model. This is empirically false. The classical system has its roots throughout the Muslim world Chamberlain 1994, 1997; Eickelman 1994). Indeed, Ware (2014) has argued that classical education in Africa still perpetuates a system that once characterized the Muslim world as a whole. It is important to insist that the categorization and dichotomization of educational systems as traditional or modern is a feature of an ideology of modernity intrinsically tied to the kind of education that colonizers of whatever stripe tried to impose on their subjects. Colonial schooling was very self-consciously modern, especially in an Africa stigmatized as primitive and consequently radically backward. Muslims were (only sometimes) considered less primitive than others, though perhaps for that very reason more recalcitrant.

Educational Material, Material Education

The introduction of blackboards has, to my knowledge, largely escaped the attention of scholars of colonialism in Africa. Blackboards have been passed over in favor of clocks, looking glasses, and other sexier symbols of European technological modernity (Comaroff and Comaroff 1991, xi, 170–97). The homely blackboard, perhaps because so many of us take it for granted, has remained virtually invisible.[3] Yet there are similarities as well as differences between writing boards and blackboards. They are, after all, similar pedagogical tools, on which texts are inscribed for the benefit of pupils, only to be erased and replaced with new and different texts. But the differences outnumber the similarities. One writes with pen and ink on a writing board, just as one writes on a sheet of paper. It is important to bear in mind that, before the advent of colonial rule, paper itself was a relatively precious commodity, which certainly would not have been wasted on the training of young pupils but kept for manuscripts intended to be preserved, especially in the absence of printed books.[4] To the extent that writing boards were reserved for sacred texts, if not exclusively for passages from the Qur'an, the very act of writing on them partook of the domains of sacrality and even of (relative) permanence. Indeed Santerre (1973, 107), in his study of classical Islamic education in northern Cameroon, notes that writing boards were not to be taken home but were always left in the keeping of the teacher (see also Fortier, this volume). Santerre's suggestion that this was a means by which teachers preserved their monopoly of pupils' education by ensuring that no one else would copy passages on a pupil's writing board is uncharitable. Such boards needed to be treated with some of the reverence accorded to manuscript copies of the Qur'an. By contrast, blackboards are an intrinsically impermanent medium. Unlike pen and ink, chalk is reserved exclusively for blackboards, where writing is destined to be erased, however sacred the text may be. The ink washed off writing boards was not infrequently drunk as "medicine," its virtues depending on the text in question. It is hard to conceive of the chalk erased from a blackboard put to a similar use.

This difference, while it conveniently encapsulates and symbolizes the contrast between two radically different systems of education, also calls attention to the material supports essential to each system and the very different embodied dispositions they inculcate. Discussions of Islamic education, particularly those that have focused on explicitly modernizing projects of reform,[5] have centered on the ideological dimensions, admittedly both real and pertinent, often to the exclusion of the material and embodied realm. In particular, Foucault's (1975) analysis of modern disciplinary regimes treats schools as one institution (among others) committed to creating docile bodies.[6] Foucault's approach has been most notably employed by Mitchell (1988) in his analysis of the nineteenth-century colonizing of Egypt. Mitchell argues that the very concept of education as an autonomous domain reserved for youth is entirely a product of the disciplinary regime of the modern school. According to Mitchell, neither the scholarship dispensed by the lessons of learned doctors at al-Azhar nor the apprenticeship dispensed by village *fiqi* in the appropriate recitation and use of words from the Qur'an constituted education. Their misapprehension as such by European observers led to their characterization as simultaneously disorderly and ineffective.

Mitchell's contrast is perhaps too stark, and not always helpful in African countries where both forms of instruction have coexisted and in many cases remain either complementary or in competition. Qur'anic instruction is, after all, also a disciplinary project, but the difference between writing boards and blackboards entails the different natures of the two projects. The disciplinary practices associated with writing boards are directed toward the text as an object. The way one holds the board and the rocking motion one makes with one's whole body while psalmodying the text are geared to instilling a reverence for the exact words and intonations, either as recited or written. The practices associated with the blackboard are directed to a qualitatively different object: the lesson. Pupils are seated in orderly rows at their desks, not in an improvised circle on the ground. They are enjoined to silence unless called on to contribute to a lesson directed not specifically to them but to the entire class. Success is measured by examination, not recitation. For Gradgrind, the caricatural schoolmaster in Charles Dickens's *Hard Times*, the goal of education was to instill "facts," not "words."

Writing boards are also a concrete token of the direct and personal link between master and pupil. Only the master, his delegate—an advanced student of the master, acting as his assistant—or the pupil himself (or, more rarely, herself) at the master's instruction would write on the board. The pupil was responsible for mastering the text by reciting it correctly, aloud and melodically. Indeed, the proper recitation of the Qur'an is a fundamental Islamic discipline in and of itself (Nelson 1985). Only when a pupil had mastered a text was it washed off and replaced by another. Consequently, each pupil proceeded at his or her own pace. Lessons involved several pupils, simultaneously reciting different passages.

Blackboards, on the other hand, exemplified the relative depersonalization of the educational process. They belonged to neither the teacher nor the student but instead to the school, the institution. Their purpose was not to convey a text but rather a lesson. The lesson was not aimed at a particular student but to an entire class,[7] who were generally responsible for writing down the lesson in their notebooks. It is the notebook that permitted the student to learn the lesson—perhaps by rote—at home, at her own leisure. Reciting the entire lesson aloud was generally beside the point and usually inappropriate. Students may have been called upon—in turn and not simultaneously—to provide appropriate answers rather than to recite the text as a whole. Success was measured by examinations rather than by recitations. There is nothing, of course, to prevent a blackboard from purveying religious education, Muslim or Christian. This is indeed frequently the case. But the same blackboard may convey a passage from the Qur'an at one moment, a problem of arithmetic at another. A blackboard is, after all, only a blackboard.

The Clash of Educations?

Nowhere is the antithesis between the classical Qur'anic and the modern colonial systems of education more powerfully expressed than in Cheikh Hamidou Kane's novel, *L'aventure ambiguë* (1961). The novel opens as the central protagonist, Samba Diallo, is being beaten by his teacher Thierno for having inadvertently garbled the verse he was reciting. The brutality of the punishment is paradoxically a token of the master's deep affection for his best pupil, from whom he demands and expects nothing less than perfection. But it is not Samba's destiny to pursue his Qur'anic education. Scion of a princely family, he is selected by his family as a pioneer and leader, the first to attend colonial school and ultimately to pursue his studies in Paris. Such a portrayal of colonial schooling as a radical rupture with tradition is common to other African, especially francophone African, novels, most notably Camara Laye's *L'enfant noir* (1953).[8] However, in Kane's novel, tradition is squarely situated in the context of Qur'anic education. These two types of schools embody the contest for Samba's allegiance, and ultimately his very soul.

Of course, the notion that classical Islamic and colonial systems of education were, to some extent (if not radically), antithetical was hardly restricted to novelists. Modern education was central to the colonial project of winning over the minds (if not the hearts) of colonized subjects. Qur'anic education was, from such a perspective, an unwelcome alternative to colonial schools that lured away potential pupils while (from the point of view of the colonizers) serving no useful purpose. In the words of a colonial report on education in Zanzibar in 1925: "It cannot be seriously said that Koran schools make any real contribution to meet the educational needs of the Protectorate. They are in fact a hindrance to progress" (cited in Loimeier 2009, 47).

The education provided in Qur'anic schools was derisively characterized as "parrot talk"—the mechanical repetition of words not understood. Another colonial memorandum insisted that "It is difficult to imagine anything more deadening to potential intellect than to read aloud from morning till evening, for a period of two or three years, words of which nothing is understood.... It is indeed true that the intellectual development in the tropics, the vital importance of bringing children under proper control at the earliest possible age is obvious" (cited in Loimeier 2009, 244–45).

This combination of disdain for Qur'anic schools and distress at their resilience was hardly restricted to British colonizers. It is striking that in most sub-Saharan African colonies—and nowadays in most independent African nations—the ability to read and write Arabic was never counted as "literacy" in official statistics. French administrators were generally more apprehensive of Islam than were their British counterparts (Harrison 1988; Triaud 1974). The British, traumatized by the Indian Revolt of 1857, were haunted by the perspective of a "nativist" uprising against which Muslims constituted potential allies; 'Abd al-Qadr's resistance to the French in Algeria left them constantly apprehensive of the possibility of a pan-Islamic revolt. Seen in this light, Qur'anic schools constituted a potential menace, and the French kept files on all Qur'anic teachers as well as other ulama in their colonies.

In turn, Muslim parents could be just as apprehensive of colonial schools. For example, Dyula Muslims in the town of Korhogo, in Côte d'Ivoire, refused as long as they could to send their children to school. A friend of mine recounted how, in the early 1950s, soldiers came to the neighborhood to escort him and other boys his age, the first cohort to attend French school, by force. Such reluctance to send children to school was hardly exclusive to Muslims, nor were Muslim reactions to European education uniform. Nevertheless, the anxieties of many Muslim parents were far from irrational. They perceived the schools as purveyors of foreign ideologies, potentially if not actively hostile to Islam: Christianity and secularism.

However, it would be imprudent to make sweeping generalizations about the reactions of Muslim parents (or, for that matter, Muslim children) without taking into account the substantial differences in educational practice and policy between, and sometimes within, different colonial empires. It has long been a commonplace to contrast the French and British empires in Africa in terms of their respective preferences for direct or indirect rule, or their ideologies of assimilation or of racial difference. Subsequent scholarship has demonstrated that such differences were in fact far less pronounced. Oddly enough, the very real difference in educational policies between colonial powers has received less attention despite the centrality of the educational project to the enterprise of colonization as a whole. By and large—with important exceptions—the British were happy to leave the task of educating Africans to the missionaries. Indeed, the missionaries had preceded the imposition of colonial rule in parts of southern Africa as well as Nigeria (Comarof and Comaroff 1991; Peel 2000). Colonies were often partitioned along mission spheres of influence to avoid unseemly quarreling. Wherever it could leave the missionaries free rein, the colonial administration could dispense with the expense of providing education for its subjects. What British taxpayers at home might object to paying in the form of taxes to underwrite the administration of the empire could be freely donated in church collections to finance the missionary task of saving the minds and souls of Africans. Missionaries also played an important role in the educational systems of Belgian and Portuguese colonies; however, in both empires, the Catholic Church enjoyed an official monopoly, quite unlike the British case.

Elementary education in British mission schools was generally in African languages. Pupils who acquired literacy in their own language could thus read translations of the Bible. This was a radically different mode of conceiving the relationship between literacy and religion than in Qur'anic schools, where sacred texts were to be recited aloud in Arabic, not read privately in one's own language. Literacy was, however, only one aim of the mission schools; their goal more generally was to transform Africans into good Christians and useful subjects. However, even in schools directly run by the British administration, instruction was in local African languages, at least in primary schools.

The situation was radically different in French colonies, precisely because education had been a divisive issue in France in the late nineteenth and early twentieth centuries. The French state managed to wrest control over education from the Catholic Church, imbuing public education with an ideology of *laïcité*, or secularism. The outcome of the Dreyfus Affair, in which the army and the Church were tightly allied, represented a further triumph for secularism, with direct repercussions for colonial administration as well as education in Africa. In the early years of the twentieth century, the army lost control over the colonies, which was handed over to civilian administrators. The very bureaucracy that had successfully battled to keep the Church from controlling education at home was not about to allow it to assume control over schools in the colonies. The ideal was to teach African children in public schools staffed by teachers trained and certified in France, following a standard curriculum also determined in the metropole. Such a system was extremely costly and difficult to staff, and its expansion was seriously hampered. Under the circumstances, mission schools were tolerated, but only under the condition that they be carefully monitored and that they rigorously follow the national curriculum.

Unlike the British mission schools, instruction in the French schools was exclusively in French, from the first day of school. African languages were rigorously excluded. (In all fairness, such linguistic exclusion was enforced even more severely in France; pupils caught speaking languages such as Breton or Occitan as well as patois—regional dialects—on school premises were systematically punished and humiliated.) French colonial schools prepared their pupils for positions in the French colonial bureaucracy.

These differences in colonial systems of education had important repercussions for conditioning the attitudes of colonial administrations toward integrating the religious education of Muslim pupils into the formal educational system. These differences have generally gone unmentioned, if not unnoticed, largely because different accounts of the interaction between colonial (and postcolonial) educational institutions and Islamic religious education have focused on specific cases. Most notably, Brenner's (2001) pioneering study of the movement to reform Islamic education in Mali is framed entirely within the context of the French educational system, just as Loimeier's (2009) comprehensive study of Islamic education in Zanzibar is set within the British system. One of the aims of this volume is to present different cases detailing the workings of Islamic education under British (Thurston, Loimeier, Seesemann), French (Babou, Launay, and Ware), and Portuguese (Bonate) rule to provide a context for drawing out the implications of these contrasts.

The French system was generally hostile to all forms of religious education, a fortiori to Islamic education, within the confines of state schools. Admittedly, in the early years of the twentieth century, the French administration did open a few *médersas* in Jenne (which quickly failed), Saint Louis, and Timbuktu (Brenner 2001, 41–54). These schools combined education in French and in Arabic with the aim of attracting the children of Muslim notables. Their goal was clearly to provide a French education with an Islamic veneer—an experiment that proved quite unsuccessful largely due to French reluctance to engage Muslims on their own terms. In this respect, the British system was far more flexible. On one hand, religious education was openly accepted, if not encouraged. On the other hand, no church or denomination enjoyed an official monopoly in any colony, although they often enjoyed de facto monopolies in specific regions. While British administrators shared a disdain for classical Qur'anic schools with their French, Belgian, and Portuguese counterparts, they had no reason to object to Islamic education *in principle* as part of a school curriculum. Roman Loimeier's chapter in this volume describes how colonial officials in Zanzibar eventually co-opted Qur'anic teachers into government schools, making them responsible for a curriculum in religious education, successfully attracting Muslim pupils who had heretofore avoided British schooling (see also Loimeier 2009). In a very different vein, the British in northern Nigeria established the Northern Provinces Law School, renamed the School for Arabic Studies, with curricula in both Arabic and English, as a modern institution for training Islamic notables, notably *qadis* (Umar 2001). Such an incorporation of Islamic religious education into a British-controlled schooling had already been pioneered in Egypt (Starrett 1998) and Sudan (Thurston, this volume).

The Best of Both Worlds?

These British schools combined Islamic religious instruction in Arabic with modern pedagogy: classrooms, blackboards, a set curriculum, and (of course) examinations. Even in British colonies, the initiative for creating such schools was not always in the hands of the colonial authorities. The Yoruba Muslim scholar Kamalu 'd-Din established primary schools in Lagos (1926) and in his hometown of Ilorin (1943) that emphasized instruction in Arabic language and *tafsir*, Qur'anic exegesis. In 1947, he began to introduce the study of Western subjects as well, and his school in Ilorin was eventually recognized by the British government in 1956 (Reichmuth 1993, 184–86). Not surprisingly, similar initiatives were undertaken in French colonies beginning in the late 1940s (Brenner 2001, 54–84). A number of such schools were opened by young Muslim intellectuals who had studied abroad, particularly at al-Azhar (Kaba 1974). Such a project for modernizing Islamic education was not by any means unique to Africa but was rather common throughout the Muslim world (see, for example, Grandin and Gaborieau 1997; Lukens-Bull 2005; and Hefner and Zaman 2007).

Such schools were not simply an alternative to classical Qur'anic education. They were frequently associated with movements such as Subbanu-l-Muslimīn and yan Izala that explicitly challenged established structures of religious authority. The critique extended to the condemnation of legal formalism, the production and use of amulets and other forms of Islamic "medicine," and the legitimacy of Sufi brotherhoods among other institutions and practices. Indeed, Brenner, in his pioneering study of Islamic educational reform in Mali, has contrasted these modes of education in terms of an "esoteric" as opposed to a "rationalistic" *episteme* (2001, 7). Such a dichotomy deliberately echoes Max Weber's notion of the "disenchantment of the world" (or, in this case, a fortiori, the word). He is absolutely right to echo Foucault and to situate this dichotomy in epistemic terms (see Launay and Ware, this volume), though the characterization of these modes of education as either esoteric or rationalistic is somewhat limited. Admittedly, Sufi mystical knowledge and practice—not to mention all the activities that are grouped in francophone Africa under the general rubric of *maraboutage* (amulets, Islamic divination, astrology, and so on)—all qualify as forms of esoteric knowledge. However, the knowledge transmitted within the context of classical Islamic schools was emphatically exoteric. The association of Qur'anic schools with Sufi brotherhoods was regionally variable.[9] Even more strikingly, the mode of transmission of amulets and other forms of "secret" knowledge was often kept separate from religious education (Launay 1992, 152–57; Hamès 1997, 226–27). What the critics of classical Islamic education contest is the very legitimacy of the separation of knowledge into secret and public domains.

The central bone of contention was the very nature of knowledge and its transmission. For proponents of the new schools, the very principle of *taqlīd* (imitation) was derided as the means by which illegitimate *bid'a* (innovations) were perpetuated in local Islamic practice. Classical Islamic education embodied the evils of imitation, most obviously through its valorization of rote memorization. Admittedly, not all pupils were expected to memorize the Qur'an as long as they could recite it accurately from a written text. Still, memorizing the text was considered superior to the mere ability to recite it or even to read it with understanding. I vividly remember one *'ālim* in Korhogo chanting aloud a passage from a legal treatise while explaining it to a student. When I asked him for a copy of the text, he confessed that he did not remember where he had placed it. A colleague of his, who later became Imam of Korhogo, insisted that his knowledge was not located in his library but in his head, in the texts he had committed to memory.

More profoundly, critics objected to the principles of authority embodied in the classical system, specifically its emphasis on personal transmission. For Qur'anic teachers and their students, the quality of religious knowledge could never be divorced from the identity of its transmitter, and ultimately of the entire chain of transmission of which the teacher was only the last link. For those trained in the Middle East but also, significantly, in colonial schools, knowledge was quintessentially abstract and impersonal.

In short, these new Islamic schools combined the content of classical education with the form of the colonial school. Seen from a modernist perspective, such schools were a perfect example of Weberian rationalization, establishing set levels of progress, curricula corresponding to each level, and examinations to gauge the individual pupil's competence within such a set scheme. More recently, the writings of Foucault (1969, 1975) and Bourdieu (1977, 1979, 1984, 1989), among others, have called into question the taken-for-grantedness of such a paradigm of educational rationality. Seen in this light, the form as well as—arguably even more than—the content of education creates and perpetuates relations of power and inequality.

In any case, these new Islamic schools have by now become an established part of the educational landscape and have taken on quite different forms. In some instances, religious instruction in Arabic alternates with instruction in English or French in secular subjects such as arithmetic, the national (ex-colonial) language, history, and geography. At the other extreme, some of the Qur'anic teachers have adopted benches, blackboards, and classrooms without radically modifying the content of the education they provide. Just as the virulence of the opposition to colonial schools tended to diminish over time without ever necessarily disappearing altogether, so the acrimony that divided partisans of Qur'anic schools and modern Islamic education has tended to abate, though education remains a potentially divisive issue.

Educational Landscapes[10]

Postcolonial African nations are all characterized in varying degrees by educational pluralism, by competition between different educational institutions as well as broader systems of education. Parents are faced with the choice of what kind of school to send their children, and to which school in particular. Individual schools compete with one another for resources. Schools that rely on tuition fees to provide the funds to cover the expenses of running the school compete directly for enrollment. In state schools, the relationship is often inverted; additional enrollments may deplete rather than provide resources. Even so, the state, as an actor in the competitive system, relies on the commitment of some parents to continue to send their children to state schools. Such a situation evokes a neoliberal vision of a free market for education, a vision that presupposes that education is a commodity. There is no doubt that education has been increasingly commoditized, as evidenced by the existence of entrepreneurs who open schools exclusively with the aim of making a profit. However, even now, the very real competition between modes of education can hardly be reduced to the operations of the market, and in the past this was even less the case.

The free market paradigm, however inadequate, does highlight the existence of alternative forms of education within any educational landscape. Different modes of education coexisted and interacted, though not always competitively. Complementarity and hybridity are (not necessarily mutually exclusive) alternatives to competition. The interaction of specific modes of education within any specific historical context depends in part on the overall nature of the field of alternatives, non-Islamic as well as Islamic. The openness of British administrators to the incorporation of Islamic religious instruction into state-supported educational institutions was due, at least in part, to the prevalence of mission schools of varying denominations. This differed significantly not only from the aggressively secular French system, which discouraged public religious education in any form, but from the Belgian and Portuguese colonies, where the Catholic Church enjoyed an official monopoly in the formal educational field.

The contextual interaction between different systems of education depends, of course, on the stakes involved. It is essential, in this respect, to avoid the temptation to reduce education to a system of transmission of knowledge. Seen in this light, one could evaluate systems of education in terms of the content of the knowledge they transmit and the cost-effectiveness of the mode of transmission. This is not, of course, to suggest that the content of knowledge is irrelevant; I do not want to throw the baby out with the bath water. But if the content alone is the primary objective, then the commoditization of education makes perfect sense. But education is also something else, better conveyed by one of its French synonyms, *formation*, "forming, molding." In other words, education *forms* a youth into a type of person. Formation is the inculcation of specific dispositions, what Bourdieu (1977) terms *habitus*, dispositions that include (but are not limited to) the deployment of knowledge. Even academics are not *only* what they know.

The relationship between education and different types of personhood is perhaps more transparent in precolonial contexts. Even among Muslims, Islamic schooling was by no means universal. Girls were sometimes (though not invariably) excluded. In much of West Africa, Muslim societies were divided into warrior and clerical lineages. Typically, only youth from clerical lineages were routinely provided a religious education. Among the Dyula of the Korhogo region in Côte d'Ivoire, warrior youths were initiated into *lo* societies (Launay 1982, 1992). These two contrasting forms of education served to mold two complementary types of person. Each large warrior lineage had its separate society associated with its own sacred grove. Initiates were collectively submitted to a series of grueling ordeals, though festivities would also take place in the sacred grove. Cohorts were mercilessly hazed by their immediate predecessors, whose instructions they had to obey. More generally, they were subjected to the authority of their seniors, especially the lineage elders, whose fields they had to cultivate. The values and behaviors inculcated by such a formation included parochial allegiance to the lineage, strong ties of solidarity within one's cohort, and a pervading respect for hierarchy (but only within the kin group) entailing the privilege of making (sometimes unreasonable) demands on one's juniors at the expense of obeying such demands from one's seniors.

Classical Islamic education formed a different kind of person. Like the initiation societies, it stressed submission, but in this case the highly personalized submission of the pupil to his master as a paradigm for the believer's submission to God in Islam. Such submission might transcend kin group affiliation, unless (as was not infrequently the case) one's teacher was a senior kinsman. Such submission was perpetual and inseverable, although a single individual, especially one who pursued his studies at an advanced level, might accumulate several bonds to different teachers. On the other hand, especially given that each student proceeded at his own pace, there was virtually no institutional emphasis on cohort loyalty. This is not to suggest that pupils studying at the same time under the same master might not develop important ties of friendship or that these were irrelevant to the educational process itself. Eickelman's (1985, 98–104) illuminating description of peer learning at the Yusufiyya in Marrakesh in the early twentieth century demonstrates the importance of such ties, which nonetheless remained under the radar, so to speak, precisely because they received no institutional recognition, much less reinforcement.

The submission of pupil to master extended outside the strictly religious domain. Colonial officials were quick to condemn exploitation by those Qur'anic teachers who relied on their pupils to cultivate their fields. (Such condemnations conveniently ignored the fact that the losers, if any, were not the pupils themselves but rather their parents or other senior kin who would otherwise have relied on their labor.) However, the central aim of submission was the absolutely precise recitation and ideally the memorization of the Qur'an (paradigmatically) and other religious texts (by extension).[11] Such submission fostered the disposition to monitor scrupulously the performance of sacred speech as well as sacred activities, specifically in the context of daily prayer. Even more broadly, this stress on corporality and corporal discipline (see Umar, this volume) was designed to ensure that pupils would, in the most literal sense, incorporate the sacred Word (Ware 2014).

In short, the person formed by such an education was (ideally) scrupulously attentive to the performance of religious duties and able to deploy sacred texts appropriately as necessary. Equally importantly, he saw his personal link to his teacher as part of a vast network of ties that transcended both local and kinship loyalties. Such individuals were not necessarily learned by any means. Few pursued their education beyond acquiring the ability to recite the Qur'an (and not always the entire Qur'an, for that matter). Cleric, in the sense of a member of a clerical lineage, was one of a variety of possible hereditary social identities—including warrior, farmer, herder, craftsman,[12] or slave—corresponding to different sorts of dispositions inculcated by different (though sometimes overlapping) modes of education. A small—but absolutely critical—proportion of such clerical students went on to pursue a far more extensive education in such disciplines as *fiqh* (law), *tawhid* (theology), hadith (traditions of the Prophet), *tafsir* (Qur'anic exegesis), and even poetry (Wilks 1968; Tamari 2002; see also chapters in this volume by Fortier, Umar, and Tamari). In some communities, this education was strictly restricted to boys until relatively recently. However, in other localities, girls, particularly from clerical lineages, might receive formal religious instruction, and in a few instances might become prominent scholars in their own right. The most notable example is Nana Asma'u (1793–1864), daughter of Usman dan Fodio, leader of the jihad in northern Nigeria and founder of the Sultanate of Sokoto, who became not only a teacher but a prolific author (Boyd 1989; Mack and Boyd 2000; Boyd and Mack 2013).

The complementarity between different forms of education (including classical Qur'anic schooling) and different types of person hardly implied any idyllic state of coexistence. The jihads of the eighteenth and nineteenth centuries pitted clerical lineages (though not unanimously) and their allies against aristocratic warriors. Even so, such movements did not seek to establish a single mode of personhood but only to reverse relationships of dominance. Colonial rule, however, was far more effective in undermining such a complementary paradigm of personhood, paradoxically paving the way for mass conversion to Islam and the formation of an "Islamic sphere." (Launay and Soares 1999; Launay 2010) Qur'anic education became a means of not simply forming but of transforming persons, of marking the passage, if not of converts, at least of their children into this new Islamic sphere.

Needless to say, colonial systems of education were also attempts to transform Africans into particular kinds of persons. There were, of course, significant differences between colonial schools. Primary instruction in mission schools and even in government schools in British colonies was conducted in African languages. From the very beginning, pupils in French colonial schools were only allowed to use French in the classroom; the experience was even more radically disorienting than in British schools. One result was a high failure rate; some pupils were simply unable to manage the abrupt transition. The elitism of such a system mirrored the elitism of French metropolitan education, where access to the most prestigious schools (such as the École Normale Supérieure or Polytechnique) depended on one's performance in highly structured competitive examinations. Degrees from such elite schools guaranteed government employment in positions of power and prestige. Similarly, one's level of performance in French colonial schools qualified students for positions in the colonial administration. By way of comparison, patterns of elite education in Britain—public schools, Oxford and Cambridge—were not so easily adapted to the colonial context. Of course, missionary educators were more concerned with forming good Christians and decent, hardworking, loyal subjects than with educating future civil servants. For such purposes, education in African languages, giving access to the Bible (duly translated) and to edifying literature, was perfectly adequate.

Of course, compared to classical Qur'anic education, the similarities between colonial educational systems outweighed the differences, however real. Colonial schools all imposed a new conception of time, rigidly structuring the school day, the school week, the school year. Pupils were situated in terms of an abstract, impersonal grid. They were at a certain grade level, but a grade was hardly a cohort; an individual could, in principle, transfer from one school to another. To each grade corresponded a curriculum covering a variety of subjects in which the pupil was tested by examinations. This system of examinations was qualitatively different from the pupil's public recitation of the sacred word in the context of Qur'anic education. Such a recitation constituted a watershed, a demonstration that the pupil had achieved a specific level of mastery, identical for every individual. Students could take as long as necessary; for that matter, failure to achieve such mastery hardly impinged on one's career other than to disqualify one for a career as a scholar. Examinations, on the contrary, were all to be taken simultaneously by students of a given grade, and they measured the performance of one against another. Intrinsically competitive, they were gauges of abstract competence, not of individual virtuosity. The allegiance such a system of education fostered was to an institution, not to an individual, a cohort, a kin group, or a village.

In the process, colonial education created a whole new conception of literacy centered on the disenchantment of the word (see Launay and Ware, this volume). In classical Islamic education, the word is intrinsically sacred. Written, it is treated with precautions; recited, it is to be reproduced with exacting precision. One way or the other, the word is never reducible to its content, to a meaning that is elusive and that, with learning, can progressively be approached but not necessarily attained with certainty. Even in missionary schools, it is the message—not the word in and of itself—that is sacred. The proof is, at least in Protestant schools, that the Bible remains essentially the same in whatever language it is translated. Texts are meant to be read and above all understood; recitation is incidental to the process, and mispronunciation is a mark of incompetence but not impiety.

Colonial rule unintentionally facilitated mass conversion to Islam at exactly the same time that colonial administrations were very intentionally introducing new paradigms of education. This particular conjuncture exacerbated the competition between colonial and Qur'anic education. It was, of course, possible to send children to both kinds of schools, especially since Qur'anic schools did not have a schedule as such, in the manner of colonial schools. Pupils could attend Qur'anic school early in the morning and in the evening, before and after formal school; or on Sundays and other days when formal school was not in session. Santerre (1973, 116) documents such attempts in Cameroon (see also Launay 1982, 103–4). The results were often unsatisfactory, no doubt given the conflicting and contradictory demands made on such pupils, who often abandoned Qur'anic schooling after a few years (however, see also Butler, this volume).

As we have seen, British administrators were much more willing than their French, Belgian, or Portuguese counterparts to experiment with developing a hybrid system. The systematic incorporation of Qur'anic teachers into the Egyptian educational system provided a paradigm for such hybridization (Starrett 1998). The case of Zanzibar is instructive. Faced with disastrously low enrollments in government schools, administrators added religious instruction to the curriculum in the 1920s, with only moderate success. The integration of Qur'anic teachers as religious instructors into the schools, in the course of educational reforms in 1939–1940, effectively reversed the trend. The majority of Zanzibari children enrolled in the government schools, and education in colonial Zanzibar became, from the British point of view, a spectacular success story (Loimeieir 2009).

It is essential to bear in mind that this hybridization was never on equal terms. The incorporation of religious instruction, indeed of Qur'anic instructors, came at the price of the wholesale adoption of the *habitus* of the colonial school: schedules, curricula, textbooks, examinations, and of course the substitution of the blackboard for the writing board. However, this hybridization was not limited to British government schools that incorporated an Islamic curriculum. The Islamic schools founded by young intellectuals in French colonies after the Second World War as rivals to both Qur'anic and colonial schools were little different in this respect. It is not irrelevant that many of these intellectuals were educated at al-Azhar—that is, in a milieu that had already experienced the British experiments in hybridization for at least a generation. Indeed, according to Mitchell (1988), the colonial project of education in Egypt considerably predated the imposition of British rule. These independent French schools had (at least in the short term) a much more limited impact that British hybrids; their determination to contest both French colonial and established Islamic authorities polarized local Muslim communities, galvanizing the opposition.

Starrett (1998) has compellingly argued that this process of hybridization, the incorporation of religious instruction into Egyptian public schools under British rule, led to a profound reformulation of the ways in which Egyptians understood Islam, as what he terms "the functionalization of religion," as well as the decentering of religious authority away from the monopoly of the ulama. In a similar vein, Eickelman and Piscatori (1996) have suggested that such processes have fostered an "objectification" of Islam, the notion that Islam constitutes a fixed and finite body of knowledge that it is possible to master. Among the many unintended effects of this process was that it opened new spaces for the active involvement of women, both as students and teachers, in religious education (see chapters by Alidou and Soares, this volume; also Alidou 2005). Alongside such institutional instruction, women's piety movements that appeal to Muslim women, as Mahmood's (2005) pioneering work has demonstrated, have blossomed not only in Egypt but throughout the Muslim world—for example, in Bangladesh (Huq 2008, 2009) and Indonesia (van Doorn Harder 2006), and, of course, in Africa (Masquelier 2009; Schulz 2012; see Sounaye, this volume). These piety movements, whether they are explicitly aimed at women or target both genders, appeal particularly to younger individuals who are literate in languages other than Arabic and who feel a radical disconnect between their level of education in general and their religious education in particular.

Paradoxes of Independence: The Ivoirian Example

The decolonization of Africa was certainly not accompanied by the decolonization of the educational system. Independent African nations took over the administration of the former colonial schools, occasionally accompanied by a token Africanization of the curriculum. However, the trajectory of Islamic education can only be understood in terms of the relationship between available forms of education available in a given nation at a given time: Qur'anic schools; state schools; hybridized Islamic schools; and other schools, for example (but not only) mission schools. The divergent political and economic situations of different nations generated different trajectories, even among former French, British, Belgian, and Portuguese colonies.

This book explores some of these trajectories. In this introduction, I briefly consider the development of religious and other forms of education in Côte d'Ivoire, not because this example is typical (I do not believe there exists any typical example, in any case) but because it illustrates ways in which the changing conjuncture has affected the kinds of education Muslim parents actively seek (or avoid) for their children.

The immediate aftermath of independence afforded lucrative forms of employment for those Ivoirians who had successfully navigated colonial school.

Indeed, the supply of relatively well-paying jobs in the state sector exceeded the supply of qualified candidates. At the same time, Côte d'Ivoire was experiencing an economic boom, the so-called Ivoirian miracle, largely based on the export of coffee and cocoa. In fact, French expatriates—*coopérants*—continued to occupy many of these administrative posts (in principle to allow for the training of a new generation to replace them).

A sizable educational as well as economic gap existed between the north of the country—far from the cocoa and coffee plantations as well as from the capital and also home to a sizable proportion of the country's Muslims—and the south. All of a sudden, Muslim parents became convinced of the benefits (at least economic) of state schooling as a sine qua non for accessing employment in the state sector. Simultaneously, the Ivoirian government embarked on the project of furnishing universal primary education to all children. In the short run, it seemed as if the blackboard had triumphed over the writing board, French over Arabic (or local African languages), secular over religious education.

The triumph proved to be relatively short-lived, and by the 1970s, cracks in the system started to appear. The economic miracle began to recede in the face of declining prices for coffee and cocoa. As the economy contracted, the population continued to expand, so that it would have been necessary to continue an aggressive policy of building schools and hiring teachers simply to maintain the quality of universal state education. However, in the face of mounting debts, Côte d'Ivoire was obliged by the international community to embark on a policy of structural adjustment, and in particular to rein in government spending. Under such constraints, expanding the educational system was out of the question. The educational infrastructure began to deteriorate, the size of classes expanded, and the failure rate—always high in schools where young pupils were parachuted into an alien linguistic environment and expected to keep up with the curriculum—mushroomed. At the same time, the real salaries of government employees (especially at the lower and middle levels) continued to shrink. Teachers, needless to say, were among the first victims.

The inadequacies of public education created lucrative opportunities for entrepreneurs to open private schools. Even here, the highly centralized model of French education still applied. Such schools, if they were to be accredited, had to adhere to the curriculum as established by state authorities and were subject to inspection by state functionaries. Only with such accreditation were students able to transfer from the private to the public educational sectors—for example, from a private primary to a public secondary school or from a private secondary school to a public university. Admission to public secondary or university education also depended on passing examinations, the primary school certificate (Certificat d'Etudes Primaires), or the Baccalaureate; but admission also required a transcript from an accredited school. Of course, private schools differed widely in quality and cost. One consequence of structural adjustment was to privilege the children of the elite, whose parents often spoke French at home (thus providing them with a substantial head start) and who could afford to send them to private schools.

Under these conditions, Islamic private schools emerged as yet another alternative. In particular, Franco-Arabic schools came into existence as a new kind of hybrid, offering instruction in both French and Arabic (for similar developments in Mali, see Brenner 2001). Aside from religious instruction, they prepared pupils for the Certificate of Primary Studies. Admittedly, pupils spent significantly fewer hours per week studying the official state curriculum than pupils in state schools. On the other hand, class sizes were often smaller, allowing teachers to give pupils more individualized attention. It was certainly not a foregone conclusion that a pupil in a well-run Franco-Arabic school was far less likely to pass the certificate examination than a student in a public state school. However, the Ivoirian government staunchly refused to accredit Franco-Arabic schools. A pupil with a Certificate of Primary Studies from any of these schools was unable to pursue his or her education at the secondary level in the state system for lack of an acceptable transcript. Nor were there, at least initially, any Franco-Arabic schools that continued at the secondary level. In the 1980s, certain countries, primarily on the Arabian Peninsula, offered a limited number of scholarships for pupils from such schools to pursue their education abroad. Such opportunities, however real, were extremely limited.

The neoliberal reforms imposed on the Ivoirian government generated a (more or less) free market in education, pitting state schools, secular private schools, and Islamic schools in competition with one another. As the availability of positions in the state sector decreased sharply in tandem with salaries (if and when they were actually paid), the value of diplomas plummeted accordingly. The highest-paid positions were generally reserved for holders of university degrees from European and North American institutions, and even then, students who obtained such degrees were likely to seek employment abroad. Needless to say, this was a strategy available mostly to children of the elite. Outside the public sector—admittedly a large and important sector of the overall economy—few jobs required formal diplomas. Many more, even in the so-called informal sector, might require literacy (in French! Arabic literacy was generally not acknowledged as such) and numeracy. For example, candidates for a driver's license had to pass a written exam as well as a driving test. In the informal sector, graduates of Franco-Arabic schools were not necessarily at a competitive disadvantage.

Such a hybrid system of education was particularly attractive to Muslim parents who had been educated in state schools. Unlike Qur'anic schools, the education they provided corresponded to taken-for-granted notions—notions that, of course, had been inculcated in the course of their own education—to what school should resemble: set grade levels, curricula, notebooks, examinations, and so on. Learning, whether in French or in Arabic, involved the mastery of crucial skills and the absorption of a determined content within the confines of an institution. Singular devotion to an individual master was out of place; teachers were interchangeable and the process of learning explicitly depersonalized and abstract. Parents were also all the more likely to be convinced of the value of French literacy. The Franco-Arabic schools represented a relatively inexpensive and ideologically attractive avenue to such literacy, certainly as compared to many secular private schools. Even state schools were not cost-free by any means; parents of pupils were obliged to purchase uniforms, textbooks, and school supplies for their children and were otherwise required to make extra official or unofficial monetary contributions to the schools.

During all this time, Qur'anic schools have continued to exist, if only on the fringes of this educational free market. In a real sense, they are not selling the same commodity. Indeed, within the framework of classical Qur'anic schooling, education is not a commodity at all. One can, not entirely metaphorically, evaluate the market value of different diplomas. A classical Qur'anic education has no market value whatsoever, nor should it. Precisely for this reason, it remains an option for parents who see no need for their children to acquire literacy in French and for parents who simply cannot afford to send their children to school.

In other words, the nature of Islamic religious education, as well as of secular education, is likely to vary according to socioeconomic categories. In the past, this has created bitter ideological splits within the Muslim community. For the time being, the acrimony has subsided, not least because political developments in Côte d'Ivoire have generated anti-Muslim xenophobia among some (certainly not all) non-Muslim Ivoirians. Under such situations, Muslims have necessarily closed ranks. But the roots of the divide remain, and it is still the case that writing boards and blackboards are forming two very different kinds of Muslim persons in Côte d'Ivoire.

The contemporary interplay between competing or simply coexisting styles of educations and different histories and political and economic conjunctures is bound to vary widely from country to country, though all of them have, in one way or another, been confronted by international demands for structural adjustment that have constrained central state authority and fostered the development of different sorts of educational free markets. In every case, however, the nature of Islamic religious education has remained a central concern for Muslims, confronting them with choices whose consequences, in the long term, are neither neatly predictable nor reducible to varieties of religious ideology.

Of Writing Boards and Blackboards

The essays in this book consider in depth the different forms of Islamic education throughout the continent. The first three chapters describe the classical system of Islamic education in considerable detail, furnishing a historical baseline and a basis for comparison with newer systems of Islamic education. Tal Tamari provides a valuable comparison of classical schooling in in Mali, Guinea, and The Gambia, at both the elementary Qur'anic and the advanced level, with attention to overall similarities within a broadly unitary system and to local and regional variability in methods and emphasis. She authoritatively refutes common stereotypes about classical Islamic education—that it amounts to nothing more than rote memorization; that pupils are routinely treated with brutality; and that they are shamefully exploited—with a much more nuanced account. This multisited comparative approach is unique in the literature on classical Islamic education in Africa. Corinne Fortier provides a rich examination of classical education in Mauritania, again at both the elementary and advanced levels. She deftly analyzes the metaphorical assimilation of learning to incorporation, in the most literal sense of the word, in the classical tradition and, by extension, the privileging of orality over writing. Muhammad Sani Umar examines the career and teachings of the northern Nigerian scholar Umar Falke as a vehicle for examining the classical theory and practice of higher Islamic learning. He identifies three critical dimensions of Islamic learning: the corporeal, the use of bodily techniques to promote the physical incorporation of the text by the learner; the corpus, the existence of a shared body of texts to be mastered; and the corporate, the constitution of recognized scholarly networks. These chapters all engage with classical Islamic education on its own terms and not as a premodern and radically outdated form of education.

The next four chapters examine the transformation of systems of Islamic education, often in the shadow of state institutions but also in conjunction with colonial and postcolonial state educational establishments. Liazzat Bonate describes how, despite the systematic Portuguese disparagement of Islam and Islamic education in the Angoche region of Mozambique, colonial rule coincided with the fuller integration of Angoche into Indian Ocean Sufi networks who introduced madrasas, which continue to coexist alongside classical Qur'anic schools. Chapters by Alex Thurston and Roman Loimeier demonstrate that the British colonial administration, unlike the Portuguese (for example), was far more willing, at least in certain circumstances, to engage actively with forms of Islamic education. Thurston discusses the importation of Islamic teachers into northern Nigeria from Sudan, considered at the time less radical than Egypt. Loimeier explains how Islamic education was integrated into colonial schools in Zanzibar, if only as a means for convincing the population to send its children to British schools. All three of these chapters (as well as later chapters by Rüdiger Seesemann and Cheikh Anta Babou) demonstrate ways in which Islamic education in specific African countries was fundamentally integrated into wider regional networks either within the African continent (with the incorporation of Sudanese teachers into the Nigerian Islamic educational establishment) or outside it, with Mozambique, Zanzibar, and Kenya all included within a broader Red Sea network that involved scholars from Oman and Hadhramaut. Ashley Leinweber's chapter documents a very different kind of institutional incorporation of Islamic education into state schools, detailing the success of Islamic-run public schools in the Democratic Republic of Congo, a nation where, under colonial rule, only Catholic mission schools were recognized. The Congolese case demonstrates the paradoxical repercussions of structural adjustment and institutional breakdown in postcolonial African nations; the Congolese government has looked to religious organizations—even Islamic ones—to run schools.

These institutional transformations were often the deliberate result of the actions of individual innovators or of specific networks of reformers. Chapters by Cheikh Anta Babou and Ousseina Alidou discuss the careers of particular pioneers of educational reform. Cheikh Babou details the creation of the al-Azhar school network in Senegal by the Murid Sheikh Murtalla Mbakke. Alidou discusses the pedagogical accomplishments of Bi Swafiya in Kenya, testifying to the growing involvement of women in Islamic education as teachers as well as students. Rüdiger Seesemann describes how scholars linked to the Hadhramaut in Yemen were particularly active in Kenya, associating the spread of Islamic scholarly networks in the Indian Ocean and with new educational projects. Abdoulaye Sounaye describes novel attempts to re-educate Muslim populations through innovative means of reaching new audiences, particularly women and youth, who are the specific targets of *makaranta*, religious study groups in Niamey. The essays by Alidou and Sounaye signal the changing role of women in Islamic education, both as teachers and as avid consumers of new forms of Islamic education.

Finally, the last three chapters consider the modalities of hybridizing forms of Islamic education in terms of both new possibilities and fundamental contradictions. Robert Launay and Rudolph Ware III take their point of departure from educational controversies in Côte d'Ivoire and Senegal, attempting to understand the cleavage between classical and modernizing forms of Islamic education in terms of fundamental epistemic differences, entailing radically differing conceptions of what it means to read a text. Benjamin Soares examines a new generation of Muslim public intellectuals, new stars of mass media in Mali and Senegal, none of whom were educated in the secular state system but who have attempted to synthesize classical and modernizing styles of Islamic teaching and preaching in very different ways. Finally, Noah Butler examines the ways in which students and their parents in Niger deploy strategies to combine different forms of education in their scholastic careers—for example, through "book-ending," attending classical Qur'anic school in the early morning and evening and state secular or Franco-Arabic schools in the daytime. All these chapters examine the ways in which contemporary Muslims in Africa are actively debating, reformulating, and negotiating different ways of acquiring and deploying an Islamic education.

NOTES

1. Santerre (1973) is a pioneering study, broadly sympathetic but nevertheless limited by its tendency to characterize classical Islamic education as outdated.

2. It is in this chronological, rather than a teleological, sense that Loimeier (2009, 163) uses the phrase.

3. Paradoxically, the diffusion of new forms of technology, screens on which projectors display PowerPoint presentations from laptops, has helped draw a little attention to blackboards as a form of superannuated educational equipment.

4. On the trade in paper as a precious commodity, see Lydon (2011).

5. Discussions of Qur'anic and classical systems of education have been more consistently attuned to the material and corporal dimension (Santerre 1973; Fortier 1998, 2003, this volume; Tamari 2008, this volume; Umar, this volume; Ware 2004, 2014).

6. See, for example, his discussion of handwriting (1975:178–79). Foucault's focus on disciplinary projects has been fruitfully applied to Islamic piety movements (Mahmood 2005; Hirschkind 2006).

7. For a history of the development of classes in European education, see Ariès (1960).

8. The theme is less pronounced in anglophone African literature, perhaps because elementary education in British Africa was conducted in African languages rather than, as in French Africa, in the language of the colonizers.

9. In Korhogo, Sufism was entirely absent from the curriculum of Qur'anic schools (Launay 1992, 179–95).

10. My use of "landscapes" as a metaphor is intentionally derived from Bourdieu's (1977, 1993, 1996) notion of a "field."

11. Such an emphasis on memory and recitation were by no means peculiar to Africa; cf. Eickelman (1985) for Morocco, Chamberlain (1994, 1997) for medieval Damascus.

12. Of course, there were distinct kinds of craftsmen—blacksmiths, sculptors, and griots, for example—whose identities were not necessarily merged.

REFERENCES

Alidou, Ousseina. 2005. *Engaging Modernity: Muslim Women and the Politics of Agency in Postcolonial Niger.* Madison: University of Wisconsin Press.
Ariès, Philippe. 1960. *L'enfant et la vie familiale sous l'Ancien Régime.* Paris: Plon.
Bourdieu, Pierre. 1977. *Outline of a Theory of Practice.* Translated by Richard Nice. Cambridge: Cambridge University Press.
———. 1979. *La distinction: critique sociale du jugement.* Paris: Editions du Minuit.
———. 1984. *Homo Academicus.* Paris: Editions du Minuit.
———. 1989. *La Noblesse d'Etat: grandes écoles et esprit de corps.* Paris: Editions du Minuit.
———. 1993. *The Field of Cultural Production.* Edited and introduced by Randal Johnson. New York: Columbia University Press.
———. 1996. *The Rules of Art: Genesis and Structure of the Literary Field.* Translated by Susan Emanuel. Stanford, CA: Stanford University Press.
Boyd, Jean. 1989. *The Caliph's Sister: Nana Asma'u, 1793–1865, Teacher, Poet, and Islamic Leader.* London: Frank Cass.
Boyd, Jean, and Beverly Mack. 2013. *Educating Muslim Women: The West African Legacy of Nana Asma'u (1793–1864).* Oxfordshire, UK: Interface.
Brenner, Louis. 2001. *Controlling Knowledge.* Bloomington: Indiana University Press.
Chamberlain, Michael. 1994. *Knowledge and Social Practice in Medieval Damascus, 1190–1350.* Cambridge: Cambridge University Press.
———. 1997. "The Production of Knowledge and the Reproduction of the A'yan." In *Madrasa: la transmission du savoir dans le monde musulman,* edited by Nicole Grandin and Marc Gaborieau, 28–62. Paris: Arguments.
Comaroff, John, and Jean Comaroff. 1991. *Of Revelation and Revolution: Christianity, Colonialism, and Consciousness in South Africa,* vol. 1. Chicago: University of Chicago Press.
Eickelman, Dale. 1985. *Knowledge and Power in Morocco: The Education of a Twentieth-Century Notable.* Princeton, NJ: Princeton University Press.
Eickelman, Dale, and James Piscatori. 1996. *Muslim Politics.* Princeton, NJ: Princeton University Press.
Fortier, Corinne. 1998. "Le corps comme mémoire: du giron maternel à la férule du maître coranique." *Journal des africanistes* 68 (1–2): 199–223.
———. 2003. "'Une pédagogie coranique': modes de transmission des savoirs islamiques (Mauritanie)." *Cahiers d'études Africaines* XLIII (1–2), 169–70, 235–60.
Foucault, Michel. 1969. *L'archéologie du savoir.* Paris: Gallimard.
———. 1975. *Surveiller et punir: naissance de la prison.* Paris: Gallimard.
Grandin, Nicole, and Marc Gaborieau, eds. 1997. *Madrasa: la transmission du savoir dans le monde musulman.* Paris: Arguments.
Hamès, Constant. 1997. "L'enseignment islamique en Afrique de l'Ouest (Mauritanie)." In *Madrasa: la transmission du savoir dans le monde musulman,* edited by Nicole Grandin and Marc Gaborieau, 219–28. Paris: Arguments.
Harrison, Christopher. 1988. *France and Islam in West Africa, 1860–1960.* Cambridge: Cambridge University Press.

Hefner, Robert, and Muhammad Qasim Zaman, eds. 2007. *Schooling Islam: The Culture and Politics of Modern Muslim Education*. Princeton, NJ: Princeton University Press.

Hirschkind, Charles. 2006. *The Ethical Soundscape: Cassette Sermons and Islamic Counterpublics*. New York: Columbia University Press.

Huq, Maimuna. 2008. "Reading the Qur'an in Bangladesh: The Politics of 'Belief' among Islamist Women." *Modern Asian Studies* 42 (2/3): 457–88.

———. 2009. "Talking *Jihad* and Piety: Reformist Exertions among Islamist Women in Bangladesh." *Journal of the Royal Anthropological Institute* (N.S.) 15 (1): 163–82.

Kaba, Lansine. 1974. *The Wahhabiyya: Islamic Reform and Politics in French West Africa*. Evanston, IL: Northwestern University Press.

Kane, Cheikh Hamidou. 1961. *L'aventure ambiguë*. Paris: R. Juliard.

Launay, Robert. 1982. *Traders without Trade: Responses to Change in Two Dyula Communities*. Cambridge: Cambridge University Press.

———. 1992. *Beyond the Stream: Islam and Society in a West African Town*. Berkeley: University of California Press.

———. 2010. "New Frontiers and Conversion." In *New Cambridge History of Islam*, vol. 6, *Muslims and Modernity; Culture and Society since 1800*, edited by Robert Hefner, 254–67. Cambridge: Cambridge University Press.

Launay, Robert, and Benjamin Soares. 1999. "The Formation of an 'Islamic Sphere' in French Colonial West Africa." *Economy and Society* 28 (4): 497–519.

Laye, Camara. 1953. *L'enfant noir*. Paris: Plon.

Loimeier, Roman. 2009. *Between Social Skills and Marketable Skills: The Politics of Islamic Education in 20th Century Zanzibar*. Leiden: Brill.

Lukens-Bull, Ronald. 2005. *A Peaceful Jihad: Negotiating Identity and Modernity in Muslim Java*. New York: Palgrave Macmillan.

Lydon, Ghislaine. 2011. "A Thirst for Knowledge; Arabic Literacy, Writing Paper, and Saharan Bibliophiles in Southwestern Sahara." In *The Trans-Saharan Book Trade: Arabic Literacy, Manuscript Culture, and Intellectual History in Islamic Africa*, edited by Graziano Krätli and Ghislaine Lydon, 35–72. Leiden: Brill.

Mack, Beverly, and Jean Boyd. 2000. *One Woman's Jihad: Nana Asma'u, Scholar and Scribe*. Bloomington: Indiana University Press.

Mahmood, Saba. 2005. *Politics of Piety: The Islamic Revival and the Feminine Subject*. Princeton, NJ: Princeton University Press.

Masquelier, Adeline. 2009. *Women and Islamic Revival in a West African Town*. Bloomington: Indiana University Press.

Mitchell, Timothy. 1988. *Colonizing Egypt*. Berkeley: University of California Press.

Nelson, Kristina. 1985. *The Art of Reciting the Qur'an*. Austin: University of Texas Press.

Peel, J. D. Y. 2000. *Religious Encounter and the Making of the Yoruba*. Bloomington: Indiana University Press.

Reichmuth, Stefan. 1993. "Islamic Learning and Its Interaction with 'Western' Education in Ilorin, Nigeria." In *Muslim Identity and Social Change in Sub-Saharan Africa*, edited by Louis Brenner, 179–97. Bloomington: Indiana University Press.

Santerre, Renaud. 1973. *Pédagogie musulmane d'Afrique noire*. Montreal: Les Presses de l'Université de Montréal.

Schulz, Dorothea E. 2012. *Muslims and New Media in West Africa: Pathways to God*. Bloomington: Indiana University Press.

Starrett, Gregory. 1998. *Putting Islam to Work: Education, Politics, and Religious Transformation in Egypt*. Berkeley: University of California Press.
Tamari, Tal. 2002. "Islamic Higher Education in West Africa: Some Examples from Mali." In *Islam in Africa, Yearbook of the Sociology of Islam*, vol. 4, edited by Thomas Bierschenk and Georg Stauth, 91–128. Münster: Lit.
———. 2008. "L'enseignement islamique traditionnel de niveau avancé: cursus, pédagogie, implications culturelles et perspectives comparatives." *Mande Studies* 8: 39–62.
Triaud, Jean-Louis. 1974. "La Question musulmane en Côte d'Ivoire (1893–1939)." *Revue française d'histoire d'outre mer* 61 (225): 542–71.
Umar, Muhammad Sani. 2001. "Education and Islamic Trends in Northern Nigeria: 1970s–1990s." *Africa Today* 48 (2): 127–50.
van Doorn Harder, Pieternella. 2006. *Women Shaping Islam: Reading the Qur'an in Indonesia*. Urbana: University of Illinois Press.
Ware, Rudolph. 2004. "Njàngaan: The Daily Regime of Qur'anic Students in Twentieth-Century Senegal." *International Journal of African Historical Studies* 37 (3): 515–38.
———. 2014. *The Walking Qur'an*. Chapel Hill: University of North Carolina Press.
Wilks, Ivor. 1968. "Islamic Learning in the Western Sudan." In *Literacy in Traditional Societies*, edited by Jack Goody, 162–97. Cambridge: Cambridge University Press.

THE CLASSICAL PARADIGM

2.
STYLES OF ISLAMIC EDUCATION: PERSPECTIVES FROM MALI, GUINEA, AND THE GAMBIA

Tal Tamari

෴

THIS CHAPTER SUMMARIZES my field observations on Islamic education, made primarily in Mali but also in Guinea and The Gambia. Whereas in earlier publications, I stressed features common to several, primarily Manding-speaking, areas in Mali, in this presentation, based on research within a wider geographical region, I would also like to recognize diversity.

Research in Mali was conducted in Segou and nearby villages, San and nearby villages (1998), Touba (Cercle de Banamba, 2005), Dia and several villages of the Masina region (2004–2008), Diakhaba (2010), Djenné (2007, 2011), and Timbuktu (2006) as well as Bamako. It has thus involved areas with Bamana-, Maninka-, Dyula-, Soninke-, Bozo-, Fulfulde-, Songhay-, Moorish-, and Tamachek-speaking majorities. Briefer inquiries took place in Mandenka-speaking areas of The Gambia (2004, one month) and the Kankan (Maninka-speaking) area of Guinea (2005, 2011, five months).[1] This, then, is an updated—but still interim—report on ongoing fieldwork.

My recent observations, as well as an analysis of the literature, strongly suggest that two traits of the educational process, identified in my earlier publications, are widespread in West Africa (and beyond). As first noted by Renaud Santerre (1973), there is a distinction between two educational levels or cycles: the elementary one, consecrated to the recitation, reading, copying, and memorization of the Qur'an; and the complementary or advanced level, consecrated to the study, with comprehension, of Arabic books. However, certain types of Qur'an memorization and recitation are constitutive of advanced rather than elementary study.

The second common trait is the use of local languages—rather than classical Arabic—for oral communication in the instructional context. Thus, nearly all reading and writing take place in Arabic, while nearly all oral explanation and discussion are conducted in a local language (or, in some situations, several local languages). Oral translation into local languages appears to be the basic pedagogical tool of advanced-level Islamic education in West Africa: in the course of oral reading, the Arabic text is parsed into syntactical units, each unit being followed by one of equivalent meaning in a local language. Thus, brief strings of Arabic words alternate with ones in the African language. Translation is based on neither the isolated word (except when—infrequently—it constitutes a syntagm unto itself) nor the whole sentence, but on the syntactical unit.

Analysis of several sources suggests that a distinction between two levels of study may have been characteristic of much of the Islamic world until recently, while a dichotomy between the use of classical Arabic in writing and local languages in oral communication may be characteristic of many non-Arabic speaking areas.[2]

A third common trait of traditional Islamic education in West Africa, stressed by both Santerre (1973) and Louis Brenner (e.g., 1993, 2001), is the highly individualized nature of instruction: although pupils may meet collectively, each receives his or her individual lesson. While individual instruction in Qur'an recitation and memorization may be the general rule in the Islamic world, its extension to advanced education could be regionally more restricted. Lectures and seminars also may have been more characteristic of advanced education in West Africa at certain times in the past (see Diakité 1991; Hamès 1997) and are an important feature today of the transmission of religious knowledge to adults in nonscholastic contexts.

On the other hand, some aspects of the educational process reveal considerable diversity. This diversity, which is correlated to linguistic, regional, and/or "ethnic" identities, concerns such matters as: school schedules; the pedagogy of reading and writing; memorization requirements; the books and disciplines studied and the order in which they are studied; Qur'an recitation and poetry chanting styles; diplomas and other procedures for certifying competence; and the social and economic contexts of education.

For reasons of space, this chapter will concentrate on the more conservative forms of Islamic education for children and youth, though it will evoke their multifaceted relationships to the madrasa, or modern Islamic schools, and the state school systems (which operate primarily in European languages). But "traditional" education itself has been undergoing a kind of modernization—with the replacement of most manuscripts by printed books and the introduction of new books, new subjects, and new pedagogical methods with associated scholastic accessories such as blackboards. These changes, which until now have been undertaken largely at the initiative of individual teachers, may be expected to accelerate as government departments and nongovernmental organizations attempt to "improve," "reform," and control.[3]

Traditional schools still provide the only form of Islamic education available in many rural areas, and in some cities and large villages, including Dia and Djenné, all children attend for some time. The number of schools has increased in some localities, though it has decreased in others.[4] Children and young people from regions and populations where local religions were until recently dominant are now attending in large numbers, whether in their home areas or ones where Islam has been established longer.[5] The educational practices and curricula of these more conservative forms of education have also had, as I have shown elsewhere (Tamari 2009), a determining impact on the madrasa and other newer forms of Islamic education.

Types of Schools, Recruitment of Pupils and Teachers

Elementary Qur'anic instruction and the advanced study of books are designated by distinct terms in the several languages of the region. For clarity's sake, in this chapter, I refer to establishments offering the first level (or, in some instances, both levels) of study as Qur'anic schools and those offering the second level as *majlis* (from an Arabic term connoting a learned assembly, widely used in the region to refer to the upper level of study).[6]

In addition, one must distinguish at least two types of schools: sedentary ones and ones in which both teachers and pupils may change places of residence several times a year, every year. All the cities and villages visited have sedentary schools run by resident teachers. These teachers may also accept pupils from out of town (or out of the village), who reside with them year-round, often for several years. On the other hand, the Fulbe (whether or not they are still nomadic) and the Bella (former dependents of the Tuareg) have some schools in which pupils, most of whom are recruited within a given geographical area, follow their teachers on a circuit. Every year, they return to some of the same places, staying in each place for a few days to a few months. Relatively large and prosperous settlements with a tradition of learning, such as the cities of Djenné, Timbuktu, Segou, and San, are considered especially appropriate for longer stays, since teachers and pupils rely on local populations to donate food. These school groups may either camp on the periphery of towns and villages or seek accommodation within them. For the past several decades, Mossi teachers and pupils from Burkina have also been itinerant in Mali; at present, they are particularly numerous in the Segou area.

In Djenné, a further distinction between teachers who have studied and settled in the city but cater exclusively to out-of-town pupils, often from their own home areas, and autochthonous (or fully assimilated) teachers, who cater to both in- and out-of-town pupils, is also pertinent.

Some normally sedentary teachers may go on pupil recruitment trips, especially in recently Islamized areas; they may also accept new pupils while traveling for other purposes. On any trip, they may take their regular pupils with them; alternatively, they may leave them in the care of their associates or assistants or of another teacher.

In the places visited, most sedentary teachers are native to the villages or cities in which they teach or to nearby areas. Furthermore, most have received much or all of their religious education in their current teaching locality—sometimes primarily or exclusively within their own families; Touba is the most extreme example. However, nearly all have had more than one teacher. On the other hand, in Diakhaba (perhaps because local traditions of learning were interrupted), it is considered preferable to also study elsewhere; Jaabikundaa, a village of the Diakhanke of Guinea Bissau, is the most usual destination.[7] Nevertheless, some students and scholars travel extensively in search of teachers who can instruct them in particular books. Certain towns and villages—including Djenné, Segou, and Dia—attract large numbers of out-of-town students. Many may be from the immediate periphery of these towns, but others come from distant places in Mali and from neighboring countries—most frequently Guinea, Guinea Bissau, or Burkina. Diakhaba, though it sends many of its own students abroad to Guinea Bissau, receives students from Senegal. I have encountered two scholars, one in Djenné and one in Timbuktu, who spent several years studying Maliki *fiqh* (law and cultic obligations) in Sudan.

Certain schools regularly receive pupils from a particular village, and fathers who have studied in a particular school often send their children there—to study with their own teacher, his son, or his grandson (or even his granddaughter; see below). In some areas, including Djenné and Dia, one may speak of teaching lineages and lineages that supply them with students—whose members may or may not, as a matter of family custom, go on to teach themselves. Younger out-of-town pupils usually lodge with their teachers; older ones (unless there is a particular link between the two families) often seek another host.

All teachers in the traditional sector have been trained in it. However, some have also attended state schools or the madrasa—sometimes to a high level. For example, I encountered a Djenné teacher who had been through the seventh grade and another who had successfully completed secondary school. A University of Bamako sociology student helps teach the Qur'an and some beginner-level books at his uncle's school in Dia. The director of one of Kankan's largest Qur'anic schools (offering both levels of study) had attended the local state schools, returning from many years living and working in New York City to assume this responsibility at his family's request. Some madrasa directors, including several who have engaged in lengthy study in Arab countries, also run Qur'anic schools and/or *majlis*. A fair number of younger Qur'anic teachers have studied at madrasa, leading them to introduce aspects of their methods and curricula into their own schools (see below).

Few schools, even the smallest, are entirely taught and run by one person. The director (i.e., the person who has ultimate responsibility for the welfare and progress of the pupils)[8] nearly always has one or more associates or assistants; these are usually pupils, former pupils, or members of his immediate or extended family. Some teachers and schools offer both elementary Qur'anic instruction and the advanced study of books, whereas others specialize in one level only. Many Qur'an instructors do not possess the knowledge to teach books, but some persons who are fully competent in both fields may choose to teach only one. In establishments that offer both courses, the director usually concentrates on books, while his assistants or associates teach beginning Qur'an pupils. However, a director may also (for example) concentrate on Qur'an pronunciation or recitation and leave book instruction to his associates.

As noted in the literature, school enrollments are highly variable: pupil numbers may vary from a handful to several hundred. Nowadays, many directors keep lists of their pupils' names. Teachers and pupils typically meet in the director's (permanent or temporary) home, in a vestibule or an inner room. However, in some larger establishments, several rooms, or even a house, may be reserved for this purpose. According to oral traditions, certain structures have been reserved exclusively for scholarly purposes for more than a century; these are usually, though not always, located within the compounds of scholarly lineages.

The itinerant schools accept only boys. In contrast, all other schools visited are currently coeducational. In Touba, this is said to be a recent development: both Malikis and Wahhabis state that they began teaching girls as a result of Wahhabi emphasis on female education. Elsewhere, this seems to have been the case for at least some generations. Nevertheless, girls are nearly always in a minority, because they typically spend fewer years in school than boys. Yet several schools in Dia and Diakhaba have some older girls, who have completed the recitation of the Qur'an and are studying books, in attendance. One Dia teacher has several advanced adult women students. Girls, even older ones, are not usually spatially separated from boys.

Although the overwhelming majority of Qur'an and *majlis* teachers are men, there are a few women scholars. In Dia, one woman runs a Qur'anic school. She has a male assistant and teenage boys as well as young children among her out-of-town lodgers. A second woman, who is currently studying books, provides most Qur'anic instruction at her brother's school. A third woman (who has since left to join her husband in another village) used to have her own school there, and she now runs a school in the second village. Another Dia woman, who died in the 1980s and was likely born in the 1920s or earlier, used to teach with her husband. A woman scholar from Djenné, who died in 2007 and was probably born in the 1930s, used to teach both Qur'anic school and *majlis* with her husband; after his death, she continued on her own. All but the last-mentioned woman came from scholarly families and studied primarily within their extended families. All were married to scholars; the last-mentioned woman studied primarily with her husband. The first- and third-mentioned Dia women are admitted to read the Qur'an and devotional poems on ceremonial occasions, on a par with men; they are also well known for their ability to do esoteric work, and one travels extensively, and internationally, for this purpose. The now-deceased Dia woman commented the Qur'an publicly, to mixed audiences, in Ramadan, as did the woman from Djenné. All these women (with the exception of the second-mentioned) teach *majlis* subjects to youths and men. The Djenné woman also organized and taught religious knowledge classes specifically for women. Several women from scholarly families in Segou are reputed for their Islamic knowledge, though they do not teach.[9]

Study Programs

School Schedules and Holidays

School schedules vary greatly. A common scheme, characteristic of Dia, Djenné, San, and Kankan, is to hold instruction in the morning, from shortly after sunrise until about noon, then again from just after the *zuhr* prayer (early afternoon; about 1:30–2:00 p.m.) until the ʿ*asr* prayer (midafternoon; about 4:00 p.m.); in many schools, the teacher or an older pupil leads the ʿ*asr* prayer. However, in Timbuktu and Touba, as well as at some schools in The Gambia, study begins before sunrise, about 4:00 a.m.; pupils break for the dawn prayer and breakfast, then resume study. In Touba and Timbuktu, they may return for an afternoon session. In Touba, Timbuktu, and The Gambia, as well as at Fulbe schools in the Masina, there is a night session after the ʿ*isha'* (nightfall) prayer (8:30 or 9:00 until 10:00–10:30 p.m.). In Djenné, students from scholarly families (but few others) add an evening study session: older family members may help the younger ones understand and review their lessons in a relaxed, congenial atmosphere. In the historic village of Diakhaba, most schools have an early-morning session, just after sunrise, ending at about 8:00–8:30 a.m., when children return to their homes for breakfast, and an evening study session, after the ʿ*isha'* prayer. However, some Diakhaba schools have an evening session only. Nowadays, Qur'anic schools in Segou, where a significant percentage of children have been attending state schools and/or madrasa for decades, meet only in the morning; in the past, they also met in the afternoon.

In all establishments and localities visited, no classes take place on Thursday. Several teachers explained that the day is considered inappropriate—"unblessed"—for study. In the great majority of schools, classes are also in recess on Wednesday afternoon and Friday morning. However, in some Fulfulde-medium schools in Djenné, pupils study Wednesday afternoon but have both Thursday and Friday off.

Book students are not usually required to be in attendance at all hours; in most instances, they make an appointment with their teacher for their individual lesson within the framework of the above schedules. However, a few *majlis* may opt for a schedule (for example, only in the morning or only at night) that does not correspond to that of the local Qur'anic schools. Each lesson may last from about five to thirty minutes (five to fifteen is most usual). Depending on his other occupations, a student may stay on school premises to revise his lessons or listen in on lessons for other students.

Agricultural activities have a considerable impact on school schedules. In large villages such as Dia and Djenné, younger pupils attend both morning and afternoon sessions all year round. However, in rural schools in The Gambia as well as in the village of Diakhaba, the morning session may be curtailed or canceled for all pupils or for all but the youngest pupils during the planting and especially the harvest seasons. In Diakhaba, Djenné, Dia, and in the Masina, young men may completely suspend their study at these times—bringing many *majlis* to a standstill.

For about a century and increasingly over the past few decades, Qur'anic school schedules have also been influenced by the constraints of school attendance. Thus, in urban areas, the afternoon session may be canceled and both morning and afternoon sessions abridged for school attendees. In Dia, where majority school attendance is more recent, there is a constant tension between the teachers of the state and Qur'anic schools, who mutually remonstrate with each other for keeping the children overlong. In Mali generally, many older pupils attend early-morning sessions or on weekends only. In Timbuktu and Kankan, where many families are not involved in agriculture, many Qur'anic schools have hugely expanded enrollments during the state school holidays, especially during the long vacation from early July through the end of September. These seasonal pupils often concentrate full-time on their religious studies at these times.

Religious holidays also impact school schedules. In general, every effort is made to keep younger pupils in near-continual attendance. These pupils usually have three days off for ʿId al-adha, also called al-ʿId al-kabir, the Sacrificial or Great Festival, and for ʿId al-fitr or al-ʿId as-saghir, the Festival of the Breaking of the Fast or Lesser Festival, marking the end of Ramadan. They also usually have off one to three days—occasionally a whole week—for Mawlid (the Prophet's birthday). For older or advanced pupils, regular instruction is suspended during Ramadan (or at least the afternoon and evening study sessions). These pupils attend the Qur'an commentaries and other ceremonial readings that are organized for scholars and the wider public at this time. Older or more advanced pupils may also have up to about two weeks off after the Sacrificial Festival. In the month leading up to the Prophet's birthday, their evening study sessions may be given over, or evening study sessions may be added, to practice the reading and chanting of compositions commemorating this event. All pupils may have one to three days off for ʿAshura' (Tenth Muharram, often described as an Islamic New Year). In Djenné and the Fulbe villages of the Masina, all study is suspended for two weeks beginning on Laylat al-Qadr (the Night of Destiny, 27 Ramadan, commemorating the inauguration of the revelation of the Qur'an to the Prophet), on which school closing ceremonies may be held.[10]

The total amount of time a pupil may devote to his studies thus varies according to the locality, age, and social background. Pupils from well-off scholarly families in Touba may spend nearly all their waking hours studying, revising even during the daily breaks or on off days, and seeking advice from their teachers as necessary. On the other hand, a poor, out-of-town student may have to work full-time during the agricultural season and for much of the day the rest of the year—studying at best a few hours per day, for a few months of the year.

Elementary Qur'anic Study

All children in Dia, Djenné, and Diakhaba and all the children from Maliki families in Touba currently attend Qur'anic school for several years, as do most children in Timbuktu. Many children in Segou also attend. Both boys and girls attend, though boys typically stay on for longer than girls, and in at least one instance (Touba), Qur'anic school attendance for girls appears to be recent.

Pupils are said to have been traditionally inducted into school at about age seven; bright children from scholarly families may be inducted at about age six. Younger children may, however, sometimes accompany older siblings to school. In Segou, many three- to five-year-olds attend before entering a state school or a madrasa—but this appears to be a development of the past few decades.

Pupils usually begin their Qur'anic studies on an auspicious day, as determined by astrological calculations. For this reason, several children may be inducted at the same time—though with the exception of holidays and inauspicious times, admission may be continuous throughout the year. Almost invariably, the teacher begins by writing blessings on the pupil's hand, which the pupil then absorbs by licking.[11]

In nearly all schools, the pupil begins by learning how to read the *basmala*—the words *bi-smi llahi*, "In the name of God," which introduce all the suras of the Qur'an (except sura 9) and must be pronounced before undertaking any important activity. The teacher may have the pupil repeat these words after him and explain how the letters are read. Then the pupil starts to read the Qur'an, beginning with the Fatiha (first sura), then proceeding to the last sura (sura 114), then working his way forward in the Qur'an. Learning to read involves three distinct phases. First, the pupil is taught the names of the letters of the Arabic alphabet, learning them in the order in which they appear in the Qur'an. After the pupil has learned to recognize and say aloud the name of each letter, he goes back over the same suras, this time learning to read and recognize the different syllables. In the third phase, the pupil learns to read and pronounce whole words and verses. Again, he or she begins with sura 1 (the Fatiha), proceeds to sura 114, and then, preferably, at least until sura 78 (the first sura of the last *juz'* [thirtieth division] of the Qur'an). Pupils with time and ability will then proceed to the beginning of the Qur'an (sura 1). This first reading may be followed by one or more additional readings. Priority, then, is given to the Qur'anic text, rather than the alphabet, in learning how to read.

In and around Timbuktu, pupils first learn the letters of the alphabet and the various syllable combinations before acceding to the Qur'anic text. This pedagogical method is called *abatasha*, with reference to the newer ordering of the Arabic alphabet, in which letters are grouped according to their shape (as distinct from the *abajada* alphabet, which is the same letters but in an order inherited from earlier Semitic alphabets that determines their numerical values). At each lesson, the teacher will first trace one or more very large letters in the sand; he will require the pupil to remember their names. To ensure that the pupil has indeed understood the relationship between the form and the name of each letter, the teacher will, after some days or weeks of practice, modify the order in which he presents the letters to his pupil. When he feels that the latter has fully mastered the individual letters, the teacher introduces the signs denoting the short vowels, vowellessness, and nunation as well as the consonant-vowel combinations corresponding to the long vowels. The pupil will be tested with all possible combinations, presented in different orders, before being allowed to proceed to the next phase—the Qur'anic text. In the interval, the teacher will have progressively reduced the size of the characters he traces in the sand. It is only in the next phase that the teacher will write on the writing board—beginning with the first sura of the Qur'an, then proceeding to sura 114 and forward to the beginning of the Qur'an (as in the pedagogical method summarized above). Even the oldest persons I interviewed in Timbuktu (about age 75) could remember no other method for learning how to read, which suggests that it must date from at least the 1930s.

Teachers state that, with this method, which they claim is traditional in Timbuktu, even the dullest child will learn to read within a few months.

A somewhat similar method in which the letters are learned in the order of the *abajada* alphabet has been reported of some schools in Senegal, where it was considered an exceptional and innovative pedagogy (Ndiaye 1985, 42). A Diakhaba Qur'anic teacher who had studied in a madrasa for some time has introduced collective reading exercises, taken from madrasa booklets, for his beginning and intermediate Qur'anic school pupils (in their first four years of study). One Dia teacher (though he had not studied in a madrasa) introduced madrasa-style reading and grammar exercises, written on a blackboard, for some of his pupils.

Manding, Soninke, Fulbe, Bozo, and other linguistic groups have their own names for the letters of the Arabic alphabet.[12] These names are similar, though rarely identical, to the classical Arabic ones (employed in the madrasa and in Western textbooks). Qur'anic schools nearly always refer to the older, *abajada* order of the alphabet; except in Timbuktu, the *abatasha* order is associated with the madrasa. Qur'anic schools always teach the Maghrebi form of the Arabic characters; this is now rare in the madrasa.

Children begin learning how to write only after they have achieved a certain proficiency in reading. Most teachers say they evaluate each child's readiness individually; but one complete reading of suras 1 and 114–78 appears to be a minimum requirement. The instructor may outline the letters on the writing board, using the blunt end of his reed pen or an empty ballpoint pen, and have the pupil go over these traces (known in Bamana as *tiiri*) with ink. Alternatively, the instructor may write a short text (initially, in large letters) and ask the pupil to copy it. Often an initiation involving tracing may be followed by practice in freehand copying. At some schools, the instructor may guide the beginner's hand. Only very advanced students and full-fledged scholars write on paper—a skill particularly important for the preparation of charms.

In schools offering two or more study sessions per day, each session has a specific content. In most establishments, the pupil begins the morning session by revising his lesson. He then reads aloud from his writing board to the instructor. If his reading is correct, the instructor will write out a new text (or read out loud to the pupil the next portion of the text if it is already on the writing board). The pupil will repeat these words or syllables once or twice to the instructor, who will, if necessary, read the text aloud again. The beginning pupil will then spend the rest of the morning session, and usually the afternoon and/or evening sessions, repeating the text out loud to himself as he gazes upon his writing board. If the pupil is confused, he may ask the instructor to read it to him yet again. Except when the teacher has not had time to listen to all his pupils in the morning, or for unusually bright pupils at some schools, writing is done only in the morning session. Pupils generally wash off their writing boards—usually into jars where the precious runoff is kept—in the morning only. Beginners may initially study only one or a few syllables. More experienced pupils may study several words, then one or more verses, per day.

External observers often consider that this kind of reading is a form of memorization. Indeed, the pupil does his best to remember his teacher's pronunciation. But he or she is also expected to understand the relationship between the graphs on the board and articulated sounds (though in fact some children do not). Furthermore, the pupil is not expected to be able to reproduce the syllables or words without the graphic support even a few days later. This, then, is not memorization (except perhaps of a very short-term kind), nor is it necessarily reading as commonly understood; the process is perhaps best described as recitation, aided by both aural memory and graphic recognition.

Transition to Advanced Study: Qur'an Memorization Requirements

Qur'an reading, recitation, and memorization requirements (and ideals) vary considerably as a function of geographical area and of cultural, linguistic, and ethnic affiliations. The most familiar paradigm, characteristic of many Manding (Malinke, Bamana, Dyula-speaking) and Fulbe-speaking areas, is the requirement that the Qur'an be read three times; the third reading involves long-term memorization of the oral form of the Qur'an—that is, the expectation that one will be able to recite it without a graphic support and remember this recitation indefinitely.

Among the Soninke, the Mandenka of The Gambia, and some Fulfulde speakers, students may go through the Qur'an three, four, five, or even six times to achieve flawless verbal recall. In addition, the ability to write out the Qur'an from memory is highly regarded. It is only after the Qur'an has been read and recited at least three times that a student will attempt to learn to write it from memory. His achievement may result in the production of a full manuscript of the Qur'an, written on fine paper.[13]

According to several Soninke scholars in Touba, there are two curricular options: one aims for total memorization of the Qur'an plus basic study of a few books, and one opts for in-depth study of a large number of books but a lesser knowledge of the Qur'an. Different lineages may specialize in one or the other of these two curricula. Qur'an memorization techniques in Touba are highly formalized, with the most advanced students revising one *thumn* (one-eighth part of a *juz*'; local pronunciation *sumunu*) at a time.

In contrast, in Dia, pupils are only required to read and recite the Qur'an twice before going on to other studies. At this stage, they are not always able to read the Qur'anic text fluently. Many Dia scholars do in fact know the Qur'an by heart, but this is a knowledge that comes from repeated practice in reading and teaching. In Kankan, memorization of certain suras only—including the Fatiha, the short suras at the end of the Qur'an, S. Maryam (19, "Mary"), and S. Ya Sin (36)—is required. S. Ya Sin is considered especially protective throughout the Islamic world. In Kankan, Maryam is considered particularly significant, in part because it describes how, in her childhood, Mary, the mother of Jesus, was miraculously provided with food. Among the Moorish speakers of Timbuktu, apt pupils are encouraged to memorize the entire Qur'an. However, it is recognized that, for others, the memorization of the longer suras is a nearly impossible task.

Not only do Qur'an memorization requirements vary according to milieu, but so do Qur'an recitation styles. In most of the localities visited, most scholars in reciting the Qur'an take into account only the signs used in ordinary writing. Though they claim that they are conforming to a particular recitation system—usually Warsh, the one most widely recognized in the Maghreb—because their manuscripts or printed volumes are arranged and punctuated accordingly, in fact they are rarely familiar with all the relevant rules. However, among the Fulbe of Djenné, persons considered to be *hafiz* (memorizers of the Qur'an) have studied one or more of the recognized recitation systems.[14]

In addition to recitation styles deriving from the early Islamic received tradition are local or "ethnic" ones. The Fulbe have a very rapid recitation style, which allows them to recite the entire Qur'an in less than fifteen hours (the various Near Eastern rapid recitation styles require at least forty hours). The Songhay of Djenné may sing the shorter suras at certain ceremonies—for example, that in which former Qur'anic schoolmates come to greet and congratulate the bridegroom some days prior to his wedding. Qur'an recitation in Dia, in the context of the ceremonial Qur'anic exegesis held in Ramadan, can be very melodious, with each verse being initially read, in a kind of chorus, by all three persons involved in the performance; the rhythm of this chorus and of the Bozo oral translation recalls that of the Segou epic.[15] Segou and San once had similar Ramadan Qur'an recitation styles, but these have been abandoned.

Some Qur'anic schools have specific ceremonial or ritual Qur'an recitation practices. The woman teacher in Dia ended each day's study by chanting from the Qur'an with her pupils and asking them to repeat certain verses after her—one of the rare instances in which Qur'anic pupils are required to recite as a group. She explained that this custom went back to her grandfather. A teacher in Djenné chanted the Qur'an to his pupils every Wednesday, just before the weekly break—a practice inherited from his father. In Diakhaba, several schools close the evening or the week with Arabic songs recently introduced by a Qur'an teacher who had studied in a madrasa. All the schools in Diakhaba hold once or twice weekly evening sessions, in which the recitation of Qur'an verses from memory, mostly by younger pupils, is followed by a blessing ceremony.

As a consequence of the lesser memorization requirements, pupils in Dia and Kankan may begin the study of books in their early to mid-teens. In Touba and the Masina, some advanced memorization pupils may undertake the study of shorter books, while others wait until they have terminated this process. Where full memorization (three or more recitations of the Qur'an) is required, the in-depth study of books does not begin until age 18 (for the most precocious); usually it begins for students between 25 and 40 years of age. Nowadays, in many localities, memorization requirements are no longer strictly observed. For example, in Djenné, many out-of-town students are admitted to the study of books after only two readings of the Qur'an.

Study of Books

Depending on the locality, pupils may begin their study of books either with *tawhid* (theology) or *fiqh* (law and cultic obligations). Starting with theology is more characteristic of rural areas. As one scholar, hailing from a small village in the Cercle de San, remarked, *tawhid* is important because it teaches one "to know oneself, to know God." Furthermore, he added, one cannot know oneself without knowing God, nor God without knowing oneself. Where *tawhid* is the first subject, it is usually studied from brief, often manuscript texts. Some of these texts consist in extracts from the Algerian Muhammad as-Sanusi's (1435–1490) *al-ʿAqida as-sughra* ("the lesser credo"; also known as *Umm al-barahin*, "the source of decisive proofs")—the book itself being considered a topic of advanced study. A pupil who begins with one of the smaller *fiqh* booklets may go on to a brief theological treatise, or he may immediately pursue the study of additional *fiqh* texts.

Introductory *fiqh* books studied include (often in this order): *al-Muqaddima al-qurtubiyya*, also known as the *Urdjuzat al-wildan*, by the Andalusian Yahya al-Qurtubi (1093–1172), which also includes some elements of theology; the *ʿAshmawiyya*, so named after its sixteenth-century author ʿAbd al-Bari al-ʿAshmawi; *al-Muqaddima al-ʿizziyya* by the Egyptian ʿAli al-Manufi (1453–1532); and the *Mukhtasar fi 'l-ʿibadat*, often known simply as *Al-Akhdari*, by the Algerian ʿAbd ar-Rahman al-Akhdari (1514–1576).[16] The last-mentioned book, exclusively consecrated to the ritual obligations, is considered the fullest treatment of prayer and therefore sometimes as an already advanced work.

The *Risala* (Epistle) by the Tunisian ʿAbd Allah b. Abi Zayd al-Qayrawani (922–996) is considered a comprehensive, advanced text, with chapters devoted to family, marriage, and inheritance as well as sections on prayer and the holy days and such questions as the legitimacy of amulets. The most advanced texts, studied by only a few, include the *Tuhfat al-hukkam* (Gift for judges), a versified manual for judges, also known as the *ᶜAsimiyya* after its author, the Andalusian Muhammad b. ᶜAsim (1359–1426), and above all, at the summit of the legal curriculum, the *Mukhtasar* (Abridgment) by the Egyptian Khalil b. Ishaq al-Djundi (d. ca. 1374), studied with the aid of commentaries. The *Muwatta'*, attributed to the founder of the Maliki school, Malik b. Anas (ca. 716–795), and the *Sahih* of the Iranian Muhammad al-Bukhari (810-870), one of the largest and most authoritative collections of hadith (deeds and sayings of the Prophet), are widely studied in Timbuktu (and read, but rarely studied with a teacher, elsewhere).

In some places and with some teachers, *fiqh* is virtually the only subject studied. However, in other places, the study of several *fiqh* books (often through the *Mukhtasar fi 'l-ᶜibadat* or the *Risala*) may be followed by the study of other disciplines, such as Arabic grammar, language and literature, and advanced theology.

Grammar texts include the *Lamiyyat al-afᶜal* (Poem about verbs, rhyming in *l*), by the Andalusian Muhammad b. Malik (1203–1273), for the study of *sarf* (morphology), and the *Alfiyya* (Thousand verse composition), also by Muhammad b. Malik, as well as the *Muqaddima* (Introduction), also known as the *Adjurrumiyya*, by the Moroccan Muhammad b. Adjurrum (1273–1323), for the study of *nahw* (syntax). These textbooks are standard throughout the Islamic world.[17] The *Adjurrumiyya* is generally studied with a commentary; in Segou, some now use *at-Tuhfa as-saniyya* (The gleaming gift), an early-twentieth-century work that includes exercises and was initially introduced by the madrasa. The *Qatr an-nada wa-ball as-sada* (Dewdrops for the quenching of thirst), written by the Egyptian ᶜAbd Allah b. Hisham (1309–1360) and highly praised by Ibn Khaldun, is considered the fullest and most advanced treatment of syntax; it is studied by some erudite scholars.

Scholars who teach Arabic grammar routinely give examples in their students' native languages to illustrate grammatical concepts (such as the parts of speech and the functions of different words and word groups in the sentence). They also recognize that there are significant differences in the nature of Arabic morphology and that of the local languages.

However, Arabic grammar is not studied in all localities. According to still-vivid oral traditions, a knowledge of Arabic grammar was only introduced to Dia by the great nineteenth-century mystic Alfa Bokar Karabenta, who had studied it in Sibila, a then-famous village about sixty kilometers northeast of Segou.[18] Many scholars in Djenné have never studied grammar, though others are expert in it. In Diakhaba, Arabic grammar is not taught or studied except by those who have attended a madrasa. Furthermore, Diakhaba scholars claim that it is a rare subject among the Diakhanke of Guinea Bissau.

Lugha (literally, language) is recognized as a distinct discipline, encompassing both religious and profane literature. Religious poems studied may include *Banat Suʿad* (Suad has gone away), also known as the *Burda* (Prophet's mantle), a poem in praise of the Prophet by Kaʿb b. Zuhayr, his contemporary; another and much longer *Burda* (full title: *al-Kawakib ad-durriyya fi madh khayr al-bariyya*) by the Egyptian Muhammad al-Busiri (ca. 1212–1296); the *Dala'il al-khayrat* (Proofs of divine favor), a collection of prayers and litanies composed or compiled by the Moroccan Muhammad al-Djazuli (d. 1465); and the *ʿIshriniyyat* by the Andalusian ʿAbd ar-Rahman b. Yakhlaftan al-Fazazi (d. 1230), often studied in an amplification by the Moroccan Muhammad b. Mahib and with several recent commentaries. These texts may be studied in preparation for the Mawlid festival (the Prophet's birthday) or—especially the *Dala'il*—for blessing ceremonies, where they are frequently recited.

But the study of *lugha* also encompasses two of the recognized masterpieces of earlier Arabic literature: the *Maqamat*, or rhymed prose stories incorporating some verse, by the Iraqi Abu Muhammad al-Qasim al-Hariri (1054–1122), and an anthology of pre-Islamic poetry known as the *Diwan sittat ash-shuʿara'* (Anthology of six poets), compiled by the Andalusian Yusuf al-Aʿlam (1019–1083). These were, respectively, the third-to-last and next-to-last books of the curriculum. The "Six poets," a collection of some 135 poems, includes several of the *Muʿallaqat* (Suspended or, in some acceptations, *Mudhahhabat* or Golden odes)—a collection of six to ten poems (there are different medieval editions). However, except in Timbuktu and Mauritania, the *Muʿallaqat* are not studied as such.[19] The "Six poets," though known to some nineteenth-century European scholars on the basis of an early Andalusian manuscript, was only rediscovered in the Arab world in the early twentieth century, on the basis of Mauritanian and Timbuktu manuscripts. Based on manuscript catalog citations, it appears to have been a common text throughout West Africa.[20] In Mali at least, the poems of this anthology are sung or chanted rather than recited, as is common in the Arab world; one can distinguish different styles, correlated to locality and scholars' native languages.

Except in Timbuktu, the *Maqamat* of the Iranian Ahmad al-Hamadhani (968–1008), which served as a model for al-Hariri's, are little studied. On the other hand, the *Hulal as-sundusiyya*, mystical compositions in rhymed prose and verse by the Syrian-born Ahmad b. ʿAbd al-Hayy al-Halabi, who settled in Fez (d. 1708), are studied in both Segou and Timbuktu. The book, which has yet to be printed, circulates in manuscript. A Timbuktu library owns the autograph manuscript, and the library of Ahmad b. al-Hadj ʿUmar Tal, Tukulor ruler of Segu (reigned ca. 1864–1890), contained at least three copies of this otherwise little-known work.[21]

One standard commentary of the *Maqamat* of al-Hariri, widely circulated in the Arab world and often studied in Mali, may owe something to traditions of interpretation conserved in sub-Saharan Africa. Although it has long been printed anonymously, it was in fact compiled by Muhammad at-Tunisi, who, in the mid-nineteenth century, traveled extensively in what are now Chad and Sudan before finally settling in Egypt.[22] A second work by al-Hariri, the *Mulhat al-i'rab* (Subtleties of inflection), an advanced work on morphology, is also widely studied in Mali.

The ultimate subject of the curriculum is *tafsir*, or Qur'anic commentary. This consists in conveying the overt meaning of the Arabic text while recalling the historical context of the Revelation and developing some of its doctrinal implications; some scholars also emphasize linguistic and stylistic analysis. Although some persons claim to have studied exegesis from a teacher who made no explicit reference to any book other than the Qur'an itself, correspondences to written Arabic commentaries are so close as to suggest that they are in fact their principal sources. In all localities visited, the *Tafsir al-Djalalayn*, composed by the Egyptians Djalal ad-Din al-Mahalli (1389–1459) and his pupil Djalal ad-Din as-Suyuti (1445–1505), was said to be the oldest and most widely studied commentary. However, for several decades now, this succinct work has been largely superseded by its much fuller metacommentary (*Hashiya*) by the Egyptian Ahmad as-Sawi (1761–1825).[23] Scholars in Segou explain the recognition granted this work by the author's status as a Maliki and a member of the Shadiliyya Sufi order (which has many affinities with the more recently founded Tidjaniyya). Many other works on Qur'anic exegesis, representing a great variety of doctrinal standpoints, may now be studied by individual scholars, who import them from abroad.

Thus, *tafsir* is only studied by a minority of erudite scholars. However, a greater number—and many members of the general public—have some knowledge of the contents of the Book, acquired mainly through attendance at Qur'an exegesis sessions held in Ramadan.

Individual scholars may study a range of other disciplines, including metrics, rhetoric, the ancillary Islamic sciences, and the large medieval dictionaries—but these subjects are not very common. Logic and medicine were probably more widely studied in the past, and they are clearly attested in some other regions of West Africa.[24] However, there is reason to believe that, on the whole, the scope of the curriculum has been broadening rather than contracting over the past century. The importation of printed books, which have largely replaced manuscripts, has greatly facilitated the diffusion of knowledge. Masina scholars told me that *tafsir*, now commonly taught there, was an extremely rare subject through midcentury. As noted above, Arabic grammar also used to be a rare subject.

The specialized vocabulary and specific syntactical structures developed by scholars to better translate Arabic into their native languages have been analyzed in other publications (Tamari 1996, 2002, 2005, 2008, 2013a, 2013b, forthcoming). Here, it may be stressed that it is considered incumbent upon the instructor to, as much as possible, teach each student in the language the student knows best. Therefore, some instructors may teach in more than one language; this is particularly common in Dia and Djenné, where advanced-level religious instruction for in-town students takes place primarily in Bozo and in Songhay, respectively, whereas most out-of-town students receive their lessons in Bamana. Fulbe scholars in Djenné have long instructed Dogon converts in Fulfulde, but for some years now, Dogon scholars trained in Fulfulde have been teaching other Dogon in their own language. This development incidentally suggests that these Dogon are currently engaged in processes of major linguistic innovation and lexical creation. Mandenka-speaking scholars in The Gambia insisted to me that, until the end of the nineteenth century, all Islamic teaching there was done through the medium of Soninke; Mandenka who had studied in Soninke, whether with Mandenka or Soninke masters, had long taught in that language.

The degree of comprehension of the Arabic language by West African scholars has been a matter of persistent controversy. Some Western and Western-trained researchers have claimed that West African scholars' attainments are based on memorization rather than comprehension. However, scholars who have studied several books can read, with comprehension, materials that are presented to them for the first time and—contrary to a widely held view—can speak Arabic if necessary (to an interlocutor who has only this language in common with them or on certain formal occasions). I have encountered several scholars who compose poems or elegant prose. Therefore, and also in view of the long history of composition in Arabic in West Africa, the view that scholars may not really understand the texts they study and own would appear to be a relic of long-held negative representations about Africa, reflecting on the observers rather than the observed.

It does seem probable that scholars' aural and oral Arabic skills have improved over the past decades because of access to radio and television. Many traditionally trained scholars listen regularly to Arabic radio and television programs—which proves both that their initial training has led them to understand this language and that their skills are honed through continued practice with the new media.

The role of memorization in traditional Islamic education has also been controversial; many Western and Western-trained researchers maintain that, in this cultural context, learning consists primarily in rote memorization. However, as described above, full memorization of the Qur'an is required in some regional traditions only. Many scholars and pupils think that to attain full mastery of these subjects, it is best to memorize the introductory textbooks pertaining to Arabic syntax and morphology. One or more (or even all) of al-Hariri's *Maqamat* and the poems of the pre-Islamic anthology may also be memorized, but this is always considered a matter of personal choice.

From repeated observation of advanced students revising their lessons, I can affirm that they read the Arabic texts several times to themselves, silently or aloud, and that in oral reading, they will often also repeat out loud their teacher's oral translation into the local language, proceeding, as in the lesson, by syntactical units. Thus, strong mental associations are established between Arabic words and syntactical units and those of the local language. However, there may be variants in the precise choice of words between the teacher's and the student's renditions and also between a student's successive renditions. This, then, is a learning process in which memory has a significant role, but word-for-word retention of the Arabic text is not always, and of the local language translation never (in my experience), an objective. I have several times collected two or more commentaries of an Arabic text at different times from the same scholar; the local language commentaries were never identical. These commentaries might differ greatly not only in length and emphasis or in the points developed but even as concerns the translation properly speaking, only the keywords remaining constant.[25]

The roles of memorization and comprehension, in elementary and advanced education, are not the same. The elementary Qur'an pupil is required to understand the general relationship between graphic forms and articulated sounds, to mentally retain his teacher's pronunciation, and (depending on the locality, cultural and linguistic affiliations) to retain a variable number of suras by heart; yet in some areas, he may be told little or nothing about the meaning of the Qur'anic text. In contrast, the aim of book students, as they and their teachers stress, is to understand these works: they read for comprehension, which must precede (optional) memorization.

Recognition of Knowledge

Unlike the situation described by Ivor Wilks (1968) for certain populations of northern Côte d'Ivoire and eastern Ghana, in the various places visited, it is not customary for the teacher to write out a diploma (*idjaza*, "license" to teach) for a student upon the completion of a book or books. However, in Dia, Djenné, and Touba, it is customary to hold a ceremony for pupils who have completed several recitations of the Qur'an (two recitations in Dia, three in Djenné, two or more in Touba). A ceremony may be organized for one or more pupils; in Touba, a single ceremony may be held for pupils who have achieved different levels of study (two to six recitations). Each pupil reads out the verses on his board (written by the teacher in Dia; in other localities, often by the pupils themselves); then the assembled scholars recite blessings. Generally, scholars from neighboring villages as well as from the teacher's village of residence attend, as do many Qur'anic pupils (from the same or other schools) and the teacher's and pupil's families and friends. The ceremony usually takes place in the teacher's home. The pupils' families cook food for all or provide the means to prepare a meal. Each pupil's family also is expected to provide the teacher with substantial gifts and compensation. As one exception, in a ceremony I attended in Segou, the pupil's father, a resident in a small village, was so poor that the teacher paid for food and refreshments for the guests.

In Kankan and its area, accomplished scholars who have completed advanced book as well as Qur'anic studies are recognized in a ceremony in which they are authorized to wear a certain turban, thus becoming *namutii* (literally, "turban-bearers" or "masters of the turban"). Similar forms of recognition have been noted among Manding speakers of the northern Côte d'Ivoire (Marty 1922, 262–64, 320) and Senegambia (Sanneh 1979, 155–58).

Social and Economic Conditions

Discipline

Westerners and the Western educated tend to have a negative image of discipline in traditional Islamic education. Though it expresses admiration for the West African Islamic spiritual heritage, Cheikh Hamidou Kane's (1961) *L'aventure ambiguë* (*Ambiguous Adventure*) depicts the master as inflicting severe physical punishment on his pupils, especially his favorite, Samba. Amar Samb's memoir (1973) is extremely critical of the Qur'anic school experience. On the other hand, Lamin Sanneh's (1975) and Yakouba Diarra's (1999) memoirs evoke moments of intellectual pleasure, fun, and enthusiasm.

In fact, circumstances vary. In Segou and Dia, children are rarely beaten, though the threat of the whip is ever present. Many persons in Dia explain that Alfa Bokar Karabenta, the great nineteenth-century saint, said that since children are future adults, they should be treated indulgently and allowed to listen to adult conversations. In some schools in Touba, where most pupils may be members of the extended family, even the threat of physical punishment is rare. In Timbuktu, perhaps because of the influence of long-established French-language state schools, which most Qur'anic pupils also attend, I have never seen children physically punished. In one school in Kankan, which I visited several times, no punitive instrument was visible, perhaps because the director—who had attended the local French-language schools and lived in New York City—subscribed to modern pedagogical preferences. In Djenné, on the other hand, I have seen children whipped severely, including on the head. In all these places, physical punishment tends to be limited to small children (up to about age eight). Where physical punishment exists, it may be meted out to girls as well as boys. Teachers explain that, because they have attained understanding, older children no longer require physical punishment.

In Dia, schoolmasters may look after small children during study sessions, often cradling babies (those of their neighbors and extended families as well as their own) in their arms as they teach.

Severe physical punishment may be applied to small and adolescent boys in the itinerant schools. State school and medical personnel in the Djenné and Timbuktu areas told me that severe beatings, resulting in permanent injury to pupils and even death, occur regularly. These officials, as well as outraged neighbors, report such cases to the police, who remonstrate with teachers and may cause them to leave the area, but so far, do not fine or imprison them.

Many persons who have not attended a Qur'anic school believe that it must be a grim experience, characterized by mindless rote repetition as well as harsh physical punishment. But this perception does not always correspond to pupils' or former pupils' experiences (whether actual or remembered). In Dia, where many children attend both Qur'anic and state schools, they often enjoy both. Some children prefer Qur'anic school, and spend as much time as possible revising their lessons—at the expense of homework for the French-language state school, family chores, and even games. In Dia especially, I have seen children rushing to Qur'anic school with beaming faces[26]; some children even arrange to study their boards in their teachers' vestibules beyond school hours or—very rarely—to take them home. These children apparently enjoy the cognitive activities involved as well as personal relationships with their teachers and other pupils. Almamy Maliki Yattara, a Masina scholar who later collaborated with several Western and Western-trained researchers, recalls how he persisted in attending Qur'anic school, despite severe physical punishment by an older relative (Yattara and Salvaing 2000).

Many adults, especially in Timbuktu, remember their Qur'anic school experience as a happy one. Some even describe it as an extension of the family experience, with warm, emotionally nurturing relationships. Indeed, in Timbuktu, children's age groups—to which they will adhere throughout their lives—are formed on the basis of Qur'anic school attendance. Choice of a Qur'anic school is, in turn, largely based on neighborhood of residence, and neighborhoods are mostly congruent with ethnic affiliations, family origins, and wealth. Whereas Qur'anic schools are coeducational, some age groups admit members of one sex only. Groups that admit both sexes provide a framework for friendly, egalitarian lifelong social relationships among men and women. All the age groups provide the context for at least some interethnic and status mixing, solidarity, and social intermingling among rich and poor (given, especially, that individual fortunes may fluctuate considerably over a lifetime).[27]

Advanced memorization and the study of books are nearly always, in my experience, remembered as happy experiences; often as—similar to how at one time college and university study in the West supposedly were—the best part of life. Former students emphasize the joys of intellectual discovery and academic progress as well as sincere camaraderie. Only those who endured the severest material hardships (for example, Almamy Yattara, who came from a poor family and studied against its wishes) have a more nuanced recollection.

In the Segou area, common attendance at a *majlis*—much like secondary school and university attendance in the West—is often the basis for lifelong friendships. Former schoolmates often visit one another, happily reminiscing about their studies. They may also visit their teacher, individually or collectively, organize reunions with him, or hold memorial commemorations after his death.

Economics

Westerners tend to perceive traditional Islamic education as economically exploitative. However, this is not how its teachers see the situation; many view themselves as supplying all their pupils' and students' needs.

Particularly in Dia, teachers may claim that they provide Qur'anic instruction without any view to material reward. They and other teachers may cite authoritative Arabic texts, according to which Qur'an instruction should not be subject to payment—though it has long been recognized throughout the Islamic world that it is a practical necessity to provide the teacher with some compensation. In the various places I visited, in-town pupils bring their teachers some small coins every Wednesday,[28] but this offering is so small that it is sometimes considered symbolic. Pupils in Dia who fail to bring this amount are not turned away. In general, out-of-town pupils, especially if they are lodging with the teacher, as well as members of the teacher's extended family, do not pay. On the other hand, some pupils may give more, especially prior to the holidays; in Diakhaba, it is customary for pupils to bring their teacher 500 CFA (francs of the African Financial Community; approximately equivalent to one dollar) before each of the two main Islamic holidays (the Sacrificial Feast and the Breaking of the Fast). In Timbuktu, teachers may charge a higher weekly fee to pupils—especially children of Timbuktu families resident elsewhere in Mali—who only study over the long vacation. Indeed, Timbuktuans so prize the city's Qur'anic schools and are so skeptical of other forms of religious education that they attempt to send their children back to the city to study over these vacations.

In the semirural milieu of Dia, young pupils accomplish several chores for their teacher and his (or her) extended family: collecting firewood, fetching water, sweeping courtyards, pounding millet. Throughout the region, older pupils, especially ones studying books, are expected to accomplish substantial (usually agricultural) work for their teacher or supply him with cash or foodstuffs.[29] Pupils in Diakhaba, rural Gambia, and Touba may work full-time or almost full-time on their instructor's fields at peak times of the agricultural year, and they may provide substantial labor at other times; they may also care for his herds. Older students in Djenné, Dia, and the Masina are often away in the rainy and harvest seasons, working on others' fields. Itinerant pupils may work, sometimes along with their teachers, in the fields of farmers who will later compensate them with a portion of the crop. In Diakhaba and Touba, out-of-town students generally accomplish more physical, particularly agricultural, labor than the teacher's sons or relatives, who may also be studying with him. In Touba, advanced memorization and book pupils, studying within their families, may be excused from physical labor altogether—and thus devote all their time to their studies.

A teacher in Djenné explained that, in earlier times, there was "no problem" in that city. Students worked on their master's fields, and the rice harvest was sufficient to satisfy the needs of all—masters and pupils; a master could even organize a favorite student's marriage. But in recent years, both the rain and the flood have failed. Once a rice-exporting zone, Djenné is obliged to import this basic foodstuff. Students have to engage in odd jobs, not always compatible with their dignity, or make long trips to earn grain or money elsewhere—taking precious time away from study. Approved jobs include working as porters at the large, weekly Monday market; hawking at the daily or weekly markets is not always approved. Several students sell bread in the evening in the esplanade near the mosque. Djenné's teachers have recently formed an association with the aim of bettering the living standards of both masters and pupils. They would like to establish a large, irrigated vegetable garden to be administered in common to provide suitable employment and income to their students.

A Fulbe student from a rural area who spent many years studying in Segou obtained income from his herds, whose active care he had entrusted to others, and he initiated and ran a bookshop. Almamy Yattara has described the different kinds of jobs during his youth in the Masina (ca. 1930s–1950s) that might be accomplished by students—including, for many, collecting and selling firewood or performing agricultural work and, for himself, looking after a shop in Mopti.[30]

Students may also obtain employment more closely connected to their studies: for example, acting as an assistant to their teacher (or, more rarely, another teacher); reading or reciting the Qur'an at funerals or on other ceremonial occasions; and copying manuscripts for their teacher, other scholars, or the general public. *Majlis* students often run their own Qur'anic schools. Some persons with a full-fledged school study with a yet more advanced teacher. A state primary school teacher assigned to a village near Dia pursued *majlis* studies there—his state school salary in effect serving to further his Islamic education. Some atypical, older students may live on their savings—for example, the truck driver from the Sikasso area who had been studying the Qur'an in Timbuktu for six months at the time I met him.

Numerous teachers, especially in Dia and Djenné, stress that they are responsible for their live-in pupils' upkeep. Because parents may or may not send money, grain or other foods, or even clothes, teachers must rely on gifts or on activities not directly related to their teaching function to cover costs.

Many teachers, especially at the *majlis* level, engage in esoteric work (French *maraboutages*; Bamana *moriya*) for clients. If the clients are satisfied, they may provide substantial compensation and renew their gifts regularly.

Many teachers, especially in Dia, go on tours of the countryside in the harvest season, with the expectation of receiving gifts. In any locality, a well-known scholar may receive a gift as a mark of respect. Such gifts also procure blessings to the givers.

Some Dia teachers benefit from the help of prosperous parents who may, for example, send a large quantity of rice or fish every year, sometimes enough to cover the whole school's needs for several months, or donate clothes for all the pupils. These parents—or their son—may continue making annual gifts to the teacher well after the son has completed his education. Children from poorer families, who achieve prosperity after completing their studies, may also make large gifts to their teacher. Wealthy individuals not directly connected to a school may also contribute to it.

Whereas many Westerners and Western-educated Africans criticize begging by Qur'anic school pupils, they and their teachers insist on its advantages and moral value. Mendicancy is a practice largely restricted to pupils from itinerant schools, which are characteristic of certain ethnic groups only (Fulbe, Bella, Mossi). Furthermore, begging is primarily characteristic of younger children (through early adolescence). Fulbe explain that begging allows small children to procure needed resources rapidly—thus freeing time for study. Furthermore, Fulbe teachers, scholars, and former pupils add that it trains children in humility and endurance, promotes detachment from worldly goods, and thus leads them to value learning. Each mendicant pupil is expected to obtain food and cash daily, which the teacher will share out among all the pupils, reserving a part for himself (and his family, if they are traveling with him).[31] Older pupils may be entrusted with the supervision of younger children or may be required to engage in pastoral or agricultural labor.

Itinerant and, more generally, out-of-town pupils and students may benefit from lodging provided by benefactors. Wealthy families—or, more simply, ones who just have some extra space—may provide living quarters such as a house, room(s), or a courtyard to itinerant teachers and pupils and to out-of-town pupils studying with sedentary teachers. Such families may also contribute to the upkeep of their guests or assist with emergency (e.g., medical) expenses. Hambarke, a major trader in Dia and Mopti in the 1950s and early 1960s, hosted scores of pupils every year. Not only are his beneficence and piety still vividly remembered, but they are the subject of at least one Arabic poem. Former beneficiaries still come to greet his descendants, most of whom are not particularly wealthy. The Ndiaye family of Segou has hosted out-of-town religion pupils, Qur'anic and later also madrasa, since its first establishment in that city in the early to mid-nineteenth century (preceding al-Hadj ʿUmar). Some former guests, now scholars in their own right, remember being treated as members of the family, with whom they have maintained close ties.

Out-of-town pupils studying with sedentary teachers may also find hosts on an individual basis. Increasingly, however, those who come to Segou, Djenné, and especially Bamako for advanced education may be obliged to pay rent.

Nevertheless, most out-of-town, especially itinerant, pupils and students suffer from inadequate lodging; many itinerant pupils sleep outside (in principle, in courtyards but sometimes on the streets or in fields or gardens) most of the year, especially in northern Mali. However, one itinerant teacher, who spends several months of every year in Timbuktu, proudly showed me the makeshift wood and synthetic fabric structure that he had his pupils build for themselves and the knapsacks in which each kept his personal belongings. One of the few itinerant teachers to eschew physical punishment, he explained that he also paid for medical care for his wards.

In contrast, in Touba and Djenné, scholarly families attempt to provide their children with the best possible material conditions during their studies.

It is customary for a pupil's family to provide a teacher with substantial material compensation when their son has completed two or more readings of the Qur'an, completes another significant phase of his education, or is withdrawn from school (and thus deemed to have completed his education). Two head of cattle, or their equivalent in cash, is quite frequent; some families may add gold or clothes for the teacher. However, only teachers with large schools and many long-term pupils can benefit from this on a regular basis. Furthermore, the compensation cannot be forced, though a pupil whose parents are unable to pay will attempt to provide it himself, through his own endeavors, as soon as possible. This is not only a matter of honor and respect but is considered necessary for the disciple to fully benefit from his teacher's blessing. An itinerant teacher should also receive substantial compensation (often provided in the form of grain) upon returning a pupil to his parents at the end of his studies.

Methods of teaching in the Qur'anic schools are evolving through the emulation, voluntary or imposed, of madrasa and state school models. Thus, governments and some nongovernmental organizations are pushing to introduce new methods for the study of reading, as well as arithmetic and elements of geography and hygiene, into Qur'anic school curricula. They also aim to provide better food and lodging, vaccinations, and medical care to Qur'anic school pupils. Especially in Mali, reading and arithmetic exercises, together with blackboards, are being introduced into spaces that sometimes are beginning to look like Western classrooms. The world-traveled Qur'anic school director in Kankan has introduced physical education and games for his pupils (up to about age thirteen). Moreover, these exercises are coed.

Conclusion

In summary, the Qur'anic schools and *majlis* of Mali and the Manding-speaking populations of The Gambia and northern Guinea are characterized by a complex pattern of shared and variable traits. Whereas in some areas, the Qur'anic school experience can be a joyous one, marked by a sense of discovery and warm social relations, in others, it can be a time of physical and perhaps also emotional deprivation. In some areas, certain pupils may be able to devote nearly all their time to study, progressing rapidly through Qur'an recitation or memorization and reading with comprehension of numerous books, whereas others may require decades to acquire a smattering of knowledge. Recognized scholars often have a thorough knowledge of written Arabic. At least in Mali, elementary Qur'anic instruction may undergo significant transformations in the near future as an increasing number of teachers introduce new subjects and pedagogical methods.

As remarked at the outset of this chapter, many of the West African educational practices surveyed here—including the recourse to the oral use of local languages—may have more in common with those of the central regions of the Islamic world than has been generally realized. Some other, apparently more specific, features, such as the emphases on individualized instruction and student labor at the advanced level, may be responses to adverse economic conditions. These traits allow individuals with no resources, in societies with a limited surplus, some opportunity for pursuing their studies: interrupting then resuming them, progressing each time at their own pace. As a scholar who ran a reputed *majlis* in Segou once commented to me: "We are not accustomed to villas or fine clothes. As long as the rains have come, as long as we have obtained a good crop, we can study."

NOTES

1. Earlier publications (Tamari 2002, 2008) summarize research conducted in Mali through 2000 and 2003, respectively. Research specifically about Islamic culture and education in Mali now amounts to about three years, conducted primarily since 1992. In the process, well over a hundred scholars have been interviewed and their schools visited. Extensive recordings of oral commentaries on Arabic texts have been obtained from some fifteen scholars (10 to 150 hours each) and briefer recordings from many more. My first trip to Mali dates back to 1979; other research topics pursued there include social hierarchies, traditional religions, and oral literatures. Major studies of Islamic education in Mali include Sanankoua (1985), Sanankoua and Brenner (1991), Mommersteeg (1996), and (mainly concerning the madrasa) Kaba (1974), Brenner (2001), Kavas (2003), and Bouwman (2005). Sanneh (1989 [1979], chapter 7) is the fullest study of Islamic education in a Gambian society. Condé (1992) is a fine historical study, based mostly on oral traditions, of the development of Islamic learning in Kankan, Guinea. For reasons of space, in this essay, bibliographical references have been kept to a minimum; please consult the documents thus cited for additional references.

2. See, for example, the Egyptian scholar Taha Husayn's autobiography (1929–1939) and the biography of a Moroccan scholar reported by Dale Eickelman (1985); concerning the interaction of Arabic and other languages, see, for example, Eickelman (1985, 54, 68–69) and Prabowo and Guillot (1997).

3. Attempts to modernize the Qur'anic schools are well discussed by Roman Loimeier (2001, 364–74, 2002) in the context of neighboring Senegal, where government and other externally imposed initiatives date back to the early 1990s.

4. For example, Charles Monteil (1903, 106–11) and Paul Marty (1920, 2:252) mention that Djenné had about twenty-five schools, whereas currently the city counts over a hundred, as reported by Roberto-Christian Gatti (1999) and confirmed by my observations in 2007 and 2011. Dia currently has forty-five schools, enrolling just under ten to more than three hundred pupils.

5. For example, a significant proportion of the *majlis* students in Touba and Djenné come from outlying (and until recently non-Muslim) Bamana villages. It seems likely that with growing Islamization, the percentage of children attending Qur'anic schools as well as, of course, such pupils' absolute numbers have increased over the twentieth century; compare the statistical information reported, for example, in Bouche (1974, 1:279–320, 2:703–54) and Sanankoua (1985).

6. Thus, in Bamana, *morikalan* and *bulonkònòkalan* are general terms for traditional Islamic study, *kuranakalan* (literally, "study of the Qur'an") refers to all aspects of Qur'anic study except exegesis, and *kitabukalan* (literally, "the study of books") refers to all other fields of study (including Qur'anic exegesis). *Kalan* ("to read or study") is derived from the Arabic *qara'a* ("to read or recite"); *mori*, from Arabic *murabit* ("marabout"; plural *al-murabitun*, sometimes with the specialized meaning "the Almoravids," referring to the eleventh- and twelfth-century political and religious movement), signifies "Muslim" or "Muslim scholar"; *kitabu*, from Arabic *kitab*, signifies "book" while *bulon* signifies "vestibule," and *kònò* signifies "in" (with reference to the area in which study typically takes place). Phonetically and etymologically similar terms are used to refer to the two levels of study in other Manding languages as well as in the Soninke of Touba and the Bozo of Dia and Djenné. The Maninka of Mali and Guinea as well as the Mandenka of The Gambia use the word *kalanta*, which may

be translated as "school," to refer to the locale where instruction is dispensed as well as the social unit formed by a teacher (or set of associated teachers) and their pupils. Bamana did not possess until recently a term that could be translated as "school"; furthermore, *lakòli*, borrowed from the French *l'école*, is not applied to Muslim establishments, whether conservative or modernizing. Songhay employs the word *tirahu*, from *tira*, "talisman," "writing," and *hu*, "house," to designate both Islamic schools and the education that is dispensed there; establishments providing advanced study may be referred to as *kitabu tirahu*. In Timbuktu, the term *hadith* refers to the study and devotional meetings of adult men; this term probably reflects the prominence accorded this domain in Timbuktu curricula and culture (though it should be noted that in Arabic, *hadith* means "saying" or "conversation" as well as "Prophetic tradition"). The Fulbe of Mali distinguish between *taalibaaɓe alkuraan* ("Qur'anic pupils") and *taalibaaɓe dewte* ("book students"), from Arabic *talib* ("student") and *daftar* ("copybook"); they furthermore distinguish several stages of scholastic progress, taking into account pupils' ages as well as educational achievements. The Fulfulde word *dudal* (probably deriving from its homophone, which designates a large fire, around which study may take place) may be translated as "school." In all the languages and regions considered, the Arabic word *majlis* ("assembly" or "study group") is used, in addition to local terms, to refer to the advanced level of study and the establishment in which it is dispensed.

7. Some information about Islamic intellectual traditions and educational practices in Guinea Bissau may be gleaned from, for example, Carreira (1966) and Giesing and Vydrine (2007).

8. One could also speak of the "senior teacher."

9. The Djenné woman scholar is also mentioned by Geert Mommersteeg (1996, chapter 1; 1998, chapter 4). Amber Gemmeke (2008) discusses female esoteric practitioners in Senegal. Important recent publications about women's learning and educational activities include Dorothea Schulz (2012) with respect to Mali, and Ousseina Alidou (2005) and Adeline Masquelier (2009) with respect to Niger.

10. For further illustration of the wide variation in school schedules and holidays, one may refer, for example, to Ware (2004, 524–30) and the works of Paul Marty (1920, 1921, and 1922) for the regions under consideration here.

11. As already noted, for example, by Mommersteeg (1991, 1996, 1998) and Ware (2004), who stress the ritual, initiatory character of this induction.

12. In the same vein, Ndiaye (1985, 38–57) has noted that the Wolof, Fulfulde, and Manding speakers of Senegal each have their own set of appellations for the letters of the Arabic alphabet. Ndiaye's book, which focuses on the Wolof of Senegal, provides by far the most detailed description of the processes of learning to read, recite, copy, and memorize the Qur'an in a West African society. Mommersteeg (1991, 1996, chapter 3) provides excellent descriptions of the process of learning to read in the Songhay milieu of Djenné.

13. I thank Peter Weil of the University of Delaware for providing me with a photocopy of such a Qur'an, which was given to him in The Gambia in 1967 by Fodee Suleemaan Demeba, the Mandenka scholar who wrote it out ca. 1942. (Peter Weil, personal letter, April 5, 1995.)

14. Most commonly, Warsh and Qalun, the two variants of Nafi^c, the recitation system predominant in North Africa. Each of these systems is named for one of its key transmitters, Warsh (d. 812) and Qalun (d. 835) having been disciples of Nafi^c (d. 785). Concerning the recited text of the Qur'an, see, for example, Gade (2004) and Leemhuis (2004). It is generally thought that Bornu is the region, within western sub-Saharan Africa, where recitation rules were granted the greatest attention; but compare, for example, Bobboyi (1992, 48–49, concerning Bornu) and Sanankoua (1985, 361) and Cissé (1999 [1941], 114–15, concerning the Fulbe of Mali).

15. According to noted ethnomusicologist Lucy Duran. (Comment made at the Mande Studies Association conference, Lisbon, June 2008.)
16. West Africans nearly always adhere to the Maliki school.
17. For example, they are studied as far afield as Egypt (see Husayn 1929–1939), Morocco (Eickelman 1985), and Bali (Prabowo and Guillot 1997).
18. This saint is mentioned in Amadou Hampaté Bâ's and Jacques Daget's study of the history of the Masina (1962, 177, 185). Robert Pageard (1961), Maria Grosz-Ngaté (1986), and Jean Bazin (1988) provide some information about the history and social structures of Sibila and its area.
19. The references to the *Mu^{c}allaqat* in the catalog of the Segou royal library (conserved in Paris) are erroneous; the texts in question are, in fact, excerpts from the "Six poets." (Catalog compiled by Ghali, Mahibou, and Brenner 1985.)
20. The European and Arab rediscoveries of this anthology are analyzed by Tamari (2013a).
21. I am preparing a critical edition and translation of portions of the autograph manuscript, including comments on its diffusion in North and West Africa and its interpretation in Mali.
22. As I have shown (Tamari 2005) through comparison of the successive editions of this commentary, first printed in 1850 in Cairo.
23. The *Tafsir al-Djalalayn* is one of several works fundamental to many Manding (especially Diakhanke and Dyula) curricula and that, according to oral and written traditions analyzed by Ivor Wilks (1968), may have been introduced by al-Hadj Salim Suware, the putative founder of the Diakhanke group of scholarly lineages, who probably hailed from Dia in the Masina and lived in the fifteenth century. Nevertheless, according to the oral traditions I collected from scholarly lineages in Djenné, this work was only introduced to the city in the first decade of the twentieth century, while as-Sawi's metacommentary was introduced in the 1940s.
24. See, for example, Rebstock and Mayer (2001) on Mauritania, and Hiskett (1957, 1975) concerning the Sokoto caliphate.
25. See the example of two commentaries on a pre-Islamic poem collected from the same scholar at two years' interval (Tamari 2013a).
26. Not at all John Greenleaf Whittier's "The feet that, creeping slow to school, / Went storming out to playing!" ("In School-Days," first published 1870; collected in Whittier 1894, 407–8).
27. For descriptions of Timbuktu age groups in earlier times, see Dupuis-Yakouba (1910) and Miner (1953, esp. 164–74). However, Miner's ethnography, based on just seven months' fieldwork in 1940, may not be entirely accurate.
28. For the past twenty years in Mali, this amount has been twenty-five to fifty CFA, depending on locality (equivalent to about five to ten U.S. cents at current rates of exchange). It is said that in earlier times, it was just five francs (the smallest denomination coin).
29. Often 500 to 2,000 CFA per week or a lump sum or some bags of grain after a season spent away working.
30. Yattara and Salvaing (2000, esp. 201–8). I have also personally collected his reminiscences about these and many other topics.
31. For a (nearly) inside view of the moral value of mendicancy, see Cissé (1999 [1941], esp. 40–46, 110–13), in which he describes the experience of a younger brother.

REFERENCES

Alidou, Ousseina D. 2005. *Engaging Modernity. Muslim Women and the Politics of Agency in Postcolonial Niger*. Madison: University of Wisconsin Press.

Bâ, Amadou Hampaté, and Jacques Daget. 1984 [1962]. *L'Empire peul du Macina (1818-1853)*. Abidjan: Nouvelles éditions africaines. Paris: Ecole des Hautes Etudes en Sciences Sociales.

Bazin, Jean. 1988. "Princes désarmés, corps dangereux. Les "rois-femmes" de la région de Segu." Special issue, *Cahiers d'études africaines* 28 (111–112): 375–441.

Bobboyi, Hamidu. 1992. "The 'Ulama of Borno: A Study of the Relations between Scholars and State under the Sayfawa, 1470–1808." PhD diss., Northwestern University, Evanston, IL.

Bouche, Denise. 1974. "L'enseignement dans les territoires français de l'Afrique occidentale de 1817 à 1920. Mission civilisatrice ou formation d'une élite?" 2 vols. Dissertation for the degree of *docteur d'Etat*, Université de Paris I.

Bouwman, Dinie. 2005. "Throwing Stones at the Moon: The Role of Arabic in Contemporary Mali." Doctoral diss., School of Asian, African and Amerindian Studies, University of Leiden.

Brenner, Louis. 1993. "Two Paradigms of Islamic Schooling in West Africa." In *Modes de transmission de la culture religieuse en islam*, edited by Hassan Elboudrari, 159–80. Cairo: Institut français d'archéologie orientale.

———. 2001. *Controlling Knowledge. Religion, Power and Schooling in a West African Muslim Society*. Bloomington: Indiana University Press.

Carreira, António. 1966. "Aspectos históricos da evolução da islamismo na Guiné portuguesa." *Boletim cultural da Guiné portuguesa* 84: 405–55.

Cissé, Bocar. 1999. *Devoir de vacances. Une école coranique que vous avez fréquentée et que vous connaissez bien*. Bamako, Mali: Jamana. [Summer assignment submitted to the Ecole Normale William Ponty in 1941, first published in 1999.]

Condé, Boundiala. 1992. "L'Université traditionnelle coranique de Kankan, des origines à l'implantation coloniale." MA thesis, Mémoire de diplôme de fin d'études supérieures, Université de Kankan, Guinea.

Diakité, Drissa, 1991. "Les fondements historiques de l'enseignement islamique au Mali." In *L'Enseignement islamique au Mali*, edited by Bintou Sanankoua and Louis Brenner, 25–44. Bamako, Mali: Jamana.

Diarra, Yacouba. 1999. *Du Kouttab à la Sorbonne. Itinéraire d'un Talibé*. Paris: L'Harmattan.

Dupuis-Yakouba, Auguste Victor. 1910. "Note sur la population de Tombouctou (castes et associations)." *Revue d'ethnographie et de sociologie* 1: 233–36.

Eickelman, Dale F. 1985. *Knowledge and Power in Morocco: The Education of a Twentieth-Century Notable*. Princeton, NJ: Princeton University Press.

Gade, Anna M. 2004. "Recitation of the Qur'an." In *Encyclopaedia of the Qur'an*, vol. 4, edited by Jane Dammen McAuliffe, 368–85. Leiden: Brill.

Gatti, Roberto-Christian. 1999. "Le scuole coraniche di Djenné. Retaggi culturali-Censimento-Problemi-Prospettive." Thesis for the *laurea* degree, Faculty of Education, University of Genoa.

Gemmeke, Amber B. 2008. *Marabout Women in Dakar. Creating Trust in a Rural Urban Space*. Münster, Germany: LIT.

Ghali, Noureddine, Sidi Mohamed Mahibou, and Louis Brenner. 1985. *Inventaire de la bibliothèque ᶜUmarienne de Ségou (conservée à la Bibliothèque nationale—Paris)*. Paris: Editions du Centre National de la Recherche Scientifique; also accessible on www.bnf.fr.

Giesing, Cornelia, and Valentin Vydrine. 2007. *Ta:rikh Mandinka de Bijini (Guinée-Bissau). La mémoire des Mandinka et des Sòoninkee du Kaabu*. Leiden: Brill.

Grosz-Ngaté, Maria. 1986. "Bambara Men and Women and the Reproduction of Social Life in Sana Province, Mali." PhD thesis, Michigan State University, East Lansing.

Hamès, Constant. 1997. "L'enseignement islamique en Afrique de l'Ouest (Mauritanie)." In *Madrasa. La transmission du savoir dans le monde musulman*, edited by Nicole Grandin and Marc Gaborieau, 219–28. Paris: Arguments.

Hiskett, Mervyn. 1957. "Materials Relating to the State of Learning among the Fulani before Their Jihad." *Bulletin of the School of Oriental and African Studies* 19 (3): 550–78.

———. 1975. *A History of Hausa Islamic Verse*. London: School of Oriental and African Studies.

Husayn, Taha. 1929–1939. *Al-Ayyam*. Cairo: Dar al-Maᶜarif. 1st ed., vol. 1, 1929, vol. 2, 1939. Vol. 1 translated by E. H. Paxton as *An Egyptian Childhood* (London: George Routledge, 1932); vol. 2 translated by Hilary Wayment as *The Stream of Days. A Student at the Azhar* (Cairo: Al-Maaref, 1943).

Kaba, Lansiné. 1974. *The Wahhabiyya: Islamic Reform and Politics in French West Africa*. Evanston, IL: Northwestern University Press.

Kane, Cheikh Hamidou. 1961. *L'aventure ambiguë*. Paris: Julliard. Translated by Katherine Woods as *Ambiguous Adventure* (London: Heinemann, 1972).

Kavas, Ahmet. 2003. *L'enseignement islamique en Afrique francophone: les médersas de la République du Mali*. Istanbul: Centre de recherches sur l'histoire, l'art et la culture islamiques. (Organisation de la conférence islamique.)

Leemhuis, Frederik. 2004. "Readings of the Qur'an." In *Encyclopaedia of the Qur'an*, vol. 4, edited by Jane Dammen McAuliffe, 353–63. Leiden: Brill.

Loimeier, Roman. 2001. *Säkularer Staat und Islamische Gesellschaft. Die Beziehungen zwischen Staat, Sufi-Bruderschaften und islamischer Reformbewegung in Senegal im 20. Jahrhundert*. Münster, Germany: Lit.

———. 2002. "Je veux étudier sans mendier. The Campaign against the Quranic Schools in Senegal." In *Social Welfare in Muslim Societies in Africa*, edited by Holger Weiss, 118–37. Stockholm: Nordiska Afrikainstitutet.

Marty, Paul. 1920. *Etudes sur l'islam et les tribus du Soudan*. 4 vols. Paris: Ernest Leroux.

———. 1921. *L'islam en Guinée, Fouta-Diallon*. Paris: Ernest Leroux.

———. 1922. *Etudes sur l'islam en Côte d'Ivoire*. Paris: Ernest Leroux.

Masquelier, Adeline. 2009. *Women and Islamic Revival in a West African Town*. Bloomington: Indiana University Press.

Miner, Horace. 1953. *The Primitive City of Timbuctoo*. Princeton, NJ: Princeton University Press.
Mommersteeg, Geert. 1991. "L'éducation coranique au Mali: le pouvoir des mots sacrés." In *L'Enseignement islamique au Mali*, edited by Bintou Sanankoua and Louis Brenner, 44–61. Bamako, Mali: Jamana.
———. 1996. "Het domein van de marabout. Koranleraren en magisch-religieuze specialisten in Djenné, Mali." Doctoral diss., University of Utrecht, Netherlands.
———. 1998. *In de stad van de marabouts*. Amsterdam: Prometheus; slightly adapted and updated French translation: *Dans la cité des marabouts. Djenné, Mali*. Brinon-sur-Sauldre, France: Grandvaux, 2009; slightly adapted and updated English translation: *In the City of the Marabouts. Islamic Culture in West Africa*. Long Grove, IL: Waveland, 2012.
Monteil, Charles. 1903. *Soudan français. Monographie de Djenné, cercle et ville*. Tulle, France: Imprimerie de Jean Mazeyrie.
Ndiaye, Mamadou. 1985. *L'enseignement arabo-islamique au Sénégal*. Istanbul: Centre de recherches sur l'histoire, l'art et la culture islamiques. (Organisation de la conférence islamique.)
Pageard, Robert. 1961. "Note sur le peuplement de l'est du pays de Ségou." *Journal de la Société des Africanistes* 31 (1): 83–90.
Prabowo, Taufiq, and Claude Guillot. 1997. "Les *pesantrèn* ou centres d'enseignement de l'islam à Java." In *Madrasa. La transmission du savoir dans le monde musulman*, edited by Nicole Grandin and Marc Gaborieau, 185–98. Paris: Arguments.
Rebstock, Ulrich, in collaboration with Tobias Mayer. 2001. *Maurische Literaturgeschichte*. 3 vols. Würzburg, Germany: Ergon.
Samb, Amar. 1973. *Matraqué par le destin, ou la vie d'un talibé*. Dakar, Senegal: Nouvelles editions africaines.
Sanankoua, Bintou. 1985. "Les écoles 'coraniques' au Mali: problèmes actuels." In "Islamic Religious Leaders in West Africa." Special issue, *Canadian Journal of African Studies* 19 (2): 359–67.
Sanankoua, Bintou, and Louis Brenner, eds. 1991. *L'enseignement islamique au Mali*. Bamako, Mali: Jamana.
Sanneh, Lamin. 1975. "The Islamic Education of an African Child: Stresses and Tensions." In *Conflict and Harmony in Education in Tropical Africa*, edited by Godfrey N. Brown and Mervyn Hiskett, 168–86. London: Allen and Unwin.
———. 1989 [1979]. *The Jakhanke Muslim Clerics. A Religious and Historical Study of Islam in Senegambia*. Lanham, MD: University Press of America.
Santerre, Renaud. 1973. *Pédagogie musulmane d'Afrique noire. L'école coranique peule du Cameroun*. Montréal: Presses de l'Université de Montréal.
Schulz, Dorothea E. 2012. *Muslims and New Media in West Africa. Pathways to God*. Bloomington: Indiana University Press.
Tamari, Tal. 1996. "L'exégèse coranique *(tafsir)* en milieu mandingue. Rapport préliminaire sur une recherche en cours." *Islam et sociétés au sud du Sahara* 10: 43–79.
———. 2002. "Islamic Higher Education in West Africa: Some Examples from Mali." In *Yearbook of the Sociology of Islam: Africa*, vol. 4, edited by Georg Stauth and Thomas Bierschenk, 91–128. Münster, Germany: Lit.

———. 2005. "La prose littéraire arabe en traduction bambara: une *maqama* d'al-Hariri." In *Paroles nomades. Ecrits d'ethnolinguistique en hommage à Christiane Seydou*, edited by Ursula Baumgardt and Jean Derive, 431–63. Paris: Karthala.

———. 2008. "L'enseignement islamique traditionnel de niveau avancé: cursus, pédagogie, implications culturelles et perspectives comparatives." *Mande Studies* 8: 39–62.

———. 2009. "The Role of National Languages in Mali's Modernising Islamic Schools (*Madrasa*)." In *Languages and Education in Africa: A Comparative and Transdisciplinary Analysis*, edited by Birgit Brock-Utne and Ingse Skattum, 163–74. Didcot, UK: Symposium.

———. 2013a. "Un poème arabe en traduction bambara: la *Mu^{c}allaqa* d'Imru' l-Qays." In *Les ruses de l'historien. Essais d'Afrique et d'ailleurs en hommage à Jean Boulègue*, edited by Bertrand Hirsch and François-Xavier Fauvelle-Aymar, 441–87. Paris: Karthala.

———. 2013b. "A Bamana Commentary on *Surat al-Waqi^{c}a*: A Linguistic and Stylistic Analysis." Special issue, *Journal of Qur'anic Studies* 15 (3): 123–183.

———. forthcoming. "Qur'anic Exegesis in Manding: The Example of a Bamana Oral Commentary on *Surat al-Rahman*." In *Approaches to the Qur'an in Sub-Saharan Africa*, edited by Zulfikar Hirji. Oxford: Oxford University Press and The Institute of Ismaili Studies.

Ware, Rudolph T. 2004. "Njàngaan: The Daily Regime of Qur'anic Students in Twentieth-Century Senegal." *International Journal of African Historical Studies* 37 (3): 515–38.

Whittier, John Greenleaf. 1894. *The Complete Poetical Works*. Boston: Houghton Mifflin.

Wilks, Ivor. 1968. "The Transmission of Islamic Learning in the Western Sudan." In *Literacy in Traditional Societies*, edited by Jack Goody, 162–95. Cambridge: Cambridge University Press.

Yattara, Almamy Maliki, and Bernard Salvaing. 2000, 2003. *Almamy*. Vol. 1: *Une jeunesse sur les rives du fleuve Niger*. Vol. 2: *L'Age d'homme d'un lettré malien*. Preface by Adame Ba Konaré. Brinon-sur-Sauldre, France: Grandvaux.

3.
ORALITY AND THE TRANSMISSION OF QUR'ANIC KNOWLEDGE IN MAURITANIA

Corinne Fortier

(translated from the French by Robert Launay)

Masters and Forms of Knowledge

Two Levels and Two Types of Masters

The analysis of Qur'anic education in Mauritanian Moorish society[1] calls into question the appropriateness of the term *Qur'anic school*. In this formerly nomadic society, there is no specific term for Qur'anic instruction at the elementary level: The Arabic word *kuttāb* (from *kitāba*, "writing") is never used, unlike North and West Africa and other Muslim regions. In Ḥassāniyya, the Moorish dialect of Arabic, the expression that signifies that a child is following such an education is "He is studying his writing board" (*yagra lawḥū*), which is linked not to any specific place but rather to the central tool of instruction, the writing board (*lawḥ*). It is striking that, wherever the pupil receives instruction—in a tent (*khayma*), in desert pastures (*bādiyya*), or in a luxurious villa in Nouakchott, the capital—the writing board remains the key symbol of Qur'anic instruction.

The writing board, the fundamental element in Qur'anic learning, is a thin rectangular plank of *aglal* wood (*Mitragyna inermis*) whose upper corners have been rounded. On one hand, this board signals the interpersonal nature of transmission from master to pupil, independent of the mediation of books. On the other hand, as this movable instrument suggests, teaching may take place anywhere, provided it remains under the master's control, whether in his house or during his travels. In fact, according to Maliki jurisprudence (Ibn Saḥnūn 1953, 97)— the rite observed by Moors since the introduction of this rite in North and West

Africa in the eleventh century by the Almoravids—it is not permitted to recite the Qur'an while walking except when one is learning it.

Moorish society is a Bedouin society where each person belongs to a tribe (*qabīla*) which bears a name that sometimes refers directly to the eponymous ancestor of the tribe through patrilineal descent and where each member has rights and duties toward the tribe according to the logic of tribal solidarity (*'aṣabiyya*). Moorish society is also hierarchical, including nobles—marabouts (*zwāya*) and warriors (*ḥassān*)—tributaries (*znāga*), and non-nobles—former slaves (*ḥarāṭīn*) as well as two castes, blacksmiths (*m'allimīn*) and griots (*iggawān*). Although most children pursue some level of Qur'anic instruction, the length of study varies with status and gender (Fortier 1997). Children from maraboutic tribes, given their specialization in religious knowledge, receive a more extensive education. It is also striking that in eastern Mauritania, in the Hawdh region, children of blacksmiths also receive an extensive religious education, which can be explained partly by the preponderance of maraboutic tribes in the region but also by the fact that their occupation allows them to stay sedentary, allowing them to give elementary instruction to girls as well as boys (Fortier 2002, 2006).

Because there is no clergy in Sunni Islam, religious instruction—such as leading prayer or the practice of law—is not professionalized. It is not unusual for an individual with another occupation to teach the Qur'an on the side.[2] Often, a master will continue teaching while pursuing his other business, provided it does not prevent him from listening to his pupils. For example, pupils may recite the Qur'an in the presence of a teacher who is selling in his shop if he is a merchant, who is herding his animals if he has any, or if he is making a tool if he is a smith. Mobility does not disrupt teaching, which continues while the teacher goes to the mosque or when he is herding his animals. Such a system of instruction is easily mobile, partly because the central tool of instruction is the writing board on which the pupil writes his lessons and partly because knowledge is thought not to reside in books (*kutub*) but in the heart (*qulūb*).

At the elementary level, a male Qur'anic teacher is called *mrābaṭ*, and a female teacher is called *mrābaṭ*, both from the Arabic name for the Almoravids, *al-Murābiṭūn*. In the east, a teacher is also called *ṭalāb*, from the Arabic verb *ṭalaba*, "to seek knowledge." Throughout Mauritania, the pupil is called *talmīdī*, an Arabic word that more generally designates a disciple. Unlike primary instruction, advanced teaching, involving a considerable number of students and sometimes several teachers, is designated by another term. This is not the term *madrasa* frequently used in North and West Africa but rather *maḥāḍra* (pronounded *maḥāẓra* in hassāniyya), derived from the Arabic *ḥāḍara*, "session." Throughout this chapter, I will use the term *maḥāẓra* instead of university—a term that misleadingly evokes the Western history of this institution. In Moorish society, the scholar who teaches several disciplines is called an *ʿālim*, and a specialist in jurisprudence (*fiqh*) is called a *fqīh*.

Boys from maraboutic tribes who pursue their studies at an advanced level leave their homes to seek knowledge from a renowned master (Fortier 2003, 2007). This journey of initiation (*riḥla*) is only undertaken by young men; young women cannot leave their natal homes until marriage. A student in search of a master looks for a scholar who will exhort him to begin the lesson simply by commanding "Recite!" or literally "Proceed!" (*mashshī!*), without mentioning which subject the student wishes to pursue. Moreover, a scholar should be capable of answering any question without consulting a book or manuscript. The intellectual itinerary of a nineteenth-century scholar, Nābigha al-Ghallāwī[3] is paradigmatic. After having studied with his maternal uncle, he left his tribe, the Laghlāl, and his region, the Hawdh, in search of a multidisciplinary education. Whenever any masters he consulted in the course of his travels asked him which discipline he wanted to study, he continued on his way. Finally, he settled in Daykan with Aḥmad wuld al-ʿAqil of the Trarza tribe of the Awlād Daymān (Idabḥum), who answered all his questions and whose very first word was the one he was waiting for: "*mashshī!*" He married a kinswoman of his teacher and stayed in the Iguidi for the rest of his life. As this example shows, the search for knowledge could lead a student to integrate permanently through marriage into the master's group.

Given the considerable number of students in the *mḥāẓar*, scholars often chose to specialize in only one discipline, leaving other disciplines to their colleagues. In the early eighteenth century, one *maḥāẓra* of the Idadjba tribe in Brakna was called the "yellow and brown *maḥāẓra*," referring to the colors of the tents in which instruction took place: one brown, made of camel hair; the other beige, from sheep's wool. Students might pass a considerable part of their lives, even as much as thirty years, in the *maḥāẓra*.

The Qur'anic Teacher and His Pupils

The modalities of Qur'anic instruction in Moorish society are more or less the same as in other Muslim societies. Indeed, there is an extraordinary pedagogical unity throughout the Muslim world in teaching the Qur'an, as indicated in Ibn Saḥnūn's[4] (ninth century) *Kitāb ādāb al-muʿallimīn* (Book of rules for the behavior of school teachers).

Space is organized to take into account pupils' different levels of instruction. Teaching generally takes place out in the open, in the courtyard of a house or in a tent. The teacher is seated on a mat or on a sheepskin. He faces the pupils, who squat on their heels and hold their writing boards vertically. In the first rows, side by side, sit those who have yet to learn how to write and who decipher the suras that the teacher has written out for them; in the next rows sit more advanced pupils to whom the teacher dictates the lesson. Clustered according to levels of competence, the pupils can correct one another as they recite their lessons. According to Ibn Saḥnūn (1953, 91–93), the teacher can encourage collective study among pupils as well as competition, as long as he monitors it. In Moorish society, the teacher encourages the students to not only emulate but punish one another. As a sign of excellence, the teacher may order his best pupil to spit on his incompetent peers or to pour sand on their head as forms of punishment. The worst student is additionally called a donkey or an "egg in the hole," a reference to an egg that remains in the nest without hatching. The other pupils make fun of him by hanging a necklace of dried camel turds around his neck. The teacher can, of course, punish pupils himself by pulling their ears, tapping them with a stick, or tying them to one of the tent poles. Ibn Saḥnūn (1953, 87) stipulates the number of blows a teacher can give his pupils: "When they abandon themselves to play or are inordinately lazy, he can strike up to ten blows; but as concerns the recitation of the Qur'an, he should not hit them more than three times."[5]

Aside from corporal punishment, this instruction is consistently embodied. For example, in Moorish society, pupils generally do not eat before going to their teacher's home, because their family considers that an empty state favors the incorporation of the suras. The attention that students devote each morning to religious instruction is considered a measure of their success throughout the rest of the day; there is a saying that "One must not sleep in the morning, because this is the time when God allots everyone their share of luck." At noontime, the pupils take a break, and their families oblige them to nap. They resume their lessons when the sun begins to set after the early afternoon prayer (*aẓ-ẓuhr*). When instruction lasts after the evening prayer (*al-maghrib*), the pupils light a fire with the straw they have brought. At night, such fires are the symbol of Qur'anic instruction: around it, the various voices in recitation break the silence.

Classes are interrupted each week from Wednesday afternoon until midday Friday. Sometimes the pupils lack the requisite reverential fear of their teacher by composing unflattering verses behind his back. Some of these verses express the pupils' desires to extend the weekly pause—for example, "On Wednesday, may our teacher be bitten by a viper." In general, pupils who also attend modern school wait until vacations to pursue their religious education. Occasionally some pursue both forms of education throughout the school year, taking a break after their classes in modern school and resuming Qur'anic instruction at nighttime. Nowadays, in upper-class circles in the capital, some teachers come to the homes of their pupils, though such practices are sometimes criticized as debasing the status of religious knowledge and its transmitters. Daily lessons are obviously shorter for those who simultaneously attend modern and Qur'anic school. Although they are allowed to take their writing tablets home with them to study their lessons, only the teacher is authorized to write a new lesson. On the other hand, pupils who are receiving only religious instruction leave their writing boards at their teacher's home so that he alone controls their instruction. The teacher considers that his presence is indispensable at every stage of instruction, on the ground that, once a serious error is engraved in the memory, it is very difficult to erase.

Foundations of Religious Learning

After the alphabet, teaching invariably begins with the Qur'an, the foundation of all other sources of Islamic knowledge (jurisprudence, the life of the Prophet, etc.). Nonetheless, other texts are taught besides the Qur'an. In the east, the study of the Qur'an must be completed before learning any other text,[6] but in other regions courses of study are diversified earlier on. In Mauritania, every region stresses a different kind of knowledge. In general, after they have memorized part of the Qur'an, pupils begin to study theology (*'aqida*) and jurisprudence (*fiqh*) in works of increasing difficulty. At this first stage, pupils learn the twenty attributes of God as well as the "personal duties" (*furūḍ al-'ayn*) necessary for religious devotion (*'ibāda*), encompassing rules of purification (*ṭahāra*), prayer (*ṣalāt*), fasting (*ṣawm*), religious taxation (*zakāt*), and the pilgrimage (*ḥajj*).

The works studied in Mauritania are generally identical to those studied in Mali (Tamari 1996, 48) and in the Fuuta Tooro (Schmitz 1998). For example, the basic works of Maliki jurisprudence, the *Risāla*, *Khalīl*, and the *Ajrūmiyya*, as well as the basic text for grammar, the *Ajrūmiyya*, are all taught. Moreover, for most disciplines, Mauritania and Niger share the same standard reference works: for jurisprudence, *al-Akhḍarī*; for grammar, the *Alfiyya* (also taught in Iran [Naraghi 1992, 48]); for poetry, the *Mu'allaqāt*; and for exegesis, *al-Jalālayn*, as well as aṭ-Ṭabarī's commentary on the Qur'an.

There exists a shared core in the religious cultures of Muslim societies that is due in large measure to the study of identical texts. References to the same basic writings explain the similarity of certain institutions and representations in otherwise culturally diverse Muslim societies. Most of these works are better known by the names of their authors than by their titles. Thus, *al-Akhḍarī* (sixteenth century, Algeria) is the first author studied for jurisprudence, followed by *Ibn 'Ashir* (seventeenth century, Morocco), whose first chapter deals with theology (*'aqīda*), the second with jurisprudence (*fiqh*), and the third with mysticism (*taṣawwuf*). The history of the early days of Islam (*sīra*) is studied in al-Lamṭi's (sixteenth century, Morocco) *Qurat al-Abṣār*. For their part, girls study a short collection of hadith called *Dalā'il al-khayrāt* (The path leading to good works) by al-Djazūli (fifteenth century, Morocco).

At a more advanced level, the sons of marabouts study the required social duties (*mu'āmala*) in more extensive legal texts. These include "collective duties" (*furūḍ al-kifāya*)—those that any given individual does not have to perform as long as they are undertaken by others (for example, teaching the Qur'an or reciting funeral prayers)—as well as "personal duties" (*furūḍ al-'ayn*), in domains such as marriage, commerce, inheritance, and penal law. Between the ages of ten and fifteen, they begin by studying the *Risāla* of al-Qayrawānī (tenth century, Tunisia), which, in Chinguetti (in the Adrar region), is known in a version put into verse by 'Abd-Allah wuld Ḥajj Ḥamāhullah, a local eighteenth-century scholar from the maraboutic Laghlāl tribe (Hamel 1992, 368, n. 167). Indeed, such texts are often versified throughout the Muslim world in accordance with the rules of Arabic prosody (*'aruḍ*) to facilitate their memorization and oral transmission. Later, between the ages of fifteen and twenty, they are taught the *Mukhtaṣar* of Khalīl (fourteenth century, Egypt) and, after they reach the age of twenty, the *'Aṣmiyya* of Ibn 'Asīm (late fourteenth to early fifteenth centuries, Andalusia) before undertaking the study of ever more complex legal texts.

Pedagogical Techniques

Mnemonic Devices, Formulas, and Quizzes

The *maḥāẓra* employs mnemonic devices to facilitate learning Islamic jurisprudence and Arabic prosody. For example, the sentence "Live as long as you have the means" (*'ish laka rizq*) contains the initials of the seven obstacles to inheritance in Maliki jurisprudence (Khalīl 1995, 453). The *'ayn* is the initial of the word "stillborn"; the *shīn* of uncertainty about who died first in an accident; the *lām* of refusal to acknowledge paternity; the *kāf* of infidelity; the *rā'* of slavery; the *zāy* of illegitimacy; the *qāf* of voluntary homicide. This mnemonic formula, used in *mḥāẓar* in Mauritania, is cited by certain Maliki commentators (Ibn 'Asīm 1958, 430, n. 1132). This demonstrates that, in a country like Mauritania, where essential knowledge is constituted with reference to Muslim scriptural sources, its transmission is effected by pedagogical methods that date back to the early years of Islam. In grammar, poems in the local *Ḥassāniyya* dialect of Arabic help students memorize rules of syntax—for example, that the fundamental units of any nominal or verbal phrase are the subject and the predicate. Similarly, short mnemonic poems in classical Arabic are used for learning the metrical structure of poetry.

In certain maraboutic families in the Trarza region, various disciplines are taught at home alongside instruction in the *maḥāẓra*. Women play an important role in teaching the life of the Prophet (*sīra*). Thus, grandmothers or maternal aunts who are knowledgeable in the subject repeat to a young student before he goes to sleep the twenty names of men in the Prophet's paternal line, the fourteen names of women in his maternal line, the four names of his sons, the four names of his daughters, the two names of the mothers of his children, and the names of the four caliphs and of the ten companions who were admitted to Paradise. Later, when the student has reached the age of fourteen, they teach him the names of warriors who fought in the Prophet's twenty-eight battles against unbelievers.

Indeed, the local reference work on the life of the Prophet was written by a scholar, al-Badawī, who sought to remedy his own ignorance on the subject, as revealed to him by a woman who questioned him about the name of Muhammad's guide during the *hijra*. When he was in his thirties and still studying in the *maḥāẓra*, he met an old woman in a camp of the Idablḥsan tribe who enquired of his patronym. Like most women her age, she was well acquainted with the intricacies of tribal genealogies and demonstrated her knowledge of his prestigious ancestry with a formula that acknowledges nobility, learning, or piety: *wakhayrt*. After having praised the erudition of his family, she gave him the chance to prove his own by interrogating him about the life of the Prophet, asking the name of his guide when he fled Mecca for Medina. Because he did not know the answer, al-Badawī decided to remedy his ignorance by writing two works on the subject: the first, *Naẓm ansāb al-arab*, on the genealogies of the Arabs; the second, *al-Ghazawāt*, on the early conquests of Islam. The first book begins with the name of the Prophet's guide during his exile, the answer to the question that had stumped al-Badawī.

In certain families, the pupil's father or maternal uncles play an important role in his education by quizzing him. This kind of quiz is called *zarg*, "to throw," as in throwing a ball, which the pupil must throw back (*jawāb*) by giving the answer. These quizzes may cover any subject: jurisprudence, grammar, poetry, theology. This kind of teaching in the family has a playful character in contrast to the rigidity of study under a Qur'anic master. The student is rewarded for giving the right answer rather than punished for mistakes. For example, if a young boy answers a quiz correctly while his father or uncle is preparing tea, he is exceptionally allowed a glass of this precious drink. Old men often have a chest with them containing treats (dates, biscuits, peanuts) reserved for pupils who give the right answer to quizzes.

On their own, children invent group games of poetry recital to bolster their knowledge and exercise their memory. Ten-year-old pupils will form a little group. The first will recite a verse of Arabic poetry; the second must continue with a verse that starts with the last letter of the first verse; and so on, until all but one is eliminated. This kind of exercise is called an "invitation" (*nadwa*); when a young man arrives as a stranger in a camp, he is invited by the youth of his age group to practice this kind of poetry contest as a way of incorporating him into their circle. Even the Qur'an can be the subject of such games played by children away from their teacher. Once the class is over, even though they have left their writing boards with their master, supposedly preventing them from studying the lesson in his absence, pupils continue to interrogate one another. This collective study is similar to a game in which each pupil recites a section (*ḥizb*) of the Qur'an as stipulated by the group. If the person who is challenged does not remember it, he is eliminated. As a result, the person who best knows the Qur'an wins the game.

Reading, Reciting, and Writing the Qur'an

The first phase of Qur'anic learning consists in its oral recitation (*qirā'a*). This education, which is generally provided by the mother in maraboutic families, begins with teaching the letters of the alphabet even before the child learns to read. This process takes into account regional differences in pronunciation.[7] First, the child learns to distinguish different letters in terms of the number of diacritical points above or below the character. Second, he learns to recognize the vowel markers and the sign for doubling consonants. Once this phase is finished, the pupil will decipher the shortest suras of the Qur'an. As in the rest of the Muslim world, the memorization of the Qur'an begins with the first sura (*al-fātiḥa*), followed by the shortest suras at the end of the Qur'an up to the longest suras at the beginning, from the 114th sura, the People (*an-nāss*) to the 2nd sura, the Cow (*al-baqara*).

The pupil learns the passage his master has written on his writing board by heart. He withdraws a bit in order to read his lesson out loud as many times as it takes to memorize it. To count the number of recitations it takes to memorize the text, he marks the sand with a dot for each reading, sometimes forming a triangle or rectangle of fifty dots. This technique of learning through repetition holds for all the suras of the Qur'an except for the first to be taught; these suras are effectively known to the pupil even before he learns to read, because he has already heard his comrades recite them incessantly. To facilitate study, the Qur'anic text is divided into sixty sections (*azhāb*), each with its own name. The first section, named for the three mysterious initials (*alif, lām, mim*) that open the sura, The Cow, is taught last, while the last section, known as *sabīh*, is the first to be taught. Each of these sections is in turn divided into eight subsections.

The pace of teaching is adapted to each pupil. The master is the only person authorized to judge whether a pupil can begin learning a new sura. Suras are qualified as "cooked" (*sūrtu ṭāyba*) or "tender" (*niyya*) according to whether the pupil has assimilated them. Someone who has a "hard head" (*rās gāssi*)—the expression in Ḥassāniyya compares memorization to engraving—will take more time to memorize a passage than one who has a "soft head" (*rās liyyin*). Only after the pupil has exercised his memory and learned to read will he finally be taught to write. A much higher value is placed on reciting the Qur'an (*tilāwa*) than on writing it down (*kitāba*).[8] Only when the pupil knows from two to four sections of the Qur'an by heart will he begin to learn to write. His quill (*qalam*) follows the trace made by his master until the teacher finally authorizes his pupil to write on his own. The most advanced pupil may also become an assistant to his master, writing verses on the writing boards of beginners and correcting their recitation. Writing is first executed according to the dictation of the master or his assistant. Once the pupil has mastered the recitation of the Qur'an, he can copy it directly on his own. To remain as faithful as possible to the original text, such copies must never omit vowel markers.

After the definitive memorization of a sura, the writing board is washed so that other verses may be written on it. Once the text has been copied, learned, and recited, this gesture of erasing from the writing board what one knows by heart—the Arabic expression is "on the back of the heart" (*'an ẓahri qalb*)[9]— is the inverse of its engraving in the memory: That which is no longer written is acquired; that which is no longer objectivized is interiorized. The beginning pupil drinks the water that has been used to wash the sacred text from the writing board, a ritual that underscores the oral ingestion of the Qur'an.[10] When it has not been drunk, the water is poured into a place where no one will step on it irreverently, out of respect for the sacred word that has been dissolved into it. According to Ibn Saḥnūn, in the era of the companions of the Prophet, pupils dug a hole in the ground where they poured the water that had erased the contents of their writing boards. These practices testify to the ways in which learning the Qur'an has been assimilated to a process of incorporation, and even of ingestion. I have noted elsewhere (Fortier 1998) that Qur'anic instruction for boys is the equivalent of force-feeding for girls—no longer practiced in Moorish society—a process that took place in the same phase of their lives and that shared the corporal logic of ingestion, whether of large quantities of milk on one hand or verses of the Qur'an on the other.[11]

Modes of Transmission and Types of Texts

A Qur'anic Recitation above Reproach

Reading and writing are ultimately subordinated to memorization and recitation,[12] the ultimate object of Qur'anic instruction. It relies in particular on hearing in the attention given to accentuation, intonation, the cadences of suras as uttered by the master, their tireless repetition (*tikrār*) out loud, and their rhythmic recitation, as if memory were constituted through audition. The rhythm of the torso rocking back and forth to the rhythm of Qur'anic verses facilitates the process of memorization. Although all pupils are simultaneously reciting different verses, the master, like the conductor of an orchestra, is listening for any error, which he signals by tapping the pupil with his rod. At a more advanced level, children answer the teacher's questions by tracing the letters of the answer on their arm, leg, or hand, concealing it from the other students. If the answer is valid, the master approves, or else he shakes his head and supplies the answer. The dominance of hearing for the transmission of knowledge explains why a blind person, but never a deaf-mute, can serve as a teacher.[13]

Even though the pupil acquires literacy by means of the Qur'anic text, reciting it remains more essential than reading or writing it. Moreover, this recitation should be perfect[14] out of respect for the Divine Word, which is unique, final, eternal, and unchangeable. As al-Qayrawānī (1968, 301–3), the tenth-century Maliki jurist, recommended: "You are not permitted . . . to recite the Qur'an with accented rhythms as in profane singing. The majesty of God's Book does not allow for any recitation other than in a serious manner and in such conditions that you are sure that God would be satisfied and find it agreeable; and in bringing all your attention to bear on this pious recitation."

Unlike most texts in classical Arabic, where only the consonants are written down, the Qur'an includes vowel markers to preclude any ambiguity in reading it. Among the ten styles of reading the Qur'an, seven of which are quite common throughout the Muslim world, Malikis have adopted the *Nāfi'* style, which includes two variants: *Warsh*, where the hamza is distinctly pronounced, and *Kalun*, where it is omitted. In Mauritania, the Qur'an is first taught according to the first variant; the student who wants to diversify his reading style learns the second afterward. Different styles of reading may have implications for the very meaning of the Qur'anic text. For this reason, the diversity of readings accounts in part for the divergent interpretations among Islamic schools of jurisprudence. Consequently, jurists (Khalīl 1995, 78) have even considered the question of whether prayer is invalidated because of a faulty reading of the suras; a mispronunciation of certain letters can be problematic.

In Mauritania, regional differences exist in the pronunciation of certain letters. They have sometimes led to heated controversies about the recitation of the Qur'an—for example, about the pronunciation of the letter *jim*. Throughout the country, the letter is pronounced as a soft *j* in dialectical Arabic or even in profane classical texts (poems, genealogies, etc.). However, when reciting the Qur'an or hadith, Moors from Adrar, Tagant, and Hawdh pronounce this letter with a hard *j*, whereas Moors from Trarza (except for the Idawa'li, who are originally from Adrar and Tagant), pronounce it with a soft *j*. The "quarrel of the *jim*" inspired an important exchange of legal opinions (*fatāwā*) in eighteenth-century Mauritania, notably between a scholar from the Tanwājyū maraboutic tribe in the east, Sīdī 'Abdallah wuld Abū Bakr at-Tanwājīwī (d. 1145 AH/1732–1733 CE), a partisan of the hard *j*, and a scholar from the Idawday maraboutic tribe in Trarza, Muḥammad al-Yadālī (d. 1166 AH/1752–1753 CE), an advocate of the soft *j*. The biography of Sīdī 'Abdallah in the *Fatḥ ash-Shakūr* describes him as a notable imam, specialist in the seven readings of the Qur'an, which he learned under Sīdī Aḥmad al-Ḥabīb al-Lamṭī as-Sijilmāsī, and who, upon returning to Mauritania, corrected the faulty reading of his companions, in particular the pronunciation of the letter *jim* (Hamel 1992, 418, n. 200). Ever since, the majority of Mauritanians adopted his way of reciting the *jim*, known as the *jim* of the Tanwājyū tribe, when reading the Qur'an.

The art of chanting (*tajwīd*) the Qur'an follows different rhythms: the fastest (*ḥadr*) is used for learning the Qur'an, a moderate rhythm (*tadwīr*) for reciting long prayers during Ramadan, and the slowest (*tartīl*) for daily prayer. Chanting the Qur'an requires discipline, as this verse indicates (LXXV, 16–18): "Do not wiggle your tongue while saying it in order to go faster!" (Blachère 1980, 626). Perfect chanting is a token of respect toward the Divine Word and one form of Divine worship (*'ibāda*); thus, the Book (LXXIII, 4) exhorts its meticulous practice: "Chant the Predication with care" (Blachère 1980, 621).

Slaking the Thirst for Knowledge

In certain maraboutic tribes, a child frequently learns the whole text of the Qur'an in five to seven years. The linguistic proximity between the language of the Moors, *Ḥassāniyya*, and classical Arabic, the language of the Qur'an, facilitates the process. A young man who knows the entire Book (*al-Kitāb*) is called *ḥāfiẓ*,[15] a word designating a guardian or keeper (Kazimirski 1944, 1:460) and which, in classical Arabic, alludes to the indestructible and indelible nature of the Word (Chabbi 1997, 484). Indeed, it is the Divine Word which the reciter contains within himself; his person is invested with the Qur'an, this saying in Ḥassāniyya suggests: "He recites and carries the Divine Book" (*ḥāfiẓu wa ḥāmilu Kitābi Allahi al-'azīzi*). Carrying the Qur'an inside oneself also means one carries within oneself the beneficent *baraka* of the Divine Word; a hadith affirms that "The carriers of the Qur'an are the elect of God, his close associates" (Ibn Saḥnūn 1953, 83). Consequently, the reciter is an intercessor between God and other humans. The numinous character of the student invested with the Divine Word comes to the fore at dangerous moments of "passage" such as burials. It is said on such occasions that he who knows the entirety of the Qur'an has "ceased wandering" (*aqsar dhihāba*)—in other words, that he is on the right path, the path of God.

The new status of the pupil who has finished learning the Qur'an is made visible in Moorish society by coloring his hands and feet with henna. One of the Moorish expressions used to designate the student who has finished memorizing the Qur'an refers to this practice: "We have put henna on his hand or his arm." As soon as the henna dries, the pupil thrusts his right hand into a jar of butter. Pupils who have not finished their education lick off the butter that covers his arm in order to incorporate the Divine Word that has been internalized by their comrade.

It remains for the student who has, according to common practice, memorized the Qur'an in reverse order to take it up again, this time in the proper order. After this repetition, which generally lasts less than a year, the student acquires a new status. The termination of Qur'anic study is marked by a rite of passage whereby the student, over a period of two days, recites the entire Book before his master and two witnesses. Before beginning his recitation, he utters a conjuration designed to protect against any error inspired by the devil: "Cursed be the devil who has been stoned!" If the two scholarly witnesses consider that the pupil's Qur'anic knowledge is sufficient, they deliver an *ijāza*, a certificate of transmission. This very common term is based on the same radical as *ajāzā*, "to authorize." As its name suggests, the *ijāza* authorizes the student to teach, which is to say that he can in his own right become a master. It is written in the teacher's hand, using on this occasion colored ink for certain signs, such as vowel markers; such ink is normally reserved for copies of precious books, and its use for the *ijāza* testifies to the importance of this document. Its official character is underscored by the formula at the end of the document, "certified authentic" (*ṣaḥah wathabata*). This has all the characteristics of a legal document, as the names of the two witnesses are added to the seal of authenticity. In addition, the student's level of proficiency is evaluated by a grade (*takhdīr*) decided upon by the master and the two witnesses: "very good" (*ḥassan jidan*), "good" (*ḥassan*), or merely "passable" (*mutawaṣṣiṭ*).

The *ijāza* also includes the name of the teacher. As it happens, the chain of transmission (*sanad*) does not go back further than the master, proof that his reputation suffices to ensure the legitimacy of the knowledge that has been transmitted. This preoccupation with continuity in oral transmission is similar for those who collected the sayings of the Prophet. If the content of knowledge depends on the imitation (*taqlīd*) of those who came before, it is essential that knowledge be transmitted through a reliable chain of transmitters. Consequently, the biographies and the *ijāzāt* of Islamic authors list, before their works, the names of their teachers, in turn part of a genealogy of transmitters of knowledge (*sanad* or *silsila*). The hierarchy of modes of transmission reflects the value placed on specifically oral transmission. Thus, an *ijāza* which testifies that a work has been recited (*qirā'a*) before a master without having been enlightened by his explanations carries less weight than an *ijāza* which specifies that the knowledge was learned by listening (*as-sam'*) to the master. Least prestigious is the *wijāda*, a sort of *ijāza* in absentia given to someone who has studied a work on his own without a master guaranteeing an accurate reading.

The Moorish term designating the process of transmission from master to student is particularly telling: The word *iṣadar* refers to a human or animal who, once he has satisfied his thirst at a well, continues his journey. In an *ijāza*, the expression used to indicate that a student holds his knowledge from a particular teacher can be approximately translated as "So-and-so has slaked his thirst from so-and-so." This formula explicitly shows that learning the Qur'an is conceived as a physiological process of ingestion. Moreover, the expression compares the Qur'anic teacher to a spring from which the student slakes his thirst for knowledge. The disciple effectively chooses the teacher from whom he desires to learn, according to his level and his field of specialization. In this quest, associated with physical travel, it is only once the student is "filled" with his master's knowledge that he is authorized to leave him in search of another master. Once the student has progressively acquired an elevated level of knowledge, his intellectual wanderings come to an end. Nourished by the knowledge accumulated from a succession of masters, he himself becomes a fixed point attracting new students. Of those who are potential masters, it is said that "they have taken the *ijāza*."

In Moorish society, the *ijāza* is limited to the Qur'an and does not include other forms of knowledge. This is because of the specificity of such knowledge, which consists of a single book committed to memory over a limited time, however long. If Qur'anic knowledge is limited, this is not the case for other forms of knowledge, whose depth is limitless like the sea (*al-bāhr*), to which they are generally compared. Given their limitless character, their study has no end; the mastery of one book leads one to study another, and so on, indefinitely. The *Mukhtaṣar* (Précis) of Khalīl is such a dense work that a common expression in Ḥassāniyya to refer to someone with perfect knowledge of a subject simply echoes the first and last words of the text. It is said that Khalīl finished the *Mukhtaṣar* with the aphorism, "Now, you are only just capable of praying,"[16] suggesting that, even after having mastered the work, the scholar cannot rest content, given the immensity of what he still has left to learn. The reference to prayer, at the heart of Islamic practice, can be explained by the fact that knowledge of its intricacies symbolically represents religious knowledge in general; the Moorish expression used to praise a scholar's knowledge is "He knows the rules of prayer" (*yaraf ḥukum ṣalātu*). The saying attributed to Khalīl, marked by humility, invites the reader to pursue his quest for knowledge without succumbing to the illusion that he has plumbed its depth while he is still only at the surface. Consequently, an *ijāza* cannot attest to the transmission of such knowledge, which, given its amplitude, surpasses the capacity of the human mind.

A Specifically Qur'anic Education

The transmission of the Qur'an should thus be distinguished from that of other forms of Arab-Islamic knowledge (e.g., grammar, jurisprudence). Because the

Book is unique, learning it is, by its very nature, finite; on the other hand, for other branches of knowledge, the number of works varies with the nature and level of specialization, and their study is in principle unlimited and infinite. Above all, Qur'anic instruction can only take place under the supervision of a master who rigorously controls learning, whereas other forms of learning can in principle be self-taught without the mediation of a teacher. Consequently, during the time strictly limited to the study of the Qur'an, the pupil is not authorized to review his lesson by bringing his writing board home, lest a third party lead him into error. By contrast, in maraboutic families, the teaching of other subjects can take place within the family; students are often tutored by women in the family about the early history of Islam as well as traditions of the Prophet and by men about grammar and jurisprudence. In addition, whereas the Qur'anic text is learned by heart, disciples (tlāmīd) in the maḥāẓra often resort to mnemonic devices to remember certain grammatical or legal rules. Furthermore, the only means of controlling knowledge of the Book is by recitation, while other subjects are tested through questioning, and learning is based on not only memorization but comprehension. Finally, punishment constitutes an essential means for teaching the Qur'an, while other subjects may be learned through play. It is necessary to qualify the notion that there is a single form of Islamic pedagogy valid for the acquisition of different forms of knowledge (Qur'an, grammar, jurisprudence, etc.). Diversity of pedagogical style follows from the different natures of the subjects taught; the *how* of transmission seems intimately linked to *what* is being transmitted. The specificity of the mode of teaching the Qur'an is strictly a function of the very singularity of the text. The status of this text is not comparable to that of any other scriptural reference; called The Book (*al-Kitāb*), it is considered by Muslims to be the very manifestation of the Divine Word.

The Qur'an is conceived to be timeless and intangible, not subject to any human modification.[17] The divine status of the text determines the attention given to its exact memorization. It must be learned word for word to reproduce the Qur'anic discourse exactly. Moreover, its recitation must not undergo any alteration, and it is not permitted to ask questions while studying it. Thus, a Muslim would prefer to abstain from citing any verse he does not know precisely rather than botch its recitation. This concern for exactness is not only cognitive but religious, because it testifies to a respectful faith in the Word of God.

The study of the transmission of Islamic knowledge raises the question of the relationship between writing and orality in the Muslim world. The mode of learning described in this chapter testifies to the importance of memory acquired through hearing, recitation, and repetition. The primacy of orality over writing in the transmission of knowledge is confirmed by numerous practices in the intellectual and religious world of Islam. The very foundation of Islam testifies to the predominance of orality over writing, given that the Qur'an, even before becoming the Book, was the Divine Word. The very name of the Qur'an stems from the first word revealed to the Prophet: "*'Iqra'!*" ("Recite!") (XCVI, 1), an injunction that is proper to a discourse that has been heard and not read. Because the Qur'an is considered to be the expression of the Divine Word, appropriating it is to make the message flesh, in order that it remain indefinitely alive. This explains on one hand why the necessary remembrance of the Divine Word is a leitmotif in the Qur'an: "Let the Reminder be heard, because it is good to remember!" (LXXXVII, 9). On the other hand, it explains why learning and teaching the Qur'an are religiously meritorious acts, as asserts a hadith: "The best among you is he who has learned the Qur'an and who has taught it" (Nawawi 1991, 280). Chanting the Qur'anic text leads the way to Paradise, as suggested by this saying of the Prophet: "They will say to he who is familiar with the Qur'an: Read and arise, chant it as you chanted it in this world, as your final home shall be determined by the last verse you read" (Nawawi 1991, 281).

Uttering verses or even simple words of the Qur'an is obligatory in all Muslim ritual, whether in prayer, where several suras are recited; for marriage, where the *fātiḥa* is spoken aloud; or even when initiating any action, by pronouncing the word *bismillah*. Compared to the foundational texts of other religions, the Qur'anic text is not only the fundamental reference for how to live an ethical life, but its verses are frequently uttered in accomplishing ritual practices. In addition, given the supernatural quality of the Word, its knowledge confers superhuman powers on he who recites it. Unlike other forms of knowledge, Qur'anic knowledge is also power. The absolutely unique status of the Qur'an explains the singularity of its mode of transmission and accounts for the existence in Muslim societies of a veritable "Qur'anic pedagogy distinct from modes of learning other texts.

Finally, the mode of transmission of learning in Islam, in contrast to Western modes of transmission, subordinates writing to orality. The very content of the concept of orality differs in the two civilizations, referring, in Western civilization, to freedom of imagination and to the spontaneity of creation, and in Arab-Muslim civilization, to the taming of imagination and to the continuity of transmission. Yates (1975) explained that the foundation of Western "art of memory" was a system of images and spaces inherited from the Greeks and that appealed to the sense of sight. The study of the transmission of learning in the Muslim world shows that the Muslim art of memory, which is remembrance (*mudhākara*), relies essentially on the sense of hearing and on oral ingestion—orality in the full sense of the word.[18]

NOTES

1. There are Peul, Soninke, and Bambara communities in Mauritania in addition to Moors.
2. On the subject of gifts to teachers and pupils who are from another locality, and on the services that pupils provide their master in Moorish society, see Fortier (1997).
3. The real name of Nābigha al-Ghallāwī is Muḥammad wuld 'Amar. He died in Tanawbak in 1254 AH (1829–1830 CE).
4. Muḥammad ibn Saḥnūn (Tunisia, 817–870) was the son of Saḥnūn *ibn Sa'īd* (Tunisia, 76–856). The latter, author of the *Mudawwana*, is considered largely responsible for the introduction of the Maliki doctrine in the Maghreb at the expense of the Hanafi school. Ibn Saḥnūn's manual is apparently unknown in Mauritania.
5. However, Ibn Saḥnūn (1953, 91) forbids teachers to hit their students in the face or to withhold from them food or water.
6. In Nigeria as well, it is only after the complete recitation of the entire Qur'an that pupils begin learning other texts (Reichmuth 1997).
7. In certain Trarza tribes, until about thirty years ago such education could be conducted in the Berber language (*klām znāga*).
8. In teaching the Torah—for example, among Moroccan Jews—learning to write is also less important than recitation: "L'écriture, considérée au niveau élémentaire comme non indispensable à la poursuite des études, n'est enseignée que bien tard" (Zafrani 1998, 65).
9. On the heart as an organ of memory in Islam, see Fortier (2001, 2007).
10. According to Ibn Saḥnūn (1953, 86), there is no problem with erasing the writing board by licking off the ink.
11. In both cases, the ingestion involved subjection to corporal punishment (Fortier 1998).
12. Eickelman (1978, 493) remarks that the memorization of the Qur'an is assimilated to its recitation.
13. Colonna (1981, 198, n. 30) notes the expression employed in a community in the Aurès for how a blind person studies: "He learns by ear."
14. A similar preoccupation with perfection is found in the teaching of the Torah: "The correct reading of the liturgical texts of the Bible implies a perfect knowledge of the fine points (*diqduqim*) and the accents (*te'amin*) of the Torah. Chanted reading of the scroll of the law where neither vowel marks nor inflections are written down is one of the fundamental elements of the service. The child is progressively familiarized with it through repetition and memorization. The audience of believers scrupulously monitors the chanting and brusquely signals any errors on the part of the reader, who has to repeat the fragment of the verse correctly" (Zafrani 1998, 64).
15. Someone who has memorized the entire Qur'an is less commonly known in Moorish society as *muqri*, a term that refers in classical Arabic to a Qur'anic reciter.
16. It would seem that this is a remark posthumously attributed to Khalīl; this sentence was not included in the Arabic edition I consulted. Even if the comment is apocryphal, it suggests a certain attitude toward knowledge.
17. Muslims insist on the definitive and fixed character of the Qur'an, compared to the "too human" corrections of the Bible. The status of the Qur'an and the Bible are very different from an Islamic viewpoint: Whereas the Qur'an is the literal Word of God, the Bible is simply a text written by humans, even if both sacred books are considered divinely inspired.
18. Jousse (1974) noted the importance of oral ingestion in processes of transmission in general.

REFERENCES

Blachère, R. 1980. Traduction du *Coran*. Paris: Maisonneuve et Larose.
Chabbi, J. 1997. *Le seigneur des tribus. L'islam de Mahomet*. Paris: Noêsis.
Colonna, F. 1981. "La Répétition. Les *tolba* dans une vallée de l'Aurès." In *Le Maghreb musulman en 1979*, 188–203. Paris: CNRS.
Eickelman, D. F. 1978. "The Art of Memory: Islamic Education and Its Social Reproduction." *Comparative Studies in Society and History* 20 (4): 485–516.
Fortier, C. 1997 "Mémorisation et audition: L'enseignement coranique chez les Maures de Mauritanie." *Islam et Sociétés au Sud du Sahara* 11: 85–105.
———. 1998. "Le corps comme mémoire: Du giron maternel à la férule du maître coranique." *Journal des africanistes* 68 (1–2): 199–223.
———. 2001. "Le lait, le sperme, le dos. Et le sang? Représentations physiologiques de la filiation et de la parenté de lait en islam malékite et dans la société maure de Mauritanie." *Cahiers d'Études Africaines* 40 (1), 161: 97–138.
———. 2002. "De la forge à l'écriture. De l'indépendance à l'aliénation. Le statut ambivalent du forgeron dans la société maure." In *La forge et le forgeron*, vol. 1, *Pratiques et croyances*, 125–53. Paris: Harmattan (Eurasie).
———. 2003. "Une pédagogie coranique. Modes de transmission des savoirs islamiques (Mauritanie)." *Cahiers d'Études Africaines*, 43 (1–2), 169–70: 235–60.
———. 2006. "Intelligence pratique du berger et art magique du forgeron dans la société maure de Mauritanie." In *Les Cahiers du Laboratoire d'Anthropologie Sociale*, edited by Salvatore d'Onofrio, 55–65. Paris: L'Herne.
———. 2007. "Blood, Sperm and the Embryo in Sunni Islam and in Mauritania: Milk Kinship, Descent and Medically Assisted Procreation." In "Islam, Health and the Body," special issue edited by D. Tober and D. Budiani, *Body and Society* 13 (3): 15–36.
Hamel, C. 1992. "Hommes de lettres, disciples et enseignement dans le Takrûr du XVIe au début du XIXe siècle. Fath ash-shakur." Doctoral thesis, Université de Paris I-Panthéon-Sorbonne.
Ibn 'Asīm, M. 1958. *'Āsmiyya*. Translated by L. Bercher. Algiers: Institut d'études orientales, Faculté des Lettres d'Alger.
Ibn Sahnūn, M. 1953. "Le livre des règles de conduite des maîtres d'école." Translated by G. Lecomte. *Revue des études islamiques* 21: 77–105.
Jousse, M. 1974. *L'Anthropologie du geste*. Paris: Gallimard.
Kazimirski, A. B. 1944. *Dictionnaire arabe/français*. Beirut: Librairie du Liban.
Khalīl, M. 1995. *Le précis*. Beirut: Dar el-fiker.
Meunier, O. 1997. *Dynamique de l'enseignement islamique au Niger*. Paris: Harmattan.
Naraghi, E. 1992. *Enseignement et changements sociaux en Iran du VIIe au XXe siècle*. Paris: MSH.
Nawawi, I. 1991. *Les jardins de la piété. Les sources de la tradition islamique*. Paris: Alif.
Qayrawānī, M. 1968 *La Risāla. Épître sur les éléments du dogme et de la loi de l'Islam selon le rite mâlékite*. Translated by L. Bercher. Algiers: H. Pérès.

Reichmuth, S. 1997. "A Regional Centre of Islamic Learning in Nigeria: Ilorin and Its Influence on Yoruba Islam." In *Madrasa. La transmission du savoir dans le monde musulman*, edited by N. Grandin and M. Gaborieau, 229–45. Paris: Arguments.

Schmitz, J. 1998. *Zuhūr al-Basātīn*, t. 1. *Histoire des musulmans noirs du Fuuta Tooro (vallée du Sénégal)*, vol. 1, *La révolution des torobbe musulmans*. Paris: CNRS.

Yates, A. 1975. *L'art de la mémoire*. Paris: Gallimard.

Zafrani, H. 1998. *Deux mille ans de vie juive au Maroc*. Paris: Maisonneuve et Larose.

4.
ISLAMIC EDUCATION AND THE INTELLECTUAL PEDIGREE OF AL-HAJJ UMAR FALKE

Muhammad Sani Umar

THIS CHAPTER EXPLORES various educational and intellectual aspects of Islam in West Africa through an analytical reading of Umar Falke's (1893–1962) *Mafākhir al-Jīl al-Kirām wa Tarājim al-'Ulamā' wa al-'Awliyā' al-A'lām*, in which he traces his educational and intellectual pedigree in the genres of biographical dictionaries (*tarājim*), hagiography (*manāqib*), and hierarchy/ranking of scholars (*ṭabaqāt*). Such an analysis can contribute to our understanding of traditions of Islamic learning, such as the master–disciple reading of texts; intellectual networks connecting Muslim scholars through the various regions of West Africa and beyond; certification for texts studied with particular masters; the core curriculum of Islamic learning in West Africa; and the polemical exchanges among scholars. Beginning with brief sketches of the author and the corpus of his writings, the chapter frames the relevant context of the text to illuminate an important subsector of Islamic education chiefly concerned with Islamic learning beyond the memorization of the Qur'an that constitutes the primary level of Islamic educational system. Using three significations of the body—as corpus, corporeality, and corporation—this chapter demonstrates the centrality of bodily ideas and practices in traditional Islamic education.

The Scholar and His Corpus in Context

Born in a village near Kano to a Tuareg father and a Fulani mother, Umar Falke began his Islamic education with members of his family, learning recitation of the Qur'an and the elementary texts of Maliki *fiqh* from his cousin, Abū Ja'far Qāsim b. Ismā'īl. In 1921, Falke relocated to Ilorin to join his father's trading business. Here he was initiated into the Tijaniyya in 1922, renewing his affiliation several times in later years. The impact of the Tijaniyya on Falke is profound and clear in all his writings but especially in the *Mafākhir al-Jīl al-Kirām*. Through the rest of his life, Falke pursued his studies and trading activities, traveling in the long-distance trade that earned him the nickname of Falke—the Hausa word for a long-distant merchant—and giving him the opportunity to meet and study with scholars in different towns and regions in Nigeria, Ghana, and Senegal. When he took residence in Lagos in 1927, Falke had the opportunity of studying with local and visiting scholars from Shinqit and the Maghreb, including Tijanis such as Sharif Aḥmad b. Ṣāliḥ, who arrived in Lagos from Marrakech in 1935; Sharīf Aḥmad b. Muḥammad al-Amīn al-Shinqīṭī, who came to Lagos in 1936; Aḥmad b. Abī Bakr al-Fāsī al-Idrīsī, who appeared in Lagos in 1937; and ʿAbd al-Latī al-Shāmī al-Hāshimī (Hunwick 1995, 276–79). In 1946, Falke traveled to Koalack in Senegal to study with al-Shaykh Ibrahim Niasse, the most prominent Tijani in West Africa from the 1930s to the 1970s.

From this biographical sketch, we can locate the active years of Falke's life in the context of colonial Nigeria during the first half of the twentieth century. Of the many events during the colonial era, improved conditions for long-distance travel—particularly with the introduction of modern means of transportation such as trains and motor vehicles—are relevant for understanding the eventful life of Umar Falke. His exposure to many teachers and scholars, including visiting scholars from outside of Nigeria, was greatly facilitated by the improved security on the trading routes following the cessation of interethnic warfare that ravaged the region in the second half of the nineteenth century. The increased volume of traffic across West Africa as well as between West and North Africa allowed the steady flow of people and ideas, more than would have been possible in the nineteenth century. In particular, the Tijaniyya seems to have spread faster through the transportation networks that connected many Tijani communities across vast distances. Both French and British colonial authorities were apprehensive about the movement of Tijani adherents, ideas, and ritual practices, as evidenced in colonial reports of surveillance on itinerant teachers. Colonial authorities feared that Tijaniyya networks were potential conduits for spreading anticolonial sentiments among Muslims, especially among the surviving veterans who fought against the French colonial conquest of the Umarian Tijani empire, who had migrated into many parts of Nigeria following the fall of their capital to the French (Umar 2000).

By the 1920s, these Tijani communities had already reconciled themselves to colonial rule; there were no efforts to mount any overt resistance to colonial authorities (Harrison 1988; Robinson 2000; Umar 2005). Rather, the polemical exchanges between the Tijaniyya and its anti-Sufi opponents were a far more important preoccupation for the Tijanis, since the polemics had also spread via the same networks of transportation made possible by the colonial regimes (Seesemann 1998, 1999). Some of the Tijani anxieties arising from the spread of anti-Tijani polemical ideas are reflected in the writings of Umar Falke. Arguably, by documenting the saintly lives of his Tijani teachers in *Mafākhir al-Jīl al-Kirām*, Umar Falke was working with a polemical subtext as implied in the full title of the work: These saintly and deeply learned scholars of the Tijaniyya are quite different from their untutored opponents.

According to *Arabic Literature of Africa* (Hunwick 1995, 276–79), Falke is the author of twelve titles and twelve poems, mostly on Sufi themes. *Mafākhir al-Jīl al-Kirām*, a short treatise of sixty-seven folios divided into three major sections, is perhaps the most important historically, because it provides accounts of the educational career and spiritual quest of Falke from his childhood through 1938, when the work was completed. Section one of *Mafākhir al-Jīl al-Kirām* comprises twenty-three biographical entries on Falke's teachers in Qur'anic studies, law, theology, Arabic language and literature, and other branches of Islamic learning. Section two is focused exclusively on his Sufi mentors who inducted him into the mystical universe of gnosis. Section three is a miscellanea of exhortations and excerpts of poems. The rest of this chapter presents a preliminary analytical reading of selected passages from section one, analyzing the Islamic educational ideas and practices through the three conceptions of the body: the corporeal, the corpus, and corporate.

Section 1: Corporeal

The transmission of Islamic education entails significant bodily practices that are readily discernible in the *Mafākhir al-Jīl al-Kirām*. The doxology alludes to the bodily practices of obeying the commands of the Almighty against following the fanciful desires of the *nafs* (soul/self), which is one of the four elements that constitute a human *(al-insān)* in Qur'anic discourse. First, *al-insān* is made of clay *(ṭīn)*, a mixture of water and earth that forms the raw material that God used to fashion the physical body of humans (Qur'an 6:2, 7:12, 23, 32, etc.). Second, *al-insān* also entails spirit *(ruh)*, which is the vital element of life animating the human body in its basic functions (Qur'an 15:27–29). Third, *khayāl* (imagination) is an integral part of *al-insān* defined by its lack of stability due to its constant change, and hence it is utterly unreliable for knowing God. As the locus of human volition, will, initiative, and moral agency, the *nafs* is always in a complicated relationship with the physical body of humans (Murata and Chittick 1993, 100–3). The Qur'an portrays these complicated relationships in terms of the potential of *nafs* to go astray by yielding to the demands of the body and the fantasies of the imagination *(al-nafs al-'ammāra bi al- sū'*, as in Qur'an 12:53) that could also result in human arrogance and boastful pride *(tazkiyat al-nafs*, as in Qur'an 53:32). But *nafs* also possesses the capacity to recognize its moral failings *(al-nafs al-lawwāma*, as in Qur'an 75:2, 53:12) and to struggle toward piety and righteousness, thereby achieving contentment and satisfaction in its obedience to God (*al-nafs al-muṭ'ma'inna*, as in Qur'an 89:27). The ultimate goal of Islamic education is to subject the *nafs* to physical and moral discipline that will elevate it through spiritual progression from *al-nafs al-'ammāra* to *al-nafs al-muṭ'ma'inna*.

This educational goal is especially prominent among Sufis, who emphasize *tarbiyya*—that is, spiritual mentoring and moral development through education. Hence, the Sufi conception of Islamic education entails, first, the simple comprehension of spiritual progression of *nafs* that could be gained from the written corpus; second and more importantly, Sufi educational practices of *tarbiyya* require the mastering of the spiritual techniques that enable *al-nafs al-muṭ'ma'inna* to prevail over the other types of *nafs*; and, third, controlling *al-nafs al-muṭ'ma'inna* over the demands of the physical body. This more important progression is not possible through simple intellectual mastering of the written corpus; it requires face-to-face learning from an accomplished teacher to master the various techniques of disciplining the physical body through ascetic practices that include prayer, night vigil, and fasting.

There are linkages of the corpus to the corporeal as well as the corporate, as discussed below. Such linkages could be either positive or negative, as can be seen in Falke's references to Sufi maxims such as "the person without a spiritual mentor will be guided by Satan" and "the person who does not know his/her *nafs* could not possibly know his/her Creator." These maxims indicate that the knowledge derived solely from the written corpus without the guidance of the corporeal (mentor) is devoid of insight and could be dangerous because it may lead to *inkār*: the stubborn denial of the authoritative spiritual insights of the master reliably transmitted through the sound spiritual genealogy (*silsila*) and intellectual pedigree (*sanad*) of the corporate body of knowledgeable masters to their disciples. In contrast to the dangers of *inkar*, the positive linkage serves as a conveyor of spiritual insights embodied in the acknowledged masters and transmitted through the corporate body of their disciples. In fact, Falke's precise reason for writing *Mafākhir al-Jīl al-Kirām* is to document his own *silsilas* and *sanads*, because, he argues, it is imperative for the Sufi seekers of knowledge to be thoroughly acquainted with the individuals comprising their respective *silsila* and the *sanad*. When positively linked, the three bodies of knowledge work harmoniously to save the corporeal body of the disciple by ensuring the correct comprehension of the reality embodied in the corpus of written texts as reliably transmitted to the corporate bodies of disciples. When negatively linked, things go awry: The corporeal is endangered by the presumption that reality could be comprehended directly by disembodied intellectual engagement with the written corpus and without the imperative mediation of the corporate body of masters and disciples. Although these educational ideas and practices are particularly strong among Sufis, they are also important even among non-Sufi Muslims.

Several passages in the *Mafākhir al-Jīl al-Kirām* highlight the various aspects of the corporeal constitution of knowledge through specific pedagogical ideas and practices. For example, introducing himself in the formulary of "the poor servant in need of His creator's mercy," Falke states his intention to document the names of his "parents in the sciences of *fiqh* (Islamic jurisprudence), *tariqa* and *haqiqa* (Sufism)." Two important points are worth highlighting here: (1) reference to the master–disciple relationship in parental (corporeal) as well as familial (corporate) terms and (2) knowing biographical and hagiographical details (corpus) of the individual scholars (corporeal) and their standing among their peers (corporate). These points once again indicate not only the connections among the different conceptions of body but their centrality in Islamic education.

A second example can be seen in the enumeration of subject matter and areas of specialization in the written corpus of *fiqh*, *tafsir* (Qur'anic exegesis), *adab* (literature), and so on, which, together with using superlative laudatory adjectives to describe the vast learning and deep insights of his teachers, are clear illustrations of the formulary developed among Muslim scholars (corporate) for writing (corpus) about individual scholars and teachers (corporeal). The intricate linkages among the three different bodies can also be discerned when we shift analytical focus from the corporeal to the corpus.

Section 2: The Corpus

The textual features of *Mafākhir al-Jīl al-Kirām* illustrate several elements constituting the corpus of Islamic knowledge. First and foremost, the corpus of Islamic knowledge comprises several genres, disciplines, and areas of specialization. As already noted, *Mafākhir al-Jīl al-Kirām* is written in the genres of *tarājim*, *manāqib, and ṭabaqāt*. Arguably, it is also an autobiography of sorts, chronicling the author's intellectual odyssey, even though autobiography is not very common in the Islamic intellectual traditions. In a sense, *Mafākhir al-Jīl al-Kirām* is modeled after—if not explicitly inspired by—the *'Idā' al-nusūkh* of Abdullahi b. Fodio (Hiskett 1957). Although both texts apparently document no more than the singular experiences of their respective authors, they do provide valuable materials that can be teased to analyze several themes and features of the production of Islamic knowledge. Leonard Binder (1988, 21) observes that, although "the technique of analyzing a single text in great depths" lacks generality, the counterargument "is that the general does not exist as an empirical reality, so that one is as well served by developing the larger implications of a significant particular as in surveying a larger number of relatively insignificant cases." Thus, for example, Table 4.1 identifies the texts and Table 4.2 the branches of Islamic learning that Falke studied with different teachers, building upon the concept of the "core curriculum" of Islamic learning in West Africa as articulated by Stewart and Hall

Table 4.1. Subjects and Fields of Study Mentioned in Mafākhir al-Jīl al-Kirām

1	Stylistics	البديع
2	Composition	البيان
3	Semantics	المعاني
4	Qur'an recitation	قرآة القرآن
5	Poetry	القصائد
6	Literature	الأدب
7	Arabic	العربية
8	Grammatical conjugation	الصرف
9	Wills and testaments	الوصية
10	Asceticism	الزهد
11	Jurisprudence	الفقه
12	Arabic grammar	النحو
13	Tinajiyya litanies	اوراد التجانية وآدابها
14	Sufi order	الطريقة
15	Sufism	التصوف
16	Theology	التوحيد
17	Preaching/sermon	الوعظ
18	Qur'anic exegesis	التفسير
19	Arithmetic	الحساب
20	Poetic rhyme	العروض والقافي
21	Theological divination	علم التوحيد الرملي البرهاني
22	Principles of sand divination	قوعد خط الرمل

(2011). *Mafākhir al-Jīl al-Kirām* confirms a number of their observations, notably the absence of incompatibility between Sufism and jurisprudence and the use of different renditions (abridged, versification, commentary) of a particular title in teaching. It also provides an additional indication of the common titles found in other collections and sources across the region. Perhaps even more interestingly, *Mafākhir al-Jīl al-Kirām* provides tangible evidence of the specific Sufi texts in the core curriculum that Stewart and Hall could not identify in their sources.

Mafākhir al-Jīl al-Kirām has glosses written by a different hand on the margins, thereby pointing to the important element of commentary (*sharḥ*) in its diverse forms from the simplest explanation of vocabulary, including Hausa translation of difficult words, to brief observation (*taʿlīq*) and more complex commentaries that engage with some of the author's main points. The critical importance of commentarial intervention in the constitution of the corpus of Islamic knowledge has rarely been sufficiently appreciated, especially in light of the

Table 4.2 Titles of Books Mentioned in Mafākhir al-Jīl al-Kirām

الاخضري
حرز اليماني
الدلائل الخيرات
مقامات الحريري
الحكم العطائية
الموطأ
(الباجي (شرح الموطأ
(الزرقاني (شرح الموطأ
المودودية في المد والقصر
الحصن
لامية الافعال
ارشاد السالك للامام الاسكري البغدادي
مختصر الخليل
العصامية
ابي مقرع للحساب
عقود الجمان
حسن الصنيع في البيان
والمعاني والبديع
الفريدة للشيخ السيوطي
الالفية بن مالك
الشفاء للقاضي عياض
دليل العقائد في التوحيد
العقيدة السنوسية في التوحيد
الياقوتة الفريدة في الطريقة التجانية
كتاب ديوان الفارض
كتاب سلاح التجانيين تاليف العلامة الفهامة الشيخ محمد الامين بن الامام مالك الفوتي اجوبة شيخه القطب الولي الصالح المحدث الشيخ الفا هاشم بن محمد الفوتي المدني رضي الله عنهما
كتاب روض الشمائل تاليف السيد احمد بن حم جد الشريف اجدود بن محمد الكبير
ورد كتاب طيب الفائح في صلاة الفاتح تاليف القطب الشريف السيد محمد بن عبد الواحد النظيفي

conventional periodization of Islamic intellectual history in which the era of producing commentaries and supercommentaries is viewed as the hallmark of intellectual decline allegedly characterized by lack of originality, dilettantism, and obsession with the superficial, banal, and trivial. In contrast with the originality and brilliance of the earlier periods of *ijtihād* (independent thought), the corpus of the commentaries and supercommentaries are the stale imitations (*taqlīd*) of the era following the supposed "closing of the door of *ijtihād*." Although such views have come under well-deserved criticism not only in the works of Hallaq (1984) but even earlier in Hodgson's magisterial *The Venture of Islam* (1974), the critical roles of commentaries in constituting the corpus of Islamic knowledge remain to be investigated in a systematic fashion. Here I can only suggest that commentaries are constitutive of the recognized canon and are far more creative in their engagement with the primary text they comment upon than is usually credited, as can easily be seen in the master template of the commentarial: *Tafsīr al-Qur'an*. Exegetical strategies of asserting and contesting the meanings and significations of Qur'anic text, specifying its generalizations and generalizing its specifics, and the divergent perspectives reflecting legal, theological, mystical, historical backgrounds, and agendas of the exegetes combined to suggest the immense impact of commentary in the formation of the Islamic corpus.

Section 3: The Corporate

As we can discern the corporeal formation of the body of knowledge in the opening doxology of *Mafākhir al-Jīl al-Kirām*, we can equally see the allusion to the corporate aspects of Islamic education. The doxology invokes the Qur'anic and hadith references to the ulama as the only group among God's servants who possess the religious virtue of the fear of God, and also as being the heirs entrusted with the prophetic legacy, hence deserving inclusion in the pious prayer to God to be counted with them along with the Prophet, his companions, and their followers ad infinitum. Another early allusion to the corporate aspects of Islamic education comes in the preliminary remarks of the author explaining his objective of composing the work to refute the *inkār* of the opponents of the Tijaniyya.[1] As the order of al-Shaykh Ahmad al-Tijani's Sufi disciples (corporate), the Tijaniyya facilitates the acquisition of spiritual knowledge through observance of its program of spiritual discipline (corporeal), including the observance of the *wazīfa*, the daily recital of set litanies (corpus) required from all adherents of the order. Falke's polemical intent points also to intellectual exchanges between Tijanis and their opponents as a component of Islamic learning through which both groups seek to: (1) define their group identity; (2) discharge the intellectual responsibility of the leadership to articulate and defend in writing (corpus) the doctrines of the order; and (3) assert the obligations of the followership to cultivate and display disciplined loyalty, which could take the form of bodily practices (corporeal) of performing unique ritual, wearing a long beard, carrying a rosary, bearing the image of the master, displaying symbols of the order, or adorning a particular garment.

In the second and third entries of *Mafākhir al-Jīl al-Kirām*, we read that the author began his education by learning the Qur'an from members of his immediate family, and entry fifteen mentions al-Shaykh Muhammad b. Abdullah, who belonged to the House of Wizara in the emirate of Bida. These entries hint at the phenomenon of clerical families who have historically been central to the spread of Islamic learning across West Africa (Sanneh 1976, 1989; Stewart 1976; El-Hamel 1999). Significant features of the clerical families across West Africa indicate the corporate aspects of Islamic education in the region as well as the already demonstrated linkages to both the corporeal and the corpus. To begin with, a clerical family originates from a particular individual (corporeal) who becomes the eponymous ancestor after whom the family is named. Paralleling the historical evolution of Sufi orders, schools of law, theological sects, and ruling dynasties, the clerical families are not always composed exclusively of the biological descendants of the founder but often include other disciples attracted to the founder because of his piety and learning. As the group of descendants and disciples grow numerically, they acquire a distinct group identity defined by their traditions of learning and the corpus of texts constituting the canon of their curriculum and libraries. Additional corporate features of Islamic education include the system of certification and credentialing; the structure of authority and leadership; rank and hierarchy among the disciples; particular ritual practices; distinct modus operandi of interacting with the political authorities and other sectors of the society; and narratives of origin (Wilks 2000). Obtaining grants of land and special privileges from rulers encoded in legal instruments (*mahram*) as well as in charters and chronicles are the final stages in the historical evolution of the clerical families as corporate bodies who have historically played critical roles in the production of Islamic knowledge in West Africa (Bobboyi 1993; O'Fahey 1996; Spaulding 2002). A point worth emphasizing here is that, although the institution of *waqf/hubus* provides both legal incorporation as well as a permanent stream of revenue for educational institutions in other regions of the Islamic world, the *mahram* is the more common instrument of legally incorporating educational institutions in sub-Saharan Muslim societies (O'Fahey and Vikor 1996; O'Fahey and Hunwick 2002).

Entries twenty to twenty-three focus on itinerant scholars visiting from the Sahara and North Africa who taught the author, thus pointing to networking as an important feature of the corporate dimension of Islamic education (Reese 2004). Both teachers and students travel to teach and to learn as well as to grant and receive *ijaza* (certification). Again we can observe the linkages among the corporeal, the corpus, and the corporate dimensions of Islamic education, with each taking various forms. Among the forms of the corporeal are the particular individuals traveling in the circuits of the scholarly networks and physically enduring the hardship of long-distance travel before the modern era. In addition to gaining the Islamic knowledge that motivates their travel in the first instance, the itinerant aspects of Islamic education entails exposure to different lands, cultures, and languages. The movement of the corporeal in the search of knowledge enjoys the authorization of the Prophet Muhammad in the famous tradition urging Muslims to seek for knowledge even in faraway China, and in Qur'anic verses urging Muslims to travel on earth to gain understanding of the signs and powers of God as manifested in different communities and regions.

Seeking to obtain particular texts to study with a known expert indicates that scholarly networks are significant corporate dimensions of Islamic education; other corporate practices include libraries/manuscript collections and the material requirements of pen, ink, and paper for writing different types of texts. It is important to point out that the written corpus requires the mediation of the corporeal, because in Islamic education the centrality of learning directly from the master has often meant that the written text enjoys no more than a problematic autonomy as a source of knowledge. Still, the epistemological privileging of corporeally mediated knowledge must be counterbalanced by the many practical advantages of writing, making it virtually indispensable, if only for facilitating the memorization (corporeal) dictated by the epistemologically privileged status of the nonwritten corpus.

Perhaps it is a consequence of the epistemologically problematic status of the written corpus that we do not have as much information on the seemingly mundane but indispensable aspects of the material production of the written corpus, for whereas we know so many authors/scholars, we know barely the names of only a few scribes/copyists and their various fonts and styles of writing. But even more seriously, we could hardly name particular manuscript illustrators; manufacturers and merchants of ink, pen, and paper; and bookstores and booksellers. While we know a great deal about authorial conventions of writing different types of texts, we know precious little about the scribal conventions observed by scribes and copyists as critical players in corporate formation of Islamic texts. Recent studies have significantly enriched our knowledge of the production and transmission of Islamic corpus in West Africa, including the commercial aspects of books and papers, archival collections of manuscripts, and the canonical texts in the "core curriculum" of Islamic education in West Africa (Krätli and Lydon 2011). But as Brigaglia (2011) has demonstrated with specific reference to northern Nigeria, the major changes in the writing and printing of Islamic texts remain poorly understood; similarly, the changes in pedagogy and curricula of Islamic schools (Brenner 2001; Umar 2003) are still in need of more case studies as well as comparative analysis of the ongoing transformations of Islamic schools across West Africa.

In the scholarly networks, the bonds that connect the corporeal in the form of particular individuals with the corporate body of scholars constitute a key thematic focus of the *Mafākhir al-Jīl al-Kirām*, for among the author's objective is to document his spiritual genealogies (*silsila*) in the Tijaniyya as well as his intellectual pedigree (*isnad*) in the legal, theological, and scriptural branches of Islamic learning. Umar Falke is meticulous in documenting his assiduous quest for the numerous *ijazas* he obtained from his teachers, often by rereading the same text with different itinerant scholars even if he had already obtained certification for the same text from other teachers. As an important pointer to the epistemological premium on the corporeal mediation of the written corpus, Umar Falke calls attention to different kinds of reading a text at the feet of a master, thereby indicating the different types of learning and teaching that transpire between the master and the disciple. Thus, in entry twenty, Umar Falke states that when he encountered a new teacher he would undertake rereadings of *baḥth* (research) and *tadabbur* (contemplation) of the same texts that he had already studied with previous teachers—presumably in a different fashion of reading. Apart from the important function of cementing the bonds between the masters and their disciples, amassing *ijaza*, *silsila*, and *sanad* as well as following multiple strategies of reading a text with different masters also serve other purposes for both the masters and the disciples. For the master, they spread his scholarly fame, spiritual authority, social and political influence, and revenue from disciples' gifts; for the disciple, they impart insights, enhance comprehension, confer blessings, and credentialize knowledge. In other words, they play critical roles in the corporate practices of Islamic learning.

Conclusion

This chapter has highlighted key aspects of Islamic education in West Africa through an analysis of educational ideas and practices as manifested in the intellectual odyssey of one Muslim. The central importance of bodily conceptions and practices in the Islamic education are not unique to the Islamic educational experiences of this particular individual; they are readily observable in the broad traditions of Islamic learning (Arjomand 1999; Eickelman 1985; Humphreys 1991; Makdisi 1981, 1991; Petry 1981; Reese 2004). Although many observers have long noted that memorization and corporeal discipline are key features of Qur'anic schooling (Boyle 2004; Şaul 1984; Ware 2004), few have paid attention to the critical roles of the three forms of embodiment in other sectors of Islamic education. In Islamic traditions of learning, a disembodied knowledge, learned or transmitted without the bodily agency of the teacher, is arguably suspect, if not useless. Such knowledge lacks the *baraka* (blessing), or moral authority and spiritual insights, that can only be obtained by the disciple through long years of toil, perseverance, and dutiful apprenticeship under the master; only the master can unveil the implicit knowledge inscribed in written texts to those of his disciples who have exhibited the appropriate disposition. Thus, the corpus, the corporeal, and the corporate are integrally connected in Islamic education.

NOTE

1. For analysis of the important Tijani discourses on *inkār*, see Hiskett (1980) and Seesemann (2001).

REFERENCES

Arjomand, Said A. 1999. "The Law Agency, and Policy in Medieval Islamic Society: Development of the Institutions of Learning from the Tenth to the Fifteenth Century." *Comparative Studies in Society and History* 41 (2): 263–93.

Binder, Leonard. 1988. *Islamic Liberalism: A Critique of Development Ideologies*. Chicago: University of Chicago Press.

Bobboyi, Hamidu. 1993. "Relations of the Borno 'Ulama with the Sayfawa Rulers: The Role of the *Mahram*." *Sudanic Africa* 4: 175–204.

Boyle, Helen N. 2004. *Quranic Schools: Agents of Preservation and Change*. New York: Routledge.

Brenner, L. 2001. *Controlling Knowledge: Religion, Power, and Schooling in a West African Muslim Society*. Bloomington: Indiana University Press.

Brigaglia, Andrea, 2011. "Central Sudanic Arabic Scripts (Part 1): The Popularization of the Kanawī Script." *Islamic Africa* 2 (2): 51–85.

Eickelman, D. F. 1985. *Knowledge and Power in Morocco: The Education of a Twentieth-Century Notable*. Princeton, NJ: Princeton University Press.

Hallaq, Wael B. 1984. "Was the Gate of Ijtihad Closed?" *International Journal of Middle East Studies* 16: 3–41.

Hamel (El), C. 1999. "The Transmission of Islamic Knowledge in Moorish Society from the Rise of the Almoravids to the 19th Century." *Journal of Religion in Africa* 29 (1): 62–87.

Harrison, C. 1988. *France and Islam in West Africa, 1860–1960*. Cambridge: Cambridge University Press.

Hiskett, M. 1957. "Material Relating to the State of Learning among the Fulani before Their Jihad." *Bulletin School of Oriental and African Studies* 19 (3): 550–78.

———. 1980. "The Community of Grace and Its Opponents, the Rejecters: A Debate about Theology and Mysticism in Muslim West Africa with Special Reference to its Hausa Expression." *Africa Language Studies*, vol. XVII, 99–140

Hodgson, M. 1974. *The Venture of Islam*, vol. 3. Chicago: University of Chicago Press.

Humphreys, R. Stephen. 1991. *Islamic History: A Framework for Inquiry*. Princeton, NJ: Princeton University Press.

Hunwick, John O. 1995. *Arabic Literature of Africa*, vol. 2, *The Writings of Central Sudanic Africa*. Leiden: Brill.

Krätli, Graziano, and Ghislaine Lydon. 2011. *The Trans-Saharan Book Trade: Manuscript Culture, Arabic Literacy and Intellectual History in Muslim Africa*. Leiden: Brill.

Makdisi, G. 1981. *The Rise of Colleges: Institutions of Learning in Islam and the West*. Edinburgh: Edinburgh University Press.

———. 1991. *Religion, Law, and Learning in Classical Islam.* Brookfield, VT: Variorum.
Murata, Sachiko, and W. C. Chittick. 1993. *The Vision of Islam.* New York: Paragon.
O'Fahey, S. R. 1996. "They Have Become the Privileged of God and His Prophet: Mahram and Zawiya in Sudanic Africa." In *The Cloth of Many Colored Silks: Papers on History and Society, Ghanaian and Islamic in Honor of Ivor Wilks*, edited by John Hunwick and Nancy Lawler, 339–54. Evanston, IL: Northwestern University Press.
O'Fahey, S. R., and Knut Vikor, 1996. "A Zanzibari *Waqf* of Books: The Library of the Mundhiri Family." *Sudanic Africa* 7: 5–23.
O'Fahey, S. R., and J. O. Hunwick. 2002. "Some *Waqf* Documents from Lamu." *Sudanic Africa* 13: 1–19.
Petry, C. 1981. *The Civilian Elite of Cairo in the Later Middle Ages.* Princeton, NJ: Princeton University Press.
Reese, S., ed. 2004. *Transmission of Islamic Learning in Africa.* Leiden: Brill.
Robinson, David. 2000. *Paths of Accommodation: Muslim Societies and French Colonial Authorities in Senegal and Mauritania.* Athens: Ohio University Press.
Sanneh, Lamin O. 1976. "The Origins of Clericalism in West African Islam." *Journal of African History* 17 (1): 49–74.
———. 1989. *The Jakhanke Muslim Clerics: A Religious and Historical Study of Islam in Senegambia.* Lanham, MD: University Press of America.
Şaul, Mahir. 1984. "The Quranic School Farm and Child Labour in Upper Volta." *Africa: Journal of the International African Institute* 54 (2): 71–87.
Seesemann, R. 1998. "The *Takfīr* Debate. Sources for the Study of a Contemporary Dispute among African Sufis, Part I: The Nigerian Arena." *Sudanic Africa* 9: 39–70.
———. 1999. "The *Takfīr* Debate. Part II: The Sudanese Arena." *Sudanic Africa* 10: 65–110.
———. 2001. *The Divine Flood: Ibrahim Niasse and the Roots of a Twentieth-Century Sufi Revival.* Oxford: Oxford University Press.
Spaulding, J. 2002. "A Charter of Sultan Badis b. Nol of Sinnar, 1145/1732/3." *Sudanic Africa* 13: 37–40.
Stewart, C. 1976. "Southern Saharan Scholarship and the Bilad al-Sudan." *Journal of African History* 17 (1): 49–74.
Stewart, C., and Bruce Hall. 2011. "The Historic 'Core Curriculum' and the Book Market in Islamic West Africa." In *The Trans-Saharan Book Trade: Manuscript Culture, Arabic Literacy and Intellectual History in Muslim Africa*, edited by Graziano Krätli and Ghislaine Lydon, 109–174. Leiden: Brill.
Umar, M. Sani. 2000. "The Tijaniyya and British Colonial Authorities in Northern Nigeria." In *La Tijaniyya: Une confrerie musulmane a la conquete de 'Afrique*, edited by Jean-Louis Triaud and David Robinson, 327–55. Paris: Karthala.
———. 2003. "Profiles of New Islamic Schools in Northern Nigeria." *Maghreb Review* 28 (1–2): 146–69.
———. 2005. *Islam and Colonialism: Intellectual Responses of Muslims of Northern Nigeria to British Colonial Rule.* Leiden: Brill.
Ware, R. 2004. "Njàngaan: The Daily Regime of Qur'anic Students in 20th Century Senegal." *International Journal of African Historical Studies* 37 (3): 515–38.
Wilks, Ivor. 2000. "The Juula and the Expansion of Islam into the Forest." In *The History of Islam in Africa*, edited by Nehemiah Levtzion and Randall L. Pouwels, 373–96. Athens: Ohio University Press.

INSTITUTIONAL TRANSFORMATIONS

5.
DIVERGENT PATTERNS OF ISLAMIC EDUCATION IN NORTHERN MOZAMBIQUE: QUR'ANIC SCHOOLS OF ANGOCHE

Liazzat J. K. Bonate

BASED ON HISTORICAL archival material as well as fieldwork conducted in 2007, this chapter examines Qur'anic schools in the city of Angoche in northern Mozambique.[1] This type of school remains the main and often the only institution for the transmission of Islamic knowledge in the city and the district of Angoche. However, rather than embodying only one style of Islamic education, the schools represent a range of divergent conceptions that have resulted from the influences of the colonial and postcolonial contexts and local, national, and transnational relations of power. The first part of the chapter provides a historical overview for the emergence of different types of Qur'anic schools in Angoche and in northern Mozambique in general, and highlights how state policies of education as well as the emergence of various Islamic actors and groups affected this diversity. The second part outlines the results of field research involving interviews of administrative and teaching staff of the Qur'anic schools as well as of prominent members of Muslim communities, including women. In addition, the physical structure, curriculum, teachers' profiles, teaching material, financial and social base, and ideological and organizational orientations of some of the schools in Angoche City were explored comparatively.

Angoche is an administrative district in the northern Mozambican province of Nampula. Its name was derived from that of an island, also known as Ngoji. The island and the adjacent region were conquered by the Portuguese in 1910, although a small military garrison was stationed in a continental strip since 1862 in a town called Parapatu, later renamed António Enes, which became the city of Angoche after the independence. Until then, the island, ruled by a sultan, had been an independent constituent of the regional Swahili trading and cultural networks for centuries. The ethnic name of the people of the island is Koti, and their language, a variant of Kiswahili, is called Ekoti.

The island is composed of various settlements, including Qatamoio, Yaruba, Kilwa, and Maziwani, each of which local residents identify as a separate island because almost all of them can be reached only by boat. During the colonial period, the Angoche region was integrated into the District of Mozambique, and the city comprised Portuguese, Koti, Indian, and Makua settlers. In the early 1930s, the Portuguese regime created a special ward called Inguri for the Koti, who were removed from the prime land plots of Quissanga and Puli to give way to white settlers.

As in the rest of Mozambique, the Qur'anic schools in Angoche are termed *madrasa*, though there is a differentiation between the very basic or elementary-type school, called by the Kiswahili name *chuo* as well as *kioni* in Ekoti and *oshakko* in Emakhuwa (the language of the Makua), and the more advanced madrasa, called *ilimu* (from Arabic, *'ilm*, knowledge). The *ilimu* madrasas have been emerging since the 1990s in other parts of the country, especially in major cities such as Nampula, Pemba, Beira, Quelimane, Inhambane, and Maputo, but not in key historical Islamic centers such as Angoche, Mozambique Island, and Pemba, because these regions have recently become economically weak and have been gradually marginalized. Before that, northern Mozambican Muslims generally used to seek advanced levels of Islamic learning in these local centers of Islam, and in the case of Angoche, in the settlements on the island that had famed teachers and *shaykh*s. They also went to the East African coast—in particular Zanzibar, the Comoros, Lindi, and also sometimes to Hadhramaut in Yemen—through their *sharifian* (from Arabic, *sharif*, descendants of the Prophet Muhammad) kinship ties to the Ba Alawi or ash-Shatiri families.

More modern, local, higher-level madrasas began to appear in the late 1990s and were created by the Indian Comunidade Mahometana (Dar ul-Ulum seminaries in Maputo, Quelimane, and Beira) and by the Mozambican national Islamic organization called the Islamic Council (for example, a boarding school called Hamza in Matola City near Maputo) (Bonate 2009b). The new postcolonial organizations, such as the Islamic Council and the Islamic Congress of Mozambique, have also been offering scholarships to Islamic universities abroad—in Saudi Arabia, Egypt, Libya, Sudan, Algeria, India, Pakistan, and South Africa.

Qur'anic Schools and Literacy before the "Effective Occupation"

With the campaigns of "effective occupation" (1895–1913), resulting from the European "scramble for Africa," the 1884–1885 Berlin Conference and the 1890 British proposal on the future borders between the Portuguese and its own colonies, Portugal began conquering African territories with the aim of imposing full administrative and political control (Botelho 1936, 351–98; Axelson 1967). Military officers who undertook these campaigns, the so-called generation 1895, included Mousinho de Albuquerque, João de Azevedo Coutinho, Pedro Massano de Amorim, Eduardo do Couto Lupi, Ernesto Jardim de Vilhena, among others, who later served as governors, published memoirs, and left firsthand reports. Interestingly, they found the practice of exchanging letters with Africans in Arabic script to be a particularly humiliating sign of the weakness of the Portuguese presence in northern Mozambique (Lupi 1907, 219–20).

Since the time of their first arrival, the Portuguese carried letters in Arabic from the king of Portugal to local rulers, who read and answered them, prompting further correspondence, as attested to, for example, by the 1517 letter from Sharif Muhammad al-Alawi, the ruler of Mozambique Island to King Manuel of Portugal (Sousa 1788–1789, 85–86). This initial royal communication set forth a pattern of relationships between the Portuguese and Africans that lasted for almost four centuries and resulted in a voluminous correspondence in Arabic script kept in the archives of Portugal, Mozambique, and possibly Goa in India (Bonate 2008c, 2010a). It also made, as Nancy J. Hafkin (1973, 47) points out, "the *lingoa do estado* (literally, 'tongue of the state')" the position of a scribe "who handled Arabic script correspondence with Makua chiefs, Swahili shaikhs, Comoro sultans and the sultan of Zanzibar" one of the most crucial posts of the Portuguese administration in Mozambique.

In a region that has been primarily matrilineal, even among Muslims, not only male chiefs but female ones corresponded with the Portuguese in Arabic script. To cite some examples, letters from several nineteenth-century women Muslim chiefs, such as famous Namarral queen Nagima (Naguema in Portuguese sources) and Fatima binti Zacariya of Mogincual can be found in Mozambique historical archives. Even African rulers of the deep mainland who were not Muslims and presumably were not literate had routinely exchanged letters in Arabic script with the Portuguese (Hafkin 1973, 47, n. 40; Bonate 2010a). And, finally, correspondence between Africans themselves, including with the East African coast and the Comoros, was also written in this script.

Aside from official correspondence, regional dynastic histories, poetry, religious and esoteric literature, and other genres were written either in Kiswahili or local languages in the Arabic alphabet (e.g., see Rzewuski 1991a, 1991b). At the end of the nineteenth century, the proponents of effective occupation such as Lupi (1907, 152) and Amorim (1911, 120) witnessed commercial contracts as well as wills being customarily written down in Angoche.

All these writing activities had seemingly put a *khatib* (a scribe, local vernacular from Arabic) in an as esteemed a position within African societies as that of the *lingoa do estado* within the Portuguese administration (see Silva Neves

1901, 18). However, it was the *mwalimu* (local vernacular from Swahili, sing., pl., *walimu*, from Arabic, teacher) who was truly central to literacy and the life of a Muslim society as a whole. The main occupation of a *mwalimu* was teaching at a madrasa (Silva Neves 1901, 17). "There is not a Black Muslim settlement without a [Qur'anic] school," wrote one of the military conquerors of the region, João de Azevedo Coutinho (1941, 67). Lupi (1907, 176) mentions the abundance of these type of schools in Angoche, while the captain-major of the time, F. A. da Silva Neves (1901, 17), states that there were ten such schools at the island of Angoche alone, with very high attendance rates. Children between the ages of five and twelve attended in the morning and the afternoon, for three hours each time. Silva Neves (1901, 17) also describes the material used at these schools: "For writing, instead of paper they use a flattened rectangular wooden board, more or less half a meter of length, which is called *nimbao*; it is whitewashed with a type of lime made of some marine plant, which is sun-dried and reduced into powder in stoop; the ink is made of cinders dissolved in water. When *nimbao* is full of characters [i.e., writing], they wash it, and whitewash again. The pen (*m'tati*) is made of the stalk of a narrow corn [millet]."

Qur'anic schools in northern Mozambique molded the religious identity as well as the personhood of someone destined to become a legitimate member of a Muslim community. To that end, the authority of a *mwalimu* was based not only on his religious and educational credentials but on the fact that, as a member of the ruling elites, he undertook vital societal rituals, such as writing appropriate Qur'anic verses and other religious formula for oath taking as part of the application of justice at chiefs' courts. He also played a pivotal role in settling disputes, divination, and the production of amulets when pursuing warfare, travel, and initiation rites (Amorim 1911, 95–98; see also Bonate 2007). In Angoche, one of the most celebrated *mwalimu* at the turn of the nineteenth century was Shah Daud, originally from Ngazidja of the Comoros, who by 1907 had lived in Angoche for more than thirty years (Silva Neves 1901, 22; Lupi 1936, 151).

The habitus of writing along with the proliferation of madrasas sustained high literacy rates among Muslims of northern Mozambique. Lupi (1907, 152) mentions that the vast majority of the "musulmanised natives . . . know Kiswahili writing," while Ernesto Jardim de Vilhena (1905, 56) is adamant that "the influence of islamism is manifested . . . by a diffusion of instruction [i.e., literacy] limited to their own [i.e., local, African] languages or suaili [*sic*] in Arabic characters, and to the reading of religious texts" (see also Coutinho 1941, 67). Silva Neves (1901, 17) maintains that, at Angoche Island, almost all Muslims "know how to write in their own languages in Arabic characters; even many women know how to write and read."

After the effective occupation, the Portuguese abandoned the use of Arabic writing in official correspondence, but this type of literacy persisted in northern Mozambique, and in 1930–1933, the Portuguese Inspector for Indigenous Affairs, Captain Armando Pinto Correia, noted that, in the District of Mozambique, due to the pervasive presence of the Qur'anic schools, "those who could not read or write in Swahili were rare."[2] However, the official concept of literacy ceased to include the ability to write in a non-Latin script, especially with the banning of African languages and the introduction of the Portuguese language both in schooling and in official bureaucratic state apparatus in 1921. In this, the Portuguese followed the French rather than British example, whereby missionaries taught in local African languages, at least at the elementary school level (Launay, introduction to this volume). Illiteracy came to mean the inability to write or read in Portuguese, despite the fact that many Africans wrote and read their own languages in Arabic script, and sometimes used this script for writing in Portuguese. The 1930 census established that the illiteracy rate among Africans was 99%, dropping only 1.5% by 1954 (Mazula 1995, 59; Gómez 1999, 63–64). Literacy in Arabic script became offstage and invisible, but it is still transmitted in most of the Qur'anic schools of the region. Even today, on graduating from a madrasa, children are required to write a letter to parents in their own language using Arabic characters. Thus, this type of literacy has been a historical tradition of *longue durée* among northern Mozambican Muslims.

The *Indigenato*, the Catholic Missions, and Survival

After the effective occupation, African Muslims of northern Mozambique, unlike in previous historical periods, suffered a complete marginalization in relation to European rule. In addition to the loss of political and economic independence, their religious identity became a hindrance for social mobility within the new context. Although the colonial regime opened two avenues for ascension for Africans—one through the acquisition of the identity card and the other through European education—both remained largely unattainable to African Muslims.

The identity card pathway resulted from the imposition of a colonial administrative and legal system called the Regime do Indigenato, which was fashioned on the French Code d'Indigénat. It started with forced labor, direct taxation, and arbitrary punishment laws of 1899, 1904, and 1907, and reached its apogee during the Estado Novo (1926–1974), which in 1928 introduced the Native Labor Code, thus formalizing de facto the Regime do Indígenato. This regime was strengthened by the legal reforms of the 1930s, such as the 1930 Acto Colonial and the Carta Orgânica do Império Colonial Português, and, finally, the 1933 Reforma Administrativa Ultramarina (Administrative reform of the overseas territories), which clearly discerned between African and European legal rights and civil statuses. Africans became colonial "native" *subjects, os indígenas*, living within the jurisdiction of local "traditional customs and usages" administered by the appointed chiefs, the *régulos/regedores* (Portuguese, small-scale king, territorial chief; Bonate 2007). Europeans, on the other hand, became *citizens* of the metropolitan state and subject to its laws. However, similar to the French, Portugal adopted an assimilationist approach, and Africans could apply for a status of *assimilado* corresponding to the French *évolué* and acquire an identity card as long as they could prove to have adopted Portuguese customs, language, and culture, including the European dress code (Errante 2003, 19–20). This position was endorsed by a particular piece of legislation, a 1917 Portaria do Assimilado, strengthened by the Native Assistance Code of 1921 and by the 1933 Overseas Administrative Reform (Errante 2003, 20; Cross 1987, 558–59). In practice, Africans faced innumerable barriers, and in 1950 there were only 4,353 *assimilados* out of an estimated total population of 5,733,000 people in Mozambique, and in 1961, they only comprised 2.55% of the population (Mondlane 1975, 37–48; Gómez 1999, 52).

It was even harder for northern Mozambican African Muslims to become *assimilados*, not only because the Portuguese culture was largely linked to Catholicism but because the vast majority of them lived under the *indigenato* rule of the old ruling clans feeding the ranks of the *régulos* incorporated into the colonial administrative system (Bonate 2007). These old clans often remained in place, because, as opposed to the south of the country, which became linked to South African economic interests and experienced a relative economic boom and greater African migration and mobility in pursuit of economic opportunities, the north continued to be dominated by monoculture plantations such as cotton. The legitimacy of the *régulos* in this context was crucial for the labor compliance of African peasants. Thus, the Portuguese rule sought whenever possible to have the so-called legitimate chiefs incorporated into the new administrative system. In Muslim regions, this legitimacy was built upon the dual historical foundation of Islamic cultural identity and African traditions of (mostly) matrilineal kinship (Bonate 2003; 2005b; 2006). This status quo was challenged at the turn of the nineteenth century by the new Sufi orders (locally, *d/tiqiri* from *dhikr* in Arabic, religious litany of the orders; Arabic, sing., *tariqa*, pl., *turuq*), the Shaduliyya Yashrutiyya, and the Qadiriyya, which generated an Islamic identity based on the religious knowledge (Arabic, *'ilm*) and the chain of transmission (Arabic, *'isnad*) (Bonate 2010b, 2015). Therefore, the *turuq* in northern Mozambique impacted on the separation of the religious from the mundane and claimed to respond to and represent the religious sector, leaving the mundane affairs up to the chiefs and the colonial regime. But after a great deal of struggle, the old chiefly clans managed to take control of the Sufi orders by the 1930s, thus bringing Islam back into their domains of power (Bonate 2007).

The second avenue for acquiring the status of *assimilado* was opened to Africans in 1930 when a new educational reform was introduced by the colonial administration, allowing Africans who successfully completed a three-tiered formal schooling to attain this status. The new reform divided the system of education in two parts. One was called the Official System and was in effect a government school system following the metropolitan curriculum set up for the children of the Europeans and *assimilados*. The other part was called the Indigenous (or Native) System, and it had three levels: (1) rudimentary school (later schools of adaptation), (2) professional school, and (3) normal/official school. Without successfully completing the first level, which formally lasted for three years but was much longer in practice (often up to six years), an African child could not pass to the next levels and hope to become an *assimilado* in the future. Such disciplines as Portuguese language, geography, and history as well as arithmetic, hygiene, and religion were taught at a rudimentary level in classrooms using textbooks and blackboards.

However, the Estado Novo that upheld Catholic faith to be a crucial marker of the Portuguese national and cultural identity gave the control of the rudimentary schools to the Catholic missions. This fact made the attainment of *assimilado* status through education impossible for African Muslims. Catholic missions had already controlled education in colonies since the second half of the nineteenth century, though they lost some ground to lay missions, the so-called Missões Civilizadores (Portuguese, civilizing missions) and especially to Protestants (Cruz e Silva 2001; Sheldon 1998, 602; Saúte 2004, 27; Saúte 2005). The idea of the civilizing mission was yet another French influence on Portuguese colonialism (see Conklin 1997; Mendy 2003). It was emphasized by the military leaders of the effective occupation campaigns, such as António Enes, Mousinho de Albuquerque, and others, but it became more pronounced after the proclamation of the republic in Portugal in 1910, and especially during the Estado Novo. However, in contrast to the French republican, anticlerical, and secular ideological policies of *mission civilizatrice*, the Portuguese regime viewed the Roman Catholic Church as capable of bringing "about cultural and educational change in African society" and leading Africans from "savagery" into "civilization" (Cross 1987, 556; Sheldon 1998, 605). Thus, the Estado Novo, characterized by an intense nationalism, saw the Church as the most adequate tool of the assimilationist agenda, able to nationalize (*nacionalização*) and "Portugalize" (*portugalização*) its colonial subjects. The Catholic missions were expected to "gradually lead the indigenous people from the state of savagery to the state of the civilized, and form in them the consciousness of Portuguese citizens" (Mazula 1995, 81).

The state imposed on the missions the task to "civilize, Christianize, nationalize and capacitate" Africans and, to that end, gave them financial support, tax exemptions, and pensions for senior officials (Mazula 1995, 59, 81–85; Cross 1987, 561). Catholic missions from other countries, and especially Protestants, were harassed and persecuted because of their supposed denationalizing tendencies due to their alleged closeness to foreign European interests (Cruz e Silva 2001; Cross 1987, 556). The regime's commitment to Catholicism was deepened by the 1940 Concordata agreement with the Vatican, and the 1941 Estatuto Missionário (Missionary statutes), both aimed at strengthening the Church's position in the colonies. Education was declared to be based on Christian values with obligatory teaching of the precepts of Catholicism (Errante 2003, 15–16). Already in 1921 the government issued a decree banning the use of African languages in education and official use, and the Concordata reinstated the privileged position of the Portuguese language in schooling (Cross 1987, 557; Sheldon 1998, 614–15).

In Mozambique, there were 2,239 rudimentary schools run by Catholic missions by 1958, with a total of 2,389 teachers and auxiliary staff and 299,782 pupils.[3] Of these students, 82,109 were studying in northern Mozambican territories run by the Nampula and Cabo Delgado Dioceses. However, African Muslims could hardly become *assimilados* through education, because children in rudimentary schools were often baptized without their parents' knowledge, were fed pork, were obliged to learn the basics of Catholicism, and were given Christian names registered in official documents, though they already had Muslim ones. This situation somewhat resembles what was taking place in the Belgian Congo (Leinweber, this volume). Many Muslims of northern Mozambique not only resisted sending their children to mission schools but sometimes burned the schools down (Monteiro 1993b, 97–99). Pan-Islamic and anti-European sentiments were also widespread. For example, in 1937, the Portuguese regime intercepted leaflets depicting the Abyssinian defeat of the Italians at Adwa in 1896 and became so alarmed that it endorsed the 1929 Legislative Diplomas 167 and 168, requiring educational and cultural institutions to obtain licenses in order to function legally. Many mosques and madrasas did not have such licenses and were closed. This led to violent clashes between Muslims and local Portuguese administrative officials. The 1930–1933 Inspector for Indigenous Affairs in Mozambique, Captain Armando Pinto Correia, found these kinds of suppressive measures to be futile, while the 1952 inspector, Manuel Metello, maintained that "the closing of the mosques only served to fanaticize natives."[4]

Despite the spread of the Catholic missions, conversion to Islam between the 1930s and 1950s, as well as the number of Qur'anic schools, increased considerably, mainly due to the expansion of the Sufi orders and their African leadership. Pinto Correia noted the pervasive presence of the Qur'anic schools, functioning "in simple huts" symbolizing "their accessibility [to Africans] to which Portuguese efforts [to launch mission schools] could not match up to date."[5] However, by and large, the madrasas of northern Mozambique were not viewed as threatening as Protestant-run institutions because they were considered to be part of Islão Negro. This concept, which was similar to and is likely to have derived from the French concept of *Islam noir*, meant that Islam in this region was perceived to be akin to local African "usages and customs" and therefore was "backward," "uncivilized," and distant from the "true" "de-Europeanizing" "Islam of Asians" (Harrison 1988, 2–4, 99–136; Brenner 2001, 154–155, 164; Bonate 2007, 2008a). Actions were taken to restrict the influence of the "foreign brands of Islam" between the late 1950s to the 1970s. But overall, the alleged association of Islão Negro with African culture was viewed as nonmenacing because it seemingly prevented the madrasa from offering alternative avenues to Africans to become civilized by assimilating into a rival non-Portuguese, European, or Asian (and therefore antinationalist) culture.

The Islão Negro idea led the Portuguese to believe that the advancement of the Catholic missions would gradually and "naturally" disenchant Africans from Islam. For example, in his 1948 report on Nacala region, another Portuguese Inspector for Indigenous Affairs in Mozambique, Hortênsio Estêvão de Sousa, pointed out that Islam had a stronghold there because of the absence of Christian activity, as the only Catholic mission and the only rudimentary school could not meet either African aspirations for "civilization and education" or tackle the influences of Islam effectively.[6] Like his predecessor, Pinto Correia, de Sousa suggested increasing the number of Catholic mission schools in the region. In 1952, Manuel Metello recommended expanding mission schools as well, arguing that "natives" "wanted to learn" but often had no alternatives available other than the Qur'anic schools.[7]

By the 1960s, Portugal became concerned with the spread of the decolonization, and as a measure to maintain its hold over Africa, introduced in 1961 the Reforma Administrativa Ultramarina (Overseas administrative reform), which conceded equal legal rights to all citizens independently of race, culture, or creed. The 1964 Educational Reform Decree eliminated the duality of the school system and the monopoly of the Catholic missions over African education and made primary education compulsory to all children between the ages of six and twelve. These laws finally opened the assimilation option to African Muslims, but their mistrust of the Portuguese schools ran deep, and most kept their children away from studying there.

In the 1960s, Portugal was also troubled with possible Islamic influences emanating from such newly independent countries as Algeria, Egypt, and Tanzania. Realizing that Catholic Portugalization of Muslims had failed, the regime decided instead to control and "domesticate"—or, as the Portuguese officials put it, nationalize and Portugalize—the Islão Negro and isolate it from the influences of "foreign brands." This idea again seems to have been influenced by the French, who undertook nationalization of Islam in West Africa by creating Franco-Arabic *mederses* in the first half of the twentieth century (Brenner 2001). This is not surprising given that the most comprehensive efforts were undertaken in Mozambique by a secret service branch called the Services for Centralization and Coordination of Information (SCCI, or SCCIM for Mozambique) in 1965–1973 under the leadership of Fernando Amaro Monteiro, a graduate of a French university in Aix-en-Provence. The SCCIM collected data on Islam in general and Muslim leaders in particular, with the objective of obtaining detailed information on Islamic networks and means of communication between various Muslim regions and so-called poles of religious authorities and on their susceptibility to the ideology of independence (Monteiro 1993a, 280–81, 305–7). Afterward, it attempted to create a state-sponsored Islamic umbrella organization, a local center of religious authority, independent and autonomous of such centers abroad. When these attempts also failed, the SCCIM concentrated on nationalizing Islam by encouraging the use of the Portuguese language as the language of Islam. This meant translating the key Islamic texts into Portuguese and promoting Qur'anic education and religious services in that language. In 1968, the regime obtained approval of twenty-one major Sunni Muslim dignitaries of Mozambique for the translated publication of the hadith by al-Bukhari (Monteiro 1993a, 283–84). Between 1969 and 1973, the SCCIM was leading the administration in the direction of sponsoring Qur'anic education in Portuguese (Branquinho 1969, 412–15; Monteiro 1993a, 244). But the Catholic missions—in particular, the Nampula Diocese in Mozambique District—put up such a fight that the government decided to halt the project out of fear of further aggravating the enmity between the diocese and Muslims.

Sufis and Wahhabis

The era of the effective occupation coincided with the arrival of two Sufi orders that came to northern Mozambique along the regional Swahili networks. The Shadhuliyya Yashrutiyya was brought in 1897 by its founder, Shaykh Muhammad Ma'arouf bin Shaykh Ahmad ibn Abu Bakr (1853–1905) of the Comoro Islands (Carvalho 1988, 61). In 1905 (or 1904), the Qadiriyya came with a Shaykh 'Issa ibn Ahmad, who probably was 'Issa bin Ahmad al-Ngaziji (also al-Msujini) al-Barawi, a disciple of Shaykh Umar Uways bin Muhammad al-Barawi (1847–1909), the leader of the Qadiriyya, known also as the Uwaysiyya in East Africa (Carvalho 1988, 63; Martin 1976, 157, 159, 174; Nimtz 1980, 57, 202, n. 10). The orders disentangled the historical link between Islamic identity and a membership in a Muslim community united around a ruling clan that provided a chief who was assisted by *walimu*, and in which the ethnic and religious identities as well as loyalties to Islam and the chiefly clan were interchangeable (Bonate 2007). Instead, the orders brought forward a competing idea of a Muslim community, which, on one hand, was much broader, both spatially—through *tariqa* connections to its global branches—and temporally—by its location within the chain of transmission (Arabic, '*isnad* and *silsila*) since the time of the foundation of the order, if not of Islam itself. On the other hand, this community was also much smaller than the one linking individuals to a particular ethnic Muslim chief or clan, because it was locally built around a delegate of a *tariqa*, the *khalifa*. Islamic authority itself was transformed; it no longer had to be linked to the chiefly clans, because the legitimacy of a Sufi *shaykh* was based on his '*ilm* (Arabic, religious knowledge), his situation within the '*isnad* chain of transmission, and the authority that a *silsila* (Arabic, a document confirming the legitimacy of a Sufi *shaykh*) conferred upon him.

The orders thus introduced changes with respect to Islamic practices and conceptions (Bonate 2007; 2015). However, in the 1960s, they faced an increasing critique by religious leaders whose stance was formed in Tanganyika, Nyassaland, Deoband seminary in India, and, especially, in Saudi Islamic universities (Bonate 2008b). Initial conflicts were about funeral rites, whereby the loud Sufi practices involving the recitation and singing of the *dhikr* were condemned as *haram* (Arabic, illicit) and un-Islamic by the reform-minded *shaykhs*, dubbed *sukutis* (from Arabic, *sukut*, silence) (Bonate 2005a). In 1968, Shaykhs Hasan 'Ali "Côncaco" and Musa Ibrahimo Siraj, both from Angoche Island, who returned home from Nyasaland and Tanganyika, stirred up violent conflicts with Sufis, whom they hailed as *nashidi* (the noisy ones, from Arabic, clapping hands) and *twaliki* (from Arabic, *tariqa*).[8] Disagreements were so acute as to require the intervention of the Portuguese, who solicited Shaykh Momade Sayyid Mujabo of Mozambique Island to issue a fatwa (legal opinion on the dispute).[9] In 1972, the conflicts were reignited when a group of young *sukutis* attacked the *tariqa shaykhs*, waving machetes at them and even assaulting one of them and destroying a Qur'anic school in Angoche City (then António Ennes) (Monteiro, 1993a). The same year, the Portuguese asked Sayyid 'Umar b. Ahmad b. Sumayt al-Alawi (1896–1976), who was the chief *qadi* of Zanzibar in 1942–1960, for a fatwa on the dispute.

The ranks of the *sukutis* were augmented by the Deobandis and the so-called Wahhabis, graduates of the Islamic University of Medina, who all together made up a group of Islamists, a local brand of a global phenomenon. Broadly speaking, they demanded a literal interpretation of the Islamic sources, the Qur'an, and the hadith and ubiquitous application of the sharia (Islamic legal principles) (Brenner 1993, 61–62, 67–71, 74–75; Eickelman and Piscatori 1996, 60–69). In particular, they opposed Sufi-associated rituals, such as *mawlid* (Arabic, anniversary of the Prophet Muhammad or Sufi saints), *ziyara* (Arabic, a ritual visitation of the tombs of the saints or deceased in general, and *dhikr*, as well as esoteric practices, such as Prophetic medicine and writing *hiriz* (Swahili, talismans). They not only consistently portrayed these practices as the manifestations of *shirk* (Arabic, polytheism) and *bid'a* (Arabic, abominable religious innovation) but tended to reduce them to the status of *kufr* (Arabic, unbelief) and, in Mozambique, to folklore and African traditions and customs.

The most vocal of the so-called Wahhabis was Abubacar Musa Ismael "Mangira," who returned to Mozambique in 1964 after graduating from the Islamic University of Medina (Monteiro 1993a, 413; Monteiro 1993b, 92–95, 104–5). He was from the southern Inhambane region and of mixed-race Indian African descent. As Benjamin Soares (this volume) points out, the Islamic University of Medina has successfully propagated Salafi ideas, including vehement anti-Sufism, among its graduates (see also Thurston, this volume). In fact, they were educated in accordance with the Wahhabi principles of the Saudi kingdom that laid ground for Salafism in Egypt, which emerged later. Mangira was no exception, judging by his incessant attacks on Sufis. However, he sought recognition from the colonial administration by claiming that he was better educated and more modern than "ignorant" and "incompetent" Sufis and therefore was well suited to be a nationwide Islamic authority (Monteiro 1993b, 93–95). Knowing that the SCCIM was thinking of sponsoring Qur'anic education in Portuguese, he suggested opening a "new Islamic college for girls and boys in separate blocks," where "the Portuguese language and Islamic doctrine in Arabic would be taught." In 1971, the most eminent Sufi *shaykh* of Mozambique, Sayyid Habib Bakr, threatened to take action against the Wahhabis, or otherwise orchestrate a simultaneous violent uprising in three districts of northern Mozambique, if the Portuguese did not intervene decisively to end the conflicts (Monteiro 1989, 85). Because the independence war was already under way, and because the SCCIM studies identified Sufi orders as holding significant geographical, numerical, and religious power in northern Mozambique, the Portuguese decided to support Sufis instead of Mangira.

After independence, Mangira became close to the ruling Frelimo party, and, with its support, he rose to the leadership of the national Muslim organization called the Conselho Islâmico de Moçambique (Islamic Council of Mozambique) (Bonate 2008b). This organization, considered pro-Wahhabi, was opposed by discordant Muslims, who created their own organization, the Congresso Islâmico de Moçambique Sunni (Sunni Islamic Congress of Mozambique), which, besides Sufis, included the Indian association Comunidade Mahometana Sunni (Mahomeddan Sunni Community of Mozambique). Because most of the first Wahhabis and Deobandis were either Indians or mixed-race Afro-Indians, they hoped to be employed in lucrative madrasas of the Indian community. However, dominated by the Chistiyya and Qadiriyya orders and the so-called Barelwis, this community expelled them from their institutions of education after a trial period. Thereafter, the Wahhabis began launching their own madrasas with the support of the Africa Muslim Agency (a Kuwait-based Islamic nongovernmental organization) and other transnational Islamic organizations that shared their views (Bonate 2009a).

In 1985, the council tried to lay the basis of the future Islamic university in Mozambique to be funded by the Islamic Development Bank, but the project did not advance, mainly due to reservations among state officials. From 1986, the council began distributing scholarships for Islamic universities abroad, establishing relationships with the University of Medina, Jamiyat al-Dawa al-Islamiyya of Libya (which also covered the hajj expenses of the council members), al-Azhar University in Egypt, al-Merkaz in the Sudan, and Islamic Universities of Algeria. Many young black Muslims gained access to scholarships to these universities, but their presence began to be felt in the 1990s, when they started returning. In 1998, some of them in northern Mozambique abandoned the Islamic Council because of alleged racial and political reasons, and they founded an organization called Ahl al-Sunna or Ansar al-Sunna (Bonate 2008b).

Madrasas in Contemporary Angoche City

In contemporary Mozambique, as exemplified here by Angoche City, there are, broadly speaking, two types of Qur'anic schools in terms of their contents, methods, and social standing: the *tariqa*-based and the so-called Wahhabi-oriented but within each of these types there is considerable variation. Most of the *tariqa*-based schools belong to individual Sufi *shaykhs* except for those affiliated with the Indian Comunidade Mahometana, which has one madrasa in each major locality (usually attached to its mosque) and the Islamic Congress, which agglomerates Sufis seeking organizational support. The Wahhabi-oriented madrasas belong to either the Islamic Council or the Ahl al-Sunna.

No Muslim expressed any reservations against the state-run secular schools. Therefore, the resistance against the Portuguese mission schools and later colonial state schools was related to the aggressive Catholic stance rather than to opposition to Western education in principle. These days, Muslims, like other Mozambicans, make every effort for their children to attend state schools, because they believe that the secular education is important for social mobility and inclusion. But they also insist that children must necessarily attend the Qur'anic schools because otherwise they will not be considered Muslims. Children are enrolled very early on, often from the age of five, and have classes either institutionally in a school in a separate building with classrooms or privately and face-to-face in the houses of the *walimu*. Students attend the madrasa before or after their classes in the official state school, either early in the morning or in the afternoon, and adults in the evenings after work.

Table 5.1 lists some of the Qur'anic schools of the organizations in Angoche City that were examined during the fieldwork in 2007.

In addition to these, there are other types of schools that could be considered hybrids of modern Western and Islamic forms of education, though the Western side usually outweighs the Islamic one. In Angoche City, there is one such school called Hamza bin Rashid secondary school. It was built in 1999 with financial support from the Al-Maktum Foundation of the United Arab Emirates–Dubai, and it follows the Mozambican official secondary education curriculum.[10] The school teaches no specific Islamic disciplines except for classes in civic education, Arabic language, and *tawhid* (Arabic, unity of God; in this case, the science of unity of God), which are taught by two graduates of the Islamic Universities of Saudi Arabia and the Sudan. But these courses are extracurricular and thus not compulsory.

Among the rest of the Qur'anic schools of the city, the Indian one is attached to the mosque of the Comunidade Mahometana of Angoche built in 1918.[11] The madrasa was erected only in 1984; before that, Indian children studied together with African children in the houses of the individual Sufi *shaykhs*. In the late 1980s, there were twenty Indian children studying in this madrasa, but due to the generalized economic marginalization that Angoche suffered after the 1989 structural adjustment, by 2007 practically all Indians had abandoned the city. In

Table 5.1. Madrasas of the Organizations

Madrasa denomination	Organizational affiliation	Number of teachers		Number of students				Total
				Adults		Children		
		Male	Female	Male	Female	Male	Female	
Cislamo/ Khatidja	Islamic Council	4	0	0	0	42	68	**114**
Islam/Bairro Horta	Ahl al-Sunna	3	0	110	70	40	25	**248**
Markaz al-Islamiyya	Islamic Congress	2	0	16	22	0	0	**40**
Mesquita Central/ Puli	Comunidade Mahometana	1	0	7	0	17	20	**45**
Total		10	0	133	92	99	113	**447**

2007, there were thirty-seven children and eight adults studying at that madrasa with teaching in the local language, Ekoti, which they learned to write using the Arabic script. The madrasa had a classroom with school chairs, desks, and two blackboards. The blackboards were used for writing notes and explanations by the *mwalimu*, and children also copied Arabic letters and verses of the Qur'an on it as a proof of their aptitude. Pupils used notebooks and pens as in normal school. The *mwalimu* received wages from the Comunidade Mahometana, and, although he was a member of the Islamic Council, he followed the recommendations of the organization to teach the Qur'an until its completion. He mentioned that the members of the *comunidade Mahometana* and the council used to fight a lot in the 1980s and 1990s because of their opposing pro- and anti-Sufi positions, sometimes quite physically and violently, but they stopped doing that after 2000, when Mangira died.

The *tariqa*-oriented madrasas are numerous and individualized, and only two of them are associated with an organization, the Islamic Congress.[12] Association with this organization obliges any *tariqa*-based madrasa to become public, and because of its public status to turn into a modern school. In other words, in the public eye, it has to display a visible paraphernalia and respectability that the modern word "school" carries with it, including classrooms, blackboards and other furniture, and textbooks.

Incidentally, the Islamic Congress and the Islamic Council are no longer in acute conflict with each other in Angoche as they were in the 1980s and 1990s (Bonate 2008a, 2010b). On the contrary, the emergence of Ahl al-Sunna seems to have brought them together against a new opponent. In a madrasa called Markaz al-Islamiyya, the Islamic Congress teaches adults; in its other madrasa attached to the Zawiya Muridiyya, the central *zawiya* (Arabic, Sufi lodge) of Angoche City, the pupils are children. This latter madrasa uses the didactical material and teaching methods developed by the Waterval Islamic Institute in Natal in South Africa, largely considered a Deobandi institution run by the Mia family that has historical ties to Mozambican Muslims.[13] It is closely associated with the Islamic Council and distributes religious schoolbooks in Portuguese called *Darus ul-Islam* organized into five levels, subsidizes madrasa teachers with monthly wages, and undertakes annual inspection of the Qur'anic schools in Mozambique. The Waterval encourages the formation of the *hafizes*: those who memorize the Qur'an in its entirety and to whom it offers scholarships to continue their education in South African madrasas. Sufis might disagree with the views of the Islamic Council or Waterval, but the facts that the books are in Portuguese, that the instruction is elaborate and structured, and that there are incentives for the *walimu* and for the children make following this system quite attractive. On the other hand, the Waterval does not confront Sufis directly but rather tries to reform them through these kinds of measures. The Markaz al-Islamiyya teaches adults reading the Qur'an, hadith, *fiqh* mostly with respect to the prayers (*salat*), and *nahu* (explanation of the language of the Qur'an).

The *tariqa*-based madrasas resulted from the founding of the two Sufi orders: the Shadhuliyya Yashrutiyya, which in 1925 split into the Shadhuliyya Madaniyya, Ittifaq, and the original Yashrutiyya, and the Qadiriyya, which is divided into five more branches in Mozambique. In Angoche, only two Shadhuliyyas took roots—the Yashrutiyya and the Madaniyya—and there was no Qadiriyya at the time of fieldwork (Bonate 2007). Both the Yashrutiyya and the Qadiriyya were deeply implicated in proselytizing and the expansion of Islamic education as exemplified by the lives of their leaders, Shaykh Ma'arouf and Shaykh Uways. In Mozambique, too, they were responsible for the expansion of Islam and the increase of the madrasas. In particular, many *shaykhs* and women Sufi leaders began maintaining private schools belonging to specific families, houses, and Sufi lodges. Similar to other regions where Sufi orders predominated, the classroom was the home of the Sufi *shaykh/a*, and the mother tongue common to both the instructor and pupils was and continues to be to this day the medium of instruction.

The *walimu* prefer to teach children in groups, while adults might opt for individual classes depending on their level of knowledge of Islam. The more advanced they are, the more they are likely to have individual classes by reading particular books, usually classical Shafi's *fiqh* (Arabic, jurisprudence) or general theology books or specialized books on astrology, divination, healing, and dealing with jinn (spirits). Often their preference is related to their profession as healers or diviners, in which case they seek a *mwalimu* who can teach those particular subjects, and this kind of learning could last a lifetime. Even if the books from which they learn might not be considered religious or Islamic enough by modern standards, in northern Mozambique these books are usually classical texts in Arabic written by medieval Muslim scholars, and thus learning them requires an assistance from a master (*fundi* in local vernacular), a true professional in a particular field. Disciples, who come from all over the northern Mozambique to study with a renowned master, stay in his home for several months at a time; they receive or copy the books they should read on their own back home, and then they leave. They usually repeat this sequence of actions every year.

The learning at a basic Qur'anic school that is usually designed for children was limited to the transmission of knowledge aimed at concluding the reading of the Qur'an and memorizing some suras (chapters and verses), the contents and meanings of which were explained and interpreted by a *mwalimu*. In addition, students learned some hadiths, the Arabic script for writing in local languages, and basic tenets of Islamic ritual. A madrasa of a *tariqa* offers, in addition, an esoteric knowledge characteristic of Sufi orders, which included the *dhikr* of the orders as well as specific *dw'as* (Arabic, prayers) for different occasions (especially for funeral rites, healing, and other treatments called *calmas* aimed at calming the spirits), and the recitation of the *qasidas* (Arabic, devotional poetry).[14] Children in *tariqa*-linked madrasas were often required to take part in celebrations of *mawlid* together with the adults. Whereas before the coming of the orders Islamic instruction was limited to the attendance at Qur'anic school, it was now enriched by a lifelong commitment of learning from an individual Sufi *shaykh*. Although the scope of Islamic education was broadened, the learning itself continued to be centered on the knowledge of the specific textbooks (Swahili, pl., *vitabu*, sing., *kitabu*), informally transmitted to a disciple by a master, who was identified through a process of *"shaykh* seeking." In northern Mozambique, the use of Arabic script for writing local languages has continued to be transmitted in these madrasas, though Kiswahili is no longer an epistolary medium. Because the learning was individualized, and thus private and intimate, not to say spiritual, the material that a *tariqa*-based Qur'anic school used remained in essence the same as described by Silva Neves at the end of the nineteenth century. The only new items added were paper and chalk, which became more widespread during the twentieth century.

Whereas before the arrival of the two *turuq*, a *mwalimu* was part of the chiefly establishment and usually a man, afterward anyone, including women, with an adequate religious formation could teach and was sought as *mwalimu*. Traditional Islamic centers such as the Qatamoio, Yaruba, and Maziwani settlements at Angoche Island continued to boast learned *shaykhs* and *khalifas* of the *turuq*, but at the beginning of the twentieth century, many of them were lured by new economic opportunities to the city and settled in the Inguri neighborhood, which eventually also became an important center of learning. The *mwalimu* was often paid on a weekly basis on Fridays the *"juma* money" or *ki-furushi*, a practice that is still in place in most of the *tariqa*-based madrasas of northern Mozambique, though the pay is seldom substantial. The interviewed *walimu* indicated that often they were not paid at all or paid a symbolic sum, but they claimed that they teach not for the money but because it is *fard kifaya* (Arabic, individual obligation). In earlier times, students who could not pay used to work in *mwalimu*'s household or *machamba* (local vernacular for private land plots) or helped with other personal economic pursuits, but these practices are no longer followed. "Why should I allow my child to work for someone?" inquired one mother. "The Qur'an says everyone capable should teach. The *mwalimu* is just doing his religious obligation." But parents and the community as a whole continue to offer gifts to *walimu* on the occasion of the pupils' completion of the Qur'an and on celebrations of important Muslim dates and rituals. Of course, the *walimu* enjoy respect and a particular charisma that teaching Islam bestows upon them.

The Wahhabi-oriented madrasas are a late phenomenon; the first ones, which initially were attached to individual *shaykhs* and their mosques, were established in Angoche in 1968. The oldest such madrasa belonged to Shaykh Hassan Côncaco, who had a mosque called Hamza. Though after the independence most of these *shaykhs* joined the Islamic Council, which sought to create institutionalized form of madrasas enclosed within the mosques of the organization, the spread of Sufism was such that, even in 2007, most madrasa teachers had started under some Sufi *shaykh*, at least at a very basic Qur'anic school level. Table 5.2 lists how, where, and by whom the *walimu* of the various madrasas were trained.

The only madrasa belonging to Islamic Council in Angoche is a big complex with several classrooms, dormitories, rooms for administration and teachers, and a refectory. It had two *walimu* who taught children exclusively according to the *Darus ul-Islam* textbooks published and distributed by Waterval Islam, which also subsidizes the *walimu's* wages and inspects the madrasa annually. The construction, which lasted from 1999 to 2004, was financed by the Africa Muslim Agency and the Islamic Development Bank. The complex, however, was too big for a madrasa, or perhaps the council did not have enough students interested in studying in its school. Thus, nearly the entire building was rented out to a college that had nothing to do with either Islam or the Council.

As can be inferred from Table 5.1, the most popular *Wahhabi*-oriented madrasas in Angoche belonged to Ahl al-Sunna, with 248 students. The madrasa called Islam that was examined during fieldwork attracted significant numbers of students, both children and adults, and even non-Muslims. This madrasa had three *walimu*, all former members of the Islamic Council. They alleged that the abandonment was due to the laxity of the council's leaders with respect to Sufi and local conceptions and practices of Islam.[15] Unlike the council, which was organized through the association of its members with the Frelimo ruling party and enjoyed the financial support of transnational Islamic organizations, the Ahl al-Sunna was a grassroots organization, composed mostly of young Africans, with leaders trained either in Islamic universities abroad or in the Islamic Council madrasas.

Ahl al-Sunna works aggressively for proselytization of non-Muslims and Muslims alike, organizes Friday campaigns directed toward women to motivate them to continue studying Islam and knowing their rights under the sharia, and provides literacy classes in Portuguese for adults in the evenings. The organization was not official at the time of the fieldwork and had no access to formal funds, nor did its madrasas charge any money. But both madrasas and mosques

Table 5.2. *Walimus'* Profiles

Name	Organizational affiliation	Echuo/oshakka	Ilimu	Ilimu teacher's training
Hajji Omar	Islamic Council	Africa Muslim Agency, Nakala	Same place	Saudi Arabia
Ismael Lamboni	Islamic Council	Islamic Congress, Angoche, Inguri	Islamic Council, Angoche	Maputo, student of "Mangira"
Swaleh Mussa	Ahl al-Sunna	Yaruba, Angoche Island, private	Dar ul-Ulum College, Quelimane	Pakistan, India, and Sudan
Mussa Amorim	Comunidade Moametana	Angoche City, Inguri, private	—	Yaruba, Angoche Island
Bramugi Momade	Islamic Congress	Qatamoio, Angoche Island, private	Inguri, Angoche City, private	Inguri, Angoche City, private
Swaleh Shale/inherited a madrasa from grandfather	Islamic Council	Shadhuliyya Yashrutiyya, Angoche City, Inguri, private	Islamic Council, Angoche City	Maputo, student of "Mangira"
Khatidja Martin	Shadhuliyya Yashrutiyya	Maziwani, Angoche Island, private	Shadhuliyya Yashrutiyya, Angoche City	Angoche City, private
Hajji Chande	Shadhuliyya Madaniyya	Maziwani, Angoche Island, private	Shadhuliyya Yashrutiyya	Mozambique Island, and Maziwani, Angoche Island
Sharifu Bacar Swaleh	Shadhuliyya Yashrutiyya	Kilwa, Angoche Island, Island	Shadhuliyya Yashrutiyya	Kilwa, Angoche Island and Inguri, Angoche City

were built with popular donations. The madrasa Islam was built with local conventional building materials. It was, in fact, a thatched hut that the *walimu* alleged was a provisional construction to be improved with time when money becomes available. It had four classrooms, each furnished with tables, chairs, and two blackboards. The organization did not have a collaboration with the Waterval Islam but used books written in Portuguese by Shaykh Aminuddin Muhammad, the current president of the Islamic Council. Like the Islamic Council, and in contrast to Sufi-based madrasas, the Ahl al-Sunna privileges Portuguese language as medium of instruction and teaches Arabic as the true language of Islam.

Conclusion

In Angoche, as in the rest of Mozambique, various systems of education coexist alongside and influence one another. As Stefan Reichmuth (1993, 179–80) points out, the interaction between Western forms of education and religious education no longer corresponds to a distinction between traditional and modern forms of learning, but the conflict between and interaction of systems of education in a given society results in the emergence of the new models of education. In Mozambique, too, the interaction and competition between different systems of education has resulted in new models of education, including Islamic ones, such the madrasas of various organizations with the pro- and anti-Sufi inclinations examined in this chapter.

As this chapter reveals, before the imposition of colonial rule, the Qur'anic schools and their respective *walimu* educated people in northern Mozambique who lived in particular kinds of Islamic communities within which the loyalties to Islam as a religious identity and to the ethnic Muslim chiefs were interchangeable. Within such communities, the madrasa provided for a literacy that linked, among other things, Muslims of this region to those of the Swahili world through the use of the Arabic script applied mainly for writing in Kiswahili and also in local African languages. The fact that the Portuguese used this epistolary medium until the twentieth century added value to this type of literacy.

Following the imposition of the *indigenato* system and associated Catholic mission schooling, Muslims of the region became marginalized and were impeded from accessing colonial citizenship status as *assimilados*. The Qur'anic schools nevertheless persisted and even increased numerically and geographically due to the expansion of the new Sufi orders.

After independence, Islamic organizations, including Sufi orders, through their madrasas, have encouraged students, especially children, to attend formal, modern, Western-style schools and, if possible, continue into the higher education levels. They are all equally concerned with integrating and maintaining Muslims within the context of a modern society. Thus, despite the differences discussed in this chapter—in methods, styles, content, material conditions, and external appearances—and whether they are considered modern or traditional, they all try to respond to the challenges of contemporary society and modern contexts.

NOTES

1. The fieldwork described in this chapter was funded by a research project titled From Transmission of Tradition to Global Learning: African Islamic Education ca. 1800–2000, under the leadership of Professors Anne K. Bang of the University of Bergen and Shamil Jeppie of the University of Cape Town, to whom I am greatly indebted. The project was sponsored by a grant from the National Research Foundation of South Africa and the Norwegian Research Fund.
2. Pinto Correia, "Relatório duma Inspecção," Vol. 1, pp. 33, 36, and Vol. 2, pp. 80, 103–4, 173, in ISANI Collection, Mozambique Historical Archives, Maputo, Box 76.
3. "Relatório de Aplicação do Estatuto de Indígenas Portugueses," Governo-Geral, Província de Moçambique, 1958, pp. 17–20, in Mozambique Historical Archives, Box 2125.
4. Manuel Metello, "Relatório da Inspecção Ordinária ao Distrito de Cabo Delgado," feita pelo Inspector Administrativo, Manuel Metello, período 1944–1952, Circunscrição da Quissanga, p. 65, in Mozambique Historical Archives, Box 2136.
5. António Pinto Correia, "Relatório duma Inspecção," Vol. 1, pp. 33, 36, and Vol. 2, pp. 80, 103–4, 173, in Mozambique Historical Archives, Box 76.
6. Hortênsio Estêvão de Sousa, "Relatório da Inspecção Ordinária ao Distrito de Nampula da Província do Niassa," Vol. 4, "Circunscrição de Nacala," p. 752, in Mozambique Historical Archives, Box 77.
7. Metello.
8. Interviews with Shaykh Mamade Abdallah, May 11, 2000, Angoche City; with Shaykh Musa Ibrahimo Siraj, May 13, 2000, Angoche City; and with Shaykh Hasan Ali "Côncaco," May 15, 2000, Angoche City.
9. "Delegação do Distrito de Mozambique, SCCIM—Chefe da Delegação, António Ceia da Costa Monteiro para o Director de SCCIM em Lourenço Marques No 258/A/20, 27 de Janeiro de 1972," Concelho de António Enes. January 19 /March 11/March 18, 1972, SCCIM-DGS, in SCCIM, IAN-TT, Lisbon, Cx. 63, No 413, Pt. 2, pp. 506–10.
10. Interview with Omar Ali, director of the Hamza bin Rashid School in Angoche City, August 8, 2007.
11. Interview with Mussa Amorim, *mwalimu* of the madrasa of the central mosque of Angoche City, August 7, 2007.
12. Interview with Bramuji Momade, *mwalimo* of the Markaz al-Islamiyya madrasa of the Islamic Congress, August 8, 2007, Angoche City.
13. http://islamicfocusarticles.blogspot.com/2008/06/waterval-islamic-institute.html, last accessed May 11, 2009.

14. Collective interview with male Sufi *khulafa*, May 11, 2000, and female Sufi *khulafa*, May 16, 2000, AngocheCity.

15. Interview with Sualehe Mussa, *mwalimu* of the madrasa Islam, Ahl al-Sunna, Angoche City, August 6, 2007.

REFERENCES

Amorim, P. M. de. 1911. *Relatório sobre a ocupação de Angoche: Operações de campanha e mais serviço realizados, Anno 1910.* Lourenço Marques, Mozambique: Imprensa Nacional.

Axelson, E. 1967. *Portugal and the Scramble for Africa, 1875–1891.* Johannesburg, South Africa: Witswatersrand University Press.

Bonate, L. J. K. 2003. "The Ascendance of Angoche: Politics of Kinship and Territory in the Nineteenth Century Northern Mozambique." *Lusotopie* 1: 115–43.

———. 2005a. "Dispute over Islamic Funeral Rites in Mozambique. *A Demolidora dos Prazeres* by Shaykh Aminuddin Mohamad." *Le Fait Missionnaire* 17 (December): 41–61.

———. 2005b. "From *Shirazi* into *Monhé*: Angoche and the Mainland in the Context of the Nineteenth Century Slave Trade of Northern Mozambique." In *Slave Routes and Oral Tradition in Southeastern Africa*, edited by B. Zimba, E. A. Alpers, and A. Isaacman, 195–219. Maputo, Mozambique: Filsom Entertainment.

———. 2006. "Matriliny, Islam and Gender in Northern Mozambique." *Journal of Religion in Africa* 2 (36): 139–66.

———. 2007. "Traditions and Transitions: Islam and Chiefship in Northern Mozambique, ca. 1850–1974." PhD dissertation, University of Cape Town, South Africa.

———. 2008a. "O *Islão Negro*: As Abordagens Coloniais do Islão no Norte de Moçambique." *Religare*, 3 (March): 73–81.

———. 2008b. "Muslim Religious Leadership in Post-Colonial Mozambique." *South African Historical Journal* 60 (4): 637–54.

———. 2008c. "The Use of Arabic Script in Northern Mozambique." *Tydskrif vir letterkunde* 45 (1): 133–42.

———. 2009a. "L'agence des musulmans d'Afrique. Les transformations de l'Islam à Pemba au Mozambique." *Afrique Contemporaine* (Paris) 231: 63–80.

———. 2009b. "Islamic Education and State Policies of Education in Mozambique." In *Proceedings of the International Symposium on Islamic Civilization in Southern Africa, Johannesburg, South Africa [1–3 September 2006]*, edited by M. Haron and S. Dangor, 273–302. Istanbul: IRCICA.

———. 2010a. "Documents in Arabic Script at the Mozambique Historical Archives." *Islamic Africa* 1 (2): 253–57.

———. 2010b. "Islam in Northern Mozambique: A Historical Overview." *History Compass* 8 (7): 573–93.

———. 2015. "The Advent and Schisms of Sufi Orders in Mozambique, 1896–1964." *Islam and Christian–Muslim Relations*, 26 (4): 483–501.

Botelho, J. J. T. 1936. *História militar e política dos portugueses em Moçambique de 1833 aos nossos dias*, 2nd ed. Lisbon: Centro Tip. Colonial.

Branquinho, J. A. G. de M. 1969. "Relatório da Prospecção ao Distrito de Moçambique (Um estudo de estruturas hierárquicas tradicionais e religiosas, e da sua situação político-social), Nampula, 22 April 1969." In *Prospecção das Forças Tradicionais— Distrito de Moçambique, Província de Moçambique, SCCI, Secreto*, by Fernando da Costa Freire. Arquivo Histórico de Moçambique, Maputo, Secção Especial No. 20, Cotas S.E., 2 III P 6, Portugal, Lourenço Marques, December 30, 1969.

Brenner, L. 1993. "Constructing Muslim Identity in Mali." In *Muslim Identity and Social Change in Sub-Saharan Africa*, edited by L. Brenner, 59–78. London: Hurst.

———. 2001. *Controlling Knowledge: Religion, Power and Schooling in a West African Muslim Society*. Bloomington: Indiana University Press.

Carvalho, A. P. de. 1988. "Notas para a história das confrarias Islâmicas na Ilha de Moçambique." In *Arquivo* 4 (March): 59–66. Conklin, A. L. 1997. *A Mission to Civilize: The Republican Idea of Empire in France and West Africa, 1895–1930*. Stanford, CA: Stanford University Press.

Coutinho, J. de A. 1941. *Memórias de um velho marinheiro e soldado de África*. Lisbon: Livraria Bertrand.

Cross, M. 1987. "The Political Economy of Colonial Education: Mozambique, 1930–1975." *Comparative Education Review* 31 (4): 550–69.

Cruz e Silva, T. 2001. *Protestant Churches and the Formation of Political Consciousness in Southern Mozambique (1930–1974)*. Basel, Switzerland: P. Schlettwein.

Eickelman, D. F., and J. Piscatori. 1996. *Muslim Politics*. Princeton, NJ: Princeton University Press.

Errante, A. 2003. "White Skin, Many Masks: Colonial Schooling, Race, and National Consciousness among White Settler Children in Mozambique, 1934–1974." *International Journal of African Historical Studies* 36 (1): 7–33.

Gómez, M. B. 1999. *Educação Moçambicana. História de um processo: 1962–1984*. Maputo: Universidade Eduardo Mondlane: Livraria Universitária/Imprensa Universitária.

Hafkin, N. J. 1973. "Trade, Society, and Politics in Northern Mozambique, c. 1753–1913." PhD dissertation, Boston University.

Harrison, C. 1988. *France and Islam in West Africa, 1860–1960*. Cambridge: Cambridge University Press.

Lupi, E. do Couto. 1907. *Angoche. Breve memória sobre uma das Capitanias-Môres do Distrito de Moçambique*. Lisbon: Typografia do Annuario Commercial.

———. 1936. *Escola de Mousinho. Episodios de Serviço, Moçambique 1895–1910*. Lisbon: Imprensa Lucas.

Martin, B. G. 1976. *Muslim Brotherhoods in Nineteenth Century Africa*. Cambridge: Cambridge University Press.

Mazula, B. 1995. *Educação, Cultura e Ideologia em Moçambique: 1975–1985*. Porto, Portugal: Afrontamento.

Mendy, P. K. 2003. "Portugal's Civilizing Mission in Colonial Guinea-Bissau: Rhetoric and Reality." *International Journal of African Historical Studies* 36 (1): 35–58.

Mondlane, E. 1975. *Lutar por Moçambique*. Translated by Maria da Graça Forjaz. Lisbon: Livraria Sá da Costa Editora.
Monteiro, F. A. 1989. "As comunidades islâmicas em Moçambique: Mecanismos de comunicação," In *Africana* 4 (March): 65–89. Porto, Portugal: Edições de Centro de Estudos Africanos da Universidade Portucalense.
———. 1993a. *O Islão, o Poder, e a Guerra: Moçambique 1964–74*. Porto, Portugal: Universidade Portucalense.
———. 1993b. "Sobre a Actuação da corrente 'Wahhabita' no Islão Moçambicano: Algumas notas relativas ao período 1966–77." In *Africana* 12 (March): 85–111. Porto, Portugal: Edições de Centro de Estudos Africanos da Universidade Portucalense.
Nimtz, A. H. Jr. 1980. *Islam and Politics in East Africa: The Sufi Orders in Tanzania* Minneapolis: University of Minnesota Press.
Reichmuth, S. 1993. "Islamic Learning and Its Interaction with 'Western' Education in Illorin, Nigeria." In *Muslim Identity and Social Change in Sub-Saharan Africa*, edited by Louis Brenner, 179–97. London: Hurst.
Rzewuski, E. 1991a. "Mother Tongue/Father Tongue Convergence: On Swahilization and Deswahilization in Mozambique." In *Akten des 7. Essener Kolloquiums über "Minoritätensprachen/Sprachminritäten," vom 14–17.6.1990 an der Universität Essen*, edited by J. R. Dow and T. Stolz, 267–305. Bochum, Germany: Universitätsverlag Dr. N. Brockmeyer.
———. 1991b. "Origins of the Tungi Sultanate (Northern Mozambique) in the Light of Local Traditions." *Unwritten Testimonies of the African Past: Proceedings of the International Symposium held in Ojrzanów n. Warsaw on 07-08 November 1989*, edited by S. Piłaszewicz and E. Rzewuski, 193–213. Warsaw: Wydawnictwa Uniwersytetu Warszawskiego (*Orientalia Varsovenia*).
Saúte, A. R. 2004. *Escola de Habilitação de Professores Indígenas "José Cabral," Manhiça-Alvor: (1926–1974)*. Maputo, Mozambique: Promédia.
———. 2005. *O intercâmbio entre os Moçambicanos e as missões cristãs e a educação em Moçambique*. Maputo, Mozambique: Promédia.
Sheldon, K. 1998. "'I Studied with the Nuns, Learning to Make Blouses': Gender Ideology and Colonial Education in Mozambique." *International Journal of African Historical Studies* 31 (3): 595–625.
Silva Neves, F. A. da. 1901. *Informações á cerca da Capitania-Mór de Angoche*. Lourenço Marques, Mozambique: Imprensa Nacional.
Sousa, Frei J. De. 1788–1789. *Documentos Arabicos para a Historia Portugueza*. Lisbon: Offician Real das Ciencias.
Vilhena, E. J. de. 1905. *Companhia do Niassa. Relatórios e Memórias sobre os Territórios pelo Governador*. Lisbon: Typographia da "A Editora."

6.
COLONIAL CONTROL, NIGERIAN AGENCY, ARAB OUTREACH, AND ISLAMIC EDUCATION IN NORTHERN NIGERIA, 1900–1966

Alex Thurston

FROM THE ESTABLISHMENT of the Protectorate of Northern Nigeria in 1900 to the collapse of Nigeria's First Republic in 1966, policy makers and other participants in the politics of Islamic schooling consistently drew on educational models found in Arab countries, especially Sudan. Such exchanges were not new: Precolonial Northern Nigeria also knew translocal religious ties forged by traveling Hausa, Fulani, and Kanuri scholars who interacted with Tuareg and Arab teachers. But during colonial rule, new—and in many cases, more formal—educational links developed between Northern Nigeria and the Arab world. These links resulted from British policies, an increase in the number of Africans making pilgrimage to or studying in the Arab world, and Arab outreach.

Educational exchanges and experiments had wide-ranging consequences. The exchanges influenced how Northern Nigerian Muslims talked about and acted upon Islamic values. The exchanges introduced new resources, both material and cultural, into the region's political milieu. British experimentation in educational policy making, and the Muslim-run educational experiments that British policy influenced, contributed to the emergence of new kinds of mass religious politics. These forms of politics drew on and reformulated indigenous Islamic traditions, external Muslim referents, and notions of Western modernity.

To emphasize the fluid and contested nature of educational policy making in Northern Nigeria from 1900 to 1966 and contextualize the growth of Nigerian–Arab ties during this period, this chapter discusses three sets of elites and their forays into transnational educational exchanges: British colonial administrators, Nigerian politicians and intellectuals, and Arab leaders and educators. None of these groups were homogeneous, but certain generalizations are possible.

British colonialists tried to co-opt and control local Islamic schools in an attempt to bolster the legitimacy and institutional reach of Indirect Rule. They looked to Sudan as a lesson on containing perceived Islamic radicalism, a model for policy, and a politically palatable partner in educational exchanges. Northern elites, including classical religious scholars, Western-educated politicians, and Arabic-speaking Muslim intellectuals, also found inspiration in Arab educational models. In the independence period, Northern leaders maintained a relationship with Sudan and maintained colonial-era contacts in the field of education in order to solidify ties with emerging Arab powers such as Egypt and Saudi Arabia. Arab leaders in the 1950s and 1960s conducted educational and religious outreach to sub-Saharan Africa to spread their understandings of Islam, cultivate solidarity with Africans, improve their positions within inter-Arab rivalries, and counter Israeli influence. Arab educators worked with Nigerian leaders and Western scholars to reform Arabic teaching and enhance Nigerians' knowledge of Islamic history. Viewing each set of actors' perspectives will allow the argument to move beyond narratives that posit Arabs' influence over a passive African audience, or ones that minimize foreign influences in favor of a strictly local reading of agency, to more fully capture the interactive dynamics of colonial policies and Afro-Arab exchanges.

The tripartite encounter between Nigeria, Sudan, and Britain is not unique. For example, in the East African context, both Seesemann (this volume) and Loimeier (this volume) highlight how Muslim coastal communities participated in patterns of intellectual exchange with the wider Muslim world and how British colonialism affected trajectories of Islamic education in Kenya and Zanzibar. Studying such multipolar interactions can contribute to discussions about twentieth-century shifts in how Muslims talked about knowledge, practices, and traditions. To that end, this chapter concentrates on relationships between educational change and discursive change. It is not accidental that linguistic developments—such as British officials' promotion and standardization of Hausa in Northern Nigeria, the acquisition of English fluency by a Muslim political class, and the spread of spoken Arabic among new cohorts of intellectuals—occurred in tandem with the emergence of new vocabularies for contesting or asserting leadership, legitimacy, and values. In Northern Nigeria, education played a central role in shaping and spreading these discourses, as well as in forming new cadres who used them. New groups and changing discourses in turn shaped new educational projects, in some cases reinforcing the drive to incorporate foreign religious and educational models. Analysis of the different actors who participated in this process will help identify the different discourses that emerged and interacted in Northern Nigeria during the colonial period and immediately after independence.

British Control

British colonial policy in Northern Nigeria was neither static nor uniform. But amid changing policy imperatives, debates among administrators, funding shortfalls, and global political instability, experimentation ran as a thread of continuity in British educational policy from the establishment of the Protectorate of Northern Nigeria to the "indigenization" of the Ministry of Education in the early 1950s. British experiments often involved blending local forms of Islamic schooling with other pedagogical models. This process touched off debates about the roles of Arabic and English in instruction; the relationships between education, Islam, and politics; and the connections between Northern Nigeria and the Arab world. Participants in these debates did not confine themselves to strictly local or Western referents. Some educational innovators drew on policies and institutions developed elsewhere in the colonized world, especially Sudan and Egypt, to inform their initiatives. Experimentation, cross-cultural exchange, and an emphasis on the "formation of character" brought local iterations of Muslim thought into dialogue with both Western and foreign systems. Ultimately, influenced by these changes, Northern elites began to express religious and political idioms through new languages.

In the first five years of Indirect Rule, British colonial administrators pondered how to absorb and control the institutions of the Sokoto Caliphate, a nineteenth-century Muslim polity that controlled much of precolonial Northern Nigeria. British administrators set up few schools. But early policies shaped an educational space in the north that was distinct from other parts of the colonized world. Like their peers elsewhere, British leaders such as Lord Frederick Lugard (1858–1945) wanted to train elites to help run the colony. Unlike in India or Ghana, however, the British in Northern Nigeria hoped to defuse Muslim hostility to colonial rule by limiting missionary activity and co-opting the region's thousands of Islamic schools. The architects of the ban on missionary activity did not implement it universally or with absolute consistency (Shankar 2014), and missionaries built more schools and enrolled more students than the government did through at least the 1930s. Nevertheless, the colonial government's Native Authorities took primary responsibility for overseeing educational policy.

From the beginning, British attempts to manage Islamic schooling in Northern Nigeria, and the political calculus underlying this strategy, were informed by experiences elsewhere in the colonized world. British officials in Nigeria sometimes contrasted educational projects there with schooling in India, and the history of colonial education in Egypt indirectly influenced policy making in Northern Nigeria. Sudan—due to its own particularities as well as the Anglo-Egyptian influences it transmitted—had a direct and powerful impact on education in Northern Nigeria. The three British officials who most strongly affected educational policy in the first two decades of Indirect Rule in the north all spent time in Sudan. Lugard and his successor as governor, Percy Girouard, served in a military capacity in Sudan, respectively witnessing British defeat at the hands of the Mahdi in 1885 and British reconquest in 1896–1898. The first director of the Department of Education, meanwhile, was the educator and missionary Hanns Vischer. Vischer, who spoke Hausa and Arabic, toured Egypt, Sudan, the Gold Coast, and Southern Nigeria before assuming his post. Vischer's trip coincided with early experiments on the part of British Residents at blending Western and Islamic schooling, and upon his return he pursued a similar policy, thereby establishing the foundations of the government education system. It is difficult to say what impact Vischer's experiences in Sudan and Egypt had on these early experiments, but his tour established a pattern: Through the 1950s, British officials in Northern Nigeria modeled certain schools on Sudan's Gordon College and the Bakht er Ruda Institute, and British and Sudanese educators came to the north to lend a hand in educational policy making.

Sudan's relevance for British officials in Northern Nigeria owed partly to perceived similarities between the two areas and their histories. For administrators like Lugard and Girouard, remembering the British defeat at the hands of the Sudanese Mahdi, and seeing "Mahdist" rebellions in Northern Nigeria in 1905–1906, did not dispel the belief that Indirect Rule could harness Islam in its service, but it did instill wariness about Islam's potential for political radicalism. One British official, writing dismissively of African Mahdism, nevertheless noted that, "on the Nile . . . in [Chinese] Gordon's day, the battle had gone the other way, and we in Northern Nigeria were still feeling the impact of those faraway disasters" (Sharwood-Smith 1969, 52). The British hoped that co-opting Islamic schools in Northern Nigeria would increase the colony's economic self-sufficiency while reducing the likelihood of Mahdist uprisings.

Both Lugard and Girouard cited educational policies and achievements in Sudan, such as Gordon College, as models for Northern Nigeria. Islam, a religion Lugard argued "carries with it its own religious sanctions" and therefore was easier to include in standardized educational curricula, allowed Sudan and Northern Nigeria to depart from what Lugard perceived as the failure of religious education in India and southern Nigeria: "In the Government schools of the Sudan 'every boy is taught his own religion.' In Nigeria the same rule is applied," Lugard wrote, whereas "in India the teaching of religion is surrounded with special difficulties, and it has not been found feasible to introduce it in Government schools" (Lugard 1959, 437). Sudan thus acted as both a warning and an ideal for the new colony.

The British also fostered contacts between Nigeria and Sudan because they considered Sudan a less radical environment than Cairo or other educational centers in the Arab world. The educational policies of Muhammad Ali Pasha in early-nineteenth-century Egypt, which established Western-style government schools and brought some Qur'anic schools under state control, set part of the template the British applied in Sudan and, later, in Northern Nigeria. But by the early twentieth century, and especially after the Egyptian revolt of 1919, British officials in Sudan and Northern Nigeria mistrusted Egypt. British officials strove to control Egyptian influences in Northern Nigeria, denying recognition to Muslims educated at al-Azhar, refusing permission for Nigerian Muslims to study there, and screening Arabic literature coming into Northern Nigeria from Egypt and elsewhere. Sudan offered an attractive alternative to Egypt in British eyes. In Sudan, British policy makers had faced challenges similar to the ones officials dealt with in Northern Nigeria, such as opening Western-style schools, integrating rural Qur'anic schools into the government education system, creating institutions of higher learning like Gordon College, and working to counteract the appeal of al-Azhar. Sudan's wide base of Arabic speakers had also provided the British with a basis for efforts to integrate Western and Islamic education. Finally, an ethic of experimentation similar to that of colonial policy makers in Northern Nigeria characterized educational initiatives in Sudan, such as the evolution of Bakht er Ruda.

The pressures and problems that the Department (later Ministry) of Education of Northern Nigeria faced throughout its existence favored experimentation and reinforced the relationship with Sudan. External pressures included the adoption of different educational policies in the metropole, the impact of world wars and depressions, and the amalgamation of the department with its southern counterpart. Internal problems included runaway students, difficulties in supervising teachers, limited funding, and the challenge of how to co-opt Muslim schools. The political imperative of "preserving the political settlement" between local Muslim elites and British rule stayed constant, but debates about the place of Arabic and religious instruction in government schools began early and remained contentious throughout the colonial period (Hubbard 2000, 27). At first British officials made Hausa the dominant language of instruction in the North. Yet as the British brought Islamic schools under colonial control, some officials included Arabic and Qur'anic education in government school curricula to boost enrollments, popular support, and perceptions of success. Demands for Arabic competed with demands that English, a prerequisite for government employment, become the main language offered, and central authorities wavered between emphasizing Arabic and vernacular languages and confining Arabic to a language of religious instruction only. By the 1930s, Arabic ceased to represent a priority in many government schools, and by the 1940s, "Islamic elements within the government schools were clearly peripheral" (Hubbard 1975, 158). But at times when and places where the desire to improve and standardize Arabic teaching was ascendant, British administrators often looked toward Sudan.

The turn to Sudan suggests that the British had trouble finding Nigerians whom they considered suitable, either politically or pedagogically, to teach advanced Arabic, and furthermore suggests that Sudanese trained in Western-style institutions offered a suitable pool of recruits in British eyes. This thinking held sway—and seems to have begun—in areas with native Arabic speakers, such as Bornu. Despite a policy of rarely hiring outside teachers in Northern Nigeria, by 1916 Bornu's British Resident was considering "importing European-trained Islamic scholars from the Sudan and Egypt" to help integrate Western and Islamic education, and he journeyed to Sudan to explore the possibility (Hubbard 2000, 38–39). This idea was formally proposed in 1919. The first teachers, graduates of Gordon College, arrived in 1924 to teach Arabic at a primary school in Bornu. British administrators evidently considered the program successful, because they attempted to continue and expand it despite the departure of the Sudanese in 1927. Just as Western-style institutions such as Katsina College emphasized English proficiency as a way of forming elites who behaved like British officials, hiring Sudanese Arabs trained in Western-style institutions became one tool for producing Muslim elites who would, British administrators hoped, have advanced competency in Arabic and religious sciences but still adhere to Britain's vision for colonial Northern Nigeria.

Even as the importance of Arabic within the school system as a whole declined during the 1930s, the British turned again to Sudan, hiring three more graduates of Gordon College to teach at the Northern Provinces Law School. This Western-style institution, founded in 1934 and later renamed the School for Arabic Studies, used Arabic as a language of instruction. British officials intended the school to produce judges and teachers who could serve the colonial administration and the sharia courts it had co-opted. The school aimed to mold a certain kind of subject: Muslim scholars trained not by "individual scholars of repute," but formed in an institutional setting that standardized knowledge and reconciled Western education with traditional Islamic knowledge (Umar 2006, 61–62). Students progressed through ordered grades, receiving instruction on not just the technical aspects of religious life but also the moral principles underlying it. These principles, articulated by the British, hearkened back to Lugard's emphasis on education as a means of forming "character."

The presence of Sudanese teachers—who in this case remained with the school for many years—testifies to British confidence that the Sudanese could improve Nigerian students' competence in Arabic and Islamic law without disrupting the transmission of a government-directed moral and political vision. In a further indication of this confidence, the British sent Muslims from Northern

Nigeria to Sudan to study Arabic and Islamic law. These transnational educational exchanges affected only a small number of Northern elites, but the combination of Western-style schooling, access to standardized Islamic knowledge, and exposure to Arab scholars would shape the development of Islamic politics in the independence period.

The British coordinated educational exchanges between Northern Nigeria and Sudan through the end of colonial rule. British intervention in the transmission of Arabic paralleled colonial administrators' attempts to shape other languages—to standardize and promote Hausa through publications and classroom instruction, for example, and to spread English among certain classes. As the uses and roles of these languages changed under colonial rule, the languages of politics and religion changed, too. Just as educational experiments in Egypt gave rise to experiments in Sudan and, through Sudan, Northern Nigeria, educational initiatives in the north produced elites who undertook their own experiments. Education replicated and transformed education.

Transnational contacts influenced this process. The Northern Nigerian elites who began to take over the institutions of Indirect Rule in the 1940s and 1950s inherited from the British an educational system shaped in part by transnational educational exchanges, especially in the field of Arabic and Islamic education. The experimental ethic of British educational policy making would continue for the north's independence-era leaders, as would the challenge of balancing Western-style and Islamic education. Before turning to a discussion of how Northern elites shaped educational policy in the 1950s and 1960s, however, it is useful to review how Northerners approached education during the first five decades of colonial rule. Northern elites were not necessarily passive recipients of British education. Some were agents who negotiated the parameters of colonial education and pursued educational exchanges beyond the borders of Nigeria. In doing so, Northern politicians and intellectuals developed forms of Islamic politics that blended ideas of tradition and modernity as well as external models of Islamic practice.

Nigerian Agency

Indirect Rule's incorporation of precolonial Muslim trade networks, sharia courts, and emirate bureaucracies gave Northern Nigerian Muslim elites ways to establish themselves in the new system, but in terms of enrollment in Western-style schools, Muslims lagged behind—and have continued to trail—southerners and non-Muslims. Yet uncertainties around the nature and purposes of schooling, and the experimental atmosphere surrounding educational policy making, created opportunities for different groups of Northerners to shape the educational arena even before independence. These groups included classical religious scholars who negotiated with British administrators over the role of religion in schooling; Western-educated elites who experimented, as did the British, with blending Islamic and Western education; and Western-educated, Arabic-speaking intellectuals. All these groups pursued ties with the Arab world and used them to influence education in the north. Northern elites replicated, transformed, and reformulated colonial educational models. New leaders and intellectuals acted as self-conscious Muslim modernizers.

Although violence, coercion, and resistance occurred in educational contexts, Muslim elites and colonial rulers also negotiated with one another about schooling. This process shaped colonial educational initiatives from the beginning. For example, the Kano schools for *mallams* (scholars) and chiefs initially occupied land donated by the emir, highlighting the legitimacy that local rulers could give to educational projects and the ways in which education allowed rulers to make their patronage visible. Hanns Vischer incorporated Islamic elements into schooling, pressuring the government to build a mosque at a school in Kano and paying the imam himself. These moves suggest that Vischer perceived a need to assuage the concerns of local rulers and build legitimacy for colonial education by giving religion space within the colonial educational project. This policy continued after Vischer's tenure, with emirs retaining influence over religious elements in the schools—for example, the power to recommend school imams. The author of a 1930 report proposing changes in Islamic education wrote that he had discussed his suggestions with emirs and cited their approval as support for his ideas (Hussey 1930). British officials sometimes mischaracterized or ignored the power dynamics inherent in such conversations, but clearly they considered the reception policies would have among Muslim authorities.

Amid such negotiations, Sudan inspired Nigerian thinking on education just as it did for the British. Just as shared experiences in colonial practice forged connections between the British in Northern Nigeria and in Sudan, historical ties and the pilgrimage route that led from West Africa through Sudan to Mecca connected Nigerians and Sudanese. Pilgrimage and educational exchange often intersected. Muhammad Gidado, the *waziri* of Kano, visited Gordon College in the 1930s on his hajj to Saudi Arabia, and this inspired the creation of the Northern Provinces Law School/School for Arabic Studies. The shared (though differently oriented) Nigerian and British interest in Sudan facilitated the spread of Sudanese models: The emir, and eventually the colonial authorities, agreed to Gidado's suggestion. Egypt also provided educational models for Nigerian elites. Despite British wariness of Egypt, in 1937 the emir of Kano visited Cairo and "appealed to the scholars of the Azhar to come to Nigeria" (Loimeier 1997, 153). When Northern traditional elites turned toward Sudan and Egypt, they simultaneously sustained precolonial traditions, shared in British conceptions of the value of transnational exchanges, and challenged the boundaries the British tried to set on these exchanges. Northern elites seemed to feel, like the British, that Arabs possessed authoritative knowledge that could enhance Islamic education in Nigeria.

While hereditary authorities were involving themselves in interchanges and struggles over the direction of educational policy, Western-style colonial institutions, particularly Katsina College, were producing elites to administer the colony. In a way, this represented the fruition of British officials' plans, but these elites were not necessarily Westernized. Many of the Northern politicians born between 1910 and 1930, including Ahmadu Bello, attended Qur'anic school as young boys. Islam provided part of the common ground for these rising elites when they attended Katsina College. To be sure, Western-style education—which, for some, included training in England—marked these men's lives deeply. Many of them advanced to teaching positions in Western-style schools after graduation, and later to careers in Western-style politics. But young Northern teacher-politicians did not forget Islam. "The question of joining western education and religious education," John Paden (1986, 129) writes, "was of concern to the young teachers who had themselves gone through both systems."

In the late 1940s, figures on both sides of an emerging political divide began to found modernized Islamic schools with organized classes, uniforms, and elements of Western-style curricula. Around 1947, Bello and future president Shehu Shagari set up a modernized "Nizamiyya school." Meanwhile, the anticolonial leader Aminu Kano set up an Arabic school in 1950 as an explicit alternative to traditional schools. These schools drew large enrollments, testifying to their capacity to create and meet demands for blended education, but they also provoked resistance from traditional scholars and religious authorities. Schooling soon became politicized. In the 1950s, Bello's Northern People's Congress, which represented the Northern establishment, and Kano's Northern Elements Progressive Union, an opposition party, drew on Islam and Islamic education to legitimate their programs and build popular support. Islamic schooling became one of the religious services modernizing Muslim politicians offered to their constituents, a trend that continued during the transition to independence and after. For example, during the 1959 elections, Bello campaigned in part on increasing assistance to Qur'anic schools.

Political approaches that framed modernization within Islamic idioms owed much to Western-style education and, increasingly, to transnational ties with Arabs. Ahmadu Bello combined these influences with traditional notions of Islamic authority, which the growing rationalization of Muslim beliefs and practices had made relative but certainly not irrelevant. Bello used multiple vocabularies to establish legitimacy. Western schooling had given him fluency in English and administrative skills, and his descent from the founders of the Sokoto

Caliphate gave him an indigenous basis for religious authority. Embracing this hybrid background, Bello blended the political languages of modernization and Islamic piety. For example, Brian Larkin (2008, 103–104) writes that Bello "used mobile cinemas for . . . projecting himself as a new type of religious as well as political leader. . . . The same newsreels that showed him in a modernist role visiting dams and factories also recorded his pilgrimage to Mecca and to the tomb of Sultan Bello. . . . Ahmadu Bello's attempt to meld religious authority with the secular technology of cinema indicates his desire to forge a new sort of Muslim identity that rejected the artificial split between tradition and modernity." Bello incorporated foreign as well as domestic influences. His frequent pilgrimages to Mecca, personal contacts with foreign Muslim leaders, and membership in the Muslim World League, of which he became deputy president in 1962, reinforced his credentials as a modernizing Islamic leader.

Connections with Arabs gave Bello financial, political, and religious capital. Saudi, Kuwaiti, and Egyptian donations helped Bello build mosques and Islamic schools; create an organization for promoting Islam; and conduct conversion campaigns. Drawing on his relationships with Arabs enhanced the already potent blend of Western-style educational credentials with Islamic piety. For example, when Bello spoke on the occasion of reopening the Sultan Bello Mosque in 1963, he invoked themes of indigenous Islamic tradition, modernity, and international Islam. He emphasized that "our fore-fathers were known for their building of mosques," but also stated that the mosque was rebuilt "in the most modern style of our time in our country." He expressly thanked Egypt for its financial contribution, and gave special recognition to a Saudi Arabian sheikh who blessed the mosque. Praise for this man was coupled with praise for Saudi Arabia itself, a move that stressed Bello's personal relationship with the kingdom: "I, and the people of Nigeria cannot express sufficiently the hospitality shown to me whenever I visit that country. I personally consider myself as you regard me, that is a citizen of the Hejaz" (Bello 1992, 319–320, 323). As the genealogical and spiritual heir of Usman dan Fodio and an honorary Arab, Bello strove to claim the broadest possible Islamic authority.

Contacts with Arabs were important not just for Northern politicians wooing the masses but for Northern elites formulating education policy. Already in the 1940s, elites such as Kashim Ibrahim were following the British example by traveling to Sudan and studying its educational policies. By the 1950s, Northern Nigerian educational initiatives took place in an international Muslim context. In 1953, a government-sponsored Committee on Higher Muslim Education recommended extending courses at the School for Arabic Studies, hiring more teachers from Sudan, and sending Nigerians to Sudan to train as teachers and study sharia. Bello commissioned reports on Islamic schooling; set up a committee to deal with the issue and manage government assistance to schools; and dispatched a team to Libya, Sudan, and the United Arab Republic to study educational practices in those countries. As a result of Northern policy makers' efforts, by the mid-1960s, state schools in the north offered several pathways toward achievement in Arabic and Islamic studies. Experimentation sparked experimentation when Northern elites, like the British before them, blended Islamic and Western curricula as they sought to create a modern elite capable of administering the north on a Western-style bureaucratic, but also Islamic, basis.

Traditional authorities and Western-educated elites played major roles in bringing Arab models and monies to Nigeria, but many of these Nigerians, including Bello, did not speak Arabic. For that reason, Northerners who mastered Arabic and studied in the Arab world provided a critical link between Western-educated Northern elites and Arab powers. For example, when Bello made his first pilgrimage to Saudi Arabia in 1955, it was Nigerian students at al-Azhar who met his party in Cairo. Another group of young Northerners, whose plans to study at al-Azhar in the 1950s provoked resistance from the colonial administration, negotiated with the British for permission to study at Bakht er Ruda in Sudan. Members of this group later became prominent intellectuals, diplomats, preachers, educators, and politicians—roles in which they influenced Northern society and continued to link it to the Arab world. One graduate, Haliru Binji, became an education officer upon his return, represented Nigeria at a conference on Islamic education held in Dar es Salaam in 1958, and helped guide the evolution of the School for Arabic Studies.

Abubakar Gumi (1924–1992), another veteran of the Sudan trip, developed an international outlook and acquired influential Arab contacts through his own education at the School for Arabic Studies, his experience in Sudan, and his work as pilgrims' officer in Jeddah in the late 1950s. Gumi attained influence as grand khadi of the Northern Region, religious adviser to Ahmadu Bello, and founder of the anti-Sufi movement Jama'at Izalat al-Bid'a wa Iqamat as-Sunna (Society for the removal of blameworthy innovation and the establishment of the Prophet's model). In the 1960s, Gumi's international connections helped Bello obtain assistance from Gulf countries, and in the 1970s and 1980s, he assisted young Northerners in seeking Arab educations. Gumi and his peers, products of both British and Arab education, were intellectuals and activists who interpreted modernity and Islam on their own terms.

Northern elites, often working within the constraints imposed by colonial rule, influenced educational exchanges during colonialism. For traditional rulers negotiating the form of Islamic schooling with British officials, Arab countries, especially Sudan, became models and sources of inspiration. For Western-educated politicians, contacts with Arabs offered ways to build political and religious legitimacy; and for policy makers, Arab countries provided templates for change and reform. Finally, for an emerging group of Arabic-speaking intellectuals, Sudan was a site for acquiring advanced education, and the Arab world a zone where the Islamic languages and ideas learned in colonial schools took on new resonances. These exchanges made available new ways of expressing notions of modernity, tradition, orthodoxy, and piety.

Just as Nigerians were not passive in the face of British attempts at control, so Arabs were not shadowy outsiders with unfathomable motives. Telling their story is critical to understanding educational, religious, and political transformations in independence-era Northern Nigeria. The transnational connections forged through Nigerians' experiments in education intersected with the foreign policy initiatives of rising Arab powers, a process that brought Arab scholars and educators to Northern Nigeria. The next section discusses political factors that increased Arab influence in Africa and examines the work of several Arabs who worked in Northern Nigeria. This discussion will help contextualize the Arab side of Nigerian–Arab educational exchanges and highlight the contributions Arabs made to changes in the way Muslims in Northern Nigeria talked about and practiced Islam.

Arab Outreach

Nigerian–Arab contacts accelerated during the colonial period and after independence due to rising numbers of Nigerians making pilgrimage and pursuing education in the Arab world. The growing political and economic influence of Arab nations progressively magnified the impact of these contacts. The foreign policies of Arab leaders in the 1950s and 1960s had macrolevel effects on the development of Islamic education and politics in Africa, and the Arab educators who came to countries like Nigeria had microlevel effects on Arabic teaching and conceptions of Islamic knowledge.

Political and religious change in the Arab world in the early twentieth century set the stage for Arab outreach to sub-Saharan Africa in the independence era. The consolidation of Saudi Arabia under the Saudi family and the growth of Egyptian and Algerian Muslim voluntary associations in the 1920s and 1930s spread new notions of orthodoxy among West African educators and pilgrims before the 1950s, but it was the Egyptian revolution of 1952 that marked a sea change in Arab countries' outreach to Muslim communities in sub-Saharan Africa. Following the revolution, Egyptian leaders asserted Egypt's African identity and promoted unity between Arab and African Muslims. Boutros Boutros-Ghali wrote optimistically in 1963, "Arabic-speaking Islam enjoys a splendid opportunity for cultural and political expansion in Africa" ((1963, 327). Egypt wooed African Muslims in part through building schools and offering scholarships for African Muslims at Egyptian universities. Nigeria received a significant portion of this Egyptian outreach. Egypt's efforts found a favorable audience among younger Nigerians and attracted Northern leaders' sympathy. Bello met with Nasser several times, and both Bello and Gumi were given official honors in Egypt. With the end of British rule, Nigeria and Egypt could pursue the relationship whose potential had existed for decades.

New Arab actors entered the stage during this time. Kuwait and Saudi Arabia "felt threatened by the expansionist policies of Egypt" and wanted "to balance the increasing Egyptian influence on Bello." Both countries donated to Bello's projects in the early 1960s (Loimeier 1997,137). These developments reflected Saudi Arabia's changing role in the Muslim world. Prior to the 1960s, Saudi Arabian religious elites did not seek ties with African Muslim movements. Succession struggles within the royal family and the desire to combat Egyptian influence in Yemen prevented the kingdom from becoming a major donor to African countries. Under King Faisal, however, Africa became an ideological battleground between Egypt and Saudi Arabia. Saudi Arabian institutions such as the Islamic University in Medina and the Muslim World League conducted outreach to African Muslims. In 1965, Faisal toured Africa as part of his pan-Islamic organizing efforts. He and Bello became friends, and the Nigerian–Saudi Arabian ties that formed during this period prepared the ground for a flowering of contacts in the 1970s and after.

With Northern leaders able to pursue ties with Arabs in the 1950s and 1960s, education policy became one of the first official points of contact between Nigeria and the Arab world after independence, and a major conduit for Arab religious and political influences. With Sudan, educational exchanges outlasted British rule. Nigerian diplomats and scholars continued to work in Sudan; Sudanese teachers and officials continued to visit the North; and "the first African conference on Islamic education," held in 1960 in Kano, was attended by "a number of Muslim scholars from Northern Nigeria, Sudan and Zanzibar" (Loimeier 2005, 368).

Indeed, educators and scholars from all over the Arab world came to the north. Some helped make policy. Others participated in efforts to spread historical knowledge about Islam, particularly Nigeria's Islamic history. Sheikh Awad Mohammed Ahmad of Sudan, a longtime teacher at the School for Arabic Studies, served as grand khadi for the first two years after independence and coauthored a volume on Islamic history for African Muslims, *The Story of the Arabs* (Hiskett and Ahmad 1957). Aida Arif and Ahmad Abu Hakima of the University of Jordan, working with the support of Northern politicians and Western scholars, cataloged Arabic manuscripts at Jos and Kaduna from 1963 to 1965 and published their findings upon completion. Arab efforts to spread knowledge of Islamic history in Northern Nigeria complemented the efforts of Northern politicians and intellectuals to reinvigorate the symbolic language of the Sokoto Caliphate and give it broader meaning in the context of emerging transnational Muslim communities.

Nigeria also continued to invite Arab educators to help improve Arabic teaching, but now drew on a broader geographical range than just Sudan. For example, Selim Hakim, an Iraqi educator, came in 1961 to Lagos, Kaduna, and Ibadan to write a report on Arabic teaching in Nigerian schools. For Hakim, the trip had political ramifications; He spoke of the "strong and ancient ties between the Republic of Iraq and Nigeria" (Hakim 1961, 2–5). Hakim criticized Nigerian schools, but was encouraged by the desire for improved Arabic education that he found, and he believed that the visiting Arabic teachers from other countries whom he met in the north could initiate a push to modernize teaching methods. Hakim recommended increased collaboration with Arabs and urged the Ministry of Education to secure more scholarships for Nigerian students from Arab governments.

Hakim's visit overlapped with changes in the education system. In 1962–1963, the University of Ibadan inaugurated its Department of Arabic and Islamic Studies. At roughly the same time, Ahmadu Bello University was founded and began to emphasize Arabic and Islamic studies. These changes offered further opportunities for Nigerian, Western, and Arab scholars to collaborate. In 1965, John Hunwick organized a "Seminar on the Teaching of Arabic in Nigeria" with financial support from the Embassy of Jordan and institutional backing from the University of Ibadan and Ahmadu Bello University. Prominent Nigerian intellectuals, Western scholars, and Arab educators (including Hakim) attended the seminar, as did the ambassadors of Lebanon, Sudan, and Jordan, along with representatives from Iraq, Pakistan, and Saudi Arabia (Hunwick 1965). These exchanges contributed to a further institutionalization of Nigerian–Arab ties as well as a standardization of Arabic and Islamic knowledge.

In the years before the end of Nigeria's First Republic, educational and intellectual exchange represented a significant component of Arab outreach to Northern Nigeria. Northerners continued British policies of seeking outside Arab expertise but also expanded their exchanges beyond Sudan to include Egypt, Saudi Arabia, and, to a lesser extent, Arab countries such as Jordan and Iraq and Muslim countries such as Pakistan, which shared with Northern Nigeria the experience of British rule. Educational and academic cooperation with Arabs built not just on British colonial structures but on foundations laid by Nigerian–Arab exchanges in the colonial period. The increasing availability of opportunities to study with Arabs inside and outside Nigeria would influence a generation of Arabic-speaking Northerners who rose to prominence after independence. Arabs' contributions to Northern Nigerian Islam in the independence era, then, comprised both the immediate effects of published works on Islamic history and advice on Arabic teaching and other policy matters, but also a long-term legacy of religious networks. Arabs and Nigerians sometimes had divergent political motives, but also generally treated each other with good will.

Conclusion

Shaykh Uthman Dan Fodio, writing around the turn of the nineteenth century in present-day northern Nigeria, discussed Islam as a system different from other ways of life and thought and struggled in word and deed against Muslim rulers whose behavior he considered un-Islamic. His vision of Islam proved portable, as he established a Muslim polity over a large territory. But religious movements elsewhere in the Islamic world, as Ahmed Dallal (1993) has argued, only partly influenced Dan Fodio. Four generations later, Ahmadu Bello moved in an Islamic and political space that was geographically broader than Dan Fodio's and reflected more immediate effects of external actors such as the British and Arabs. Bello routinely traveled to Arab countries and drew on their support to promote forms of education in Northern Nigeria that consciously blended Western and Islamic content and style.

A nineteenth-century religious reformer like Umar Tall, meanwhile, traveled to Arabia and studied with Arabs. Roughly a century later, Abubakar Gumi did the same, but he pursued advanced education through pathways that were more institutionalized and formalized. This is not to say that no institutions existed in Tall's time or that Gumi did not build personal ties in his, but rather to point out that by the late colonial period contacts between Northern Nigeria and the Arab world were becoming routinized and standardized on a scale that was not the case in the precolonial period.

This chapter has traced the institutionalization of these transitional ties in the field of education, arguing that under colonial rule both British administrators and Northern Nigerian elites consistently turned to Arab countries—especially Sudan but also, and increasingly, Egypt, Saudi Arabia, and others—to inform or supplement local experiments with new kinds of schooling. Arab outreach also contributed to transformations in colonial-era education in Nigeria. With the approach and realization of Nigerian independence and the rising political and religious influence of Arab states in the 1950s and 1960s, Nigerian–Arab links had an even greater impact on the north. Arab educators and scholars who came to Northern Nigeria made diverse contributions to the emergence of rationalized forms of Islamic thought and politics, especially by helping to standardize and popularize understandings of Northern Nigeria's own Islamic history.

Analyzing how each group affected shifts in Islamic practice and politics in Northern Nigeria emphasizes the importance of transnational exchanges for understanding new articulations of Islamic identity that developed during and after colonial rule. In late colonial and independence-era Northern Nigeria, politicians taking the reins of power from the British acted as self-conscious Islamic modernizers. This political style owed much to Northern elites' experiences with Western-style and Islamic education during colonial rule. As such, it also owed something to the transnational religious ties forged under colonialism through educational exchange and, especially after the 1950s, pilgrimage to Mecca. These links, by exposing Northern elites to other iterations of Islamic practice and thought, helped create an environment in which politicians and intellectuals could reformulate precolonial models of Islamic leadership and authority, sometimes with the direct support of outside actors. This process of rationalization did not eliminate esotericism and tradition as major components of religious authority in Northern Nigeria in the 1950s and 1960s, either for Western-educated elites or for Sufi leaders, leaders with inherited positions, or scholars who continued to study in the precolonial style. Rather, what Ousmane Kane (2003) calls a "fragmentation of sacred authority" occurred, putting esoteric and traditional forms of authority into competition, dialogue, and combination with other claims to knowledge and legitimacy. Northern politicians such as Ahmadu Bello created self-consciously modern Islamic personas, and Northern intellectuals and activists formed in colonial Arabic schools and institutions in the Arab world increasingly drew contrasts between themselves and other Muslim scholars and authorities. Although Northern Nigerian Sufis had enjoyed translocal ties for centuries, and increasingly cultivated links with Sufi authorities elsewhere beginning in the late colonial period, transnational religious ties—often formed through education—became a powerful conduit for anti-Sufism in postcolonial Nigeria.

The importance of what happened in Islamic education in Northern Nigeria from the beginning of the colonial period through the independence era stems partly from the uniqueness of Nigeria's educational space, particularly the ban on missionary activity, and from the ways this space shaped Northern Nigerian politics and Islam. The emergence of Islamic modernizers like Bello during this period also has significance for the study of the Islamic world as a whole. A comparative gaze, looking back at Sudan and Saudi Arabia, finds parallels between Bello and other Muslim leaders of his time who drew on both inherited authority and fluency in the languages of Western modernity. Sudan's Sadiq al-Mahdi, though born roughly a quarter century after Bello, built a political following partly on the basis of his descent from the Sudanese Mahdi, but also attended university in Oxford. Bello's friend Faisal, meanwhile, was a Saudi royal and his father's lieutenant, but also an English-speaking diplomat who, as king, pursued an explicitly modernizing agenda. Western notions of modernity, pan-Islamic thought, and the desire to express inherited religious and political legitimacy through new idioms influenced all these men. Comparing their careers, and contrasting them with the careers of revolutionary Muslim and Arab leaders such as Gamal 'Abd al-Nasser, who drew on different bases of authority, could offer new insights about the ways Muslim elites grappled with the challenges of local politics, global religion, Western modernity, and indigenous tradition in the independence era, a critical juncture in the history of the Muslim world.

REFERENCES

Arif, Aida, and Ahmad Abu Hakima. 1965. *Descriptive Catalogue of Arabic Manuscripts in Nigeria: Jos Museum and Lugard Hall Library, Kaduna*. London: Luzac.

Bello, Ahmadu. 1992. "On Re-Opening of Rebuilt Sultan Bello Mosque, 1963." In *Power of Knowledge: Biographies and Speeches of Northern Nigerian Founding Fathers*, edited by Isa Kaita, 319–20, 323. Nigeria: Arewa Research and Publications.

Boutros-Ghali, Boutros. 1963. "The Foreign Policy of Egypt (United Arab Republic)." In *Foreign Policies in a World of Change*, edited by Joseph E. Black and Kenneth W. Thompson, 319–31. New York: Harper & Row.

Dallal, Ahmad. 1993. "The Origins and Objectives of Islamic Revivalist Thought, 1750–1850." *Journal of the American Oriental Society* 113 (3): 341–59.

Hakim, Selim. 1961. *The Teaching of Arabic in Schools and Colleges in Nigeria*. Ibadan, Nigeria: University College, Institute of Education.

Hiskett, Mervyn, and Awad Ahmad. 1957. *The Story of the Arabs*. London: Longmans, Green.

Hubbard, James. 1975. "Government and Islamic Education in Northern Nigeria (1900–1940)." In *Conflict and Harmony in Education in Tropical Africa*, edited by Godfrey N. Brown and Mervyn Hiskett, 152–68. London: Allen and Unwin.

———. 2000. *Education under Colonial Rule: A History of Katsina College, 1921–1942*. Lanham, MD: University Press of America.

Hunwick, John. 1965. *Report on a Seminar on the Teaching of Arabic in Nigeria*. Ibadan and Kano, Nigeria: University of Ibadan and Ahmadu Bello University.

Hussey, E. R. J. 1930. *Memorandum on Educational Policy in Nigeria*. London: Waterlow.

Larkin, Brian. 2008. *Signal and Noise: Media, Infrastructure, and Urban Culture in Nigeria*. Durham, NC: Duke University Press.

Loimeier, Roman. 1997. *Islamic Reform and Political Change in Northern Nigeria*. Evanston, IL: Northwestern University Press.

———. 2005. "Playing with Affiliations: Muslims in Northern Nigeria in the 20th Century." In *Entreprises religieuses transnationales en Afrique de l'Ouest*, edited by Laurent Fourchard, André Mary, and Rene Otayek, 349–71. Paris: Karthala.

Lugard, Frederick. 1959. *The Diaries of Lord Lugard*. Edited by Margery Perham and Mary Bull. Evanston, IL: Northwestern University Press.

Paden, John. 1986. *Ahmadu Bello, Sardauna of Sokoto: Values and Leadership in Nigeria*. Zaria, Nigeria: Hudahuda.

Sharwood-Smith, Bryan. 1969. *Recollections of British Administration in the Cameroons and Northern Nigeria, 1921–1957: But Always as Friends.* Durham, NC: Duke University Press.

Umar, Muhammad Sani. 2006. *Islam and Colonialism: Intellectual Responses of Muslims of Northern Nigeria to British Colonial Rule.* Leiden: Brill.

Williams, D. H. 1959. *A Short Survey of Education in Northern Nigeria.* Kaduna: Ministry of Education, Northern Region of Nigeria.

7.
MUSLIM SCHOLARS, ORGANIC INTELLECTUALS, AND THE DEVELOPMENT OF ISLAMIC EDUCATION IN ZANZIBAR IN THE TWENTIETH CENTURY

Roman Loimeier

THIS CONTRIBUTION HIGHLIGHTS the role of Muslim religious scholars (Arabic, ulama Swahili, *walimu*) and teachers (Arabic, *muʿallimūn*; Swahili, *walimu*) in the development of Islamic education in Zanzibar in the twentieth century. In particular, I focus on the development of the relationship between these scholars and two different administrations: the British Protectorate and Zanzibar Sultanate until 1964 as well as the Revolutionary Government of Zanzibar since 1964. While the Protectorate era witnessed the apex of ulama power in Zanzibar as well as the emergence of a second tier of scholars—Muslim government school teachers—the revolution in 1964 led to the demise of a whole social group of both religious scholars and educators. Thus, the question might be asked: What happens when the scholars are gone? My contribution is based on ten years of research in Zanzibar, where I was reading in the Zanzibar National Archives and conducted numerous conversations with local interlocutors (Loimeier 2009).

When examining the development of Islamic education in Zanzibar in the twentieth century, it is important to have some basic facts in mind: First, Zanzibar town, in contrast to other urban centers on the East African Coast such as Mombasa or Lamu, was a rather recent foundation of the early nineteenth century. Consequently, traditions of Islamic learning (beyond local mosques) have developed in Zanzibar only since the 1850s to 1860s. This late development of Islamic education and local traditions of Islamic learning was linked with the influx of scholars from either Brawa (on the southern Banadir coast), the Comoros, the Hadhramaut, Oman (mostly of Ibādhi orientation), and other places along the East African coast—in particular, Lamu and Mombasa.

Due to the lack of established traditions of Islamic learning, these scholars were quickly able to establish themselves and to develop distinct schools of learning, most often affiliated in the nineteenth century with the Sufi order of the Qādiriyya and the scholarly networks of the 'Alawiyya. The first Islamic madrasa—an Islamic school that provided advanced Islamic education to students following a distinct syllabus—only developed since 1892, however, in the guise of 'Abdallāh Bā Kathīr's Madrasat Bā Kathīr in Ukutani/Zanzibar (see Bang 2003). Most education was, in fact, done in private houses or in mosques, both in Zanzibar town as well as in the *shamba* (rural) areas. 'Abdallāh Bā Kathīr's Madrasat Bā Kathīr was inspired by a movement of educational reform that had started a few years earlier in the Hadhramaut among the religious scholars of the 'Alawiyya.

This movement of reform was initiated by 'Alawī b. 'Abd al-Raḥmān al-Mashhūr (1846/1847–1922/1923) (Bang 2003, 62, 113). In 1873–1874, al-Mashhūr had spent some time at al-Azhar in Cairo, where he witnessed the start of Egyptian educational reforms that initially came to mean a formalization of the curricula of the religious sciences. After his return to the Hadhramaut in 1881, al-Mashhūr became a teacher in the Ribāṭ al-Riyāḍa in Say'ūn. The year 1872 was a decisive one for social reforms in the Islamic world: al-Azhar introduced entry examinations, registration of students, diplomas, and final examinations (Bang 2003, 62).

These reforms had repercussions in the Hadhramaut, where they were introduced, at least in part, in the Ribāṭ al-Riyāḍa in Say'ūn that had been established in 1878–1879 by 'Alī b. Muḥammad al-Ḥibshī as well as 'Abd al-Raḥmān b. Muḥammad al-Mashhūr. Their reforms were communicated to Indonesia, India, and East Africa and discussed within the network of Hadhrami students and scholars (Bang 2003, 75). However, the Azhar reforms and those in the Hadhramaut remained confined for the time being to changes in formal structures as well as some aspects of scholarly orientation. They were not (yet) a change in "theology" (Bang 2003, 71). The new *ribāṭs* in Say'ūn and Tarīm were characterized by the fact that a group of teachers in the school gave a number of fixed courses in a four-year curriculum that emphasized *fiqh*. The students, though still sitting in circles, were organized in classes according to their abilities and progress (Freitag 2003, 284). The concept of Islamic education "in organized, academically structured institutions privately funded and privately run," as developed in the Hadhramaut, was subsequently adopted by Aḥmad b. Sumayṭ or 'Abdallāh Bā Kathīr and cultivated in East Africa (Bang 2003, 62–64 and al-Farsy 1972, 21–60).

At the same time, in the late nineteenth century, Zanzibar saw the development of three other systems of education that competed with Islamic education: mission schools (which had failed completely by the early twentieth century; see Turki 1987), Indian private schools (confined to Indian communities; see Loimeier 2009), and the British government schools (since 1905, which were open to all students, at least in theory). The competition between British government schools and Islamic schools came to dominate the development of Islamic education throughout the twentieth century and forms the focus of this essay.

The first question that arises with respect to this theme is why the British government schools became such a threat for Islamic education. Several answers can be suggested: First, British government schools, in contrast to the Indian schools, targeted the whole population of Zanzibar; second, government schools were supported by the administrative apparatus of the Protectorate administration, in the guise of a Department of Education (since 1905); third, government schools provided a complete model of education, suited to modern times, which promised to provide access to "marketable skills"[1]; and, last but not least, government schools aimed to replace existing Qur'anic schools (Swahili, *chuo*; pl. *vyuo*), which were seen as largely obsolete and superfluous by the British. Qur'anic school teaching was branded as useless "parrot talk" (Loimeier 2009, 247–48). The 1913 annual report on education, as written by the first director of education, Rivers-Smith, reflected the negative assessment of the Qur'anic schools by the British and started the colonial mantra of accusing the Qur'anic schools of providing "meaningless" education:

> The atmosphere of a native conducted class, without European assistance and supervision, is essentially bad. The teacher lacks dignity, he has little idea of discipline and none of school method. The teaching may include a rudimentary instruction in Arabic writing but more often a verbal knowledge of the Koran is all that is attempted. This in Zanzibar is meaningless, as little or no Arabic is taught in these schools and Swahili is the domestic language even of the majority of the Arabs. It is difficult, to imagine anything more deadening to potential intellect than to read aloud from morning till evening, for a period of two or three years, words of which nothing is understood. But what is more important is that the wasted years are probably the most valuable of the child's life. The question of puberty is of far greater moment in the intellectual development of the African than of the European. It is indeed true that the intellectual development in the tropics, the vital importance of bringing children under proper control at the earliest possible age is obvious. (Zanzibar National Archive, file AB 1/224)

Despite their claim to establish modern education for the whole population of Zanzibar, the British government schools model failed pathetically in the first decades of the twentieth century, while Islamic education, Qur'anic schools, and madrasas survived and blossomed. Zanzibar in fact witnessed, in the first decades of the twentieth century, the rise of several generations of respected Muslim religious scholars who earned recognition due to their scholarship not only in Zanzibar but on the East African Coast (and beyond). As a result, Zanzibar came to be seen, since the early twentieth century, as the *qibla* (Arabic, the decisive point of orientation) for Islamic education in East Africa. Government schools, by contrast, experienced a series of crises and began to make an impact on education in Zanzibar only since the early 1940s.

The initial failure of the government schools was due to three major reasons. The first was the introduction of the Latin (or Kizungu; Swahili, European) script in 1908. The Latin script was quickly branded by Zanzibar's religious scholars as areligious, or even antireligious, and was nicknamed *lā-dīnī* (Arabic, non-religious, atheist). The second reason for the initial failure of the government schools was the lack of a proper "Islamic syllabus." For a long time, the British did not understand (or accept) the social role of the Qur'anic schools and the social importance of the teaching of the Qur'an as well as other basic religious texts, which provided the essential social skills for Zanzibar's social and religious life. Finally, the government schools and their aim to become the one and only (or at least the paramount) system of education in Zanzibar threatened the very existence and survival of the Qur'anic schools and madrasas and the reproduction of their teachers, the *walimu*, Zanzibar's religious scholars. These religious scholars might be viewed, as Antonio Gramsci (1980, 223) has suggested, as a distinct social class of "organic intellectuals"—that is, local scholars who identify with their respective local community, who represent this community and fight for its rights, and who are deeply rooted in a specific local context. In Zanzibar until the 1940s, this group of organic intellectuals represented the vast majority of the educated elite and consisted of about a thousand religious scholars (of all kinds, mostly based in an equal number of Qur'anic schools and/or mosques) in a population of about 240,000 to 320,000 (in the 1920s to 1960s).[2]

As a result of these policies, *walimu* and parents opposed the government schools and boycotted them effectively: Between 1908 and 1940, many government schools had to be closed down again—in some cases, several times (see Table 7.1)—because the children of the respective school circle did not register and attend "their" government school (see Loimeier 2009, 280–81). At the same time, the Protectorate government was never able (or willing) to enforce government school attendance. The opening and closing of government schools thus became a regular feature of the British colonial administration in Zanzibar. In a letter to the secretary of state for the colonies, the British Resident attached a list of all schools established by the British since 1906 and the years of their closure, up to 1938 (Zanzibar National Archive, file AB 1/284, appendix 1).

In reaction to the failure of the government schools in the 1900s and 1910s, a period characterized by the politics of Rivers-Smith, the first director of education, the British started to reform the government school system in the 1920s (after Rivers-Smith's departure) under the guidance of the second director of education, Hendry, who held the office from 1920 to 1937 and left Zanzibar in

Table 7.1. Overview of Openings and Closings of Government Schools

Name of school	Opened	Closed	Reopened
Schools in Unguja			
Mangapwani	1906	1921	1925
Mahonda	1906	1913	
Mwera	1908	1910	1924
Mazizini	1908	1910	
Kizimkazi	1908	1912	1924
Mnyimbi	1908	1912	
Makunduchi	1908	1912	1924
Muyuni	1908	1912	1927
Bububu	1912	1914	
Bumbwini	1914	1921	
Mkokotoni	1921	1929	
Mdijani	1925		
Mkwajuni	1929		
Donge	1930		
Chwaka	1935		
Mombeni	1935		
Uzini	1936		
Schools in Pemba			
Wete	1907	1934	
Chake	1908		
Mkoani	1908	1910	1928
Matangatwani	1925	1937	
Kengeja	1926	1937	
Jongangome	1930	1936	
Ziwani	1930	1935	
Ngwachani	1934	1937	
Kangani	1934		
Uwendwe	1934		
Kiwani	1935		

1939. In particular, the British incorporated an "Islamic studies syllabus," called *diāna* (from the Arabic term *dīn*, religion) into the government school curriculum and asked several religious scholars—in particular, Sayyid Aḥmad b. Sumayṭ (as well as Ṭāhir b. Abū Bakr al-Amawī, Burhān b. ʿAbd al-ʿAzīz al-Amawī and Muḥammad al-Mundhirī)—in 1924 to give advice on this first *diāna* syllabus. However, these efforts of reform were too half-hearted to change the situation significantly, and the boycott of the government schools by *walimu* and parents continued. Parents were not willing to send their children to schools where disciplines were taught in the *lā-dīnī* script and where only a small portion of the Qur'an was memorized. This led the British to introduce a new and larger *diāna* syllabus in 1931 and to develop other strategies of reform, which, however, also miscarried, because they still failed to recognize a basic weakness of the British government schools system: the exclusion of the *walimu*.

The real revolution in the government schools system began in 1939–1940, when Hendry retired and made room for successors who were free to radically change the existing system of government school education. This political turnabout was enhanced by the fact that the British had to economize at the onset of World War II and thus rely more on local support, on the *walimu*, on the organic intellectuals. Also, and importantly, a whole generation of Zanzibari primary school teachers, groomed in the British system, had taken positions in government schools and had started to change public opinion regarding government schools. The British-educated Zanzibari government schoolteachers, in fact, came to form a second tier of organic intellectuals who would eventually complement the ulama/*walimu* as translators and negotiators of knowledge in Zanzibar.[3] What were the most important elements of reform?

In 1939–1940, the British finally realized that they could solve the problem of acceptance of the government schools by integrating existing Qur'anic schools with their respective *walimu* into existing government primary schools and to recognize the *walimu* as British government schoolteachers (for *diāna*). In the late 1950s, the government schools employed seventy-five *walimu*, supervised by an inspector of religious instruction. This inspector was Shaykh ʿAbdallāh Ṣāliḥ al-Farsy (1912–1982), a religious scholar who had gone through British government school education and who represented the *walimu* establishment. ʿAbdallāh Ṣāliḥ al-Farsy was, in fact, to become a *qāḍī* of Zanzibar in 1960 and the chief *qāḍī* of Kenya in 1968. He also inspected the *diāna* classes at Zanzibar's government primary schools from 1947 to the late 1950s. The 1931 reforms of the *diāna* syllabus paved the path for yet another reformed *diāna* syllabus that was developed in 1945–1946 by several religious scholars; this syllabus was implemented in 1946 and remained in force until 1964. The members of this committee of scholars were Shaykh ʿAbdallāh Ṣāliḥ al-Farsy; Rajab Ḥimīd; Ḥasan b. al-Shaykh Jamal al-Layl; Aḥmad Zahrān; and the Shāfiʿī Chief Qāḍī, Sayyid ʿUmar b. Aḥmad b. Sumayṭ, as well as the Ibāḍhi Qāḍī, Saʿīd, b. Rashīd al-Ghaythī.

These reforms led to the collapse of resistance against the government school system. Students started to stream into government schools, and by 1963, Zanzibar had not only a comparatively high literacy rate but one of the best-educated populations in sub-Saharan Africa. This success story was linked with the fact that an increasing number of Zanzibaris served as government schoolteachers since the 1920s (see above), joined, since the early 1940s, by a growing number of *walimu*, responsible for *diāna*.[4]

Looking back to colonial times, we can identify three generations of Zanzibari government schoolteachers. This focus on three generations of religious scholars mirrors respective generations of British administrators (as described above): A first generation of colonial teachers from 1905 to the late 1920s can be regarded as the pioneers of government school education. Scholars such as Burhan Mkelle tried to find a place in the new system of education and to translate British concepts of education into Zanzibari contexts. Often these teachers were members of families of religious scholars and were highly respected as they often continued to be active as *walimu* outside their government school jobs. Their position was not always easy, especially when it came to school discipline. Their overall number was rather small and never exceeded fifty to sixty teachers in the 1920s. Most of them were hired in the early 1920s.

A second generation of government schoolteachers, from the mid-1920s to the late 1940s, increasingly identified with the government schools and rose to leading positions in the system as headmasters of individual schools. This generation of teachers was mostly educated by Lawrence William Hollingsworth (see Loimeier 2009, 353–56), director of the Teacher Training College from 1921 to 1933 and director of Zanzibar's first secondary school from 1933 to 1940. Hollingsworth was a competent teacher and pedagogue, widely respected for his devotion to education and still remembered today by many Zanzibaris as a key educator. The second generation of Zanzibar teachers increasingly considered the government schools as their own. Their number rose to more than 110 by the late 1940s. Many teachers were still members of families of religious scholars, such as Shaykh ʿAbdallāh Ṣāliḥ al-Farsy (see Loimeier 2009, 375–400).

Since the late 1940s, a third generation of government school teachers not only identified with the government schools, which were now seen as Zanzibar's own schools, but increasingly sought full control over both schools and the Department of Education (from 1961, the Ministry of Education). Members of this third generation of government teachers, such as ʿAmīr ʿAlī ʿAmeir or Bibi Samīra al-Maʿamirī (see Loimeier 2009, 364–75), were prepared to fight against the British for their rights as teachers and administrators. As a consequence, complaints (also raised by the government school *walimu*), as recorded in the personnel files, increased considerably during this period. At the same time, the size of the staff (local teachers and administrators) of the Department of Education grew to more than eight hundred in 1963 (Loimeier 2009, 341).

However, the success of the government schools—and in particular the success of Zanzibar's Muslim scholars to define the *diāna* syllabus—had serious consequences for education: The hegemony of interpretation that Zanzibar's religious scholars had achieved by their integration into the government schools and the domination they had achieved over the *diāna* syllabus led to the development of *diāna* into a rather quotidian discipline in the government school syllabus. *Diāna* increasingly came to be seen as a discipline such as English, geography, and sports. Islamic government school education in the form of *diāna* necessarily became objectified knowledge that could and had to be examined in tests along the patterns of all other school disciplines. *Diāna*, even if defined by Zanzibar's religious scholars, thus became a discipline that followed the same institutional logic as other school disciplines in a government school, and this logic was defined no longer by religious scholars and the philosophy of Islamic education but by the British colonial administration and the logic of the Cambridge Overseas Examination system—or, after 1964, the policies of the revolutionary government of Zanzibar. By successfully integrating Islamic education into the government school system, *diāna* lost the primary rationale of education in Qur'anic schools: to provide social skills, to prepare students for a social role in life as defined by religious knowledge. Now *diāna* prepared students for an examination in a school system that essentially provided marketable skills.

The apparent success of Islamic education in Zanzibar's government schools also led to the marginalization of Islamic education at many Qur'anic schools—in particular, those whose *walimu* did not join the government schools. With the increasing attraction of government schools, children stopped going to Qur'anic schools or simply no longer had the time to attend a Qur'anic school, because government timetables conflicted with Qur'anic school temporal rhythms. As a consequence, teaching in Qur'anic schools was limited to those time slots that were not taken by the government school curriculum—that is, Saturdays and Sundays as well as some afternoons. This development can be visualized in Tables 7.2 and 7.3.

This path in the development of education continued after the revolution of January 1964. Looking at the basic data again, it appears that Islamic education was hit particularly hard by the revolution in January 1964: The Muslim Academy, Zanzibar's only higher institution of Islamic learning, which was about to become an Islamic secondary school, was closed in 1965; religious education—that is, the

Muslim Scholars | 145

Table 7.2. Timetable of the Qur'anic School until the 1940s

Times of prayer	j.mosi (Saturday)	j.pili (Sunday)	j.tatu (Monday)	j.nne (Tuesday)	j.tano (Wednesday)	khamisi (Thursday)	ijumaa (Friday)	Daytimes
subḥ	Q	Q	Q	Q	Q	Q	-	Asubuhi
Ẓuhr								Mchana
'aṣr	Q	Q	Q	Q	Q	-	-	Jioni
maghrib	Q	Q	Q	Q	Q	-	-	Maghribi
'ishā'	Q	Q	Q	Q	Q	Q	-	Usiku

Table 7.3. Timetable of Government Schools and Qur'anic Schools in the 1940s to 1970s

Hour	Monday	Tuesday	Wednesday	Thursday	Friday	Saturday	Sunday	Daytimes
5.00								Morning
6.00	Q	Q	Q	Q		Q	Q	
7.00	Q	Q	Q	Q		Q	Q	
8.00	R	R	R	R	R	Q	Q	
9.00	R	R	R	R	R	Q	Q	
10.00	R	R	R	R	R	Q	Q	
11.00	R	R	R	R	R	Q	Q	
12.00	R	R	R	R	R			Noon
13.00	R	R	R	R	R			
14.00	Q	q	Q			q	q	
15.00	q	q	Q			q	q	Afternoon
16.00	q	q	Q			Q	Q	
17.00	q	q	Q			Q	Q	
18.00								Evening

Note: q means that teaching is not done by the *mwalimu* but by one of his assistants.

diāna syllabus—at government schools was stopped in 1967; and government Qur'anic schoolteachers were also sacked in that year. In addition, the Ministry of Education was cleansed in 1967 of prerevolutionary "elements." Also, religious (like all other public) activities came under scrutiny of the Ministry of Interior, and religious events of all kinds had to formally request permission and could be prohibited (see Loimeier 2009, 461–68).

Who was responsible for the antireligious policies in the first years of the revolution? Neither Uthman Shariff, the first minister of education after the revolution, in office from January to April 1964, nor Idrissa Abdul Wakil, in office from April to December 1964, carried a grudge against Islamic education and even represented, as in Uthman Shariff's case, the values of the ancien régime. Blame falls rather on the first revolutionary president of Zanzibar, Abeid Amani

Karume, who was known for his anti-intellectualist positions, as well as Ali Sultan Issa, the third minister of education from December 1964 to 1968. Under his administration, many teachers and administrators, such as ʿAbdallāh Ṣāliḥ al-Farsy, Bibi Samīra, and ʿAmīr ʿAlī ʿAmeir, were sacked and often subsequently left the country. An examination of the statistical record of the staff in the Ministry of Education, both for schools and administration between 1963 (the last data recorded before the revolution) and 1974 (when data became available again) is quite revealing:

> In early 1964, the Ministry of Education had 827 teachers (including 52 *walimu*) and an administrative staff of 35 (as well as considerable technical staff, who are not considered here): a total staff of 862 people.
> In 1964, all British staff (20) as well as 282 local teachers left Zanzibar ("ran away," according to the respective pamphlets produced by the Afro Shirazi Party) in the context of the revolution. The total staff was reduced to about 540.
> Until 1972, another 200 teachers and staff were sacked, mostly in the context of the purges of Ali Sultan Issa in 1967, reducing the staff of the Ministry of Education to a mere 340 in 1974—about 40% of the 1963 work force of the ministry (Loimeier 2009, 494–95).

This policy can only be called a massacre; it was a policy of radical self-mutilation, imposed not only to enforce a systematic policy of Zanzibarization but as an expression of a complete shift in education, in which religion did not figure and was replaced by a new discipline called *siasa* (politics). However, Ali Sultan Issa's radical and often arbitrary measures came to an end in 1968, when he was replaced as minister of education by Hassan Nassor Moyo (in office until 1977). In Moyo's time, Islamic education in Zanzibar and Islamic education in government schools were restarted. A first sign of this revival was the reopening of the Muslim Academy as the Chuo Cha Kiislamu (School of Islam) on March 25, 1972, as approved by Zanzibar's president, Abeid Amani Karume, just two weeks before his assassination on April 7, 1972.

After Karume's assassination, the religious policy of the regime was gradually revised under Karume's successor, Aboud Jumbe. The Muslim Academy had already been reopened in 1972, and the teaching of religion and Arabic soon resumed at government schools, although there was not yet a proper syllabus. In contrast to Karume's regime, Jumbe steered his policy in a gentler and perhaps more rational fashion. Many of the changes put into effect or on their way since 1972 were linked to his personal initiative, notably within the important field of religious instruction that had been deleted from the syllabus (of government schools) between 1965 and 1972. In particular, in the 1970s, the revolutionary government started to send students to Arabic countries such as Sudan and Saudi Arabia and to employ the returnees as functionaries in the Ministry of Education, in the office of the chief *qāḍī*, and (since 2000) the office of the mufti, in the administration of the religious endowments (*awqāf*) and other state-controlled functions to extend state control over the religious sector.

At the same time, a new generation of religious activists emerged who introduced new ideas, often influenced by their training at Saudi Arabian universities and their contact with the Wahhābī critique of the *mawlid*, the festivities in the context of the *ʿīd* celebrations, or the *dhikr* of the Sufi orders, and they started to criticize the efforts of the revolutionary government and its Muslim functionaries to control religion in Zanzibar. Because there were few scholars left who were able to defend established traditions and because the government did not (yet) define its own religious position, disputes over religious issues and religious politics became increasingly prominent since the 1980s.

Since 1972, Islamic education in Zanzibar has thus recovered slowly; yet it suffers today from the same problems that affect all schools and the whole system of education in Zanzibar: lack of funds, lack of infrastructure, lack of qualified teachers, and lack of a political will to build a proper system of education. The closure of the Muslim Academy in 2007 can be seen as yet another manifestation of the unwillingness of the revolutionary regime, as led by Abeid Amani Karume's son, Amani Abeid Karume (r. 2000–2010), to invest in education—Islamic education in particular.

NOTES

1. For the concept of marketable (and social) skills in Islamic education, see Launay (1992, 93).
2. In 1939, the British estimated the number of Qur'anic schools to be about 880; by 1958, this number had risen to 1,100, but it fell to 865 in 1963 (Loimeier 2009, 263). In 1999, the number of Qur'anic schools had grown to 1,902 in a population of one million (Loimeier 2009, 497–98).
3. The Department of Education had 4 teachers in 1908 (none of them was of Zanzibari origin); this number rose to 52 (mostly Zanzibari) teachers in 1926, 107 teachers in 1932, 365 in 1955, and 775 in 1963 (Loimeier 2009, 341). By 1963, the number of Zanzibari government schoolteachers had thus reached almost the same level as that of Zanzibar's religious scholars. It must be stressed here that all Zanzibari government schoolteachers had a background in religious education and often came from *walimu* families.
4. The number of *walimu* in government schools, where they continued to conduct Qur'anic classes and teach *diāna*, grew from 2 in 1940 to 28 in 1943, 67 in 1955, and to 81 in 1960 (Loimeier 2009, 341).

REFERENCES

Bang, Anne. 2003. *Sufi and Scholars of the Sea*. London: Routledge Curzon.
Al-Farsy, 'Abdallāh Ṣāliḥ. 1972. *Baadhi ya wanavyuoni wa kishafi wa mashariki ya Afrika*. Mombasa, Kenya.
Freitag, Ulrike. 2003. *Indian Ocean Migrants and State Formation in Hadhramaut*. Brill: Leiden.
Gramsi, Antonio. 1980. "Die Herausbildung der Intellektuellen." In *Zu Politik, Geschichte und Kultur*. Frankfurt: Röderberg.
Launay, Robert. 1992. *Beyond the Stream. Islam and Society in a West African Town*. Long Grove, IL: Waveland.
Loimeier, Roman. 2009. *Between Social Skills and Marketable Skills: The Politics of Islamic Education in Zanzibar in the 20th Century*. Leiden: Brill.
Turki, B. S. 1987. "British Policy and Education in Zanzibar, 1890–1945." PhD thesis, University of Exeter.
Zanzibar National Archive (NAK), Files AB 1/224 and AB 1/284.

8.
THE NEW MUSLIM PUBLIC SCHOOL IN THE DEMOCRATIC REPUBLIC OF CONGO

*Ashley E. Leinweber**

THERE IS A dearth of scholarly work on the Muslim minority population of the Democratic Republic of Congo (DRC). Young's work (1966, 1969) on the topic in the early years of Congolese independence portrayed the community as excluded from politics and education, remaining on the fringes of society. Today, however, this situation is changing. Rising out of the ashes of a decade of war, the Muslim community has mobilized to create a plethora of associations focused not only on spiritual matters but on development goals. Following in the footsteps of the models developed by other religious organizations, the Muslim community has created an effective education bureaucracy and begun to actively build, run, and monitor what are known as Islamic public schools throughout the country.

To explain this remarkable process, this chapter focuses on three important eras in the history of Congolese education. The first details the Belgian colonial system and the remnants of its legacy in the contemporary period as well as the exclusionary and often brutal realities of educational monopoly by the Catholic

---

* The data presented here were collected in the DRC on three fieldwork trips in 2008, 2009, and 2013. The first two research phases were funded by a Dissertation Research Grant from the African Power and Politics Program (APPP), through the Center for African Studies at the University of Florida. APPP is a consortium research program funded by the UK Department for International Development (DFID), with additional support from Irish Aid, for the benefit of developing countries. The views expressed in this chapter are my own and not those of DFID, Irish Aid, or the APPP. The most recent research phase was funded by a Faculty Summer Research Grant from Missouri State University. I am grateful to these institutions for their support; Leonardo Villalon for comments on early drafts of this chapter and for organizing the panel "Education and the State in Muslim Africa" at the African Studies Association conference in New Orleans in 2009, where this work was originally presented; Robert Launay for his hard work in creating and inviting me to contribute to this important volume; and the hundreds of willing interviewees in Congo who truly made this research possible.

Church. It then describes the Muslim community of Congo, focusing on a shift from historical marginalization to contemporary mobilization. Finally, it delves into a description of rapidly proliferating Islamic public schools as a hybrid institutional form combining a secular state school with the management of the Islamic community. The chapter's contribution to this volume is in its presentation of evidence from the extremely understudied case of the Muslim minority in DRC, offering a historical analysis of the importance of colonial legacies while showcasing the agency of Muslims in their process to work with the existing system to create hybrid schools that meet the needs of their community.

History of Education in Congo

Belgian Colonial Legacy and the Catholic Monopoly

At the Berlin Conference of 1884–1885, European governments reached agreements on how they would partition the African continent among themselves. Belgian King Leopold II was personally granted control over the vast Congo territory, and in 1885 the Belgian parliament agreed to the creation of the Congo Free State. Leopold's reign in the Congo was marred by brutality and exploitation, stories of which were made public by missionaries working in the area, and in 1908, under international pressure for human rights abuses, Leopold turned over his colony to the Belgian government. The colonial period in the Congo has been characterized as rule by a trinity of the colonial administration, the Church, and large business interests (Young 1965, 10). The domain of education was presided over by the first two elements of this trinity. However, in reality, "from the beginnings of the colonial presence in the Zairian territory until after World War II, the Belgian state assumed no operational control over education but established conditions favoring the spread of Catholic missionary activity and the gradual emergence of a mostly Catholic system" (Boyle 1991, 52).

Education in the Congo was almost exclusively run by the Catholic Church, and missionaries were the primary teachers. This was the so because the Belgian government had little interest in spending large amounts of money on creating a strong education sector in its colony. Colonial-era schools in the Congo could be compared "to the small, essentially religious church schools which dotted the Belgian countryside centuries before" (Gingrich 1971, 37). Belgian colonists believed this to be the essential kind of education for its colonial subjects: "Finally, there was an even more powerful argument for religiously-based education than missionary expertise and low cost. Whatever their personal religious convictions Belgian colonialists were convinced that Congolese education had to be an essentially moral education. They concluded that state-administered secular education simply could not provide the moral instruction which the uncivilized

African needed" (Gingrich 1971, 38). Like most colonial governments, the Belgians believed their primary task in the Congo was a civilizing mission to bring African pagans to Christianity and therefore modernization.

King Leopold appealed to missionaries to take on the duty of "civilizing the natives" in his vast territory. However, even before his mandate in the region began, there had been Protestant missions in the area, beginning with the Baptist Mission Society in Bakongo in 1979 (Boyle 1991, 52). And Catholics had begun work in the Congo Basin at the time of the Portuguese explorations of the area in the fifteenth century. By 1905, there were almost ninety permanent and temporary Catholic missions in Congo as well as forty Protestant missions (Gingrich 1971, 94). In part fueled by the desire to limit the influence of Protestant evangelization in the colony, in 1906 King Leopold II and the Vatican reached a formal agreement regarding the role of the Church.

The agreement was called the Concordat, and it gave a land grant to each Catholic mission created in the Congo. The agreement had the effect of excluding Protestant missions because they were not "'national missions,' defined as those established by Catholic religious congregations based in Belgium" (Boyle 1995, 454). The Catholic Church agreed to provide the manpower to run mission schools according to the approval of the colonial governor, and the state agreed to give each mission up to two hundred hectares of land in return. Thus, the missionaries were in charge of day-to-day functioning of the schools, but the colonial government supervised the curriculum, textbooks, and administration of the schools. We can see this development as the original establishment of a form of the hybrid state–religious education system that still operates in Congo today.

The colonial insistence on a Catholic monopoly over education was the product of Leopold and the Belgian government's distrust of Protestants. This fear was less religious per se and more focused on the fact that the Protestants were primarily from Britain and the United States and were thus "foreigners." This fear was confirmed as Protestant missionaries became some of the most vocal advocates for human rights reforms in the colony and made public appalling reports of atrocities committed by the colonial state. In response, during the Catholic Party's control of politics in Belgium "from 1906 to 1914 the government granted more than 23 times as much land to the Catholic missionaries as to their Protestant counterparts" (Gingrich 1971, 178).

In fact, Louis Franck, the colonial minister in the 1920s, believed that Catholic mission schools would provide the best moral education for Congolese. As such, he decided to provide colonial subsidies only for Catholic mission schools. Conventions signed in 1925 and 1926 stipulated that government subsidies would be provided to missions as long as they implemented the education policy of the state. These conventions were not extended to Protestant missions on the grounds that these were not Belgian national organizations. As a result, "the virtual equality of educational effort in 1920 shifted until more than twice as many children were in Catholic as Protestant schools by 1938" (Gingrich 1971, 180). However, the colonial policy of ostracizing Protestant mission education began to change around the onset of World War II.

Louis Franck, in addition to championing Catholic missions, set up an educational commission in 1922–1924, which led to the outlining of six principles for education of Congolese students: "1) moral education is more important than technical or literacy instruction; 2) schools must be adapted to the native's environment; 3) native languages have to be used in primary school; 4) the State has to work with the 'national' (i.e. Catholic) missions; 5) girls have to be educated as well as boys; and 6) native teachers must be used" (Gingrich 1971, 98). In 1919, there were 74,000 Congolese students in mission schools, but this number increased rapidly to 400,000 by 1934; and by 1937 this number was 840,000 out of a total estimated population of over ten million Congolese (Gingrich 1971, 43). These numbers represented almost entirely rural classes often taught by somewhat-educated Congolese, and usually only a basic education for two years. Thus, as a result of early colonial policy, the ancestor to the current education system in Congo emerged with religious associations shouldering the majority of responsibilities for schooling, while the government's role included accreditation, provision of subsidies, and general supervision.

Education Reform and School Wars

In the period from the end of World War II to Congolese independence (from 1945 to 1960), there was much discussion about education reform in the colony. This discussion was not between the state and the Congolese people, but for the most part took place in Brussels and was between Belgian politicians. In Belgium, the Liberal Party encouraged secular public education financed by the state, while the Catholic Party wanted to keep the Catholic monopoly of private religious schools. Most of the debates about education in the Congo were specifically focused on what kind of schools European children living there would frequent. As Boyle suggested, despite increased Congolese advocacy for a secular school system, the main reason for postwar education policy change in the Congo was that many Belgian expatriates arrived in the colony after the war and began demanding schools for their children (Boyle 1995, 455).

In 1948, a Belgian Senate budget report commented on education for Congolese children in the colony and lamented that fewer than half (about 44%) of school-age children were attending colonial schools and that the education received by the minority was still not adequate (Gingrich 1971, 108). Under pressure from Belgian expats, the colonial minister in the mid-1940s, Robert Godding, created a secular school system for Europeans living in the colony. However, when pushed to extend this system to include Congolese children, he retorted that there were not enough financial resources to do so. He noted that there were twenty-five thousand primary schools training Congolese children that were almost entirely financed by Christian missions, and the colonial state simply did not have the resources to convert these to secular schools (Gingrich 1971, 135). However, as a liberal who sought to limit the colonial Catholic monopoly, he was happy to jump on the bandwagon of increased demand for government subsidies for Protestant missions that evolved at this time. Subsidies for Protestant missions were implemented in 1946 and resulted in state assistance for 60 to 90 percent of teacher salaries and 50 to 70 percent of the cost of school buildings and teaching supplies (Gingrich 1971, 184). Godding hoped that the Catholics would now face more of a threat to their stature from both secular schools for European children and Protestant schools for the masses.

The Catholics in the Belgian parliament were not happy with government subsidies for Protestant missions in Congo, and when they came back to power in 1947 the new colonial minister, Wigny, did not move quickly to execute Godding's subsidies for Protestants. Eventually Protestant missions did start receiving their promised subsidies, but at a much smaller rate than their Catholic counterparts. In fact, Catholic missions continued to receive almost ten times as much as Protestants even though they were only teaching twice as many students (Gingrich 1971, 190).

In the early 1950s, mission representatives and the colonial administration signed a convention that created a formal policy for subsidized schools. In 1951, the Catholics created an Office of Catholic Education and sought a new agreement with the state to replace the Concordat of 1906. Thus, in December 1953, the Belgian minister of foreign affairs and a representative from the Vatican signed a new agreement focusing on financial agreements between the church and state (Boyle 1995, 457).

Auguste Buisseret worked for the colonial ministry in the 1950s, visited the Congo in 1947, and wrote a report about the education system in the colony. His report requested the expansion of secular schools because it appeared that the mission schools were much more interested in recruiting new Christian followers and much less focused on providing a solid education (Gingrich 1971, 136). He pointed out that the state was already paying 50 to 90 percent of the cost of subsidized schools, so Godding's argument about the expense of creating secular schools was not wholly accurate.

Thus, upon his appointment as colonial minister in 1954 (not coincidentally the year that a liberal-socialist coalition was victorious over the Catholic-ruled Belgian government), Buisseret ordered the creation of a pedagogical mission in which three Belgians spent two months touring the colony and writing an over-three-hundred-page report titled the "Reform of Teaching in Belgian Congo." Not surprisingly, the report was very critical of missionary education and justified the minister's policy of creating more secular schools for Congolese students. In fact, "the commission proposed as an antidote the expansion of 'lay' or secular primary and secondary schools in urban and rural areas" (Boyle 1995, 459). Prior to 1954, Congolese students had no chance of receiving a secular education, but Buisseret's commission set a new standard by saying all Congolese students should have the same possibilities as Belgian children in terms of the same kinds of schools, following the same curriculum, and being taught in French and not local languages.

The Catholic missions reacted particularly harshly to this report. Buisseret planned to finance his secular school system for Congolese by providing fewer subsidies for mission schools. When he announced this plan, the Catholics countered by saying they would completely suspend all education efforts in the colony. Thus, Buisseret was forced to back down and maintain subsidies for mission schools. However, he simultaneously ordered the establishment of a few experimental schools. "Eventually a kind of uneasy truce ensued when Buisseret and the president of the Bureau de l'education catholique . . . agreed that the three main providers of schools in Congo should be subsidized according to a new formula: Protestants would receive 10 percent, as against 45 percent for both Catholic and official state networks" (Boyle 1995, 461).

Boyle argued, "Struggles between church and state for control over the direction of education demonstrate that this wing of the triple alliance was much weaker than has been presumed" (Boyle 1995, 451). The church and the colonial state did have good working relations in the education sector for most of the colonial period, but these became strained at the end of World War II. This was largely the result of non-Catholics predominating in Belgian domestic politics. The new colonial minister appointed in 1954 challenged the Catholic monopoly over the education sector, and there were external pressures for reform from the international community and the Congolese population. The 1950s in Belgium were marked by "school wars" that trickled down to the Congo colony in the form of school battles, to use a more mild terminology coined by Boyle (1995, 457). As Young notes, "The 'school war' was the metropolitan dimension of the bitter dispute over state v. church schools. . . . Baldly stated, the conflict centered on the extent of use of public funds to assist Catholic schools. The solution found . . . was through assuring adequate state support for both church and state school systems" (1965, 148).

With the Schools Pact of 1958 the state agreed to increase subsidies for both kinds of schools. As a result, state spending on the education sector increased from 10 percent of the colonial budget to 15 percent between 1954 and 1960, and most of this increase went to the establishment of sixty-seven new secular schools (Boyle 1995, 464). Thus, at independence, there were fifty thousand Congolese students in non-mission schools, but this was only 3 percent of the Congo's total, as there were over a million students in Catholic schools and over a hundred thousand in Protestant education (Boyle 1995). Despite the many criticisms of Belgian colonial education policy—such as the fact that most students only went to school for two years and it is usually acknowledged that children need four years of schooling to become literate—"it is none the less the case that primary-school enrolments in 1960 included over 70 percent of the relevant age group, twice the average for sub-Saharan Africa" (Boyle 1995, 465). However, as will be discussed in the next section, this almost-universal primary education was not extended equally to Muslim children in the Congo.

The Muslim Community of Congo: From Marginalization to Mobilization

Arrival of the Arabs and Colonial Repression

The most well known, and virtually the only, work on the politics of Islam in the Congo was compiled by Crawford Young (1966, 1969) in the early years of Congolese independence. Young's work is primarily historical, focusing on describing the arrival (in the late nineteenth century) and survival of Islam in eastern Congo. The author stresses that the Swahili Arabs, such as Tippo Tip, did not have religious conversion as their main goal; rather, they were interested in the vast amount of ivory and slaves that could be obtained in the Congo. In fact, "Tippo Tip's objectives were always primarily commercial; he assumed political authority in the region because his trading aims could be best served in this way" (Young 1969, 254).

The Belgian colonial force effectively conquered the Swahili Arabs, and the regime remained hostile toward the Muslim community when it appeared active. Partly due to their weakness, the community preferred to maintain a low profile so as not to receive reprisals from the administration. Nevertheless, the community began to grow and increase its proselytizing mission in the 1920s as it had more interaction with the outside Muslim world. Qur'anic schools were formed, men were sent to Islamic institutions in other countries to receive education in order to teach upon their return, and the Qadiriyya Sufi order made important inroads among Congolese Muslims.

Young notes that Muslims were almost entirely excluded from colonial and Christian missionary education, thus eliminating their prospects for acceptance into the civil service (Young 1969, 260). As documented above, during the colonial era, most education was provided by the Catholic Church, resulting in the harassment and expulsion of Muslim children. Harassment included forced conversion; beatings; being forced to eat pork, snakes, and other forbidden meats; and being forced to drink water during the fasting month of Ramadan.[1] In reaction to this, Muslim leaders encouraged followers not to send their children to mission schools (Tata 2003, 64). As a consequence, most Muslims dropped out of school. Those who did stay in school were only able to do so by converting to Christianity.[2] If a Muslim child was able to complete primary school, he or she was able to go to secondary school only after being formally baptized as Christian (Bureau Islamique pour la Défense des Droits Humaines 2007, 2). As further evidence of this discrimination, a UNESCO report released prior to Congolese independence, which was not focused on Muslims in particular, noted that "blacks in the Congo complain that the missionaries eliminate non-Catholic children" from education (cited in Gingrich 1971, 153).

Instead, Muslims were active merchants, continuing their heritage from the Swahili Arabs. Adherents of the religion remained marginalized by the Congolese government after independence as the religious school system represented a key area of continuity despite the withdrawal of the colonial regime. Other major religious groups were formally recognized and received subsidies for their schools, but missionary educators and administrative structures remained largely unchanged after independence (Boyle 1991, 50). Thus, Young concluded that, in the years after independence, "Islam, it would seem, remains as quiescent and isolated as it had been during the colonial period" (1966, 464). However, the first national Muslim conference was held in Kasongo in March 1964 with the purpose of selecting an official representative to interact with the state.

Co-optation in the Mobutu Era

Communauté Islamique en République Démocratique du Congo (COMICO) remains today the national organization for all Congolese Muslims. It began in 1972 at the insistence of President Mobutu as a way of co-opting an important segment of society, as most one-party states and personal rulers did throughout postcolonial Africa. In the area of education, Muslims gained more freedom in the postindependence period, but this, too, was marred by the dictatorial rule of Mobutu.

Political efforts at reform of the colonial education sector were renewed during the authoritarian rule of President Mobutu Sese Seko. In the early 1970s, Mobutu initiated a process of "Zairianization" in which he nationalized most aspects of the country's economy. By seizing profitable foreign-owned businesses and redistributing them to Mobutu's extensive patronage network, Zairianization proved politically successful for the regime, but it resulted in a devastated economy (Gondola 2002, 145). In a further effort to consolidate his power and contain the threat of the prominent Catholic Church, Mobutu also sought to take control of the education sector for the state. "In the early 1970s, most primary and one-half of the secondary schools were staffed and managed by religious groups. Their administration was centered in the government's Department of Education and they received government subsidies" (Kisangani and Bobb 2010, 152). Thus, in 1974, he nationalized all schools, most of which were run by religious organizations. This attempt at secularization of education, like other elements of the Zairianization campaign, proved disastrous for the school system.

Not surprisingly, this move met some resistance from the Church, "but the regime's nationalization efforts ultimately failed not because of unified, prophetic resistance from the church but because the state had just entered a deep economic crisis. The state could not shoulder the expanded financial and administrative burden it had assumed" (Boyle 1992). Because the government's budget was suffering as a result of the declining economy in the late 1970s, these state schools suffered from lack of adequate equipment and teacher salaries being paid several months in arrears. Teachers had to abandon their students to search for alternative economic activities, and parents were asked to subsidize salaries. Therefore, after a few years of this experiment, parents requested that the churches be allowed to take back control of schools because, in addition to these complications, there was a significant decrease in morality and discipline.

Given the rapid deterioration of the education sector in only a few years, the Congolese government wished to return administration of the school system to the churches but also retain more control of the sector than in the presecularization period (Boyle 1991; Kisangani and Bobb 2010). Thus, Mobutu agreed to give some control back to religious organizations, but under the condition that each sign a convention, or formal agreement, with the state. Another reading of the situation emphasized the agency of the church: "Perhaps fearing the state would, when once again strong, reassert control over education, it demanded approval of a new educational convention. Signed in February 1977, this agreement . . . gave them [Catholic, Protestant, and Kimbanguist churches] more managerial control than they had possessed before the radicalization" (Schatzberg 1988, 119–20).

Thus, in the late 1970s, the state and a representative of each of the four main religions—Catholic, Protestant, Kimbanguist, and Islamic—signed a document requiring religious-run public schools to register and be recognized by the state, fall under the jurisdiction of authorities of the provincial and district teaching offices, allow state inspectors to determine whether they are following national standards and regulations, and teach according to the national curriculum. The religious organizations, in turn, became wholly responsible for the day-to-day running of their institutions, but the state had organizational power over them, at least on paper. This hybrid system of institutions that are simultaneously public and religious-run remains in place today.

What was new about this phase of Congolese education was that the Muslim community was formally included for the first time. However, as several informants insisted, the impetus behind the signing of the convention between the Muslim community (which occurred two years after the state conventions with the other religious groups) and the state was clearly political. According to the former national coordinator of Islamic schools, because Mobutu was facing a financial crisis, he traveled to Saudi Arabia in 1978 to seek assistance. The Saudi government agreed to assist Mobutu as long as he allowed Muslims in Congo to establish their own schools, which led to the signing of the convention.[3]

In another version of the story presented by the current national coordinator for Islamic schools in 2009, the Saudi Arabian embassy in Kinshasa closed in 1977 because of disapproval of President Mobutu's politics surrounding the Israel/Palestine conflict. Therefore, Mobutu went to Saudi Arabia to talk to the government about their relationship and was asked whether Muslim schools existed in his country. Mobutu responded in the affirmative, even though this was not the case, and the king granted him one million dollars for the construction of three hundred modern Muslim school buildings. The money was never used for this end, and the Muslim community did not know of its existence until the COMICO legal representative at the time went to Mecca on his pilgrimage and learned about it. Upon his return to Zaire, he questioned Mobutu about the money, which had already been spent elsewhere, and they compromised by signing the school convention on August 31, 1979.[4] Although these two stories differ slightly in the details, and the reality behind the reasons for Mobutu agreeing to allow Muslims to create their own schools is likely more complex, they do illustrate the shared history of Muslim marginalization.

Corruption scandals in the 1980s and 1990s led to two periods when the government broke the education convention with the Islamic community. According to the former national coordinator of Islamic schools, in the first instance this happened because the money from Saudi Arabia had terminated. In the second episode, corroborated by numerous informants, the Muslim leadership was putting names of family, friends, and religious authorities on the list of school agents to receive state salaries even though they were not working in the schools. The state conducted an investigation and found that the Muslim community was not capable of managing its schools well, so the state took back control of these institutions.

However, the new Islamic leadership petitioned for reinstatement of schools in 1990 and was accepted. Since then there have been no more interruptions in the convention system, and community spokespeople assert that the Muslim community has drastically improved its management skills and worked to (re)build its educational infrastructure and a good image for providing quality education. Muslim public schools have indeed proliferated in the postconflict period.

Muslim Communities Today

Reliable estimates of national religious demographics suggest that Muslims constitute 5 percent of the total Congolese population, while Catholics comprise 50 percent, Protestants 35 percent, and Kimbanguists (a Christian sect, mostly located in the Bas Congo province and Kinshasa, founded by the Congolese prophet Simon Kimbangu) 5 percent (U.S. Department of State 2013). The eastern province of Maniema is the historical and present-day home to the majority of Congo's Muslim population. Islam originally came to the area in the late nineteenth century (before the arrival of Europeans) as Swahili Arab traders penetrated the hinterland from the east African coast. Tippo Tip, the most famous of these traders, not only dominated the ivory and slave exchange in the area but was involved politically as the governor of Stanley Falls appointed by Belgian King Leopold II. Tippo Tip has been the subject of much scholarly work on Islam in the Congo, which emphasizes not the role of religious expansion but the primary interest of the newcomers in ivory and slave trading. Commerce continued to be a factor in the maintenance of the Islamic community in the Congo during colonial and early postcolonial periods, as Muslim traders from Asia and other regions of east Africa continued their interior business.

Today, the total population of the Maniema province is around 1.8 million. Kindu, the ethnically and religiously mixed provincial capital, has a population of about 254,000 (Ngongo et al. 2007, 13), of which Muslims constitute about 25 percent. Kasongo is the second largest city in the Maniema province and the historical birthplace of Islam in the country. The Muslim community of this southern town constitutes a large majority, most likely between 70 and 80 percent.[5] There are also enclaves of Muslims outside of Maniema province. Kisangani, the third largest city in Congo located in the northeastern Orientale province, has the most substantial Muslim community outside of Maniema. Swahili Arab traders who originally brought Islam to the Congo made their way from Kasongo up the Congo River to settle in the Kisangani area. Estimates of the Muslim population range from 10 to 30 percent, but the most reliable sources place the Islamic community at about 15 percent of the Kisangani population. The Congolese capital, Kinshasa, also contains a substantial Muslim population and is headquarters for COMICO, the national Muslim organization.

The early postcolonial period witnessed modest scholarly interest on the topic of Islam in the Congo (Young 1966, 1969), but since then these communities have received little attention. The lack of current scholarship on the topic belies the reality of a vibrant and organized Muslim community, especially in Maniema. Little information is available about these organizations and the broader Muslim community in the region for several reasons. The Maniema province, where most

Congolese Muslims reside, is extremely poverty stricken and remote, making travel difficult. Roads are in disrepair, and expensive risk-prone airplanes are the primary mode of transportation. Additionally, insecurity in the Maniema province is a major factor, because the region borders the volatile North and South Kivu provinces, the primary location of sporadic violence for over a decade that has continued even after the formal end to conflict in 2002.

Though little information exists about the postwar social organization of the remote Maniema province, on the ground, one finds a plethora of local, regional, national, and international organizations performing development functions. In several interviews with civil society and religious associations, leaders and active members expressed their dismay at the lack of assistance they receive from their national, provincial, and local governments, which prompted the need for citizens to rally together to take care of themselves.[6] Many secular organizations have been created since the end of fighting in Maniema, around 2002, to encourage children to go to school, take care of war orphans, assist those handicapped by the war, rehabilitate ex-combatants, and assist women victims of sexual violence. Religious associations of Catholics, Protestants, and Muslims are also actively involved in these service-oriented and war reconstruction projects.

In research prior to fieldwork in Maniema, the only available news about the contemporary Islamic community came from the United Nations Organization Mission in the Democratic Republic of the Congo (MONUC). The peacekeeping mission that was charged with securing the demobilization of armed groups and overseeing the postconflict transition to democracy had a field office in Kindu. In 2004 it released a news article discussing a three-day conference held in the provincial capital by a local group, known as Collectif des Associations des Femmes Musulmanes Pour le Développement du Maniema (Collective of Muslim women for the development of Maniema), encouraging Muslim women to become active in development in the region (Bakody 2004). Beyond brief reports such as this, however, no literature was available for analyzing the current development activities of the Muslim community in the Congo.

The contemporary Muslim community boasts a variety of organizations and functions. As noted above, the principal organization for Congolese Muslims is COMICO. In recent years national women's organizations have been created in conjunction with COMICO, including the Comité Nationale Feminine de COMICO and its affiliate at the provincial level, the Comité Provinciale Feminine. There is also the national organization Union des Femmes Musulmanes du Congo, which has affiliates in the provinces.

Other important Muslim organizations active in Maniema today include the women's collective mentioned above; Ami Santé, which is an association in Kindu working to provide health care for Muslims and the broader Maniema society; the Bureau Islamique pour la Défense des Droits Humaines, which has a provincial office in Kindu and an affiliate in Kasongo; more than 130 Muslim women's organizations active in Southern Maniema which are mostly focused around community agriculture projects; the Dawa'tu Islamiyya organization of women from Mosque 18 in Kasongo; Jumiatu Islamiyya from Mosque 17; the Association de Développement Communitaire pour les Mamas Musulmanes from the Central Mosque; and the local branch of the Conseil National des Droits de l'homme en Islam, also in Kasongo. In Kisangani one finds several more active Islamic associations, such as the Union des Mamas Musulmanes pour le Développement et Droits Humaines, the Centre Sociale pour le Développement Communitaire, Mapendo, Maendeleo, and Dawati.

The national, provincial, and local Muslim associations mentioned thus far focus on a wide variety of tasks, whether spiritual or providing important services for their communities that the national state has failed to provide. The next section analyzes the extent to which Islamic organizations have begun to emulate other faith-based organizations in the provision of education in the Congo.

Islamic Public Schools: Hybrid Institutions

A postconflict World Bank report on education in the Democratic Republic of Congo described it as among the five worst countries in the world for the number of children enrolled in school (World Bank 2005, ix). Since the Congolese state's education budget was 6 percent of total government expenditure, the state had largely retreated from providing this social service, but individuals and voluntary social organizations responded. The report notes that "households finance between 80–90 percent of total expenditures in public sector institutions" (World Bank 2005, xviii). Faith-based organizations run schools attended by three-quarters of all primary school children (Titeca and De Herdt 2011, 220), and 64 percent of secondary schools are religiously run (U.S. Department of State 2012).

Public institutions in the Congolese education system include schools managed by the government (*écoles non-conventionées* or *écoles publiques*) and institutions run by religious organizations (*écoles conventionées*), each of which receive government subsidies. The conventions signed between the state and each of the main religions stipulate that the state will pay teachers and administrators, and for the most part it does so, although often in arrears. However, the amount that each educational employee receives from the state is insufficient to provide him or her a livelihood.

The state's ability to fund the education sector was severely limited beginning with the structural adjustment era, when "real expenditure per pupil dropped from US$159 in 1982 to $23 in 1987 and finally to around $4 in 2002.

Teachers' salaries dropped from $68 to $27 per month between 1982 and 1987, reaching an absolute minimum of $12.90 in 2002" (Titeca and De Herdt 2011, 221). In addition to the effects of structural adjustment in the 1980s, the state's ability to provide education was complicated in the early 1990s as Mobutu's financial resources for state functions and patronage were drying up with the withdrawal of U.S. support in the wake of the Cold War. The effect on the education sector was profound, and teachers began a major strike in 1992, but to no avail because of the low rate of pay and frequent failure to obtain salaries.

The Catholic Church was the first to demand a stop to the cycle of children not being educated because of teacher strikes, and in 1993 it created "conventions" of its own with the parents of students, in which the parents agreed to pay a monthly fee to support teachers and encourage them to return to work. "Although this was seen as a temporary coping mechanism to compensate for the lack of salaries, it soon became an institutionalized practice" (Titeca and De Herdt 2011, 222). The other religious organizations running schools quickly followed this trend, which remains in existence today despite drastic improvement in the state's educational budget. In 2003, the Ministry of Education's budget was US$20 million, but had jumped to $170 million by 2007 in large part because the country's debt was canceled through the Heavily Indebted Poor Countries Initiative (De Herdt, Titeca, and Wagemakers 2010, 27). In 2004, the Mbudi Agreement between teachers' unions and the government raised salaries from $13 (in 2001) to $35, although this was still insufficient to live on and below the poverty line (De Herdt, Titeca, and Wagemakers 2010, 28).

Despite several improvements in education salaries and budgets, the Congolese school system still relied on parental contributions to properly function. Every academic year, parents and school staff set the amount of monthly parental contributions for teacher salaries. In 2008, parents of primary school children in Kindu paid 1,000 CDF (Congolese franc, around US$2) per child per month; in 2013, this averaged between 1,500 and 2,000 CDF (still around US$2). But the parents' contribution that was initially intended as a stopgap measure to keep teachers from striking slowly began to evolve into funding for the entire school system, with some of the parental contributions paying for not only teacher salaries but district, provincial, and even national education bureaucracies (Titeca and De Herdt 2011, 222).

The World Bank estimate that households pay almost 90 percent of the cost of education reflects this evolution of parental contributions. However, this system not only operates in the religiously affiliated institutions but has extended to the official state public schools. Even though this seems like a small fee, it is often arduous for parents to pay for their children's "public" schooling, and many children are not in school for this reason. The Congolese state seems to have no plans to increase teacher salaries enough to rectify this burden on parents. In fact, the state appears quite content to allow the education sector to continue functioning in this manner by relying on the hybrid model with religious organizations supplemented by parental contributions.

With a history of Muslim marginalization from education and more than a decade of conflict in the Congo, it is perhaps not surprising that the provision of education by Muslim organizations has been a recent phenomenon. Even though the community had been running schools off and on since the 1980s, before 2002, few schools were sponsored by the Islamic community. The increasing involvement of the Muslim community in the provision of education in the postwar period was repeatedly confirmed by in-depth interviews with members of the Muslim community as well as other citizens and was bolstered by statistical evidence.

Figure 8.1 depicts the number of primary and secondary schools in the Maniema province run by the Islamic community from 2003 to 2012. Between the school years of 2003–2004 and 2008–2009, the number of Islamic primary schools more than doubled, from 29 to 76. The same trend can be seen with secondary schools, where the number increased from 19 to 42. By academic year 2011–2012,

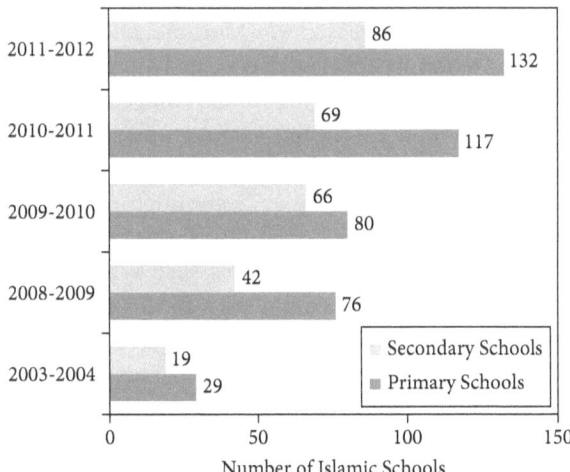

Fig. 8.1. Statistics for Islamic public primary and secondary educational institutions in the Maniema Province, Democratic Republic of Congo

Note: 2003–2004 statistics are from République Démocratique du Congo Ministère du Plan (2004, 33). 2008–2012 statistics are from the director of planning and statistics at the Provincial Division of Primary, Secondary, and Professional Teaching (EPSP), collected in Kindu, February 2009 and July 2013.

the numbers had increased to 132 primary and 86 secondary schools.[7] This trend is not limited to the Maniema province but reflects a national phenomenon. In the Orientale province, where the percentage of Muslims is not very large, the coordinator for Islamic schools since 2007 stated that when he began his job there were only ten Muslim schools in the province, but only two years later in the 2008–2009 academic year this number had grown to more than 50.[8] The national Muslim public school coordinator in Kinshasa provided the following statistics: For the academic year 2005–2006, there were 368 primary and 142 secondary Islamic schools throughout DRC. Only three years later, during the 2008–2009 academic year, the Congolese Muslim community was running more than 800 schools in the country, about 500 primary and 300 secondary institutions. By 2013, that number had increased by another 200 institutions nationwide.[9]

These Muslim schools are not madrasas, but hybrid state–religious public institutions. Though the Muslim community is a minority population in Congo, the new schools being created are not catering only to Muslim students, and therefore they provide a service that can be accessed by any Congolese child regardless of religious affiliation. In fact, many teachers, directors, and other administrators involved in the operation of these Islamic schools are not Muslim. The coordinator for all Islamic convention schools in Maniema stated that perhaps 50 percent of children in their schools are Muslim, and many teachers are also non-Muslim.[10] The primary reason why Muslim schools rely on non-Muslim teachers is that there are simply not enough educated Muslims to fill all positions, an artifact of the history of their marginalization from education.

In Kindu, Kasongo, and Kisangani, extensive research was conducted at several Muslim public schools as well as institutions run by the other religions and the state. Religious public schools, or "convention" schools, are those that were created through conventions signed between the Congolese state and representatives of the four main faith communities, such as that signed in 1979 with COMICO representing the Muslim community. In these conventions, the state has agreed to pay teacher and administrator salaries, set the national curriculum, and monitor schools through its inspection bureaucracy. The religious communities in turn have agreed to control the day-to-day operation of their institutions and are granted permission to teach a religion course.

For example, at E. P. Jihudi, a Muslim convention primary school in Kindu, and all other schools visited, this arrangement translates into two thirty-minute religion lessons per week to be taught by the class's regular teacher. If the teacher is not Muslim, then the school director or religious authorities provide instructors with materials about relevant topics to present each week. Therefore, the religious instruction received by primary school students is not very rigorous, and most parents encourage their children to attend Qur'anic schools in the evenings and on weekends to augment their religious instruction. This fact also demonstrates that religious conversion is not a primary motivating factor for the Islamic community in running Muslim public schools. Apart from the content taught during religion courses, Islamic public schools presented no discernible difference from public schools run by other main religions or the state itself. In nonconvention state public schools, instead of religion courses, students spend the same amount of class time each week studying "civic and moral education."

These new Muslim public schools are providing Muslim and children from other religious backgrounds with a high-quality education. In 2009, the coordinator for Islamic convention schools in Maniema boasted that, for the proceeding two academic years, Muslim schools had the best ranking out of all types of schools for the number of students passing national exams at the end of the year—a statement that was confirmed by the state educational bureaucracy.[11] In the past, the Catholic public schools, which have a long institutional history because they were the primary schools functioning during the colonial era, were the ones to be distinguished as the best schools. Shockingly, they came in third place in the 2007–2008 academic year in the Maniema province, falling below Muslim institutions despite the recent origin of the latter.

A similar story exists in other parts of the country. Muslim schools in the Orientale province have also demonstrated good performance. In the city of Kisangani, they came in second place with 95 percent of students passing national exams in academic year 2006–2007.[12] The year before, Muslim schools in the whole province were number one for the percentage of students who graduated, with an exceptional 96 percent who passed their exams. In addition, the state inspection office conducted a study for the years between 2000 and 2008 and found that Institut Hodari, the oldest Muslim public school in Kisangani, founded in 1990, was the best secondary school in the provincial capital, based on the number of students who successfully completed their state exams over the eight-year period.

These results demonstrate that the Muslim public schools, which are fairly young, are very competitive in terms of the quality of education they provide. Perhaps this quick success can be explained by the enthusiasm of the Muslim community and the commitment of its leaders to expand and excel in the education sector. Interviews with Muslim members of the education administration were characterized by their enthusiasm and increased momentum for their new schools. In contrast, interviews with Catholic educators and administrators revealed unhappiness with the amount of support and resources Catholic schools receive from the state and parents, and they repeated claims that poor salaries translated into little motivation for hard work and providing high-quality education.

Conclusion

The provision of education has been carried out by Catholic and Protestant organizations in the Congo since before colonial times. The Catholic Church's monopoly over the education sector was consolidated during the colonial era, with the encouragement and support of the Belgian administration. Historical texts and interviews document how the Muslim community was always marginal to Congolese state institutions. This is no doubt the direct result of exclusion and intimidation Muslims suffered during the colonial era by the foreign regime and Catholic missionaries. The education provided by the Catholic Church harassed Muslim children and offered either forced conversion or expulsion from the only available education system. As a result, Muslims reverted to trade for their livelihoods, because they did not speak the administrative language and were unable to access state institutions.

However, Islamic public schools in postconflict Congo have proliferated at an unprecedented rate, despite the Muslim minority's historical marginalization from both other religious communities and the state. Elsewhere it is argued that there are two primary causes for this radical shift from quiescence to mobilization. First, a shift in internal politics of the Muslim minority facilitated collective action and involvement in social welfare provision (Leinweber 2012). This was the result of the easing of internal conflicts (reflective of Sufi/Reformist debates across the continent) within the Congolese Muslim community itself at local, regional, and national levels. A unified development agenda emerged as the national COMICO organization elected a single leader in 2004 and local reform-minded leaders in subsequent elections.

Second, a key cause of the recent proliferation of Islamic associational involvement in DRC was the political opportunity available in the postconflict period that allowed Muslim organizations to mobilize (Leinweber 2013). For example, the postconflict Congolese state was too weak to be the sole provider of all education services. One factor complicating state provision of services was that much infrastructure, such as school buildings, was destroyed during the years of civil strife. In addition, there was a mass influx of people moving from the rural regions of the province to the capital Kindu because of insecurity caused by roaming militias during the conflict years. Demand for education has been augmented by the increasing number of girls enrolling in school. Therefore, the number of children in cities needing an education is much larger than it was prior to the conflict years, so there is demand for new schools. This has been numerically captured by Titeca and De Herdt, who found that "between 2002 and 2007 the number of children attending school increased by 11 percent per year" (2011, 221).

The needs of the Congolese people were so large in the postconflict period that other religious institutions, such as those run by Catholics or Protestants, were unable to meet all needs, thus creating a unique opening for Muslim organizations to become active. One might think that the increasing involvement of the Muslim community in such sectors displaced other religious associations and created tension. However, that was not the case; representatives of the Muslim and Christian communities affirmed that their associations were not in conflict in the education realm, because there were simply too many children needing an education and not enough schools.[13] This increased demand may have contributed to the state's willingness to continue to incorporate Muslim institutions into the hybrid state–religious education system.

However, the opportunity argument goes beyond an analysis of the weak capacity of the Congolese state to include the increased religious and political freedom of the postconflict period. The history of Muslim marginalization has ended, and a new Muslim elite has emerged to lead their community and the expansion of Muslim education. By providing Islamic public schools, the Muslim community provides future generations with the education and language skills to participate in government and economic life as well as provides salaries for teachers and administrators through the funds they garner from the state and parental contributions.

This chapter adds to the growing literature on Islamic societies in Africa by highlighting the case of the Muslim minority population of the Democratic Republic of Congo. This community has been extremely understudied in the past, and virtually no information exists about the current involvement of this once-marginalized society. What is of particular interest to scholars and students of Islamic education in Africa is the fact that the Muslim community of Congo has chosen to join the existing state–religious cooperation in the education domain. Unlike Muslim communities in other countries, especially West Africa, the Islamic minority in DRC has not chosen to reform the existing education system to move away from the kinds of secular institutions that are the legacy of European colonialism, but has instead mobilized to create a space for Islamic public institutions within the existing Congolese state–religious hybrid system.

NOTES

1. Interview with male members of the mosque in Quarter 18, Kasongo, July 5, 2008; interview with the head imam for Kindu Muslim region, Kindu, March 27, 2009; interview with the head imam for Orientale province, Kisangani, June 10, 2009.
2. Interview with the president and vice president of the Muslim Youth, Kindu, June 18, 2008.
3. Interview with the former national coordinator of Islamic schools, Kasongo, April 27, 2009.

4. Interview with the current national coordinator of Islamic schools, Kinshasa, June 18, 2009.
5. Interview with the assistant administrator for the Kasongo Territory, Kasongo, July 3, 2013. A Catholic priest, not surprisingly, asserted the smaller estimate of Muslims comprising 65% of the Kasongo population (Tata 2003, 67).
6. For example, an interview with the financial and administrative officer of Caritas, Kindu, July 2, 2008.
7. Statistics for 2003–2004 are from République Démocratique du Congo Ministère du Plan (2004, 33). Statistics for 2008–2009 were gathered from the Division Provincial d'Enseignement Primaire, Secondaire, et Professionelle in Kindu, February 2009. Statistics for 2011–2012 were gathered from the same office in Kindu in June 2013.
8. Interview with the provincial coordinator of Islamic schools, Kisangani, May 25, 2009.
9. Interview with the national coordinator of Islamic schools, Kinshasa, June 18, 2009. Statistics for 2013 are from an interview with the national coordinator of Islamic schools, Kinshasa, July 23, 2013.
10. Interview with the provincial coordinator of Islamic schools, Kindu, March 23, 2009.
11. Interview with the provincial coordinator for Islamic schools, Kindu, March 23, 2009.
12. Statistics from documentation gathered at the State Provincial Inspection Office, Kisangani, June 12, 2009.
13. Interview with the coordinator for Islamic public schools in Maniema, Kindu, March 23, 2009; interview with staff at the coordination office for Protestant public schools in Maniema, Kindu, March 25, 2009; interview with the Catholic bishop for Kindu Diocese, Kindu, March 26, 2009.

REFERENCES

Bakody, Jennifer. 2004. "Maniema's Muslim Women Speak Out." MONUC: UN Mission in DR Congo, August 24, 2004, accessed March 15, 2007, www.monuc.org.
Bureau Islamique pour la Défense des Droits Humaines. 2007. *Cahier de Charge de la Communauté Musulmane du Maniema*. Kindu, Democratic Republic of Congo: BIDH.
Boyle, Patrick M. 1991. "The Politics of Education in Zaire." Dissertation, Princeton University.
———. 1992. "Beyond Self-protection to Prophecy: The Catholic Church and Political Change in Zaire." *Africa Today* 39 (3): 49–66.
———. 1995. "School Wars: Church, State, and the Death of the Congo." *Journal of Modern African Studies* 33 (3): 451–68.
De Herdt, Tom, Kristof Titeca, and Inge Wagemakers. 2010. "Making Investment in Education Part of the Peace Dividend in the DRC." UNESCO 2011/ED/EFA/MRT/PI/09 Paper commissioned for the Education for All Global Monitoring Report 2011 *The Hidden Crisis: Armed Conflict and Education*, accessed April 12, 2016, http://datatopics.worldbank.org/hnp/files/edstats/ZARgmrpap10a.pdf.
Gingrich, Newton Leroy. 1971. "Belgian Education Policy in the Congo, 1945–1960." Dissertation, Tulane University.

Gondola, Ch. Didier. 2002. *The History of Congo*. Westport, CT: Greenwood.
Kisangani, Emizet François, and F. Scott Bobb. 2010. *Historical Dictionary of the Democratic Republic of Congo*, 3rd ed. Lanham, MD: Scarecrow.
Leinweber, Ashley E. 2012. "The Muslim Minority of the Democratic Republic of Congo: From Historic Marginalization and Internal Division to Collective Action." *Cahiers d'Etudes africaines* 52 (206/207): 517–44.
———. 2013. "From Devastation to Mobilization: The Muslim Community's Involvement in Social Welfare in Post-Conflict DRC." In "Neither War nor Peace in the Democratic Republic of Congo (DRC): Profiting and Coping Amidst Violence and Disorder," special issue edited by Miles Larmer, Ann Laudati, and John F. Clark, *Review of African Political Economy* 40 (135): 98–115.
Ngongo, Clément Putshu, Dieu-Donné Tchomba Amisi, Mwemenwa Imurani, Ndanga Omari, and Hélène Odimba Dembo. 2007. *Hadisi fupi ya Maniema tangu mwanzo mpaka leo: Bref aperçu historique du Maniema des origins à nos jours*. Kindu, Democratic Republic of Congo: GTZ.
République Démocratique du Congo Ministère du Plan. 2004. *Monographie de la Province du Maniema*. Kinshasa, Democratic Republic of Congo: Ministry of Planning.
Schatzberg, Michael G. 1988. *The Dialectics of Oppression in Zaire*. Bloomington: Indiana University Press.
Tata, Abbé Pontien. 2003. "L'Islam à Kasongo." In *Souvenirs du Centenaire et Élargissement des Connaissances sur Kasongo*, edited by S. E. Mgr. Theophile Kaboy, 49–72. Kasongo, Democratic Republic of Congo: Catholic Diocese of Kasongo.
Titeca, Kristof, and Tom De Herdt. 2011. "Real Governance beyond the 'Failed State': Negotiating Education in the Democratic Republic of the Congo." *African Affairs* 110 (439): 213–31.
U.S. Department of State. 2012. "Democratic Republic of Congo 2012 International Religious Freedom Report." Bureau of Democracy, Human Rights and Labor, accessed November 15, 2013, http://www.state.gov/j/drl/rls/irf/2012religiousfreedom/index.htm#wrapper.
———. 2013. "Democratic Republic of Congo 2013 International Religious Freedom Report." Bureau of Democracy, Human Rights and Labor, accessed August 16, 2014, http://www.state.gov/j/drl/rls/irf/religiousfreedom/index.htm?year=2013&dlid=222037.
World Bank. 2005. *Education in the Democratic Republic of Congo: Priorities and Options for Regeneration*. Washington, DC: World Bank.
Young, Crawford. 1965. *Politics in the Congo: Decolonization and Independence*. Princeton, NJ: Princeton University Press.
———. 1966. "Chronique Bibliographique: Materials for the Study of Islam in the Congo." *Cahiers Economiques et Sociaux* 4 (4): 461–64.
———. 1969. "The Congo." In *Islam in Africa*, edited by James Kritzeck and William H. Lewis, 250–64. New York: Van Nostrand-Reinhold.

INNOVATIONS AND EXPERIMENTS

9.
THE AL-AZHAR SCHOOL NETWORK: A MURID EXPERIMENT IN ISLAMIC MODERNISM

Cheikh Anta Babou

IN HIS SEMINAL work on Islamic education in former French Soudan, current-day Republic of Mali, Louis Brenner describes a paradigmatic shift from what he termed an "esoteric" episteme to a "rationalist" one (Brenner 2001, 7–8). This shift that took place in the twentieth century was made possible by two things: first, the influence of the French model of education on Qur'anic teachers and, second, the intensification of communications with the wider Muslim world. The impact of this transformation affected both people's conception of the nature of Islamic knowledge and the conditions of its transmission. Secrecy, hierarchical knowledge, and spiritual transformation through learning—all features that marked entrenched Muslim traditions of education—were undermined by a new system that championed free access to a liberating Islamic education opened to all.

This change also took place in the French colony of Senegal, which was just as exposed to French educational innovations, but its transforming power was felt differently by different segments of the Muslim community. While the Tijaniyya, especially the Sy and Niass branches of this Sufi order, are said to have embraced a rationalist and modernist view on education, the Muridiyya, the homegrown and second largest Sufi order in Senegal, continued to embody the conservative and mystical tradition associated with the esoteric episteme. It is contended that, for the Murids, highly ritualized education of the body and soul dispensed in secrecy in the so-called working schools takes precedence over the teaching of the Qur'an and other classical Islamic disciplines, whereas among other Muslims, the latter disciplines taught in open schools are given preeminence.[1]

In the Muridiyya, as in mystical Islam in general, *mā'rifa* (knowledge directly inspired by God, experiential knowledge) or gnosis occupies central importance, and alongside genealogical credentials it forms the foundations of religious authority. Exoteric knowledge, although highly valued and sought after, does not always translate into prestige and religious authority. Among the Murids, then, as in most Sufi orders, knowledge must submit to *baraka* (God-given gift of grace). But the precedence of *mā'rifa* over *ilm* (exoteric science) does not signify a lack of interest or neglect of classical Islamic education. In the Muridiyya, and I would argue in most Sufi orders, esoteric and rationalist epistemes coexist, but they relate to two different fields of knowledge that sometimes overlap but are clearly distinguishable: spiritually inspired or experiential knowledge and scripture-based knowledge. This chapter is concerned with the latter. It argues that Murid conceptions and practices of education share more similarities with other Muslims in Senegal and the Muslim world than the binary opposition between modernist (rationalist) versus mystical Sufi tradition (esoteric) would let us believe. Using the example of the al-Azhar Institute founded by the late Shaykh Murtalla Mbakke in the 1970s as a case study, I document the existence of a long tradition of modern Islamic education among the Murids.

Islamic Education in the Muridiyya

The Muridiyya Sufi order was founded at the turn of the twentieth century in west-central Senegal by Amadu Bamba Mbakke. Bamba emerged at a time of crises and rapid sociopolitical change fueled by the end of the Atlantic slave trade, militant Muslims' struggle for state building, and French colonial conquest. He belonged to a family that placed high value on Islamic education. The mastery and dissemination of the Qur'an and Islamic sciences was at the core of Mbakke identity. Bamba's forebears in the precolonial Senegalese kingdoms of Jolof, Kajoor, and Bawol were respected members of the community of *doomi soxna* (literally, son of a virtuous woman, but the expression refers more precisely to a class of wise and highly learned families). Bamba's great-grandfather, Maaram Mbakke, founder the village of Mbacke Bawol, heartland of the Mbakke clan, was a renowned teacher in Jolof and Bawol. Bamba's father, Momar Anta Sali Mbakke, was also a teacher, advisor, and *qadi* (Muslim judge) in the court of King Lat-Joor in the second half of the nineteenth century Kajoor. Amadu Bamba himself started his career as Qur'anic teacher in the village of Mbakke Kajoor and continued to teach even through exiles and house arrest until his death in 1927 (Marty 1917, 234).

Shaykh Mbakke Buso, Amadu Bamba's cousin and disciple, provides a good illustration of the centrality of Islamic education in the Mbakke family's ethos. Defending Amadu Bamba and his brothers against French accusation of political ambitions, he mentioned that, in their dealings with rulers, members of the

Mbakke family have always limited their demands to two things: first, enough land to build a house, a mosque, a school and to farm; and, second, the security needed to carry out their activities (Bousso n.d.). However, it is important to note that, although he remained faithful to family values, Amadu Bamba was not a mere imitator of family traditions. He was also open to innovations and was prepared to challenge established practices of Wolof Muslim clerics to fulfill what he perceived as his mission.

It was in the domain of education that Amadu Bamba's efforts at innovation were most clearly perceptible. The most important turning point in Bamba's conception of education can be dated from 1883 to 1884, one year after the death of his father. Soon after Momar Anta Sali's demise, Bamba left the family school of Mbakke Kajoor and engaged in an eight-month journey across the Wolof states and in Mauritania. During this extended trip, he visited many clerics, read from their libraries, followed their teachings, consulted them about questions related to Islamic practices and mysticism, and received *ijazas* (diplomas or certificates) from them.

One immediate consequence of the trip and the reflection it inspired was a radical transformation of Amadu Bamba's philosophy and practice of education.[2] Alongside the notion of *taalim* (the classical teaching of the Qur'an and Islamic sciences), he introduced the concept *of tarbiyya*. *Tarbiyya* is a holistic and universal approach to education invented by the Sufis that goes beyond the mere transmission of knowledge and seeks to transform the whole being by touching the body, the mind, and the soul. *Tarbiyya* establishes a special relationship between the *shaykh* and his disciple, who is no longer a *taaleb* (student) but a *murid* (aspirant) on the path to God who surrenders his will to his master and gives him command of every aspect of his life. Learned Muslims in Senegal and West Africa who were conversant in the science of *tasawuff* (Islamic mysticism) were certainly familiar with the notion of *tarbiyya* as theory and concept, but Amadu Bamba was among the first to use this idea as the foundation of a pedagogy.[3] For Amadu Bamba, *tarbiyya* was the best instrument to address the perceived decline in the quality of Qur'anic education dispensed in the Wolof states and to remedy the moral and political crises that have been plaguing Wolof societies for generations and which were now exacerbated by French colonization.

The implementation of *tarbiyya* soon gave birth to a new type of school: the *daara tarbiyya* (*daaray laxasaay* in Wolof), or "working school," which specialized in educating the body and spirit of disciples. This school developed alongside the traditional *daara* devoted to exclusive study of the Qur'an and Islamic sciences. The *daara tarbiyya* was primarily devoted to the spiritual education of older disciples who had passed the time of sitting at the feet of teachers to receive initiation into the Qur'an. The main goal of *daara tarbiyya* was education of the soul and heart through physical labor, meditation, *dhikr* (remembrance of Allah's sacred names), and psalmody of Bamba's spiritual poems. This institution, considered by Donal Cruise O'Brien as the most important innovation of the Murid order, has been the object of numerous scholarly investigations.[4]

The *daara tarbiyya* has become in the views of scholars of Islam in Senegal the embodiment of education in the Muridyya. Yet, in the educational system put forth by Amadu Bamba, *tarbiyya* was only one of three steps, and in his eyes, not even the most important one. Alongside *tarbiyya* and *tarqiyya*, *tālim* (formal Islamic education) was an important pillar of the Murid system of education. As Bamba observed, "Those so-called Sufis who contend that what they do is more meritorious than reading the Qur'an use false arguments and have been in reality misled by Satan" (Mbakke 1988, 90). Elsewhere, he noted that "The best among human beings are those who, after finishing the study of the Qur'an, teach it to others" (Mbakke 1988, 96).

Amadu Bamba's attitude toward teaching and reading the Qur'an was consistent with that of Sufi masters throughout history. As noted by El-Tibawi in his reconstruction of the tradition of Islamic education in the Muslim world, the provision of free Islamic education "was a natural consequence of their [Sufis'] system the essence of which was the striving for personal favor and communion with God." For this reason, as he noted, "Almost all great Sufis were also great teachers" (Tibawi 1971, 32). This opinion is shared by Ann K. Bang, who, referring, to Sufi literary tradition in Zanzibar, observes that, "In Sufi reformist literature, the word da'wa—literally, to summon or call—by the late nineteenth century had taken on the distinctive meaning of missionary or teaching activity" (Bang 2011, 90).

Scholars' failure to understand the place of classical Islamic education in the Muridiyya can be explained by the influence of ideas that have largely shaped the scholarship on Islamic education in sub-Saharan Africa.[5] First, there is the orientalists' narrowly scripture-based Islamic intellectual history that opposes the so-called rational Islam of the ulama based on Qur'anic exegesis, studies of *fiqh* (Islamic jurisprudence), and hadith (prophetic traditions) to the esoteric Islam of the Sufi centered on mystical exploration of the heart and soul; second, the French colonial concept of *Islam noir*, which denies the orthodoxy of black African Islam; and, third, scholarly fascination with the unusual and exotic.

Because of the powerful influence of these streams of ideas, scholars of the Muridiyya often overlook the centrality of classical religious education among the Murids despite the abundance of data supporting the importance that Murid *shaykhs* and disciples ascribe to this form of education. In 1913, Paul Marty, the influential French colonial administrator and scholar, provided in his survey of the Sufi orders of Senegal good evidence to support the idea of an entrenched tradition of Qur'anic and Islamic education in the Muridiyya. He described the Murid holy city of Tuubaa as a sort of *ribat* and Islamic *zawiya* composed of a small university where students were taught religious and profane disciplines, a convent where Murid *shaykhs* trained disciples in the way of the Sufi, and a pilgrimage site (Marty 1917, 135). Marty also observed that all the major Murid *shaykhs* managed Qur'anic schools, even the most business oriented among them such as Shaykh Anta Mbacke and Shaykh Ibra Fall. Marty indicated that, in Diourbel, Amadu Bamba (then under house arrest) had more than one hundred disciples in his school (Marty 1917, 135). The school of Gede founded by Shaykh Mbacke Buso at the turn of the twentieth century and that of Ndaam led by Shaykh Abd Rahmane Lo were also and still remain important Murid schools where the Qur'an and Islamic religious sciences were taught. The same Mbakke Buso named one of the first schools he founded in west-central Senegal in the late nineteenth century *lassar*, a Wolof corruption of the name al-Azhar.

There is evidence that some Murid *shaykhs* sent their sons and prominent disciples to the Middle East and North Africa to pursue advanced Islamic education at a time when this practice was rare in West Africa. In 1937, Amadu Bamba's half brother and renowned Murid *shaykh*, Shaykh Anta Mbakke, dispatched two of his sons, Mustafa Mbakke and Same Mbakke, to pursue Islamic education in Mecca. At the time, among sub-Saharan Africans, only the Haussa people of Northern Nigeria had an established tradition of sending students to the Hejaz.[6] When in the 1950s, the municipality of Dakar had started to extend grants to Senegalese Muslims to continue their education in North Africa, the late Serigne Mbakke Soxna Lo, a great-grandson of Amadu Bamba and prominent *shaykh* in the Muridiyya, was among the first generation of Senegalese to travel to Algeria to pursue religious education there.[7] Mbakke Soxna Lo's father, Cheikh Mbakke, had studied in a French madrasa. After independence in 1960, the establishment of diplomatic relations with Arab and Middle Eastern countries and the founding of international Muslim institutions such as the World Islamic League offered opportunities for Senegalese to study in countries in North Africa and the Middle East. As early as 1965, five young Murids, including three sons of the caliph, Falilu Mbakke, were sent to Saudi Arabia to pursue advanced religious education at high school and university levels.[8] One of those young Murids, Professor Khadim Mbakke of Ifan, continued his education after graduation from the Islamic University of Medina and earned a doctoral degree at the Sorbonne in 1978. Besides the official channels sending Murid students to North Africa and the Middle East, resourceful disciples, following the honored Muslim tradition of traveling for the sake of seeking knowledge (*rihla li talab al-ilm*) also found their way in schools in the Muslim world.[9]

However, although Murid *shaykhs* and disciples have been among the first Senegalese Muslims to seek an education in North Africa and the Middle East, the initiative of creating modern madrasas originated principally from Salafis (proponents of a return to the way of Prophet Muhammad and his early companions). These Salafis were staunch critics of the Sufis, whom they accused of exploiting and misleading Senegalese Muslims by perpetuating obscurantism and superstitious beliefs (see, e.g., Toure 1957). The schools they founded were a means to undermine the power and authority of Sufi *shaykhs*, yet these schools also functioned as models that inspired Sufi *shaykhs* such as Murtalla Mbacke, who gradually embraced the madrasa method of teaching.

The Development of Islamic Madrasas in Senegal

The tradition of *medersa* (French spelling) or *madrasa* (Arabic spelling) was brought to West Africa by the French. This model of schooling was first experimented with in Algeria then transposed to West Africa, where schools were opened in Jenne and Timbiktu (Mali), Saint-Louis (Senegal), Butilimit (Mauritania), and several other localities as early as the first decade of the twentieth century. Through these schools, France aimed to achieve several objectives: "to develop higher Muslim education and train the teachers of Qur'anic schools" and "to teach an elite of young Muslims how to speak and write in French and at the same time to give them proper views of the civilizing role of France in Africa" (Brenner 2001, 41; see also Bouche 1975). The ultimate goal was to undercut the influence of local institutions of Islamic education believed to stoke fanaticism and conservative and xenophobic behavior. For the French, the role of the madrasa was not so much different from those of the French language schools; they were all tools of empire mobilized to build legitimacy for and minimize opposition to colonial rule.

By the mid-1940s, new types of madrasas had appeared, founded by Muslims who shared French criticism of the conservatism of the old models of Islamic schooling but who were inspired by different motivations. Their aims were to promote what they believed were proper Islamic practices, to eradicate unlawful innovations, and to entrench a pan-Islamic identity. These Muslims, who often had been educated in North Africa or the Middle East, were looking for more efficient pedagogical methods to teach the Arabic language and religious disciplines and to dispel what they conceived as religious obscurantism.

In Senegal, Elhaj Mahmud Ba pioneered this movement. Ba belonged to the first generation of Senegalese Muslims of modern times to receive extensive training in the Islamic sciences in the Middle East. Like generations of devout West African Muslims before him, he studied the Qur'an and the Islamic religious sciences in his native land of Fuuta and in Mauritania, then found his way to Saudi Arabia by following the well-worn overland pilgrimage route to the Middle East through Tchad, Sudan, Ethiopia, Yemen, then Mecca. In Mecca, he completed elementary and middle school and then joined the Al Falah religious school, where he graduated in 1939 at the age of thirty-five after spending eleven years in the Middle East.

As soon as he returned home to Jowol in northern Senegal in 1941, Ba opened a Qur'anic school he named Vorabia after the elementary school where he had studied in Mecca. The way he organized this school and the innovations he introduced became a major bone of contention between Ba and the local Muslim clerks. He adopted the blackboard, which then was not used in Qur'anic schools in Senegal and instituted a formal weekly timetable of twenty hours around a curriculum including initiation to the Qur'an, study of the Arabic language, and physical education. He also employed new pedagogic methods and imposed mandatory prayers and the wearing of a clean uniform. But his most revolutionary and controversial innovation was the banning of begging by disciples and the requirement that parents pay fees for their sons' education. Historically, teaching Qur'an was conceived by Senegalese Muslims as a religious duty rewarded by God and for which the teacher should not accept compensation.[10] Disciples relied on families of adoption and most of the time begged for food and other needs and worked in their master's farm as free labor to help him provide for his family (see Mamadou Ndiaye 1985 and Ware 2014).

While teaching in Fuuta, Ba made several trips to Dakar and other areas in Senegal, prospecting for the possibility of opening Qur'anic schools there and weighing his chances to successfully duplicate the system he was experimenting with in Fuuta. He also counted on his networks of friends and mentors in Saudi Arabia and elsewhere in Africa and Senegal to take his project to fruition. Dakar offered greater possibilities to strengthen and maintain contacts with these potential resources (Kane 1997).

In 1944, Ba decided to move to Dakar, the capital of French West Africa, with his disciples. He was welcomed by Elhaj Ibrahima Diop, customary chief of the native African population of Dakar (the Lebou). He opened a school in the mosque of Tileen in the African neighborhood of Medina and later moved to Rue 6 in the same area.[11] Confronted by the hostility of the colonial administration that was wary of his so-called militant and politicized Islam and his frequent trips to the Middle East, Ba decided in 1946–1947 to move the headquarters of his school to Kayes in Mali. This city was a hub of trade strategically located on the international railroad linking Senegal to Mali and north of his heartland of Fuuta. In his new headquarters, Ba could count on the support of wealthy merchants who welcomed his revolutionary style of teaching and his contestation of social hierarchies that kept them from fully enjoying the prestige to which their fortune entitled them. From Kayes, Ba was able to build and operate a network of modern Qur'anic schools and mosques, spanning West Africa and beyond, graduating thousands of young men who, in turn, opened their own schools using their master's model (Kane 1997, 462).

Alongside Mahmud Ba, Cheikh Toure represents the other influential actor for the expansion of madrasa education in Senegal.[12] Unlike Ba, who was from a modest family of cattle herders, Toure was born in a prestigious Tijani family with a long tradition of Islamic learning and teaching. He was raised by his uncle, Hady Toure, who was a prominent disciple of Elhaj Malick Sy, one of the leading figures of the Tijaniyya order in Senegal. Like Ba, Toure was educated in Senegal and Mauritania, but unlike him, he received most of his education in a French-style madrasa school. He was trained by Mauritanian and Algerian teachers in Saint-Louis and Boutilimit. After graduation from the madrasa of Boutilimit, Toure returned to settle in Saint-Louis, where he opened his first school in 1952.

The same year, Toure was among six Senegalese to benefit from grants offered by the municipality of Dakar to pursue their education in Algeria. He stayed there for only one year before being repatriated because of the hostility of the colonial administration in Algeria, which was concerned about the influence of Islamism on black African colonial subjects and political changes in the leadership of the municipality of Dakar. Toure's stay in Algeria was short, but it had a transforming effect on him. He learned about the life and actions of Muhammad Ben Badis, founder of the Association des Ulamas Musulmans Algeriens (Association of the Muslim Ulama of Algeria) (AUMA) (Loiemeier 1998, 158). Ben Badis was a traditional ulama who embraced reformist and nationalist ideas, combated Sufi orders, and promoted a modern Islamic system of education in Algeria. He led the building of a network of modern schools, where Islam was taught alongside secular and scientific disciplines.

Upon returning to Senegal in 1953, with the support of some of the Algerian alumni, Toure founded Union Culturelle Musulmane (UCM; Muslim cultural union). This was a regional organization that included all eight colonies that composed French West Africa. The same year, he founded the newspaper *Reveil Islamique* (Islamic awakening). He obtained official government approval for

UCM in 1956.¹³ The association was modeled on Ben Badis's AUMA in its aims as well as in its organization. It put great emphasis on modern Qur'anic education, on combating the French policy of cultural assimilation, and on raising the political consciousness of Muslim subjects. Despite initial administrative reluctance, schools were opened in Dakar and in the other provinces of Senegal and across West Africa, offering lessons in the Qur'an and Islamic religious sciences and in geography, history, and other secular disciplines. Following the model provided by Mahmud Ba's network, graduates of the UCM schools also founded their own madrasas.

Shaykh Murtalla Mbakke's initiative to found the al-Azhar Institute should be understood as both a reflection of the tradition of Islamic learning and teaching in the Mbakke family and a result of the pedagogical innovations brought about by proponents of Islamic modernism such as Mahmud Ba and Cheikh Toure. But an examination of the trajectory of Shaykh Murtalla's own life provides useful insights for understanding his interest in education and his openness to Islamic modernist ideas.

Shaykh Murtalla: A Brief Biography

Shaykh Murtalla Mbakke was the youngest son of Amadu Bamba.¹⁴ He was born in 1921 to a mother who originated from Coki, a village in northwest-central Senegal with a long tradition of production and dissemination of Islamic religious knowledge. After completing Qur'anic studies, he traveled on his own initiative to Mauritania to further his training in the Arabic and Islamic sciences. The fact that he had decided on his own to pursue advanced education rather than settle as a *shaykh* and profit from his father's *baraka* (God-given gift of grace) constitutes an early indication of his dedication to promoting education.

After completing his studies in Mauritania, Shaykh Murtalla returned to Senegal but chose to stay in the Bambuck Valley in far eastern Saalum, away from the Murid heartland of Bawol. He consented to return to Tuubaa only after the intervention of his older half brother, Bashiir Mbakke.¹⁵ The reasons for Shaykh Murtalla's self-imposed isolation in this stage of his life are diversely interpreted. His hagiographers see this episode as a period of meditation and spiritual purification. While there may be some truth to this contention, it is also possible that his decision was motivated by more earthly concerns. The liquidation of Amadu Bamba's inheritance after his death in 1927 created great turmoil in the Mbakke family that had long-lasting negative effects on the relationships between his sons, his brothers, and his earlier disciples.¹⁶ It is probable that Shaykh Murtalla, who was only six years old when his father had died, might have been affected more negatively than his older brothers. There is evidence that, as late as the 1940s, he was still reluctant to plead allegiance to his elder brother and caliph of the Muridiyya at the time, Shaykh Mustafa Mbakke.[17]

Whatever might have been the real cause of his perceived alienation from the leadership of Muridiyya at the time, Shaykh Murtalla ended up living a life quite uncharacteristic for a Murid *shaykh* and son of Amadu Bamba. He is one of the rare Murid *shaykhs* not involved in the practice of founding *daara tarbiyya* dedicated to farming. Njote Siyaan, the village where he lived for some time after returning from Mauritania, is the only *daara* he is known to have founded.[18] He did later own orchards in the region of Kolda in southern Senegal and the region of Dakar and rice fields on the Senegal River Valley, but he was not a great peanut producer and was not known for issuing public appeal on his disciples to work on his farms, as was common among Murid *shaykhs*. He was rather attracted to the modern sector of the Senegalese economy, where he invested in transportation, bakery, and printing.

Shaykh Murtalla was atypical in other ways as well. While Murid *shaykhs*, especially the sons of Amadu Bamba, were known for their love of sedentary village life, Shaykh Murtalla, very early on in his career, developed a taste for travel, even at a time when communication was difficult. Earlier in his life, he had the reputation of traveling frequently in punishing conditions and with little means.[19] He visited many countries in sub-Saharan Africa. He took his first trip to North Africa in the late 1950s and early 1960s, and during his lifetime, he had visited almost all the Muslim countries in North Africa and the Middle East, including Iran. From the late 1970s and 1980s, when a Murid diaspora had started to form in Europe and North America, Shaykh Murtalla established a tradition of annual visits to those disciples. These trips were always punctuated by religious and cultural events that helped bind disciples together and consolidate their ties with their leaders in Senegal. In his message to the Murid abroad, Shaykh Murtalla always insisted on three things: first, the importance of Qur'anic and Islamic education, especially for the second generation of immigrants; second, hard work and honesty; and, third, the creation of institutions to strengthen the bonds between the disciples and other Muslims without discrimination. He also emphasized respect for the laws and institutions of the countries that welcomed Murid disciples.[20] His connections with Murid immigrants earned him the nickname of "marabout of the diaspora."

Shaykh Murtalla entertained discreet but good relationships with the governments of Senegal, although his relationships with Abdou Diouf, the second president of Senegal, had deteriorated in the last years of his presidency.[21] Shaykh Murtalla needed governmental support for his international travels, where letters of introduction from the president were critical to getting access to heads of state and influential people. He also needed state backing for his business and the expansion of his school network. However, unlike many Sufi *shaykhs* in Senegal, Shaykh Murtalla seemed to show great political awareness and was not shy about privately communicating his misgivings at the highest level of the state, sometimes at the risk of angering his interlocutors.[22]

The unusual trajectory of Shaykh Murtalla's life can be explained partly by his position in the Murid hierarchy of power. As the youngest son of Amadu Bamba who barely knew his father, his life was shaped more by the memory he had of him than actual experience. In the midst of the dissensions that plagued the Muridiyya in the decades following Bamba's death, he might have been skeptical about the institution that was purported to represent his father's legacy and may have strived to build his own idealized version of this legacy. Education was at the core of this idealized version because it represented the most tangible inheritance bequeathed by Bamba. As someone who had little chance of becoming caliph of the Muridiyya because of his ranking at the very bottom of the list of possible successors of his father, Shaykh Murtalla may have found in education a means for stamping his own mark on Murid history. Education was even more attractive as a vocation because it was not a priority at the time for his older brothers. His interest in the diaspora may also be seen as part of this effort to identify areas where he could acquire relevance while avoiding competition from his more powerful siblings. The domains where he chose to invest his energy and authority put him on a path to engage with issues related to modernity and the global Muslim world that were of less interest to the leadership of the Muridiyya based in the holy city of Tuubaa.

The al-Azhar Institute: An Example of Islamic Modernism

Modernism in Islam is intrinsically linked to education.[23] Educational reform has historically been one of the sites where competition between conservative and progressive Muslims was most intense. It is revealing that almost all the leaders of the reformist and Islamist movements throughout the Muslim world were also educators. In West Africa, the pioneers of Islamic reformism such as the Subanu movement in Mali, the Yan Izala founded by Abubakar Gumi in Northern Nigeria, and the movement of Mahmud Ba and Cheikh Toure in Senegal all put educational modernization at the center of their agenda.[24] The most visible aspects of this effort at modernization were related to curriculum and pedagogical innovations. New disciplines, such as *`ilm al-Qur'an* (Qur'anic sciences), *usuul al-fiqh* (foundations of Islamic jurisprudence), math, geography, and so on, which were not widely taught in sub-Saharan Africa, were introduced. The teaching environment was also transformed with the separation between schools and dwellings, the specialization of teachers, a more rigorous separation of the genders, and the introduction of the blackboard, notebook and timetable. However, one of the most significant innovations of Islamic modernists was that they promoted "a more universal profession of Islam" by detaching education from any particular place and by making the business of teaching Islam less closely tied to ethnically defined religious leaderships.[25] The al-Azhar Institute school networks reflect all these characteristics of modern Islamic education.

The project that led to the founding of the al-Azhar school network dated from the late 1950s, a period when colonial subjects had started to make significant inroads toward self-government and when in Senegal Shaykh Toure had started the building of his network of madrasas alongside the one established by Mahmud Ba over a decade earlier. The founder, Shaykh Murtalla Mbakke, then seemed to entertain the less ambitious endeavor of opening a formal Qur'anic school in the area of Tuubaa, holy city of the Murid order. He met with his older brother and second caliph of the Muridiyya, Shaykh Falilu Mbakke, to seek his blessings and support. Falilu had opposed the initiative of Shaykh Mbakke, his nephew and son of the first caliph of the Muridiyya, Mustafa Mbakke, to open a Franco-Arabic school in Tuubaa, but he endorsed Shaykh Murtalla's idea.[26] Caliph Falilu reminded Shaykh Murtalla that by the time of his death, Shaykh Amadu Bamba had only two wishes yet to fulfill: the building of the great mosque of Tuubaa and the opening of an advanced Qur'anic school in the holy city. Since Falilu was fully invested in finishing the building of the mosque, which his older brother Mustafa started in the 1920s, he considered that Shaykh Murtalla's initiative to create a Qur'anic school should be a project of the Muridiyya as a whole. The caliph suggested the village of Daaru ālim Ul-khabīr, best known as Ndaam, as site for the new school.[27] He also wrote letters of support to facilitate Shaykh Murtalla's access to the Murid disciples, to the government of Senegal, and to other sources for funding. Serigne Falilu's official endorsement allowed Shaykh Murtalla to travel to Egypt, probably with the consent of the government of Senegal, to meet with President Gamal A. Nasser and the rector of al-Azhar University in Cairo. President Nasser agreed to provide funding for the project if some conditions were met and the authorities of al-Azhar University in Cairo accepted to send teachers to help staff the new school.[28]

By the early 1970s, the school project had taken a whole new direction. Now it was no longer question of opening a classical Qur'anic school but a modern madrasa. In 1978, Shaykh Mutalla had secured official government licensing of al-Alzhar as an Islamic sociocultural institution with two major objectives: first, to strengthen the faith of Senegalese Muslims and to protect them against negative influences through a good education and, second, to contribute to the struggle against illiteracy, criminality, and joblessness (see al-Azhar Institute 2001, 2).

This ambitious agenda clearly shows a departure from traditional educational practices. The aim of Islamic schooling in Senegal has been first and foremost to make good Muslims. The fight against illiteracy, criminality, and joblessness, however relevant, was rarely put forward by educators. The new orientation initiated by Shaykh Murtala can be explained by transformations that were both internal and external to the Murid order.

The third caliph of the Muridiyya, Shaykh Abdu Lahad Mbakke, who acceded to the caliphate in 1969, was more open to modernizing ideas than his predecessors. In 1977, he built in Tuubaa the first modern public Islamic library and printing press in Senegal and planned the building of a modern Islamic University at the projected cost of six billion CFA (franc of Communaute Financiere Africaine), currency shared by most of the former French colonies in West and Equatorial Africa; at the time $1 was equivalent to 250 CFA). He also authorized Shaykh Mbakke to open the Franco-Arabic school refused by caliph Falilu. At the same time, modern Islamic education was spreading across Senegal thanks to the efforts of Union Culturelle Musulmane founded by Shaykh Toure, the Al-Fallah movement, and followers of Shaykh Ibrahima Niass of Kaolack. Shaykh Murtalla's visit to Egypt and his contacts with the leadership of al-Azhar University may have also influenced his views.

In 1974, the first unit of the al-Azhar school network was inaugurated in Ndaam, the headquarters of the institution. It was comprised of a complete elementary school cycle with six classrooms and additional facilities for providing students with lodging and other amenities. Students were accepted free of charge. Later on, modest fees were required from parents who could afford to pay for their children's education. From 1974, the al-Azhar school network continued to grow steadily with the opening of new institutes in Kaolack and Bambey in 1977, Saint-Louis and Thies in 1978, Diourbel in 1980, and Guediawaye in the suburb of Dakar in 1990. Schools were also opened outside Senegal in Côte d'Ivoire, Gabon, and Cameroon and, more recently, in New York City, where the Qur'anic school is hosted by the Malcom Shabaz mosque in Harlem. In 2004, al-Azhar counted 33,000 students in 260 schools of various sizes across Senegal.[29]

With the growth of the institution, a new model of organization was developed that distributed the schools between principal centers, secondary centers, and annexes. A principal center is responsible for supervising a number of secondary centers. It must command enough staff and resources to cover the whole cycle of education from elementary school to baccalaureate. It must also have a critical mass of students. A secondary center must cover the whole elementary school cycle and at least half of the middle school cycle. It is also tasked with supervising village schools. Annexes include village schools that do not have the staff or resources to stand alone. Although this mode of organization differs from the structures of the Senegalese national school system—which is based on the administrative division of the country—it aims at achieving similar objectives through a rational use of human and other resources and a tight bureaucratic hierarchy.

In the beginning, the creation of a school was decided and funded by Shaykh Murtalla, but now it is more common for local communities to take the initiative to build their schools and with al-Azhar providing the teacher and administrative framework. More recently, non-Muslim foreign countries, members of the Murid diaspora, and anonymous Senegalese donors have funded the building of classrooms.[30] Building and running such an enterprise requires substantial funding. But here also Shaykh Murtalla has drawn from traditional Muslim practices and modern fund-raising strategies to finance his school project.

The cost for running the school network was estimated in 2001 at nearly 400 million CFA francs (roughly equivalent to $800,000). Seventy-five percent of this amount was covered by school fees and Shaykh Murtalla's financial contribution in the form of *waqf* (al-Azhar Institute 2001, 8). The *waqf* is an inalienable religious endowment that has historically funded education and other social services in Islamic societies. The *shaykh* has earmarked most of the resources generated by his businesses to supporting the al-Azhar school network. His contribution was supplemented by state subsidies amounting to 10 million CFA ($20,000) and modest funding from the Muslim World League and the Libyan-based World Islamic Call Society.[31] Egypt and Mauritania send teachers to the schools, and Morocco provides grants to fund al-Azhar graduates continuing their education in its high schools and universities.[32]

One can clearly see that, through its objectives, mode of organization, and funding, the al-Azhar school differs markedly from classical Qur'anic and Arabic schools in Senegal. Traditionally, such institutions have functioned as family projects funded through students' labor and parental financial contributions and they aimed exclusively at religious education. The difference is even more obvious when one looks at the school's curriculum and pedagogy.

The al-Azhar curriculum is divided into four major sections: first, the religious disciplines including the Qur'an, *tawhid* (science of the oneness of God), hadith (prophetic traditions), *tafsir* (science of Qur'anic commentary), *fiqh* (Islamic jurisprudence), and *tajwid* (sciences of Qur'anic recitation); second, sciences of the Arabic language comprised of grammar, morphology, metric, rhetoric, composition, and literature; third, scientific and social disciplines, including the natural sciences, history, geography, biography of the Prophet Muhammad, civic education, French, and English; and, fourth, mathematics, physics, chemistry, sociology, psychology, philosophy, and *usul al-fiqh* (foundations of Islamic jurisprudence) (al-Azhar Institute 2001, 3). Students start the fourth section of the curriculum after completing elementary education. The textbooks used by the teachers are borrowed from North African and Middle Eastern countries.

The workweek is comprised of twenty-five hours of contact between students and teachers with more than one-third of the time (nine hours) devoted to the religious sciences and the rest dedicated to study of the Arabic language and secular disciplines.[33] Students start taking two hours of French in second grade, and at the sixth grade they split the two hours between French and English classes. Physical education is also included in the curriculum.

Clearly, the teaching of the Qur'an and religious sciences continues to occupy an important place in the curriculum of the al-Azhar schools, but unlike classical institutions of Muslim education in Senegal, greater attention is also given to secular sciences. What is even more remarkable is the introduction of religious disciplines such as *usuul Aa-Qur'an* and *usuul al-fiqh* that go beyond rote memorization and repetition—the methods favored for studying the Qur'an—and require discursive analysis and disputation. The introduction of the French and English languages and, more recently, the experimentation with technological training, shows greater awareness of the necessity to equip students not only with religious knowledge but with the skills to compete in the job market with those graduating from government schools.[34] The effort to offer a high level of modern education is also reflected in the attention given to the selection and use of teachers.

In 2001, al-Azhar counted 436 teachers in different specialties. Among those, 74 held a bachelor degree or a master's degree, 215 a baccalaureate, and 147 a brevet (al-Azhar Institute 2001, 5). By Senegalese standards this is highly qualified personnel, given that Arabic teachers in the private, and even sometimes public, schools are often poorly trained. Many of these teachers were former graduates of al-Azhar hired after they had completed their education in Senegal or abroad. They continue to perfect their training through a system of continuing education jointly organized by the managers of the al-Azhar Institute and governmental educational institutions.[35]

The personnel are composed of both men and women teachers, although women make only 11 percent of the teaching corps. But these women teachers have also benefited from advanced training; two-thirds of them hold a baccalaureate degree. It is likely that most of these teachers are al-Azhar alumnae (al-Azhar Institute 2001, 5). Until recently, women in Senegal had limited access to higher Islamic education. The effort to hire women teachers at al-Azhar and other Islamic educational institutions is certainly stimulated by the growing number of young girls frequenting those institutions and the push from UNESCO and other international bodies for the schooling of girls. The director general of al-Azhar estimated that in 2004 half the students registered in his school were girls.[36]

In addition to the awareness of gender issues, al-Azhar's modernity can be gauged through the attention given to students beyond graduation. Al-Azhar schools offer the complete cycle from elementary to secondary school. Students can choose to terminate their schooling at the end of the elementary cycle and earn a certificate sanctioning their studies; they could continue and finish the middle school or college cycle with the brevet; or they may opt to complete the secondary cycle and earn the baccalaureate that will open the door to higher education. In the 2001 school year, 115 students obtained the brevet and 43 the baccalaureate; in 2004, 1,000 students have earned the certificate capping elementary school education. Through its collaboration with countries in North Africa and the Middle East, al-Azhar sends the best and brightest among its students to pursue higher education in the Arab world. Between 2001 and 2004, it has sent 30 students to Morocco alone.

Since the school's diplomas are not recognized by the Senegalese state, students do not have direct access to the official governmental schools or jobs. But they can compete in examinations to enter the national school system at the level of the middle and secondary cycles as well as at the level of vocational schools. Many alumni now serve in government jobs, some at the highest echelon of the educational system. Beyond education, al-Azhar also facilitates employment for its students in the informal sector. Many of the employees of the businesses created by Shaykh Murtalla are graduates of his school network. They work as drivers in his transportation business and as bakers and laborers in his printing and agricultural businesses. He had envisioned al-Azhar as a self-sustained system, which could generate the resources to fund the educational operation while offering employment opportunities to graduates. The competitiveness of the jobs that al-Azhar offers its alumni is an open question, but in a country with a jobless rate of over 25 percent, recent graduates probably appreciate the opportunity the institute gives them, if only as a temporary occupation while they look for a better job elsewhere.

Serigne Murtalla's death in 2004 did not seem to hinder the development of the al-Azhar school network. His eldest son and successor, Serigne Maam Moor Mbakke, is pushing the modernization project even further. He is working with the minister of technical teaching in Senegal to introduce technology training in al-Azhar's curriculum to facilitate employment after students' graduation . He has also initiated an ambitious project to build a modern Islamic University on the site of al-Azhar headquarters in Ndaam at the estimated cost of 7 billion CFA francs ($1.4 million). But Serigne Maam Moor does not have the charisma or the prestige and authority of his late father, who was a son of Amadu Bamba. Already, some of his younger brothers are raising their voices against the idea of continuing to manage their father's asset as *waqf*, and some have sued for a settlement of the inheritance. The impact of Serigne Murtalla's death is already felt in the diminishing capacity for fund-raising that is slowing the building of the Islamic University of Ndaam. The dissolution of the *waqf* system would deal an even greater blow to the school network. The future of al-Azhar seems to depend more on the will of the parents who send their children to the school and the school's ability to meet their educational needs than on the vision of its founder.

Conclusion

Islamic education is at the core of Mbakke identity. Amadu Bamba, the founder of the Muridiyya, was nurtured in this family ethos. While abiding by family traditions, Bamba's own life experience inspired him to adopt new approaches to Islamic education that challenged entrenched family practices. Educational innovation for him required the introduction of a new discipline and methodology to accommodate the needs of different segments of the Muslim population in a period of rapid social change, but the production and transmission of Qur'anic and Islamic religious knowledge remained at the center of his preoccupation and actions. His views on education should be understood as a response more to the historical context in which he lived than to any philosophical shift about the meaning and role of Islamic education. However, because of their fascination with the organizational innovations initiated by the Muridiyya, many scholars of Islam in Senegal have lost sight of the more traditional aspect of Amadu Bamba's philosophy and practice of education.

The distinction between Muslim orders favorable to modern Islamic education and a more conservative Muridiyya tuned toward mystical education perceptible in the literature on Islam in Senegal is fundamentally an invention of French orientalists later endorsed by some scholars of the Murid order. In reality, for Sufis, esoteric and rationalist epistemes are not mutually exclusive; they belong to different fields of knowledge—that of *bāṭin* (the hidden) and *zāhir* (the open)—which are equally important for the education of the disciple.

The work of Serigne Murtalla Mbakke through the al-Azhar school network can be seen as an effort to affirm and strengthen his father's legacy in the educational domain. Like his father in nineteenth-century Senegal, Shaykh Murtalla labored to offer a model of education that, he believed, best suited the Senegalese Muslims of the twentieth and twenty-first centuries. His peripheral position on the Murid hierarchy of power and his unusual life itinerary as a global Murid *shaykh* put him in a position to understand the centrality of modern Islamic education in fostering the Muslim identity of the future. The very fact that his project, implanted in the heart of the Murid country, just a few kilometers from the holy city of Tuubaa, did not incur any hostile reaction demonstrates that the Muridiyya did not see his enterprise of modernization as a threat or incompatible with the order's ethos. The continuing popularity of the al-Azhar school networks in the Murid heartland and elsewhere in Senegal and beyond provides further evidence of the openness of the Muridiyya to modern transformations in Islamic education.

NOTES

1. This idea is rooted in the work of French orientalists such as Paul Marty and is reflected in later scholarly works such as those of Donal Cruise O'Brien on the Muridiyya. See, for example O'Brien (1971).
2. For more on Amadu Bamba's conception of education, see Babou (2003). Also see Babou (2007), especially chapter 4.
3. On a different Sufi approach to *tarbiyya*, see Seesemann (2011).
4. See Pelissier (1966) and O'Brien (1971). See also Jean Copans (1980). On the perceived centrality of *daara tarbiyya* in the Muridiyya, see O'Brien (1971, 165).
5. For a recent and extensive discussion of the scholarship on Qur'anic education in Senegal, see Ware (2014).
6. Interview with Mustafa Ceytu Mbakke, one of the sons of Shaykh Anta, who was sent to Mecca in 1937. Mbacke Gawane, Mbakke, August 3, 2000. During our conversation, Serigne Mustafa showed me a letter copied from the Senegalese National Archives related to his trip to Mecca in 1937. In the letter, dated February 19, 1937, the governor general was requesting information from the lieutenant governor of Senegal regarding the embarkation on the ship SS *Kutubiya* of Sam Mbakke and Mutafa Mbakke bound for Mecca. He regretted the fact that the lieutenant governor did not consult with him before granting the authorization for travel. He mentioned that he would have recommended that the two young men enroll in the madrasas of North Africa instead.
7. Interview with Cheikh Ndiaye, leader of the al-Falah movement, Dakar, June 24, 2006.
8. Interview with Professor Khadim Mbakke, Dakar, Senegal, May 22, 2006.
9. Doctor Muhammad Lo, a leader of the Salafii movement in Senegal, and Doctor Khadim Sylla, who graduated from al-Azhar in Cairo and the Sorbonne in Paris, are among dozens of Murid disciples who found their ways in North Africa and the Middle East to seek advanced religious education.
10. See Ware (2004). The debate about the lawfulness of requiring compensation from teaching the Qur'an has a long history in Islam. Abu Amid Ghazzali, the famous

twelfth-century Muslim philosopher, in his book, *kitab al-ilm* (the book of sciences), evokes the issue to articulate his own views. See Al-Ghazâlî (2009).

11. Interview with Cheikh Ndiaye, leader of Al-Fallah, Dakar, June 24, 2006.

12. See Loeimeier (1998) . I also refer to my interview with Cheikh Toure in Dakar in June 2001.

13. Interview with Cheikh Ndiaye, leader of Al-Fallah, Dakar June 24, 2006.

14. For biographical information regarding Shaykh Murtalla Mbakke I rely on my interview with Afia Niang, a Murid scholar and researcher, in New York, October 4, 2009.

15. Interview with Afia Niang, New York, October 4, 2009.

16. For more on the turmoil following Bamba's death, see Tidiane Sy (1969), especially the appendixes. Also see Musa Ka's Wolofal poem, *Kharnu bi* (the century).

17. One of my informants indicated that in 1947 (he probably meant 1945, the date when Shaykh Mustafa died), while he was in the throes of death, the cousin and close disciple of Amadu Bamba, Mbakke Buso, had convened all of Amadu Bamba's sons to ask them to pledge allegiance to their older brother, then Caliph Shaykh Mustafa. Everybody agreed, but Shaykh Murtalla objected mentioning that he would pledge allegiance only to someone embodying the quality of leader exhibited by Prophet Muhammad.

18. It is remarkable that, unlike with prominent Murid *shaykhs* whose names are always associated with the string of villages and *daaras* they have funded, hagiographers of Shaykh Murtalla do not attribute to him the founding of a single locality.

19. Afia Niang, New York, October 4, 2009. Also personal conversations with Akhma Faal referring to a testimony of one of Shaykh Murtalla's son and traveling companion, Washington, DC, November 2005, and Ahmadou Drame, son-in-law and traveling companion of the *shaykh*, Paris, May 2010.

20. See Moustapha Diop (1985). These values are also what the son of Shaykh Murtalla and director general of the al-Azhar Institute, Saliu Mbakke, identifies as the core teachings of his father. Interview in Ndaam, June 1, 2004.

21. During the Senegalese presidential elections of 2000, no major Murid *shaykhs* had made a public or private declaration of support on behalf of the incumbent, Abdou Diouf. It was widely rumored that Shaykh Murtalla, in particular, was a supporter of the challenger, Abdoulaye Wade. During the runoff for the elections, rumors had circulated in Mbakke and Tuubaa, major cities in the heartland of the Muridiyya, that Diouf had sent off people to solicit Shaykh Murtalla's support and that the *shaykh* had declined saying that he had already given his prayers out.

22. During one of his audiences with Abdou Diouf, former president of Senegal, Shaykh Murtalla had told him that the Senegalese people were suffering and that they needed his help. Diouf took offense at the observation and ended the audience prematurely. The *shaykh* then told the aide who accompanied him at the audience that Diouf seemed angered by his remarks but that he was happy to have let him know how the people actually felt about him. Personal conversation with A. S. B, disciple and aid to Serigne Murtalla. Dakar, Senegal, January 2000.

23. In a recent article on Islamic education in West Africa reprinted in this volume, Robert Launay and Rudolph T. Ware III argue, for example (and I agree with their view), that, although the scholarship on Islamism in Africa emphasizes the social and political dimensions of this movement, the bulk of their activities are in fact devoted to education. See Launay and Ware (2009, 128).

24. On the Subanu movement, see Kaba (1974), Amselle (1985), and Soares (2005); on Yan Izala, see Loiemeier (1997); on Ahmad Ba and Cheikh Toure, see Kane (1997). See Loimeier (1998).

25. Hefner (2009, 20) attributes these innovations to the type of Islam advocated by reformists, especially in Indonesia, but I believe that their views were also reflected in the type of education they promoted.
26. Interview with Afia Niang, New York, October 4, 2009.
27. The choice of Daaru ālim al-khabīr was symbolic because it was there where Amadu Bamba had instructed his disciple, Abdurahman Lo, to open a Qur'anic school where many of his children were educated. On this site was also located the village school Lassar (corruption of al-Azhar) opened by Shaykh Mbakke Buso in the late nineteenth century.
28. President Nasser indicated to the *shaykh* that he could not provide support to individuals but that he was willing to help if the *shaykh* were able to create a formal organization in charge of carrying out his project. Interview with Afia Niang, New York, October 4, 2009.
29. Interview with Saliu Mbakke, director general of al-Azhar in Ndaam, June 1, 2004.
30. Ibid.
31. Interview with Saliu Mbakke, director general of al-Azhar, Ndaam, June 1, 2004.
32. Ibid.
33. The length of the workweek varies from twenty-two hours for first-grade students to twenty-five hours for ninth-grade students (al-Azhar Institute. n.d.). It is worth mentioning that the time devoted to the Qur'anic and religious sciences is greater at the elementary school level. At the levels of middle and high school, more secular disciples are introduced.
34. See Diop (2009). In this article Diop reports about the pilot project initiated by the Senegalese minister of technical teaching and Serigne Maam Mor Mbakke, successor of Shaykh Murtalla Mbakke, to introduce the teaching of technology, especially, electromechanics, in the curriculum of the al-Azhar school network.
35. Interview with Saliu Mbakke, director general of the al-Azhar Institute, Ndaam June 1, 2004, and personal conversation with Gaston Sanghare, inspector of education of the district of Mbakke, Mbakke June 2004.
36. Interview with Salih Mbakke, Ndaam, June 1, 2004.

REFERENCES

al-Azhar Institute. 2001. *La lumiere sur l'Institut al-Azhar: Une publication de la Direction Generale de l'Institut al-Azhar.* Ndame: al-Azhar Institute.
al-Azhar Institute. n.d. *Program and disciplines taught at the al-Azhar Institute*, Ndame (brochure in Arabic).
Al-Ghazâlî. 2009. *Le livre de la science.* Translated by Jean Abd Al-Wadoud Gouraud. Paris: Albouraq.
Amselle, Jean L. 1985. "Le Wahabism a Bamako, 1945–1985." *Canadian Journal of African Studies/Revue Canadienne des Etudes Africaines* 19 (2): 345–57.
Babou, Cheikh A. 2003. "Educating the Murid: Theory and Practices of Education in Amadu Bamba's Thought." *Journal of Religion in Africa* 33 (3): 310–27.
———. 2007. *Fighting the Greater Jihad: Amadu Bamba and the Founding of the Muridiyya of Senegal, 1853–1913.* Athens: Ohio University Press.

Bang, A. K. 2011. "Authority and Piety, Writing and Print: A Preliminary Study of the Circulation of Islamic Texts in Late Nineteenth and Early Twentieth Zanzibar." *Africa* vol. 81 (1): 89–107, 90.
Bouche, Dénise. 1975. "L'enseignement dans les territoires français de l'Afrique occidentale de 1817–1920." Doctoral thesis, University of Paris, I.
Bousso, Mbacke. n.d. *Lettre à Monsieur Brevié*, edited and translated into French from Arabic by Khadim Mbacke in "Deux traités d'un lettre religieux." Unpublished article.
Brenner, Louis. 2001. *Controlling Knowledge: Religion, Power and Schooling in a West African Muslim Society*. Bloomington: Indiana University Press.
Copans, Jean. 1980. *Les marabouts de l'arachide*. Paris: Sycomore (2nd ed, Harmattan, 1988).
Hefner, Robert W., ed. 2009. *Making Modern Muslims: The Politics of Islamic Education in South Asia*. Honolulu: University of Hawaii Press.
Kaba, Lansana. 1974. *The Wahabiyya: Islamic Reform and Politics in French Africa*. Evanston, IL: Northwestern University Press.
Kane, Moustapha. 1997a. "La vie et l'oeuvre d'Alhaji Mahmoud Ba Diowol (1905–1978) du pâtre au patron de la révolution Al-Fallah." In *Le temps des marabouts*, edited by David Robinson and Jean-Louis Triaud, 431–67. Paris: Karthala.
Launay, Robert, and Rudolph T. Ware III. 2009. "Comment (ne pas) lire le Coran?" In *L'islam, nouvel espace public en Afrique*, edited by Gilles Holder, 127–45. Paris: Karthala.
Loiemeier, Roman. 1997. "Islamic Reform and Political Change: The Example of Abubakar Gumi and the Yan Izala Movement in Northern Nigeria." In *African Islam and Islam in Africa*, edited by E. Rosanders and D. Westerlund, 286–306. Athens: Ohio University Press.
———. 1998. "Cheikh Touré, un musulman sénégalais dans le siècle: Du réformisme à l'islamisme." In *Islam et islamismes au sud du Sahara*, edited by Ousmane Kane and Jean-Louis Triaud, 155–168. Paris: Karthala.
Ndiaye, Mamadou. 1985. *L'enseignement arabo-islamique au Sénégal*. Istanbul: Centre de recherches sur l'histoire, l'art et la culture islamiques.
Marty, Paul. 1917. *Etudes sur l'Islam au Sénégal*, vol. 1, *Les personnes*. Paris: Leroux.
Mbakke, Amadu Bamba. 1988. *Masalik al-Jinaan*. Rabat, Morocco: daar al-kitab.
Moustapha Diop, A. 1985. "Les associations islamiques sénégalaises en France," *Esprit* 102: 197–206.
O'Brien, Donal Cruise. 1971. *The Mourides of Senegal: The Political and Economic Organization of an Islamic Brotherhood in Senegal*. Oxford: Clarendon.
Pelissier, Paul. 1966. *Les paysans du Sénégal: Les civilisations agraires du Cayor à la Casamance*. Saint-Yriex, France: Imprimerie Fabrègue.
Seesemann, Rüdiger. 2011. *The Divine Flood: Ibrāhīm Niasse and the Roots of a Twentieth-Century Sufi Revival*. Oxford: Oxford University Press.
Soares, Benjamin. 2005. *Islam and the Prayer Economy*. Ann Arbor: University of Michigan Press.
Sy, Cheikh Tidiane. 1969. *La confrérie sénégalaise des mourides*. Paris: Présence Africaine.
Tibawi, A. L. 1971. *Islamic Education: Its Traditions and Modernization into the Arab National Systems*. London: Luzac.

Touré, Cheikh. 1957. *Afin que tu deviennes un croyant*. Dakar, Senegal: Imprimerie Diop.
Ware, Rudolph T. III. 2004. "Njangaan. The Daily Regime of Qur'anic Students in Twentieth Century Senegal." *International Journal of African Historical Studies* 3: 515–38.
———. 2014. *The Walking Qur'an: Islamic Education, Embodied Knowledge, and History in West Africa*. Chapel Hill: University of North Carolina Press.

10.
MWALIM BI SWAFIYA MUHASHAMY-SAID: A PIONEER OF THE INTEGRATED (MADRASA) CURRICULUM IN KENYA AND BEYOND

Ousseina D. Alidou

◦◉◦

HAVING UNDERGONE SEVERAL decades of British colonialism, all the East African countries, including Kenya, have inherited an educational system that maintains a distinction between schools designed for religious training and those for the material world. But under the impact of globalization, Muslim women educationists in this region are rethinking the question of modernity in terms of creative alternative educational setups. One of these novel approaches to Muslim education is the modernized integrated madrasa curriculum, which is intended to make learning about Islam an integral part of learning about other, secular subjects. The integrated madrasa now endeavors to prepare students for both religious and secular life. It is this alternative educational paradigm that this chapter explores by focusing on the pioneering works of its main architect, Bi Swafiya Muhashamy-Said from Mombasa, and the teachers who benefited from her training in East Africa. This social biography of Mwalimu Bi Swafiya is an important contribution to African Muslim women educationists' approach to knowledge production by integrating religious epistemology within a secular framework.

A native of Mombasa born in 1935, Bi Swafiya is unique among Swahili women of her age for having attained two university degrees—BA and MA—in her sixties. After retirement as a primary school teacher in Kenya in the early 1980s, Bi Swafiya became the founder of the Mombasa Madrasa Resource Center, a pioneering institution devoted to the promotion of an integrated (Islamic–secular) curriculum for preschool children. The center persuades traditional Qur'anic teachers to participate in the project by providing pedagogical and skills training and adopting the integrated curriculum in the running of their own madrasas. Given the success of her work, Bi Swafiya was appointed as the regional director of East African Madrasa Resource Centers covering the countries of Kenya, Tanzania, and Uganda—a position she held until her retirement in 2007. In addition to this pioneering educational initiative, Bi Swafiya has made significant contributions to and provided leadership in other important domains, which I explore in another essay.

The Formative Years

At the end of the nineteenth century, British colonialism used both missionary education and Christianity as tools for consolidating their domination in Kenya. However, as Ngome (2006, 3) rightly observes, the cultural production of African colonial agents through this educational and religious process was not uniform throughout Kenya, partly due to the way the different regions were incorporated into the colonial economy and partly because of the specific responses of local cultural communities to British colonial subjugation. The coastal strip of Kenya, though under British colonial rule, was still considered part of the East African coastal territory of the sultan of Zanzibar. Because of the nature of this relationship between the sultan and the British, the colonial authority in Kenya tried to accommodate Swahili interests by making provisions for Islamic education and the teaching of the Arabic language as a subject and for the exclusion of Christian religious education in those schools. For example, in the earlier Mombasa colonial schools known as the Arab Boys School (which later became Serani Primary School), the Arab Girls School (which became Mbaraki Primary School) and the Sir Bin Ali Primary School (later Malindi Primary School), Christianity was never taught as a subject.

Coastal Kenya indigenous *chuo/vyuo* (Qur'anic schools) were essentially in conflict with the British colonial schooling paradigm in terms of the ideologies and aims they sought to impart. As a result, the number of Muslim boys enrolled in schools during the colonial period was disproportionately lower than that of their non-Muslim counterparts. As a consequence, when Kenya finally acquired its independence in 1963, Muslims lagged far behind non-Muslim citizens. Furthermore, there was an ironic convergence of patriarchal gender ideology between the colonial administration and Muslim and non-Muslim Kenyan cultures who preferred not to send their daughters to school on the grounds that they were "custodians of traditions." African (Muslim) girls were thus incorporated into the framework of Victorian domesticity of good Christian wives (Chege and Sifuna 2006, 22–26). As a result, the more the colonial schooling was transforming the identity of African girls according to Christian parameters, the more the Muslim communities in Kenya recoiled from sending their daughters to school. It is against this background that we should understand Bi Swafiya Muhashamy-Said's comments below:

Yes! You see they started their work a long time ago to try to get to our minds through the teaching of the scripture, and Muslims resent that. The year was . . . I was very big because I was to do my Qur'an first and then go to school. It was in 1946. When my father said I should go to school in 1946, the whole community was against it except his own mother, who said, "Why not?" So when my grandmother agreed, then I was taken to a Catholic school because there were no Muslim schools. So I was taken to a private girls' community school run by Asian Goans. Even in my own family, my grand-aunt did not like the idea of sending me to school. The Muslim community's fear of the possibility of converting the children and also fear for the girls to mix with boys. But all the time, my mother would counsel me not to talk to boys. Because it is very dangerous, just talking could lead to many other things. So every night, she would ask me, "Whom we were together with? What happened today?¹"

This statement by Bi Swafiya brackets a couple of significant points. First, it reveals the concern of Muslim communities in the wake of World War II. This is another historical moment when Africans were absorbed into European internal conflicts. Second, it highlights the circulation of the colonized engendered by colonialism. Here we have the Goans, a Catholic community of Indian origin once colonized by the Portuguese, now serving the British civilizing mission through education in the East African side of the Indian Ocean. Third, the mixing of the genders was itself considered one of the European cultural vices wrought by colonial education. Even those parents who saw some value in sending their children (especially girls) to colonial schools were still worried about its alienating effects. And some, like Bi Swafiya's father, had to devise domestic strategies to limit the Euro-Christian impact of the school:

> My father was liberal, but still he has his own attitude. I am really lucky. I always thank him and pray for him that he took me to school. So he suggested that I become a teacher and I said, "All right." So I joined a teacher training here in Mombasa, Coast Teachers Training. I became a P1 [Primary 1] teacher; in fact it was a mixed school. But when I had to take the Christian scripture in form four, he was very concerned. He said, "OK! If you are not going to be converted, you are just taking it as a subject, all right!" But at the same time when I took the scripture, he came and asked me, "How many times in a week do you have scripture?" And I told him. So he marked the days I took scripture. The day I have scripture he made time to sit with me, asked me what I learnt in the scripture, and then he would refer me to Yusuf Ali's translation of the Qur'an. He would say, "Let us open this chapter and see what Islam tells us on this issue." So I learnt my Islam with my [Christian] scriptures. Every time I read [Christian] scripture in school, I read the Qur'an with my father. He would sit with me and discuss with him what our culture is saying, what is our gain. This is how I finished my school there.

The active agency of Bi Swafiya's father as an intercultural mediator between Islam and Christianity is important here. In an attempt to ground his daughter in both Islamic values and the modern secular world of knowledge, he employs a dialogic method of processing the Christian Bible through Islamic lenses. The ultimate aim of this conversation facilitated by her father was primarily to define what is useful to a Muslim from this new education—"what is our gain," as she puts it—in the shaping of a modern educated Muslim girl. Going against the grain of the Muslim community of his time, Bi Swafiya's father was able to dispel the fears of his community. As noted earlier, the more the colonial schooling was transforming the identity of African girls along European and the quasi-Christian parameters, the more the Muslim communities of Kenya recoiled from sending their daughters to school. According to Bi Swafiya, in fact, "Up to now there are people who fear education for girls, and the other reason they fear is because education came with the missionaries, with their cross. The aim was to convert people. And they won. Some of us became Christians. And I have observed also that all of us who have gone to secular schools, our thinking is Western thinking, even however religious you are, you pray five times, your way of thinking is not Islamic thinking. So there is a reason why our people fear secular education." This quote clearly demonstrates the theoretical sophistication of Bi Swafiya in her argument that different epistemologies engender different worldviews. Being a Muslim in fulfilling ritual obligations does not amount to thinking Islamically. She provides a philosophical articulation of the fears of her community with regard to the culturally alienating dimension of (post)colonial education. This concern is not unique to Muslims, but expressed throughout colonized worlds.

Bi Swafiya was among a handful of coastal Muslim girls who attended secondary school in the immediate aftermath of the Second World War. As a pioneering Muslim woman student, she had to overcome several cultural barriers. One of the challenges of her life as a student is revealed in the following elaborate self-portrait that captures the coming of age of a young Muslim woman in a society in transition, between colonialism and national liberation, having to negotiate between her yearning for a modern education and a career and societal expectations of women as custodians of tradition and identity:

> You see, I am now seventy years old and I will tell you. When I was born, now I am going to take you back to when I was born. When I was born, my mother tells me my husband's mother came with a bundle of clothes tied up in a cloth. We call that in Kiswahili *furushi*. Just *furushi*, clothes tied up in a piece of cloth, or a *kanga*, and she said, "Now I am engaging my son to Swafiya." But that happens always to anybody. But somehow rather, it stayed, and the same man got married to me. I was in secondary school; they revived [the marriage proposal]. That time I was living far away. When

I was born, we were in the same area together. But when I was in secondary school, he was somewhere else and I was somewhere else. We had not met. But his mother came from where he was and said, "Look, my word I am keeping. We want Swafiya." And actually there were already two other proposals and there was a debate between the grandmothers. My grandmother was all for Mohammed [the husband-to-be], and the other grandmothers had the other two people. In any case, my paternal grandmother won. They accepted my proposal, and I was now in form four. And then when I finished form four [grade twelve in United States], I told my father that I want to become a teacher. So they said, "Now the man is ready to marry you." But I said to them, "How would I do my training?" Then Mohammed was told. Then he said, "OK. You can do your training and get married at the same time." So I got married when I was training, and that was in my second year of training. But this time, I was nineteen. All right! And then after I got married, naturally I got pregnant. And when I got pregnant, I told my husband, "You did not want me to have a career? Now I am going to be a housewife and bring babies for you." So my husband said, "No, you can still continue." And I said, "I feel ashamed to go to the training with a womb coming up and all that. I don't want to go through that." So my husband quietly went to the principal. He was a Scottish man, a very good man, Mr. Bradley, and he told him, "My wife now does not want to continue with the training." And he asked him why. And my husband said, "Because she is pregnant, she is preparing to return the books." So he said, "Let her come with the books. I will talk to her." So Mr. Bradley took me in and closed the door and said, "Swafiya, congratulations!" I said, "What for?" My tears were rolling down. And he said, "No! This is a wonderful thing that can happen to a woman! To get a baby, it is wonderful! I congratulate you. You don't have to regret, study can go on even if you are pregnant. It doesn't matter." But then I asked him, "What will happen to me with my colleagues?" He said, "Nothing will happen, everybody is understanding." So he told me, "No, no, no, Swafiya, take your time to rest, I know what you feel like. But the doors are opened and let me tell you a story.

> *You see there was a lady in Britain who trained as a teacher. But she did not start teaching because she did not need teaching. Her husband was well off and she started getting children. And then suddenly her husband died and she had to find work. And this certificate became very useful.*

It is the same for you, Swafiya. You don't have to work. But you take the certificate. Remember in Mombasa here, there isn't a girl who has reached this stage—a Muslim girl who has taken this teaching. And something that you don't know is: Mohammed had wanted to join this training." But I told him, 'Because you know your culture, if you are interested in this girl, don't come. Take up another job.' So just remember your husband wanted to be a teacher and he was teaching as an untrained teacher. You see the trend in Mombasa was for people to become teachers. Now, he forfeited that place for you. So please take it up. Don't leave it." This was a Scottish man who was advising me. So then I said, "I will come back for you, Mr. Bradley. But today my books...." He said, "Do you want to leave your books? Take them. Then when you are decided, you come to me." This is what happened when I was a girl.

So in the end I went back to my husband and told him this is what Mr. Bradley told me, and he said, "If I were you, I would listen to what Mr. Bradley said." And I said, "It is too much work," and he replied, "I will help you. I will give all the support you want!" which he did. So there we are! I became a teacher finally, but I got a baby in between . . . [laughs] a baby boy. Everybody was excited.

This gentleman Bradley took it upon himself to take all the students and inform them. He said, "Come! I want to tell you something about Swafiya. I want you to support her because she has married and is now pregnant and I want her to continue with the pregnancy. I am requesting you all not to treat her like a stranger. Let her mix like she was used to like every student. [laughs] . . . So in fact that was what happened. Boys and girls were mixed. They were all helpful. Till I got the baby, I continued with the studies and started my teaching career. This was 1957/1958. I finished my training in 1958. I trained as a teacher in Mombasa.

Then I left the country but not as to train. In the beginning I thought I would go and further my studies when my husband was training in Britain. I insisted that I would take the children. But he said, "If you are coming, just come with one." So I picked the elder one, who then was three years old. But when I got there, it was difficult for me to go to college and I had the child. So I was a housewife then. But with my husband I traveled so much. I was exposed to the Western world. And we went to Holland, and when we came back, we went to the United States for studying with an Eisenhower Fellowship. I went with him and out of the fifty-two or fifty-three states in the USA we visited twenty states, moving all the time.

In this self-portrait, we see a modern love story emerging out of a very traditional institution of arranged marriage and child betrothal. That bond of love provides space for the remaking of cultural values of gender status to make it possible for a Muslim girl to evolve into an educated cosmopolitan woman leader. We also see that those who came to the rescue of Bi Swafiya then were not only people from her own community—her husband and other Kenyan students—but, more importantly, the representative of colonial educational administration, Mr. Bradley. During the post–World War II era, the British colonial government was under pressure to produce a class of educated elite who would take over the bureaucratic and managerial functions of the country once they departed (Eshiwani 1993, 25). Bi Swafiya might thus have been among the first Kenyan women—and certainly Muslim women—beneficiaries of this new colonial educational policy. Despite the problematics of colonial education and its continuing legacy in the postcolonial period, however, it was educational developments in independent Kenya that came to have a more decisive impact on Bi Swafiya's decision to initiate an alternative educational paradigm. And it is to this postcolonial background that we should now turn.

The Postcolonial Phase: Mwalimu Bi Swafiya's Modernist Vision of Integrated Madrasa

Like most African countries, the newly independent Kenyan state saw formal mass education as a fundamental pillar of development. To disengage from the discriminatory approach to colonial education, the new Kenyan government endorsed a politics of compulsory mass education for all children from age seven, regardless of gender and ethnicity. The success of this postindependence colonial policy is what set Kenya as one of the African countries with a high literacy rate, estimated at about 78 percent of the population. Yet, in spite of these figures, Kenya is also one of the places in Africa where the problem of Muslim children's education is most acute (Ngome 2006; Chege and Sifuna 2006).

In the early days of independence, under the banner of "de-ethnicitizing" government schools and rendering them multicultural and multiethnic and secular, the few predominantly Muslim schools of the Arab Swahili became de-Islamized in population and in curriculum, terminating the teaching of Islam and the Arabic language. Schooling in this period became the site of struggle to resolve the nation's historical contradictions in areas related to race, ethnicity, and religion (JanMohammed, 1976, 195; Strobel 1976, 208–9). Islam and Muslim-ness became almost indistinguishable from Arabism and Arab historical hegemony, especially in the minds of a great majority of non-Muslim coastal Kenyans. As a result, Muslim parents and children were increasingly disengaging from the postcolonial schools. It is within the context of this history of education that we must understand the formation of Bi Swafiya Muhashami-Said as a pioneer of a new modern educational paradigm that seeks to address the schooling needs of Muslim children.

In the past, the Qur'anic school, most commonly referred to as *chuo* in Kiswahili, was the first site of schooling where the Muslim child was initiated into the acquisition of a formalized body of knowledge, albeit religious, through acts of and practice of literacy. In fact, these early stages of Islamic education introducing the child to the verbal artistry of Qur'anic recitation and memorization, reading of the Arabic alphabet, and the ritual of *salat* (prayers) are central to the process of shaping the Muslim child's identity. Most Kenyan Muslim children undergo this faith-based early childhood schooling before entering secular primary schools in both rural and urban centers.

However, by the 1970s, this *chuo* tradition rooted in Islam gradually began to lose students as the newly introduced private secular nursery schools started to spread nationally, especially in urban centers. The new nursery school poses a challenge to the Muslim children's education on a number of grounds: (1) It further reduces, if not eliminates, the little room left to many Muslim parents to instill the early seeds of their faith-based identity, because its curriculum is molded by a secular vision. (2) Because its aim is to provide a curricular head start to primary education, it sets children of parents who can afford the fees and those of poor parents who cannot afford the fees in an unequal competition for primary educational opportunities. (3) It is in the postcolonial period that English begins to be introduced earlier in the educational structure—as early as the nursery level in many urban private schools. Children of the better-to-do families end up better prepared not only academically but in terms of English linguistic skills for opportunities in the competitive primary schools.

Aware of the ways that educational institutions (re)produce socioeconomic classes and in which educational structures are used to achieve hegemonic goals, Bi Swafiya Muhashamy-Said began to explore creative approaches to countering the alienating threats to Islamic identity posed by the newly embraced secular nursery schools as well as the class disparities it produces. As she put it:

> When I saw that the girls we teach in our Muslim women's institute do not know the Qur'an, I told my fellow women that there is a big problem here and we must all be concerned about this since our children don't know our religion because they attend the nursery schools.... So they asked me, "Now what are we going to do?" I said now in Kenya, because people are all interested in sending children to school [formal school], the Qur'an has been pushed into the corner. When we went to school, we had to finish our Qur'an before we joined school. All right but now, children are sent to [private] nursery before even going to Qur'an because madrasa will take children when they are six to seven years old. But we are sending children at three years to the nursery.

Part of the blame, of course, can be laid squarely on the teaching approach in the *vyuo*, with many of the teachers relying more on the stick than on the carrot. Muslim parents themselves were now drawn to the more enjoyable environment of the nursery school than the disciplinarian environment of the *vyuo*:

> The *mu'alim* [teacher] in the madrasas are using stick to teach. So no parents will send their children of three or four years old to the madrasa. But in nursery schools they are very happy children. They are playing, it is a secular learning. Thus, most parents are sending their children to the secular system till they start primary one, then they go to the madrasa in the afternoons. They only learn [the Qur'an] on Saturday and Sunday when they reach standard four [not four years, but the class four], because primary one, primary two and three, they will go in the afternoon to Qur'an. And because the learning system or the teaching system in the Qur'an is not

systematic, they do not acquire the reading skills in those three years when they are very young.

These observations led Bi Swafiya to the conclusion that, under the new circumstances, the only way the community can fully reclaim the *vyuo* tradition is to change both the content focus and the instructional approach of the institution:

> So I explain this [problem] to my ladies and let them understand that here in our institution, our club, we must start nursery schools which will teach both [Qur'an and secular contents]. We can prepare children to be ready for secular and at the same time to be ready for Qur'an. Then the women started to complain, "Oh Swafiya, we have our hands full already. Who is going to do that?" You know how it is with the ladies. But in my mind I kept saying, I am going to start a madrasa which is going to prepare children to Qur'an and secular content.

It is within this context that, although not an expert of early childhood education, Bi Swafiya pioneered an Islamically inspired secular nursery curriculum that integrates an Islamic perspective. This is an innovative approach now widely known in East Africa as the Integrated Islamic Nursery school curriculum, which aims not to teach Islam as one of the subjects but to have Islam as a framework of understanding whatever the subject matter, be it in the social sciences, the sciences, or humanities.

By the early 1980s, Bi Swafiya Muhashamy-Said had retired from her teaching career as a primary school educationist. She now took over the responsibility of looking after her toddler grandson in the afternoons after he returned from the nursery school. This extended contact with her grandson gave her an additional opportunity to think of the impact of the nursery school on Muslim children. It also gave her access to the curriculum content of the nursery school, which she later transformed using an Islamic framework. According to her:

> When I got my grandson, and when he started school, I began [to take care of him] because I had retired and I was teaching half day. So what I did is that I started preparing Islamic songs. For instance, the same songs which they learn in the nursery, I changed the wording, the tune. I give you an example: There is a song well known all over the world which says:
>
> *Twinkle, twinkle little star*
>
> So what I did, I said:
>
> *You are shining little star*
>
> *Who has made you as you are*

Allah Almighty subhana-l Allah

Twinkle, twinkle Masha Allah

So you see, this is what I had and started with. So I had my grandchild. I started composing nursery rhymes, and at the same time, in the afternoon I sat with the boy and started teaching him: *alif bah*. I started making simple words and associating the alphabet letter with an Islamic word or event, or I started telling stories with Islamic roots. So I started this initiative with my grandson. I said when I get some cash, I will start and open a small school madrasa with my new approach. But this was not possible without the means. As a widow with three orphans to bring up, I found it very difficult. However, people say that where there is a will, there is a way. Much later, I got an offer of starting a school, madrasa, with an Islamic orientation.

Bi Swafiya appropriated several nursery songs and Islamized them and sometimes even Swahilized them. There is a nursery rhyme, for example, that begins with the words: "Two little birds sitting on a wall; one named Peter, one named Paul." Peter and Paul are central figures in the early history of Christianity who are used to Christianize the lyrics by replacing Jill and Jack, which were the names used in the original song. In Bi Swafiya's version, in addition to other changes, the names Peter and Paul were changed to Ali and Hassan, two influential figures in the early history of Islam. Appropriating these and other British-inherited texts used in the Kenyan national curriculum was crucial for exposing Muslim children to the school contents that shape the scholastic development of their non-Muslim Kenyan contemporaries.

In addition to putting an Islamic spin on texts and activities from the British-inherited secular nursery school curriculum, Bi Swafiya drew extensively from local lore and wisdom in the crafting of her own integrated curriculum. Moreover, her curriculum introduces students to other subjects, including mathematics, environmental studies, health education, and even the more controversial subject of sex education. In the process, she developed a trilingual education program based on Swahili, Qur'anic Arabic, and English. Swahili provided the foundation for local identity; Arabic opened the door to Islamic learning and contributed to the consolidation of an Islamic identity; and English was the key to the material world of professional success and transethnic national integration.

And so Bi Swafiya's Integrated Madrasa Project finally came to fruition starting in 1986. As the newly appointed director charged with the responsibility of designing a curriculum, she received a small grant from the Aga Khan Foundation. Her commitment to bringing an Islamic perspective to early childhood education as well as her determination to modernize the traditional approach to teaching Islam to young Muslims led Bi Swafiya, at age sixty, to embark on the path of further education in this new field, first through self-instruction. She studied the national authoritative documents issued by the Kenya Institute of Education to better shape her own innovative integrated methodology.

> Ousseina: Wow! This is starting from scratch.
>
> Bi Swafiya: Yes, from scratch. Now, how did I educate myself to the learning of the nursery school? I started getting books. First, I got one from KIE, which is a guideline to preschool. . . . Kenya Institute of Education. So I got that green book which is a guideline which tells you what children should learn in the secular schools. Since I was told that I was to develop the curriculum, I suggested to my [consultative] board that we should invite *mu'alims* and sell the idea to them and we form a small task group, give each person in the group a topic like, for example, asking him about how to design the *tawhid* curricular content for nursery. What should nursery level pupils know? Another person is assigned a topic on *akhlaq* [good behavior], another is assigned the article of faith or the Qur'an to three- to four-year-old kids. Of course, the *mu'alims* were very pleased that we included them in this initiative. So within the committee, we had one school advisor who was advisor to the secular school. Mr. Basharahil brought the National Islamic Curriculum. So we took the content of standard one and moved it to the level suitable to nursery pupils. So that it connects with the rest. Actually, they gave me purely the hadith, the *akhlaq* in the hadith, what hadith should these little children be taught, which sign rituals should the nursery children learn? Then I sat and started reviewing and reforming the curriculum and brought the developed material to the board, and three members of the board examined what was given to us and the three of us should come up with what content that three- to six-year-olds should learn.

Bi Swafiya's methodology, in other words, consists of bringing an Islamic perspective to everyday life activities taught in the secular curriculum while in the process respecting the functional distribution between Qur'anic language, the child's mother tongue, and English.

> Bi Swafiya: First, I have to tell you the caliber of the teachers we are getting; we had targeted at least secondary school graduates as teachers. But it was very difficult to recruit from the second level, because most young people don't want to become teachers. So I had to be satisfied with primary school education and very few failures of secondary schools. So the caliber of the teachers was very low and it is varied. That is, from primary mixed to secondary low achievers, higher achievers like that. So we had to adjust our teachers training accordingly, and I used Kiswahili and English to train. I used to give them English classes whenever I had time. So I wanted them also to acquire some literacy in English.

As for our curriculum, I will give you a copy for you to look through. We had planned that the first year the child comes to school, we use Kiswahili. . . . In the third year, English is introduced.

Ousseina: How does the Qur'anic teaching operate?

Bi Swafiya: Qur'anic teaching, I told you is all integrated. But *qira* [reading] operates like we are teaching the alphabet. We teach the alphabet in Arabic. Like *alif, ba, ta*. But we don't teach them letters. You take a picture, with the name of Allah, *alif (ainabu)*, *be (batatun)*, *te (tetajun)*. So Arabic words like that in a song form, in a picture with a story, with few Arabic words as you are telling the story.

Ousseina: Would the words be written in Latin or Arabic?

Bi Swafiya: Arabic. The Qur'anic alphabet will be in Arabic. The words will be in English. Like all English words will be all in English, Kiswahili words all in Kiswahili. And Arabic words all in Arabic. So we are working with three languages.

At the initial stages, then, Bi Swafiya's project involved a two-tiered educational arrangement. She recruited young women from marginalized Muslim communities who had dropped out of school and provided them with training in content, pedagogy, and English language skills. For the young women, their participation in this innovative project was a source of income and professional development. This cadre of trainees was then mobilized to implement the Islamic-oriented trilingual program in early childhood education. Bi Swafiya's educational approach has earned the appreciation of many Muslim parents who feel that what their children are getting is of direct relevance to their own lives.

In fact, the feedback I got when I established the third school from the parents and many people is that some are saying, "We are learning Islam from our children." When it is snack time, besides saying "*Bissmillahi* [in the name of God]," there is a *Du'a* [prayer], we teach them the *Du'a*. So they go home and they tell their parents, "Don't eat, we have the *Du'a* to say." So the parents also come to me and say, "We are also learning along with our children," and that gave me a lot of enthusiasm and support.

As argued earlier, education is not a neutral process; it serves an ideological aim with socioeconomic consequences. As a result, the implementation of any educational curriculum requires the right combination of institutional legitimacy and funding support. Fortunately, Bi Swafiya's grassroots vision and approach coincided with the Aga Khan Foundation's mission of making early childhood education accessible and affordable to Muslims. However, because of the intra-Muslim denominational divide, Bi Swafiya, as a Muslim belonging to the Sunni majority community in Kenya, was careful to cross-check the implications of accepting funding from the Aga Khan Foundation, one of the prominent organizations of the Shia community known as the Ismaili. After consultation with her community members, she agreed to accept the offer.

> From the Aga Khan Foundation. So when I got this offer, first I was doubtful. Perhaps these people want me to sell my faith. I got worried a little bit because they are Shia and we are Sunni. And during that time—it was the time when Khomeini—many people were becoming Shia. . . . This was 1984, 1985, 1986. . . . But I retired in 1984. I was teaching half day in another private school and I was teaching standard one. I continued teaching. With the offer, I consulted the womenfolk with whom we do the *Da'wa* [proselytization]. My female *Da'wa* colleagues warned me against taking the offer, fearing that they will force me to embrace their Shia ideas and make me do this and that. When I consulted my mother, she told me that this is a great opportunity . . . to implement what I had long envisioned to do. I moved on and consulted another principal of Sheikh Kalifa School, Swabir. He was a colleague I was working with. He was working with the boys' school and I was dealing with the girls school. He said, "Well, Swafiya, I think you better take it because it will get into the wrong hands, you will be answerable to that because the offer went to you. But I know you throughout these years, nobody can change you. And if anything goes wrong you are able to stop it." So he gave me the courage. Then I went back and took the offer.
>
> The Aga Khan offer was to start madrasa schools for the very poor people who cannot afford the nursery school. When I asked them who is going to give me a curriculum for this, I was told, "One of your tasks is to conceive the curriculum." So Allah is with me *Alhamdulillah*! So I got to implement my curriculum initiative. Of course, I received their support and worked with a board to which I was answerable. I was to report every month. I started from nothing, and I had not been trained in early childhood education. I was trained as a primary school educator. So I started learning. And since my grandson was in nursery school in the morning, I was getting all the songs from him, and in the process, like I told you, I started changing many of the songs into Islamic. The board was very supportive. We started the first school in October 1986. My duties were to train the teachers, establish the school, and form a committee. Since the Aga Khan Foundation was not going to pay the teachers, it was the community that is supposed to pay. It is a community school. So I was to mobilize the community around the Madrasa and form a committee to run the school.

This experience provided an opportunity for Bi Swafiya to return to school for a university degree at age sixty, which is very unusual for women regardless of their religious background. As she noted: "As far as my own academic qualifications, I remained a P1 teacher until I joined this organization [Aga Khan Foundation]. Then I did my two degrees, BA and MA in education in my sixties. I did that with other colleagues through the Exeter University in Britain. But I did it very late when I was old, and I am still studying. [laughs] I am one who believes learning never ceases, from the cradle to the grave." Her academic advancement in the secular field now came to complement her pursuit of Islamic learning and Arabic language skills. She was now standing with one foot solidly in Islamic knowledge and the other in secular education.

> So before this BA and MA training, I was involved with the mosque doing my religious training with a woman teacher, graduate of Al Azhar University [Egypt]. She was teaching us how to do *Da'wa*. She taught us many things in religion. She lived in Egypt and she was a lecturer there. Her name was Su'ad. She was originally from Zanzibar. She took a group of ten of us and said that we must learn Arabic, otherwise we would not understand the religion. So she gave us lessons in Arabic. We went through the *nahau* [grammar]. And of course, we did a lot of Qur'anic translation. She gave us the skills, so were preaching at the mosque. Up to now it is going on, every Thursday the ladies meet and one of us presents a lecture.

Although Islam was the inspiring framework for reforming the nursery school for Muslim children, Bi Swafiya's creative methodology became an inspiration for both her secularist as well as Christian educationist colleagues:

> In fact, the people from Kenya Institute of Education, we caught them by surprise because they are the people who developed the curriculum. So when they came to our school, they were so impressed in the sense that we are rewriting education in totality. It means we are developing the children mentally, physically, socially, emotionally, and spiritually, which none of the schools do. . . . In fact, KIE, after they came to visit us and saw the day in madrasa, they started inviting the Christians to tell them what is happening. We had a consultation meeting in Nairobi, and they invited me in order to know what we are doing. And the [non-Muslim] sisters there came out to compliment us and told us, "We have not been able to do what you are doing." Although they are teaching in the church, that method of interrelating everything is not there. They teach religion as a subject. They have not integrated in it the whole system.

Through her modernist vision, Bi Swafiya thus opened up a space for a constructive interfaith dialogue on holistic ways of providing a religious perspective to a secular curriculum in both a modern and nonhegemonic manner.

Despite her pioneering role in making culturally relevant the secular nursery curriculum for Muslim children, Bi Swafiya still had to deal with the sensibilities and vested interests of the teachers in the traditional *vyuo* schools, who are predominantly men. If secular education has opened its door to women's leadership especially in early childhood education, this is not the case in *vyuo* schools, which are still controlled by the men *mu'alims*. Bi Swafiya was ready to adopt a subversive behind-the-scenes strategy if that would help transmit the new idea to conservative teachers and its testing in the communities.

> Ousseina: I have a question, if I may. When your board at the Madrasa Resource Center invited the Qur'anic schoolteachers, the *mu'alims*, and they saw a woman leader, how was their reception?
>
> Bi Swafiya: Yes, I was very sensitive and I took care of that in the sense that I took men at bay. That is, I was in the background. In the meetings, I did not appear because I knew if this has to work, I have to go by the Islamic cultural way as they understand it. Every time I had the meeting with the people, I was behind. Until the *mu'alims* themselves accepted me, and they themselves say, "Please Mama, we want to see you. You are just like our Mama . . . [laughs] . . . [you see] . . . [laughs] . . . I did not go up in the street up telling them "Do this, do that." I chose to remain behind the scene. The *mu'alims* told them, "You will do this and you will do that." And I was behind the scene. And if they ask, they say, "We would like to ask Bi Swafiya, 'Bi Swafiya, . . . '" then, I will answer behind the scene! So this is how I took care of that until they themselves wanted me to speak to them. Until we reached a stage that the *mu'alims* said, "We also want you to give hands on how to teach Qur'an in our madrasa which teach girls."
>
> Ousseina: *Mashallah!*
>
> Bi Swafiya: *Alhamdulillah*, Allah was really very kind on us! Showed us the way, this is what happened. I think in Uganda, when I went, I did the same thing. But when the ladies, the young ladies took over and started talking to men, it was resented. It was resented, and the men said, "We don't want to listen to the women. We don't want the woman like that." . . . So in my mobilization, I tell the people around, especially the women, to be aware of the strategy for success. These will be women and men. Then I will quote the prophet (PBH) [Peace Be with Bim] Salallah Alahi Wassalam, who says, "Seek knowledge, even in China." You see if it is religious knowledge, he had it in Medina. But he said, "Seek knowledge in China!" China! It is this other *ilimu* [knowledge] which is preferred. This *fard a'in* is with him, but *fard kifayah*, you have to seek to be a doctor, to be a nurse, to be all these things. So the Prophet Muhammad had no margin in between the *ilm*. Ilm was holistic for him.

In Islam, *fard a'in* refers to what is obligatory to individual Muslims (such as observing the five pillars of Islam). *Fard kifayah*, on the other hand, is what is obligatory in every Muslim community—like ensuring that there are enough doctors, teachers, engineers to meet the developmental needs of the society. By foregrounding this distinction between the two types of Islamic obligations, Bi Swafiya emphasizes once again that the acquisition of secular knowledge from the vantage point of Islam—and upon which her nursery curriculum and approach are designed—is itself an act of Islamic faith. In fact, she sees Islam as a faith that shatters the boundary between the religious and the secular, giving further credence to her integrated Islamic–secular approach. And in this understanding she adds an important gender dimension in the process: "Yes, you see, in our minds if we think that we respect our values, then we treat them properly, people accept us. They will accept us for what we are. But if we try to copy them, imitate them, and try to be like them, we are not gaining anything. Even when I visited the States all covered up, they respected me as a covered woman. So when I am training my teachers, I told them, 'You are to be proud of your dressing. If you do it that way, people respect you.' So this is my policy."

The success of Bi Swafiya's vision is appraised by the Aga Khan Foundation's latest report on educational impact as follows: "From the seed that was planted here in the Coastal Region some 25 years ago—when Bi Swafiya Said received her grant from the Aga Khan Foundation—the East African Madrasa Programme has grown to include 203 pre-schools, with nearly 800 teachers, reaching some 30,000 households and serving more than 54,000 children" (Aga Khan Foundation 2008).

Conclusion

In the Islamic world, the tension between the dimensions of the human experience is of course rooted in the history of European conquest and colonialism of the Muslim world. In the process, Muslim educational institutions seeking to modernize have often had to respond to this new challenge precipitated by its encounter with the European Other. In Kenya, Bi Swafiya Muhashamy-Said's modernist contribution is to integrate the secular and the religious into a unified curriculum. Of course, her experiment has started where it should have started: at the nursery stage of socialization.

Equally significant, however, is Bi Swafiya Muhashamy-Said's own personal accomplishment. Hers is a social biography that provides an understanding of the challenges and hurdles confronting Muslim women born during colonialism at the onset of a major struggle between an indigenous worldview and a colonial one. It is a story of great resilience against local and colonial patriarchy. And by incorporating the poor as both teachers and students, and by making students' parents participate in her educational design, she manages to challenge class boundaries rooted in local socioeconomic inequalities and exacerbated by colonial and postcolonial structures. In the final analysis, then, Bi Swafiya Muhashamy-Said is that personal embodiment of the very curriculum that she created. Like her curriculum, she is the convergence of the old and the new and of the Afro-Islamic and secular modernity.

NOTE

1. All the quotes in the chapter are selected from my fieldwork interview with Bi Swafiya conducted in 2006.

REFERENCES

Aga Khan Foundation. 2008. *The Madrassa Early Childhood Programme Experience.* Geneva: Aga Khan Development Network.
Chege, Fatuma, and Daniel N. Sifuna. 2006. *Girls' and Women's Education in Kenya: Gender Perspectives and Trends.* Nairobi: UNESCO.
Eshiwani, S. George. 1993. *Education in Kenya since Independence.* Nairobi: East African Educational Publisher.
JanMohammed, Karim. 1976. "Ethnicity in an Urban Setting: A Case of Study of Mombasa." *Hadith* 6: 186–205.
Ngome, Charles. 2006. *Mobile Schools Programme for Nomadic Pastoralists in Kenya: Pilot Project in Wajir, Ijara and Turkana Districts.* Nairobi: Government of Kenya, Office of the President, Special Programs, Arid Lands Resource Management Project.
Strobel, Margaret. 1976. "From Lelelama to Lobbying: Women's Associations in Mombasa." In *Women in Africa: Studies in Social and Economic Change,* edited by Nancy J. Hafkin and Edna G. Bay, 183–238. Stanford, CA: Stanford University Press.

11.
CHANGES IN ISLAMIC KNOWLEDGE PRACTICES IN TWENTIETH-CENTURY KENYA

Rüdiger Seesemann[*]

⁓⃝⁓

THE ENCOUNTER WITH European imperialism in the thirteenth century of the *hijra* (nineteenth century CE), and even more so the colonial experience of the fourteenth/twentieth century, raised unprecedented challenges to Islamic education and knowledge practices that have evoked a wide variety of responses.[1] These have most carefully been studied in Egypt, where Muslims reacted in different ways to the devaluation of their educational institutions, their pedagogical methods, and their "traditional" curriculum. Responses have ranged from Rifaʻa al-Tahtawi's admiration of *la civilisation française* in the mid-nineteenth century CE to Muhammad ʻAbduh's attempt to reform al-Azhar University a few decades later, from Hasan al-Banna's fundamental critique of British educational policy and rejection of secular education to later Muslim scholars who continuously emphasized the importance of seeking Islamic rather than secular knowledge.[2] In other parts of the Islamic world, the positions taken by scholars as well as ordinary Muslims followed similar and, in fact, related patterns.

The issues Muslims struggled with from the Atlantic to the Indian Ocean included questions such as: Do Islamic educational institutions, be they Qur'an schools, madrasas, or universities of the "old" style such as al-Azhar in Cairo, Qarawiyyin in Fez, or Deoband in India, still offer useful knowledge? If not, can a reform of the structure, the teaching methods, or the curriculum help to

---

[*] This is a slightly revised and updated version of an article originally published as "Between Tradition and Reform: The Hadhrami Model of Islamic Learning in 20th-Century Kenya." In *Orientwissenschaftliche Hefte* 22, 2007 (*Bildungsformen und Bildungsträger zwischen Tradition und Moderne*, edited by Stefan Leder and Hanne Schönig, 37–60. I would like to express my gratitude to Professor Burkhard Schnepel, the executive director of the publishing institution, for granting permission to republish in the present volume.

transform the institutions in ways that meet the challenges of the modern world? Can Muslims pursue education in secular institutions without compromising or forfeiting their religious identity? Can a combination of secular and religious disciplines offer a viable alternative to secular educational models that helps to maintain the religious identity of teachers and students? The present study examines some of these questions with reference to the Kenyan coast.

Perhaps a few words are in order to clarify why the case of Kenya, a place usually regarded as "periphery" in studies of the Islamic world, is relevant to the theme outlined above. First, with the introduction of air travel and, more recently, the internet, center–periphery models have arguably become obsolete. Even from a historical perspective, such models are highly questionable, because they tend to overlook how peripheral Muslim communities and their scholars participated in intellectual exchange with other parts of the Islamic world (see Reichmuth 1988; Voll 1994). Second, purported peripheries often had and continue to have their own scholarly centers. The East African coast is a case in point. Over almost a millennium, Muslim inhabitants of the coastal regions and towns, such as Barawa, Lamu, Mombasa, Tanga, and Zanzibar, to mention but a few, have cultivated religious relations with the Hijaz, the Hadhramaut (Yemen), and the Indian subcontinent. These religious links often overlapped with economic networks that connected East African Muslims with other regions across the Indian Ocean.[3]

Another reason that Kenya comes across as Islamic periphery is related to demography. By all accounts, Muslims form a minority in this country. The percentage of the Muslim population is a highly controversial issue, with estimates varying between 8 and 35 percent (see O'Brien 1995, 201). The 2009 census puts the number of Muslims at 4,304,789,[4] equivalent to slightly more than 11 percent of the total population, a result contested by several spokesmen of Muslim organizations. Undisputed, however, is the fact that the Christian majority has dominated the political, economic, and educational life in the country since national independence in 1963. Muslim observers never fail to lament the marginalization of their faith, which is, however, also due to the high degree of ethnic diversity within the Kenyan Muslim community. Ethnic cleavages were not very conducive to creating a sense of unity among Muslims, and neither was the wide array of Islamic denominations, ranging from Sunni Muslims (usually following the Shafi'i and sometimes the Hanafi School of Law) to Twelver Shiites and members of different Isma'ili factions (notably the Nizaris, known as Khojas in India and East Africa, and the Musta'lis, known as Bohoras).[5] Kenyan Muslims thus constitute a heterogeneous community, which seems to be marginalized both within the national context of Kenya and within the international context of the Muslim *umma* (see Seesemann 2005, 2009).

Be that as it may, Kenya does offer a rich Islamic culture, and studying aspects of this culture, such as knowledge practices, provides insights that can further our understanding of Islam not only in Kenya but in other parts of Africa and beyond. The present case study of Islamic knowledge practices in Kenya, and more specifically the Hadhrami tradition of Islamic learning as adopted in the college directed by Sharif Muhammad b. Sa'id al-Baydh (d. 1434/2013) and subsequently by his son Mu'taman in the coastal town of Mambrui, offers an example of how Muslims in a particular locality have responded to the challenges outlined above. Moreover, it invites us to question received wisdom about the alleged decline of so-called traditional Islam. This decline, purportedly caused by its encounter with "modernity" and its confrontation with a more "fundamentalist" brand of Islam, is perhaps not as prevalent as many observers claim. This chapter argues that it is more appropriate to conceive of tradition and reform as two segments of a spectrum that, rather than occupying opposite ends, interact with each other in a dialectic relationship.

The Hadhrami Tradition and the 'Alawiyya in East Africa

For centuries, Muslims from the Hadhramaut region in southern Yemen have played a crucial role in the propagation of Islamic knowledge and the establishment of Islamic educational institutions in many parts of the Indian Ocean world.[6] Hadhrami presence in East Africa goes back at least to the fourteenth century and was from early on accompanied by attempts to spread the teachings and practices of Islam (Martin 1971, 527–28; Sperling 1985, 34).[7] However, the events that shaped the more recent development of Islam in the region took place in the late nineteenth and early twentieth centuries. The rise of European colonial powers paralleled the decline of the Omani Sultanate in Zanzibar. At the same time, a new generation of Muslim scholars emerged, frequently with family roots in the Hadhramaut. As Martin (1971) and more recently Bang (2003) have emphasized, these scholars advocated a stronger orientation toward scripture and were instrumental in the promotion of Islamic knowledge and norms (Martin 1971; Bang 2003, 126–52).[8]

In the coastal region of what is today Kenya, the key representative of this trend was Salih b. 'Alawi (b. 1269/1853–1854 in Singani, Grand Comore; d. 1354/1935), a member of the Comorian branch of the Jamal al-Layl family, who took residence in Lamu in the 1870s.[9] As descendants of the Prophet Muhammad, the Jamal al-Layl belonged to the social class known as *sada* (sing. *sayyid*, a title indicating descent from the Prophet) in the Hadhramaut. Their status as *sada* or *ashraf* (sing. *sharif*, another term used for the Prophet's progeny) facilitated their rise to leadership within the Muslim community. Like other *sada* families, the Jamal al-Layl were part of the *tariqa* 'Alawiyya, a Sufi tradition peculiar to the Hadhramaut that goes back to the seventh/thirteenth century.[10] Being based on both a religious and a blood pedigree (*nasab dini wa-tini*),[11] the 'Alawiyya represents a case of a Sufi order where scholarly and family networks overlap even more than in other orders. Thus, 'Alawi scholars such as Salih Jamal al-Layl maintained both spiritual and genealogical bonds with the homeland of their forefathers, as well as with their relatives throughout the Indian Ocean world.

The career of Habib Salih, as he is popularly known, has been the subject of several academic studies, which have put forward divergent interpretations.[12] There is general agreement that Habib Salih established a school in the poorer, southern part of Lamu town, which subsequently developed into the famous Riyadh mosque-college. He is also credited with the introduction of a new way to celebrate the birthday of the Prophet Muhammad (Arabic, *mawlid*; Kiswahili, *maulidi*). Both the Riyadh and the new type of *maulidi* celebrations were established in the early 1890s and exercised a tremendous influence on the later course of Islam in the area. But here the agreement ends.

Lienhardt (1959), the author of the earliest study, portrays Habib Salih as a newcomer who managed to get the recognition of all sectors of Lamu society, precisely because he was an outsider not involved in the rivalry among competing factions within the Islamic spectrum of the town.[13] El Zein (1974), however, whose monograph is based on extensive field research conducted in the late 1960s, describes Habib Salih as a controversial figure in Lamu, the main reason being that he decided to teach former slaves. This activity, El Zein claims, was extremely unpopular with the so-called *waungwana* (literally, "the civilized," often translated as "patricians")—that is, the social and religious establishment in the town—and subsequently earned him the pejorative nickname "*sharif* of the slaves" (El Zein 1974, 121).[14] Against the fierce opposition of the *waungwana* Habib Salih managed to gain a large following among the recently freed slaves and Hadhrami immigrants of lower social status (merchants, artisans),[15] a success that, according to El Zein's interpretation, was mainly due to the fact that he offered the former slaves access to education and equal participation in the rituals, particularly the *maulidi* (El Zein 1974, 125–27).

In contrast to El Zein, Romero (1997) downplays the slave connection in the career of Habib Salih. Her account suggests that his scholarly standing attracted "some members of the aristocracy" who sent their children to his school, while the role of the slaves was largely restricted to supplying the labor for the construction of the Riyadh mosque-college, which was completed in 1901 (Romero 1997, 99–100).[16] Although Romero does acknowledge the role of Habib Salih as a scholar, teacher, and popularizer of the *maulidi*, she seems to favor another explanation for the rise of the Jamal al-Layl as the most prominent religious family in Lamu. She identifies Habib Salih, and even more his sons and successors, with "saint worship," the writing of amulets, and the use of musical instruments during the *maulidi* celebrations—in short, practices that were attractive to ordinary people but "alien to the Orthodox Sunni" (Romero 1997, 171). Romero links the Jamal al-Layl and the Hadhrami tradition to "popular" Islam as opposed to an undefined "orthodox" Islam, thereby postulating a dichotomy that did not exist at the time, even though it gained wide currency from the 1970s onward.

Romero's assessment differs from the conclusions offered by other authors such as Trimingham (1964) and Pouwels (1987), who connect the growing Hadhrami influence in the late nineteenth century to a wave of religious reform that swept through East Africa at the time (Trimingham 1964, 73; Pouwels 1987, 131; also Pouwels 1987, 145–62, 193–96).[17] However, Pouwels and Trimingham seem to contradict themselves. On the one hand, they portray the Hadhramis as "reformists" who pushed for "stricter adherence to the written law" (Pouwels 1987, 195); on the other, they associate Habib Salih's *maulidi* with an "alternative Islam" for the "downtrodden" (Pouwels 1987, 195) and describe the celebrations as a merger of Islamic and "traditional African" elements (Trimingham 1964, 79). These apparent contradictions are perhaps best resolved by Bang (2003), who argues that the *maulidi* celebrations and the drive toward "scriptural Islam" were in fact two sides of the same coin. Both represented attempts by Hadhrami scholars to achieve greater adherence to Islamic norms and practices (Bang 2003, chapter 7).[18]

The spread of Islamic knowledge was arguably the most important element in these attempts. While the context of Lamu society certainly influenced the activities of Habib Salih as a teacher, his educational endeavor is primarily a reflection of developments in the wider Hadhrami context.[19] The structure and curriculum of Habib Salih's Riyadh mosque-college closely followed the pattern of a mosque-college of the same name in the town of Say'un in the Wadi Hadhramaut. The latter was founded in the year 1296/1878–1879 by 'Ali b. Muhammad al-Habshi (b. 1259/1843, d. 1333/1915), who was widely considered as the *qutb* ("pole") of the 'Alawiyya at the time.[20] Al-Habshi's college was the first among similar institutions established in late-nineteenth-century Hadhramaut and known as *arbita* (plural of *ribat*). According to Freitag (1999, 171), the *arbita* put a greater emphasis on the study of Shafi'i *fiqh* in the curriculum, whereas earlier institutions focused more on theology and mysticism (*tasawwuf*).

However, the *arbita* also differed in other respects from earlier institutions of higher Islamic learning. In previous times, teaching typically took place in the so-called *halaqa* (literally, "circle"; pl. *halaqat*) (Freitag 1999, 171), a system in which the students sit in a circle around their master, who gives lectures or reads to them from a scholarly work. The students who attended *halaqat* came almost exclusively from families representing the religious and political elites. Along the

Swahili coast, where the same system prevailed until the beginning of the twentieth century, the teachers used to read the Arabic text first and then translate the text and give further explanations in Kiswahili.

The Ribat al-Riyadh in Say'un was the first Hadhrami institution to introduce a formalized curriculum. Learning now took place in a classroom setting with a structured syllabus, where a fixed amount of time was assigned to each field of study.[21] Although the question as to whether these educational reforms deserve to be called a success has given rise to some controversy,[22] the *arbita* clearly signal a new orientation with regard to higher Islamic learning in the Hadhramaut and in regions with a Hadhrami diaspora, such as Lamu. Compared to the *halaqa* system, the new institutions in Say'un, Tarim, Ghayl Ba Wazir, and Lamu provided easier access to advanced Islamic knowledge and were able to accommodate larger groups of students from different social backgrounds who received a more standardized training.

The fact that Habib Salih modeled his Ribat al-Riyadh on the mosque-college of 'Ali al-Habshi is not only indicative of the strong orientation toward the homeland among the descendants of Hadhrami migrants, but also reflects the unique relationship between these two scholars, who never met each other in person. In the words of a great-grandson of Habib Salih, the two shared a "spiritual companionship" (*suhba ruhiyya*) that enabled them to communicate without seeing each other (Badawi 1410/1989, 4–25). In other words, Habib Salih perceived himself as following in the footsteps of 'Ali al-Habshi, be it with regard to his *ribat*, the way he celebrated the *maulidi*, or any other of his religious activities.

Yet Habib Salih's college was more than the mere reproduction of the Hadhrami model in a different place. Within the context of Lamu, and the East African coast as a whole, the Ribat al-Riyadh definitely ushered in a new era in the history of Islamic education. The introduction of a more structured way of teaching advanced Islamic knowledge was an important innovation, and it paved the way for a process of educational formalization that continued well into the twentieth century, up to the point where primary education lasted for five years, and intermediate and secondary education three years, respectively (Khitamy 1995, 272).[23] More importantly, the Riyadh mosque-college signaled a break with the elitist approach of the *halaqa* model, because it opened its doors to social groups that were previously excluded from access to higher Islamic knowledge.[24] For the first time, higher Islamic education became available to people from the lower sections of Lamu society. The popularization of Islamic knowledge, whether through formal instruction or through participation in the *maulidi* celebrations, is probably the greatest achievement of Habib Salih, and also the most important feature of the Hadhrami tradition in East Africa.

Competing Knowledge Practices and Models of Education

While the Ribat al-Riyadh definitely constituted a milestone in the development of Islamic education in East Africa as a whole, the colonial period brought new educational challenges to the Muslim community in Kenya. From the second decade of the twentieth century onward, the British authorities intensified their efforts to establish modern schools. In this endeavor they cooperated closely with Christian missions, creating a situation where access to education became synonymous with visiting a Christian school.[25] As in other European colonies with a large Muslim population in Africa, the initial Muslim responses to the new education system ranged from indifference to outright rejection. The only notable exception was the Indian Khoja Isma'ili community, which seized the new opportunities from the beginning and set up its own network of modern schools throughout Kenya.[26] However, schools run by the missions were met with deep suspicion among all Muslims, because they thought of the schools as turning their children into "unbelievers."[27] Some Sunni Muslims were less suspicious to modern education as offered in government-run institutions.

But even where Muslims were open to the idea of visiting a government school, they encountered another difficulty, because British colonial policy was based on a distinction between races. In the field of education (as in other areas) priority was given to Europeans, followed by Indians and Arabs.[28] Even though the latter were still relatively well off compared to the so-called natives or Africans, they complained bitterly about what they perceived as their deliberate marginalization in the educational sector.[29] Those who fell into the category of natives were virtually excluded from access to quality education in government schools. These factors created a situation in which most Muslim parents continued to send their children to Qur'an schools and madrasas only, with the consequence that non-Muslims got off to a much better start when Kenya became independent in 1963.[30]

Only in a few instances did Muslim scholars speak out in favor of modern education, the most prominent example being Shaykh al-Amin b. 'Ali al-Mazru'i (b. 1309/1891, d. 1366/1947).[31] He was one of the first East African Muslims to propagate the ideas of the Egyptian Salafiyya movement and became a strong advocate of the need for educational reform in the 1930s. Although highly critical of both colonial and mission schools, al-Mazru'i managed to persuade many Muslim parents that Western education was not a danger for Islamic culture as long as it was assured that the children receive a sound religious instruction as well (Elmasri 1987, 230). However, Shaykh al-Amin's suggestions to improve the education of Muslims did not bear fruit during his lifetime.[32] The few attempts to add secular subjects to the religious curriculum in certain Islamic schools of Mombasa were short-lived, as was the Mombasa Institute of Muslim Education, which was turned into a purely secular school in 1947, only a few years after its establishment (O'Brien 1995, 206; Salim 1987, 70).[33]

Throughout the colonial period, opposition to Western education remained particularly strong among the representatives of the Hadhrami tradition of learning.[34] Their rejection of modern schools continued well into the postcolonial era, although 'Abd al-Rahman b. Ahmad al-Badawi, a grandson of Habib Salih better known under the name Sharif Khitamy (d. 1425/2004), taught Islamic subjects at the Mombasa Institute of Muslim Education in the mid-1940s and later sent his own sons to government schools in Mombasa. On their occasional visits to Lamu, however, his sons still felt the negative attitude toward secular schooling when their classmates publicly denounced them as *kuffar* (unbelievers) simply because they attended a modern school (personal communication, Muhdhar Khitamy, Mombasa, July 2005).

Whereas secular education as introduced in the colonial period posed a challenge to the Muslim community in general, the increasing influence of reform-oriented Muslim scholars from the early 1970s onward came as a particular threat to the guardians of the Hadhrami tradition. The emergence of the "new ulama," as Bakari (1995) has called them, as well as the spread of new Islamic knowledge practices and models of learning had the potential to undermine the religious authority of the *sada* and other scholars affiliated with the Hadhrami network. At that time, the main promoter of reformist ideas derived from the Salafiyya in Egypt and the Wahhabiyya in Saudi Arabia was Abdallah Saleh Farsy ('Abdallah Salih al-Farisi, b. 1330/1912, d. 1403/1982). Coming from a family with Omani roots, Farsy spent almost two decades in Zanzibari government service before leaving the island a few years after the 1964 revolution to take residence in Mombasa. In 1969, he was appointed Chief Kadhi of Kenya, an office he held until the early 1980s. Although not a teacher himself, Farsy was able to inspire young urban-based Muslims, some of whom went to pursue a higher religious education abroad (Bakari 1995, 182). On their return from countries such as Saudi Arabia, Egypt, and Sudan, many of the young, reform-minded scholars entered the educational sector. Since the 1980s, madrasas have mushroomed along the coast and in many Kenyan cities, often with financial support from Saudi Arabia or from so-called philanthropists from the Gulf States.[35]

The activities of the new generation of Muslim scholars had several important effects. First, their educational enterprises focused less on the teaching of Arabic, which remained prominent in the institutions linked to the Hadhrami network. Instead, they made Kiswahili the medium of instruction, relegating Arabic to a minor role. The growing body of Islamic literature in Kiswahili reflected the same tendency toward the "Swahilization" of religious knowledge.[36]

Following the example of Shaykh al-Amin al-Mazru'i, the first Muslim intellectual to publish widely in Kiswahili, Abdallah Saleh Farsy and some of his students became prolific writers. As a result, religious ideas left the classrooms and mosque circles and became easily accessible to the average Muslim (see Salim 1987, 69). This, in turn, significantly reduced the dependence of ordinary Muslims on the former guardians of Islamic knowledge, a development captured in Farsy's famous dictum, "it is not necessary to follow a Sheikh or a Sharif" (quoted in Lacunza-Balda 1997, 114).

In addition, the curriculum offered in the newly established madrasas differed from the one taught in the Hadhrami institutions. Some subjects that figured prominently in the Hadhrami syllabus, such as *maulidi* poetry, Sufism, and advanced jurisprudence, were not even mentioned in the schools run by the reform-oriented new ulama. Although most of these madrasas provided education on an intermediate level, a few institutions of higher learning were designed to produce graduates who could pursue their studies at the university level in Saudi Arabia, Egypt, or elsewhere in the Arab world.[37] The new intermediate madrasas closed the gap between higher Islamic learning and basic Qur'anic education and thus enabled the reformists to reach new and larger audiences, thereby reinforcing the effect of the dissemination of Islamic literature in Kiswahili. The proliferation of such schools especially in the 1980s and 1990s further undermined the position of the Hadhrami scholars as the sole transmitters of Islamic learning.

In some instances, the restructuring of the madrasa curriculum was not limited to dropping a few traditional disciplines. Since the 1980s, several Kenyan graduates of Islamic universities abroad have started to set up a new type of Islamic educational institutions where secular subjects were added to the curriculum. The declared aim of the so-called integrated system was to impart marketable skills to a future Muslim elite, who would be able to compete with non-Muslims in the professional sphere while maintaining a strong Islamic identity.[38] Most schools that adopted this system require the students to attend morning and afternoon lessons to cover the full range of both the Islamic and the secular disciplines. Although the long-term impact of the integrated curriculum remains to be seen, this school type seems to have the potential to emerge as a viable response to some of the educational challenges facing the Muslim community in Kenya (see Seesemann 2006b).

It was not only the rapid development of the educational projects initiated by the new ulama that put the *sada* on the defensive. The former missed no opportunity to denounce some of the religious rituals associated with the 'Alawiyya as "reprehensible innovations" (Kiswahili, *bidaa*; from Arabic, *bid'a*)—that is, beliefs or practices that are not endorsed by the Qur'an or the

Sunna (Bakari 1995, 181–85). In particular, they took offense at the *maulidi* celebrations and the visits to the graves of saintly persons, two characteristic features of the Hadhrami tradition in East Africa and elsewhere. Against such allegedly "un-Islamic" practices, the advocates of Islamic reform promoted their own understanding of Islam, which they claimed to be more authentic and occasionally also more "modern" than the "traditional" version of Islam as represented by the Hadhrami scholars.[39]

At first sight, reformist discourse seems to have gained the upper hand in the Muslim public sphere of Kenya, relegating the Hadhrami tradition, which had started into the twentieth century as an influential movement of religious education and reform, to a marginal role. The new ulama are more media savvy; they have greater resources and a stronger presence in the public sphere. It is perhaps more than a coincidence that some academic observers echo the *bidaa* theme of the reformers. So-called Swahili Islam, which, although ill defined, bears many traits characteristic of the Hadhrami tradition, appears as "popular religion" or, in more recent academic parlance, as "local Islam."[40] Both discourses grant the reformists the privilege to speak for "orthodox" Islam (whatever one may understand by "*orthodox*"); both tend to depict "popular Islam" as a relic of a superstitious past, and both suggest that the tide has ultimately turned against the Hadhrami tradition.[41]

However, as the next section shows, representatives of the Hadhrami network were able to respond to the challenges of Islamic reformism and modern education, and some have done so with remarkable success. Changes in Islamic knowledge practices provided the key to the reassertion of the Hadhrami tradition of Islamic learning and the related beliefs and practices.

Mambrui: The Renewal of Tradition

Probably the most spirited reaction to the reformist challenge came from Mambrui, a small town located on the Indian Ocean coast, about one hundred miles north of Mombasa. The initiator of this response was Sharif Muhammad b. Saʿid al-Baydh (b. 1361/1942, d. 1434/2013), the scion of another *sada* family with Hadhrami roots. In many ways the history of this family mirrors the eventful development of Islam and education in coastal Kenya.

The first member of the al-Baydh clan to live in what is today Kenya was Sharif Muhammad's grandfather, ʿAbdallah b. Saʿid al-Baydh, whose father, Saʿid b. Salim, had emigrated from the South Arabian town of Shihr to Zanzibar in the middle of the nineteenth century.[42] While in Zanzibar, Saʿid b. Salim married a woman from Malindi, where ʿAbdallah was born in 1278/1861–1862. As a young man, ʿAbdallah traveled to the homeland of his forefathers to study, following a common practice among Hadhrami migrants. One of his teachers there was ʿAli

Muhammad al-Habshi in Say'un. According to Sharif Muhammad's account, it was 'Ali al-Habshi who told 'Abdallah about Habib Salih and his activities in Lamu.[43] In 1311/1893, when 'Abdallah returned to East Africa, 'Ali al-Habshi supplied him with a letter to Habib Salih, allowing the latter to perform the *maulidi* on the last Thursday of the lunar month of Rabi' al-Awwal, as had been the practice in the *ribat* of Say'un since 1306/1888.

From 1328/1910 onward, the *maulidi* performance in Say'un, Lamu, and other places under al-Habshi's influence was based on a work composed by al-Habshi under the title *Simt al-durar fi akhbar mawlid sayyid al-bashar*.[44] A few years later, 'Ali al-Habshi ordered Habib Salih to authorize 'Abdallah al-Baydh to perform his own *maulidi* ceremony in either Mambrui or Malindi. 'Abdallah, who had in the meantime married one of Habib Salih's daughters, decided to take residence in Mambrui. He held his first *maulidi* celebration there in 1333/1915 and called his own religious center al-Riyadh, emulating the example of Lamu and Say'un.

After 'Abdallah al-Baydh passed away in 1344/1925–1926, his adolescent sons Sa'id (b. 1330/1912) and 'Ali went to Lamu to stay with their maternal grandfather, Habib Salih. On the completion of his studies, Sharif Sa'id b. 'Abdallah married a daughter of Ahmad al-Badawi b. Habib Salih and opened a wholesale business in Lamu. In addition to his career as a trader, Sharif Sa'id followed in his father's footsteps and devoted much of his time to increasing the religious reputation of Mambrui. In 1351/1931–1932, he built a new mosque in Mambrui, and eleven years later (in 1362/1943), he founded his own school, which he called Madrasat al-Nur. According to his anonymous biographer, Sharif Sa'id was an indefatigable traveler and teacher who constantly worked for the spread of Islam and Islamic knowledge, be it in his hometown or in Uganda, where he is said to have converted thousands of people to Islam and coordinated the establishment of many mosques and madrasas (*Tarekhe ya Sharif Said al-Beidh* n.d.).

Throughout the 1940s, the Madrasat al-Nur seems to have operated as a branch of the Riyadh mosque-college in Lamu. In 1949, however, a rift occurred between 'Aydarus b. Habib Salih, the head of the Riyadh at the time, and the Comorian community on the island.[45] This resulted in the exodus of most Comorian scholars, and several of them joined the Madrasat al-Nur as teachers. Mambrui's status as a center of Islamic learning received a boost in 1382/1962, when Sharif Sa'id decided to turn his madrasa into a full-fledged boarding school with a standardized curriculum and formal classes. He involved the local people in the planning and initiated the construction of a new school building, which was completed shortly before his death in 1383/1963.

The first principal of the new Madrasat al-Nur was Sharif Sa'id al-Baydh's son Muhammad, popularly known as Ustadh Muhammad. According to his own account, he ran the school with great success for more than twenty years, producing many graduates who became teachers, preachers, and imams. In the mid-1980s, however, a conflict broke out over the religious orientation of the college. Ustadh Muhammad attributed the discord to what he described as the gradual infiltration of the school by "Wahhabi" forces.[46] Whatever the case, the conflict ended with Ustadh Muhammad's withdrawal from the Madrasat al-Nur. With the financial support from Hadhrami donors he was able to acquire a piece of land adjacent to the school and the Riyadh mosque. In 1406/1986, he established an independent boarding school, the Madrasat al-Ghanna' al-Islamiyya.

From the outset, Muhammad b. Sa'id al-Baydh wanted the school to be different from others. Even though he thought the Madrasat al-Nur had provided several generations of students with a sound religious education, his earlier teaching experience left him unsatisfied with the efficiency and the speed of learning, especially at the advanced level. Higher Islamic education in Hadhrami institutions such as the Riyadh in Lamu usually consisted of studying a fixed number of scholarly works in Arabic that cover the relevant Islamic disciplines, including Arabic grammar, rhetoric and literature, hadith (Prophetic traditions), *fiqh* (jurisprudence), *tawhid* (theology), *tafsir* (Qur'an interpretation), and *tasawwuf* (mysticism) (see Khitamy 1995). Typically the teacher would read sections from the book in the classroom while the students take notes or, depending on the availability of books, follow the text in their own copies. In this system the teacher dictates the speed of learning, but most instructors tend to adapt to the pace of the slower students rather than the advanced ones. According to Ustadh Muhammad, progress was often delayed as a result.

These observations made Ustadh Muhammad think of possible alternatives. He found his solution in a system he called "individual reading" (*qira'a fardiyya*). Here, the student is supposed to read a fixed set of Arabic books covering all relevant disciplines. Instead of studying the texts in a group led by the teacher, each student reads the assigned books individually and at his own pace. Classes would still meet for certain subjects, including some that are not directly religious, such as geography, history, mathematics, and logic. But the more the student advances, the more he does his assignments on an individual basis. Twice a day the students report to Ustadh Muhammad or one of his assistants, who are either senior students or employed teachers. In these meetings each student reads portions from his text aloud in front of the instructor and translates selected phrases into Kiswahili. The instructor carefully follows how the student renders the text and corrects him if necessary. In this manner the students of al-Ghanna' al-Islamiyya proceed over a period of up to eight years, covering a wide range of Arabic books from all relevant Islamic disciplines.[47]

Although this system gave the students the freedom to study at their own pace and to determine to some extent the order in which they study the assigned books, the syllabus followed a clear and coherent structure. Ustadh Muhammad divided the complete curriculum into eight parts that are in turn divided into a total of 112 modules based on a book or lectures in any given subject. Coupled with a rigid time management, where the first period of study starts before sunrise right after *fajr* prayer, the individual reading method has apparently led to a significant increase in the speed of learning.

It may appear as an irony that the new style of instruction partly draws on teaching methods used in the Hadhramaut before the establishment of the *arbita* in the late nineteenth century CE. In fact, as Freitag (1999, 170) argues, the primary novelty of the *ribat* lay in the shift from individualized instruction to structured group instruction. The system introduced by Ustadh Muhammad constitutes a synthesis of previous and more recent educational methods, as it is tailored to accommodate the individual needs and capacities of the students while it prescribes a meticulous program of studies. Judging from my encounters with students at al-Ghanna' al-Islamiyya, the new system was tremendously efficient. The senior students were fluent in Arabic and had an impressive command of a wide variety of Islamic subjects. In addition to the more classical texts in the Islamic sciences, they are familiar with some of the most recent products of Muslim scholarship in the Middle East.

Another significant feature of Ustadh Muhammad's school is the heterogeneous student population. Since its inception, al-Ghanna' al-Islamiyya has been a boarding school, and it has usually accommodated between sixty and one hundred students at a time, with Kenyans constituting the majority. But the school has also attracted students from Somalia, Uganda, Tanzania, Malawi, and even as far as Burundi. On the completion of their studies in Mambrui, most graduates have established their own madrasas in the towns or villages of their origin, while others have started careers as imams and preachers. In any case, they played a crucial role in the creation and expansion of a new religious network coordinated by Ustadh Muhammad.

Among those Muslims who do not identify with the reformist ideas as advocated by the new ulama, the Madrasat al-Ghanna' al-Islamiyya has become synonymous with the renewal of the Hadhrami tradition of learning in East Africa. Ustadh Muhammad himself proudly referred to Mambrui as al-Manba' al-Rawwi, Arabic for "the source that quenches the thirst" (i.e., the thirst for knowledge). Although it is not the proper etymology of the name Mambrui, this epithet constitutes a wordplay that describes the small town on the Indian Ocean as a paragon of the promotion and transmission of Islamic knowledge. As such, it reveals Ustadh Muhammad's self-perception as someone who dedicated his life to the service of Islamic knowledge. Similarly, the fact that he used the title *ustadh* ("professor"; a common way to address a scholar in Arabic) instead of *sharif* indicates that he preferred his religious authority to be based on knowledge rather than on his descent from the Prophet Muhammad.

This is not to say that Muhammad b. Saʿid al-Baydh would rather have dispensed with the hereditary authority of the *sada*. But the importance he accorded to learning and knowledge clearly indicated a shift in emphasis, and conceivably also a response to the severe criticism the *sada* received from representatives of the reformist faction, such as Abdallah Saleh Farsy quoted above. Given Ustadh Muhammad's emphasis on knowledge as the proper source of religious authority and the innovative potential of his educational methods, it is perhaps not entirely accurate to describe him as "a pillar of traditionalism," as Mohamed Bakari (1995, 187) has suggested.[48] The attribute "traditionalist" only applies to Muhammad b. Saʿid al-Baydh with respect to his negative attitude toward secular education and to his staunch commitment to the traditional canon of Hadhrami scholarship. For his educational purposes, which were designed to train future madrasa teachers, preachers, and imams, secular schools only distract the students from achieving their aim. Ustadh Muhammad's reservations even included the more recent integrated schools that combine the teaching of Islamic and secular subjects. Although he claimed that he did not have objections "in principle," he maintained that, "in such schools the students lean more towards the worldly subjects than the religious ones. As long as the religious side is stronger than the worldly one, I have no objection. But this is usually not the case."[49] This attitude, which reflects the rejection of secular education among Muslims during the colonial period, is perhaps the most "traditional" aspect of Ustadh Muhammad's approach.

As far as the curriculum of al-Ghanna' al-Islamiyya is concerned, the strong Hadhrami component does not mean that the school has to be qualified as "traditional." During his frequent and extensive travels to Saudi Arabia and the Gulf states, Ustadh Muhammad has been busy making new acquisitions for his large library. He remained connected with the most recent trends in Islamic scholarship, and whenever he came across new books he believed to be useful, he encouraged his students to read them and occasionally makes a new work part of the syllabus. A good example is *al-Mawsuʿa al-Yusufiyya*, a massive compendium of scholarly arguments in support of Sufism by a contemporary Syrian author (Muhammad 1418/1998). According to Ustadh Muhammad, the study of this work helped his students respond to the arguments of the "*takfiriyyun*" ("those who call other Muslims unbelievers"). The latter term is a reference to reformists who have adopted the Wahhabi practice of *takfir*—that is, accusing other Muslims of unbelief, usually because of their alleged contravention of the principles of monotheism.

The Madrasat al-Ghanna' al-Islamiyya of Muhammad b. Saʿid al-Baydh can be considered an example of a dynamic and flexible response—and not a very traditional one for that matter—to the rise of reformist tendencies among Kenyan Muslims. His successful attempt to restructure Islamic knowledge practices, and higher learning in particular, was largely motivated by the hope to curb the influence of the new ulama through the promotion of a different religious agenda. Although secular education appears to be almost an anathema in Mambrui, Ustadh Muhammad acknowledged the importance of modern technology, and he could count on the support and donations from Muslim professionals and businessmen with successful careers in the modern sector. But he saw his mission as carrying the torch of a renewed Hadhrami tradition of learning and passing it on to future generations. Under the direction of his son, Mu'taman al-Baydh, the educational network along with its knowledge practices continues to thrive. As I was able to learn on a follow-up visit in early 2015, about nine years after my first visit and two years after Ustadh Muhammad's passing, more than sixty Muslim schools in Kenya, as well as others in neighboring Uganda and Tanzania, have adopted the curriculum first developed and successfully tested in Mambrui.

Conclusion

The study of the Madrasat al-Ghanna' al-Islamiyya can teach us several lessons. First and foremost, it disproves the conventional view that the purportedly traditional Islam associated with Hadhrami scholarship and the 'Alawiyya is on the way out. The analysis in this chapter also demonstrates that it is seriously misleading to reduce the contemporary Hadhrami tradition to a "local" or "popular" expression of Islam. The relative success of the educational enterprises run by reformist scholars, combined with the apparent dominance of the new ulama in the public sphere, might suggest otherwise, but a closer look behind the scenes reveals that the Hadhrami tradition of learning has retained much of its intellectual vigor without losing its popular appeal.

This is not to assert that everything is just as it used to be. Islamic education as taught in institutions linked to the Hadhrami network over the last 150 years has been subject to significant changes. The course of Hadhrami educational history seems to follow a cyclical pattern, in which periods of decline alternate with times of revival. In other words, a particular tradition can become subject to reform, which in turn becomes susceptible to future revisions.[50] The introduction of individual reading as a teaching method by Muhammad b. Sa'id al-Baydh is a case in point. Whereas the *arbita* of late-nineteenth-century Hadhramaut replaced individualized instruction with structured learning to improve the efficiency of learning, Ustadh Muhammad turned to a variation of the very same and presumably outdated method to bring about an educational renewal.

The dialectic of tradition and reform also manifests itself in other facets of the trajectory of Hadhrami scholarship and institutions in Kenya. In the late nineteenth century, it was the 'Alawiyya led by Habib Salih that questioned and undermined the religious authority of the *waungwana*, the local elites at the time. One century later, the Kenyan representatives of the 'Alawiyya, long established as local elites in their own right, were themselves confronted with a challenge to their authority, when the new ulama claimed the right to define authentic Islam and reached out to new and larger audiences among the Muslims of Kenya.

Interestingly, in his response to the new challenge, Ustadh Muhammad seems to have borrowed certain elements from the reformist model. For instance, his educational efforts aim to fill the gap between basic and higher Islamic education by producing future teachers of an intermediate madrasa curriculum. In addition, by emphasizing a high standard of Islamic learning as the basis of religious authority, rather than solely relying on his rank as a *sharif*, Ustadh Muhammad tried to reassert the religious legitimacy of Hadhrami scholarship. This strategy was at least partly successful in countering the attempts of the new ulama to undermine Hadhrami claims to religious leadership. The Madrasat al-Ghanna' al-Islamiyya constitutes a new synthesis of Hadhrami elements and transnational modes of Islamic expression, a synthesis that defies simple identification with either tradition or reform.

NOTES

1. In the aftermath of the September 11 attacks at the threshold of the twenty-first century, Islamic schools received much attention in the media and Western security circles. However, the post-9/11 developments are beyond the scope of the present chapter, even though they had a lasting effect on Islamic educational institutions throughout the world. See Moosa (2015).

2. For the nineteenth century, see Mitchell (1988, especially chapter 3); for the twentieth century, see Starrett (1998).

3. See the contributions to Loimeier and Seesemann (2006) for details.

4. The complete census reports are available through the internet site of the Kenya National Bureau of Statistics, http://www.knbs.or.ke (last accessed September 2, 2015). The data on religious affiliation are included in volume 2.

5. Crozon (1998) gives a good impression of the diversity within the Muslim community in Kenya. For the Shiite denominations and other Indian Muslims, see Salvadori (1983).

6. See the contributions to Freitag and Clarence-Smith (1997) for a comprehensive overview of Hadhrami activities in the Indian Ocean region.

7. The religious activities of Hadhrami families in the Lamu archipelago from 1600 onward are briefly discussed in Pouwels (2000, 261). Rich documentation can also be found in Becker (1911). On the history of Islam in East Africa to 1900 in general, see Pouwels (1987) and Trimingham (1964).

8. Of course, we should avoid jumping to the conclusion that Muslims paid little attention to scripture or to religious norms before the arrival of this new generation of Hadhrami scholars. Nonetheless, their activities provided a new impetus to Islamic scholarship and education. They also introduced a wider range of religious texts, especially in Sufism and jurisprudence.

9. On the Jamal al-Layl see Bang (2003, 25–27). A brief account of the family in Kenya, mainly based on a compilation of secondary sources, is given by Le Guennec-Coppens (1979).

10. A concise and reliable account of 'Alawiyya history and doctrines is offered by Bang (2003, 12–34). See also Peskes (2005, 173–87).

11. According to 'Alawi teachings, this Sufi order relies on two chains of transmission: One passes through the bloodline back to the Prophet Muhammad and the other, spiritual chain is connected to the Moroccan Shu'ayb Abu Madyan (d. 1197), who also figures as the *shaykh* of the founder of the Shadhiliyya Sufi order.

12. It should not go unmentioned that my informants in the field, most eminently Sharif Khitamy, one of Habib Salih's grandsons, and Muhammad b. Sa'id al-Baydh (on him more below), raised strong objections to the accounts given by academics so far. In particular, they accuse Abdul Hamid El Zein of misinformation and gross distortion of facts (see also Ahmed 1995, 163; Romero 1997, 168; Badawi 1410/1989, 19 n. 1). A history of Habib Salih that does justice to the perspective of his descendants and followers remains to be written. A good point of departure for such an endeavor is Badawi (1410/1989).

13. Contrary to what the title of Lienhardt's study promises, he does not offer an in-depth analysis of the college's social background.

14. See also the detailed account in El Zein (1974, chapter 3).

15. Social stratification is rather pronounced among Hadhramis, both in southern Yemen and in the diaspora. See Bujra (1971) for details.

16. Cf. the short but pointed critique of El Zein and Romero by Rohlinger (2005, 12–13).

17. For a critical discussion see Seesemann (2006a).

18. Bang (2003, 130) explains that "outward manifestations [of the 'Alawiyya; i.e., *maulidi* celebrations, *dhikr* sessions, grave visitations, etc.] spread *alongside* [author's emphasis] with the intellectual tradition—the ideas, principles, doctrines and tenets—in which the activities . . . were rooted."

19. This is not to suggest that Habib Salih's school was a seamless implantation of the Hadhrami model in a different environment. Local conditions in Lamu and transformations related to the end of slavery also shaped the new educational institution considerably, as did the expectations of Habib Salih's followers.

20. On him Ahmed (1995); Freitag (1999). My transliteration of this name follows East African usage. In the literature on Yemen, the name commonly appears as al-Hibshi.

21. According to Freitag (1999), the standard period of study in the *ribat* of Tarim, established in 1305/1887, was four years. It should not go unmentioned that she expresses serious reservations about the quality of education offered in the *arbita*, comparing the college in Tarim to a "secondary school" (Freitag 1999, 173).

22. Authors with an 'Alawi background used to refer to the reforms in terms of a *nahdha* ("renaissance"), while Freitag comes to the conclusion that they were rather modest. Opponents of the 'Alawiyya are of the opinion that the alleged reforms failed to address the educational crisis. For details, see Freitag (1999).

23. The sources available to me do not state when this system was introduced. While Freitag's account (1999, 173) seems to imply that the period of study was eleven years from the outset, Lienhardt's description (1959, 237) does not suggest that there was a high degree of formalization in 1958, the time of his visit.

24. As Bang (2003, 146) put it, "what was taught in al-Riyadh college in Lamu was not a revolutionary 'counter-culture', designed to cause social upheaval. . . . What was revolutionary was that it offered a path to religious authority that completely bypassed the traditional patricians."

25. See the detailed account in Bogonko (1992, chapters 3 and 4). See also Sheffield (1973, 8–12, 17–25), who describes the relationship between the British colonial government and the mission schools as "symbiotic" (Sheffield 1973, 21).

26. See the chronology of Isma'ili educational institutions in Bogonko (1992, 13–14).

27. On Muslim resistance to Western education in Kenya, see Eisemon (1988, chapter 3, especially 43–44). See also Bogonko (1992, 13–16). It should be noted that such opposition was in no way limited to Muslims; see Bogonko (1992, 42–44).

28. This comes out clearly in a confidential colonial report kept in the Public Record Office London. See PRO BW 90/71, Report by the Fact-Finding Mission to Study Muslim Education in East Africa, n.d. (ca. 1957). The Kenya Education Department compiled different syllabi for European schools, Arab and Asian schools, and African schools.

29. See, for instance, PRO BW 90/101, Sir Bernard Reilly's Report on Arab Problems in Kenya and Zanzibar, 1948, 4–5. The racial distinction, while working relatively well with Europeans and Indians, posed significant problems with regard to the categories Arab and African. Those among the coastal population who referred to themselves as Swahili defied clear identification with either group. As the British went ahead and enforced their artificial distinction, several established families within the Muslim community of the coast were excluded from the educational benefits accorded to Indian and Arab Muslims.

30. This is also emphasized by Bogonko (1992, 15).

31. On al-Mazru'i, perhaps the most celebrated Muslim intellectual in East Africa of his time, see Elmasri (1987) and Salim (1987).

32. He was also a "champion of women's education" (Elmasri 1987, 234), an idea that was not met with enthusiasm by many of his contemporaries (see Salim 1987, 67).

33. The college exists up the present day as the Mombasa Polytechnic.

34. See Romero (1997, 177–78), with particular reference to Ahmad al-Badawi Jamal al-Layl, the eldest son of Habib Salih who died in 1939, only four years after his father.

35. On the boom of Islamic schools in rural areas, see Sperling (1993). As Sperling points out, there was frequently a particular agenda connected with the donations (Sperling 1993, 206–7).

36. For details, see Lacunza-Balda (1997). I have discussed the irony of this development elsewhere (Seesemann (2006a, 242–46).

37. See Kahumbi (1995, 330–32). Higher Islamic learning with a reformist orientation and an emphasis on a good command of Arabic is offered in a few institutions in Nairobi and Mombasa, the most prominent being the Islamic Institute at Kisauni.

38. Personal communication, Sharif Hussein al-Baydh, Malindi, August 2003. Sharif Hussein, a member of a well-known *sada* family, has been involved in the establishment of an integrated school in Malindi. I borrow the expression "marketable skills" from Robert Launay (1992, 94), whose account of education in northern Ivory Cost bears considerable resemblance to coastal Kenya (see Launay 1992, chapter 4).

39. See Kresse (2003), who frames his analysis of reformist thought in terms of "enlightenment."

40. A recent example of the rather simplistic dichotomy local or popular Islam versus orthodoxy is Kim (2004, see in particular chapter 3). See the detailed discussion of terminological and conceptual questions in Seesemann (2006a).

41. Cf. Kresse's remarks on the dialectics of reform in East Africa (2006, 217); see also Kresse (2006, 211) for a critique of the concept of Swahili Islam.
42. This paragraph is based on an interview with Muhammad b. Saʻid b. ʻAbdallah al-Baydh that I recorded in Mambrui on December 25, 2005.
43. "Whenever Habib ʻAli talked about the East African coast, he mentioned Habib Salih" (Muhammad b. Saʻid al-Baydh, interview, Mambrui, December 25, 2005).
44. On the adoption of *Simt al-durar* as the principle *maulidi* text in Kenya, see Badawi (1410/1989, 19); Lienhardt (1959, 233–34); El Zein (1974, 136–37); Bang (2003, 149).
45. See Romero (1997, 171–72) (but note the inaccuracies in her account of the al-Baydh family); cf. El Zein (1974, 161). Muhammad b. Saʻid al-Baydh referred to the incident as "a small *fitna*" (personal communication, Mambrui, December 2005).
46. According to Ustadh Muhammad's version, the Wahhabis took advantage of the statutes of the madrasa, which affirmed every Muslim's right to join the school as a student or a teacher. Over time more and more Wahhabis secretly joined the teaching staff, until they claimed to hold the majority (interview, Mambrui, December 25, 2005).
47. The disciplines include Qur'anic sciences (recitation, exegesis), hadith, the life of the Prophet Muhammad and his companions, Arabic language (including grammar, calligraphy, and composition), rhetoric, classical Arabic literature (including pre-Islamic poetry and belles lettres), *fiqh* with a focus on the Shafiʻi School of Law, *tawhid*, *akhlaq* (ethics), Sufism, and *maulidi* poetry.
48. See also his portrayal of Ustadh Muhammad's madrasa (Bakari 1995, 187–88).
49. Interview, Mambrui, December 25, 2005.
50. Cf. Kresse (2006, 217). See also Loimeier (2010) for an extensive discussion of similar dynamics in Senegal and Tanzania.

REFERENCES

Ahmed, A. A. 1995. "The Impact of Hadrami Scholarship on Kenyan Islam." In *Islam in Kenya*, edited by Mohamed Bakari and Saad S. Yahya, 158–67. Nairobi: MEWA.
Badawi, Salih Muhammad ʻAli [known as Shaykh Ba Hasan]. 1410/1989. *al-Riyadh bayna madhihi wa-hadhirihi*. Copy in the archival collection Islam in Africa, Bayreuth University, Germany.
Bakari, Mohamed. 1995. "The New ʻUlama in Kenya." In *Islam in Kenya*, edited by Mohamed Bakari and Saad S. Yahya, 168–95. Nairobi: MEWA.
Bang, Anne K. 2003. *Sufis and Scholars of the Sea: Family Networks in East Africa, 1860–1925*. London: Routledge Curzon.
Becker, C. H. 1911. "Materialien zur Kenntnis des Islam in Deutsch-Ostafrika." *Der Islam* 2: 1–48.
Bogonko, Sorobea Nyachieo. 1992. *A History of Modern Education in Kenya (1895–1991)*. Nairobi: Evans Brothers.
Bujra, Abdalla S. 1971. *The Politics of Stratification: A Study of Political Change in a South Arabian Town*. Oxford: Clarendon.

Crozon, Ariel. 1998. "L'umma divisée. Les communautés musulmanes du Kenya." In *Le Kenya contemporain*, edited by François Grignon and Gérard Prunier, 169–89. Paris: Karthala.
Eisemon, Thomas O. 1988. *Benefiting from Basic Education, School Quality and Functional Literacy in Kenya*. Oxford: Pergamon.
Elmasri, F. H. 1987. "Sheikh al-Amin bin Ali Mazrui and the Islamic Intellectual Tradition in East Africa." *Journal of Muslim Minority Affairs* 8: 229–38.
El Zein, Abdul Hamid M. 1974. *The Sacred Meadows: A Structural Analysis of Religious Symbolism in an East African Town*. Evanston, IL: Northwestern University Press.
Freitag, Ulrike. 1999. "Hadhramaut: A Religious Centre for the Indian Ocean in the Late 19th and Early 20th Centuries?" *Studia Islamica* 89: 165–83.
Freitag, Ulrike, and W. G. Clarence-Smith, eds. 1997. *Hadrami Traders, Scholars, and Statesmen in the Indian Ocean, 1750s–1960s*. Leiden: Brill.
Kahumbi, N. Maina, 1995. "The Role of the Madrasa System in Muslim Education in Kenya." In *Islam in Kenya*, edited by Mohamed Bakari and Saad S. Yahya, 323–39. Nairobi: MEWA.
Khitamy, Ahmed Binsumeit. 1995. "The Role of the Riyadha Mosque-College in Enhancing the Islamic Identity in Kenya." In *Islam in Kenya*, edited by Mohamed Bakari and Saad S. Yahya, 269–77. Nairobi: MEWA.
Kim, Caleb Chul-Soo. 2004. *Islam among the Swahili in East Africa*. Nairobi: Acton.
Kresse, Kai. 2003. "'Swahili Enlightenment?' East African Reformist Discourse at the Turning Point: The Example of Sheikh Muhammad Kasim Mazrui." *Journal of Religion in Africa* 33 (3): 279–309.
———. 2006. "Debating *Maulidi*: Ambiguities and Transformations of Muslim Identity along the Kenyan Swahili Coast." In *The Global Worlds of the Swahili*, edited by Roman Loimeier and Rüdiger Seesemann, 209–28. Berlin: Lit.
Lacunza-Balda, José, 1997. "Translations of the Quran into Swahili, and Contemporary Islamic Revival in East Africa." In *African Islam and Islam in Africa*, edited by Eva Evers Rosander and David Westerlund, 95–126. London: Hurst.
Launay, Robert, 1992. *Beyond the Stream: Islam and Society in a West African Town*. Berkeley: University of California Press.
Le Guennec-Coppens, Françoise, 1979. "Les Masharifu Jamalilil au Kenya." *Annuaire des Pays de l'Océan Indien* 6: 91–102.
Lienhardt, Peter, 1959. "The Mosque College of Lamu and Its Social Background." *Tanganyika Notes and Records* 52: 228–42.
Loimeier, Roman. 2010. "Traditions of Reform, Reforms of Tradition: Case Studies from Senegal and Zanzibar/Tanzania." In *Diversity and Pluralism in Islam*, edited by Zulfikar Hirji, 135–62. London: I. B. Tauris.
Loimeier, Roman, and Rüdiger Seesemann, eds. 2006. *The Global Worlds of the Swahili: Interfaces of Islam, Identity and Space in 19th- and 20th-Century East Africa*. Berlin: Lit.
Martin, Bradford G. 1971. "Notes on Some Members of the Learned Classes of Zanzibar and East Africa in the Nineteenth Century." *African Historical Studies* 4 (3): 525–45.
Mitchell, Timothy. 1988. *Colonising Egypt*. Cambridge: Cambridge University Press.
Moosa, Ebrahim. 2015. *What Is a Madrasa?* Chapel Hill: University of North Carolina Press.

Muhammad, Yusuf Hattar. 1418/1998. *al-Mawsu'a al-Yusufiyya fi bayan adillat al-sufiyya.* Damascus: Dar Kinan.

O'Brien, Donal B. Cruise. 1995. "Coping with the Christians. The Muslim Predicament in Kenya." In *Religion and Politics in East Africa*, edited by Holger Bernt Hansen and Michael Twaddle, 200–22. London: James Currey.

Peskes, Esther. 2005. *al-'Aidarus und seine Erben. Eine Untersuchung zu Geschichte und Sufismus einer Hadramitischen Sada-Gruppe vom 15. bis zum 18. Jahrhundert.* Stuttgart: Steiner.

Pouwels, Randall L. 1987. *Horn and Crescent: Cultural Change and Traditional Islam on the East African Coast, 800–1900.* Cambridge: Cambridge University Press.

———. 2000. "The East African Coast, c. 780 to 1900 CE." In *The History of Islam in Africa*, edited by Nehemia Levtzion and Randall L. Pouwels, 251–71. Athens: Ohio University Press.

Reichmuth, Stefan. 1988. "The Interplay of Local Developments and Transnational Relations in the Islamic World: Perceptions and Perspectives." In *Muslim Culture in Russia and Central Asia from the 18th to the Early 20th Centuries*, vol. 2, *Inter-Regional and Inter-Ethnic Relations*, edited by Anke von Kügelgen, Michael Kemper, and Allen J. Frank, 5–38. Berlin: Schwarz.

Rohlinger, Louise. 2005. "Constructing Islam and Swahili Identity. Historiography and Theory." *MIT Electronic Journal of Middle East Studies* 5: 9–20.

Romero, Patricia W. 1997. *Lamu: History, Society, and Family in an East African Port City.* Princeton, NJ: Markus Wiener.

Salim, Ahmad Idha. 1987. "Sheikh al-Amin bin Ali al-Mazrui: Un réformiste moderne au Kenya." In *Les voies de l'islam en Afrique orientale*, edited by François Constantin, 59–72. Paris: Karthala.

Salvadori, Cynthia. 1983. *Through Open Doors: A View of Asian Cultures in Kenya.* Nairobi: Kenway.

Seesemann, Rüdiger. 2005. "Kenia: Muslime im politischen Wandel." *INAMO* 41: 9–12.

———. 2006a. "African Islam or Islam in Africa? Evidence from Kenya." In *The Global Worlds of the Swahili*, edited by Roman Loimeier and Rüdiger Seesemann, 229–50. Berlin: Lit.

———. 2006b. "Competing Approaches to Islamic Education in Kenya." In *Proceedings of the International Symposium on Islamic Civilisation in Eastern Africa*, edited by Abdu B. Kasozi and Sadik Ünay, 171–79. Istanbul: IRCICA.

———. 2009. "Kenyan Muslims, the Aftermath of 9/11 and the 'War on Terror.'" In *Islam, Globalization and Disengagement of the State in Africa*, edited by Benjamin F. Soares and René Otayek, 243–73. New York: Palgrave Macmillan.

Sheffield, James R. 1973. *Education in Kenya: An Historical Study.* New York: Teachers College Press.

Sperling, David. 1985. "Islamization in the Coastal Region of Kenya to the End of the Nineteenth Century." In *Kenya in the 19th Century*, edited by Bethwell A. Ogot, 33–82. Nairobi: Bookwise.

———. 1993. "Rural Madrasas of the Southern Kenyan Coast, 1971–92." In *Muslim Identity and Social Change in Sub-Saharan Africa*, edited by Louis Brenner, 198–209. Bloomington: Indiana University Press.

Starrett, Gregory. 1998. *Putting Islam to Work: Education, Politics, and Religious Transformation in Egypt.* Berkeley: University of California Press.

Tarekhe ya Sharif Said al-Beidh. n.d. Copy in the archival collection Islam in Africa, Bayreuth University, Germany.

Trimingham, John Spencer. 1964. *Islam in East Africa.* Oxford: Clarendon.

Voll, John O. 1994. "Islam as a Special World System." *Journal of World History* 5: 213–26.

ARCHIVAL SOURCES

Public Record Office London (PRO), BW (Records of the British Council).

90/71, Report by the Fact-Finding Mission to Study Muslim Education in East Africa, n.d. (ca. 1957).

90/101, Sir Bernard Reilly's Report on Arab Problems in Kenya and Zanzibar, 1948.

12.
WALKING TO THE *MAKARANTA*: PRODUCTION, CIRCULATION, AND TRANSMISSION OF ISLAMIC LEARNING IN URBAN NIGER

Abdoulaye Sounaye

◦◦◦

ONE STORMY AFTERNOON, I was scheduled to meet the leader of an Islamic organization in Niamey, and, anticipating that he would not make it to our appointment, I decided to visit some of my relatives I hadn't seen for several years. As I was sitting under the main *tanda* (shed) of the compound, sharing the news about the family with the two cowives of the household, both *hajias*,[1] I noticed the incessant and frenetic *va-et-vient* (French, literally "back and forth") of a young woman who was holding a booklet in her hands. Discretely and apparently not interested in my conversation with her aunts, she would get out of the room, come by one of the *hajia*, murmur some words while pointing at sections of a booklet, and return to her hideout. This went on for the forty-five minutes or so I spent there. Before leaving, I managed to have a look at the booklet: It was written in Hausa, with a few sections in Arabic, those the young woman was trying to decipher. On her last trip, she grew impatient and asked the cowives: "Are we done yet? Are we going to the *makaranta* today or just staying here chit-chatting? You should save the rest [of the conversation] until he revisits you." A few minutes later, one of the *hajia* responded to her injunction, cutting short our conversation: "*Zamu neman ilimi* [we are going to seek knowledge]; make sure we see you again before you leave."

Over the last few years, similar scenes of women striving to acquire higher Islamic learning have become ordinary in Niamey and in many other urban areas in Niger, where new Islamic learning initiatives have developed, complicating the already variegated landscape of Islamic learning. One of those initiatives resulted in the urban *makaranta*, an informal learning space that acquired popularity only recently (Alidou 2005) as Muslims compete to define the terms of the practice of Islam. Debates that arise within this context have usually promoted learning as a way to express religiosity and prepare for arguments, especially in increasingly transforming epistemic conditions (Sounaye 2012; Alidou 2005; LeBlanc 1999; Meunier 1997 and 2002; Brenner 2001).

Makaranta is a Hausa word that may be used to refer to any training or instructional institution. It derives from the root *karatu*, study or learning, and *ma*, a prefix attributing a quality or a function. In its most current use in the urban context, it refers to Islamic learning institutions, mainly informal study circles that emerged in the last fifteen years following a trend of activism that has created additional learning opportunities for the urbanites (Sounaye 2009b; Alidou 2005). Many of my informants, for example, see going to the *makaranta* as an opportunity to achieve higher Islamic learning and therefore ensure proper practice.

What is striking about the scene described above is less the seriousness of the young woman in her effort to grasp the content of her booklet or her lack of Hausa good manners, especially in the way she addressed her aunts, but her resort to one of the *hajia* to decipher the lines of her booklet. When did the *hajia* acquire competency in Islamic learning to be called on? I knew the two cowives used to have a *makaranta* where they would gather for Qur'an lessons and, as they usually say, "to learn enough to be able to fix a prayer" (*gyara salla*), connoting the modest degree of learning they expected from their practice. When I visited the *makaranta* with some of my students in 2000, nothing signaled that *hajia* would be tutoring someone else in Islamic learning a few years later. I had to realize that many things have changed, as one of the *hajia* would proudly tell me: "Since your departure, our knowledge has increased (*iliminmu ya karu*)," and more seekers of knowledge (*masu neman ilimi*) have joined them in their walk to the small shack they use as classroom, two streets away from their compound. As if to show me the progress she has made, she displayed the new booklet (*Kitab al Tawhid*) entirely in Arabic she was reading by herself.

This chapter provides an overview of discourses, changes, and transformations in the contemporary Islamic knowledge economy in Niger. New practices, spaces, and actors have emerged that aim to cultivate, spread, and consolidate Islamic learning. The act of walking to a *makaranta*, in many urban areas in Niger, and particularly in Niamey, epitomizes the renewed interest in Islamic learning as Muslims invest time and means to increase their *ilimi*. As I shall demonstrate, the walk translates both an attitude and an act—in particular, the act of both seeking and transmitting learning.

Today, particularly in urban areas, groups of young people and women increasingly attend *makaranta* and mosques, two spaces they have re-created and reappropriated as they engage in teaching, learning, and scholarly practices that reshape the conditions of religious and social practice. I argue that the current social transformation process in Niger is due not only to the epistemic shift that affects Islamic knowledge and its current dynamics but to the representation of knowledge and learning as qualifying factors of religiosity. Thus, knowing and learning Islam are now part of a widespread symbolic economy that has mobilized many social actors and translated into initiatives that end up redefining being Muslim, female, and literate.

Context, Problematic, Significance: Reconceptualizing Islamic Knowledge

Muslim groups and actors that emerged in Niger the past two decades have promoted a culture of learning and enlightenment deeply rooted in a perception of Islam as a reservoir of social ideas and transformative ethic. The quiet activism Islamic learning institutions have embraced has targeted learning and knowledge as the most prominent modalities of being Muslim, primarily because of their role in affecting subjectivities and reshaping ethical horizons. The opening vignette of this chapter precisely captures what I see as one of the major features of the current knowledge economy in urban Niger, where seeking and acquiring higher Islamic learning have become particularly empowering, while all sorts of claims contend for legitimacy and authenticity.

When the *hajia* referred to the "increase of their knowledge" (*iliminmu ya karu*),[2] her evocation of both a qualitative and quantitative change affecting their learning community was just an indication of a trend that has become common among many women's groups, housewives, youth, and *femmes travailleuses* (employees of the state administration and the formal economic sector). A woman invested in seeking Islamic learning outside of the domestic domain is no longer a picture out of the ordinary. In contrast, not long ago, if they existed at all, women's learning practices in the region, and particularly in Niamey, were primarily located within the domestic realm, as illustrated by several studies (Sounaye 2009a, 2011; Alidou 2005; Umar 2004; Cooper 1997; Reveyrand-Coulon 1993). The most striking feature of the women's groups I observed is that they have taken their desire to acquire higher learning to the mosque and the *makaranta*, reinventing practices, creating and reorganizing spaces. Many private homes are still the base of women's learning communities across Niamey; but seeing women over forty walking the street to the *makaranta*—sometimes alone but most of the time in groups—is a phenomenon that has become part of Muslim practice only in the past fifteen years. Although Islamic learning was not particularly popular in Niamey, some families managed to send their children to Qur'anic schools, mostly on Wednesday afternoons, on weekends, or during public school breaks. However, after a certain age, female students tended to withdraw from the

Qur'anic schools, in part because of the chores and domestic responsibilities they would usually undertake much earlier than their male counterparts. As a result, it is common to see girls dropping out from their Qur'anic school, abandoning Islamic learning, focusing their attention on domestic life. If still interested at all, most of them can only hope to return to Islamic learning after they marry and settle in their own household. And even at this point, significant challenges can hinder their efforts and discourage them, especially with the burden of running a household or simply because they are not expected to be extraordinarily learned and become scholars.

Thus, the spread of the women's *makarantu* (pl. of *makaranta*) in Niamey has represented a major shift in the social organization of Islamic learning and in how individual women are cultivating Islamic learning and defining themselves as major players in the current knowledge economy. It is, then, no surprise that women's learning practices have acquired social relevance, mobilizing power and having a significant impact on contemporary Islamic institutions in Niamey. For many (probably most) Muslims in this city, this phenomenon has changed their epistemic horizons, the way they understand their religious obligations, and even gender roles. This is even more visible among urban women who increasingly bestow the quest for Islamic learning with a devotional meaning. *Go learn! Join a makaranta instead of lazing on your bed! Get yourself a booklet instead of wasting your time listening to useless radio programs!* are injunctions that one regularly hears among women in urban Niger.

Similar trends are perceptible with many youth groups, which, adding to traditional representations, perceive their being religious as consisting in more than attending the congregational prayer at the mosque and lining up behind the imam for daily prayer. For these youth, too, investing time and energy to attend Qur'anic lessons has become an important expression of religiosity. For both categories, being a good Muslim starts with learning and assimilating in a culture that emphasizes other injunctions, such as *Know your religion! Know in order to better perform! A good Muslim should not stop learning!* These associations of learning with devotion have made the learning initiatives and practices I discuss even more important.

A look at the historical background of the current developments in Muslims' learning practices reveals a major shift occurring in the 1990s. The period was marked by a liberalization ethos that served as a catalyst for the transformation of the religious sphere in Niger (Maikorema 2009; Sounaye 2005, 2009a; Glew 1996). The institutional reform and the restructuring of Islamic learning that ensued constitute two significant dimensions of this transformation. Alidou (2005), Masquelier (1999), and Meunier (1998) have alluded to the emergence of a new episteme, a framework within which learning and knowledge become markers of religiosity. For not only has Islamic leaning gained new significance within this episteme, it has become the focus of many Muslim entrepreneurs (groups, clubs, associations) who seek to redefine being Muslim through *neman ilimi* (seeking knowledge, in Hausa), part of a discourse that has translated into the construction of numerous *makaranta*. As these entrepreneurs engage in the construction of a society they expect will fully consider Islamic norms, creating circles of production and circulation of knowledge become prime priorities of their agenda. In addition to the new modes of sociability these spaces lead to (which I have discussed elsewhere; Sounaye 2009b), they also inaugurate a cultural realm within which learning is commoditized and endowed with the quality to nurture religiosity. Among urbanites who have discovered Islam only recently, this philosophy has prompted a dynamic culture of Islamic learning as they are convinced that proper religiosity rests on a high degree of learning.

Connecting the notions of knowledge and economy is only an attempt to think about (Eickelman 1992) the processes and relationships that emerge around the production, transmission, and circulation of ideas primarily shaped by Islam and based on the assumption that, in order to be a good Muslim, one needs to know (*sani*) and learn (*karatu*) Islam. In fact, *sani* or *beyrey* (knowledge/learning), *lura* (understanding), and *ganewa* (comprehension/grasping) are concepts frequently invoked to define the attitudes Muslims should adopt or abilities they need to have not only because of the importance of these postures and skills in daily social commerce but because they improve piety. For these discourses, the Muslim subject appears as an actor who is compelled to reinvent the modes of cultivation and distribution of knowledge. Thus, the claim of the publicity of Islam characteristic of the learning communities I examine finds its most audible expression within the circles that engage in *aikin adini* (serving Islam) or *sanin adini* (knowing Islam).

The issue is not only about a mere dispensation and understanding (*sani*) of a valued religious knowledge. More than that, it is about how the high degree of learning one acquires delivers a fruitful life (*rayuwa mai anfani*). Therefore, studying the Islamic texts implies following up with acts and deeds (*aikatawa*) and should result in living by the teachings exposed in these texts. At the same time, *sanin adini* is not a mere theoretical construct designed to render more sophisticated the framework within which one operates; it is primarily the expression in practice of an improved religiosity one desires and seeks. Thus, the real objective of *sanin adini* within the learning communities I describe resides not so much in the cognitive experience of knowing but, more importantly, in practicing (*aikatawa*)—that is, living by the prescriptions of the tradition one learns. For this reason, and not surprisingly, in the communities I discuss here, the hadiths, more than the Qur'an, are the center of attention because they tell and show how the Prophet implemented and enacted the prescriptions of Islam within his community. This dimension of the current Islamic learning culture is, as we may imagine, linked to the activism that has defined the emergence of reform discourses, notably the *izala*[3] (Maikorema 2009 and 2007; Masquelier 2009; Umar 1993; Sounaye 2009a), eager to inform personal and social ethics through a sustained and strategic popularization of what they view as the reservoir of resources for a Muslim life that fully conforms to the Sunna.

Women Striving to Learn: The Quartier Abidjan Women's Makaranta

Unlike most *makarantu*, the Quartier Abidjan Makaranta has no ties with an official organization and was not inspired by a Sufi community. Its distinctive feature is its independence from organized Islam, the Islamic associations, and the Sufi organizations that have been creating and using similar spaces to promote their activities and engage in intra-Muslim rivalry since the early 1990s. In Maradi and Niamey, the rise of *izala* anti-Sufism prompted the rise of learning institutions that sought to provide Islamic learning opportunities to various social categories (Sounaye 2009a; Alidou 2005: Meunier 1998; Moulaye 1995). In Maradi, for example, the youth organization Club des Jeunes Musulmans and the civil servants' organization le Cercle des Travailleurs Musulmans de Maradi have been involved in seminars, conferences, teaching, and Arabic literacy programs in a form of activism that have transformed the institutional makeup and practices of Islamic learning in the name of *sanin adini*. In other parts of Niger and focusing on the *makaranta*, the same trend of appropriation of Islam targeted segments of the urban population that are regarded as either too secular or not learned enough to properly practice Islam. A thorough sociological analysis is needed to understand the significance of this phenomenon, but for now it suffices to note that the development discussed here has not promoted a radical rupture. On the contrary, it has sought to correct what the *izala* have viewed as a state of ignorance (*jahilci*) that has undermined proper Islamic practice.

The Quartier Abidjan Women's Makaranta is precisely one of these spaces that seeks to make this correction and establish a culture of learning among urban dwellers. Exclusively devoted to women, this learning space opened in 1998, shortly after a group of women decided to learn more than the minimum they needed to "fix a prayer" (*gyara salla*). If this was seen as a basic step, as the *hajia's* statement suggests, it is nevertheless the main foundation of pious practice. Knowing how to fix a prayer may be the minimum for the daily practice of their religion, but for many Muslims it sets the stage for a Sunna-inspired religious life. The *hajia* reiterates this postulate I have consistently heard within Muslim circles: "Islamic practice starts with a commitment to the five daily prayers" (*Alsilamataray gandji sintina gati djingar-yan*). To nurture religiosity, one must consolidate its foundation. Obviously, as my vignette suggests, the *hajia* has learned more than enough to fix a prayer.

The initial group of the *makaranta* included four housewives in their fifties. But it rapidly grew to about twenty housewives, a development that necessitated the expansion of the *tanda*, where they gather for their study. The *tanda* that serves as classroom is located in the concession of one of the founders of the group. The space previously hosted a home-based business run by a relative of one of the women. The owner was unable to secure a tenant, so the women requested and obtained its use free of charge for their *makaranta* sessions. The group meets every afternoon, except Thursdays and Fridays. This schedule was intended to accommodate members whose chores keep them busy until late afternoon, between the *asr* (around 4:00 p.m.) and the *maghrib* (around 7:00 p.m.) prayers, when they can afford to devote about an hour and half to their *makaranta* activities.

As is often the case with women's organizations in Niger, the *makaranta* set the ground for a communal chain of solidarity that is usually activated whenever a member has a wedding, a naming ceremony, or a funeral. A tontine was also set up to allow participants to save money to cover life events or any other expenses. However, the main purpose of the *makaranta* is to help the women memorize the Qur'an, study the hadiths, and acquire Arabic reading skills so they can read the texts on their own. Occasionally, preaching sessions are also held, usually on women's religious obligations, ongoing issues, or household management (*windi sadjaw-yan*).

The *makaranta* is a group-funded initiative in which each participant commits a monthly contribution of 500 CFA ($1), mainly to support the instructor, a man who runs other *makarantu* across Niamey and who has instructed this group since its inception. However, participants also contribute various gifts, including fabrics, soap, and perfumes, to show gratitude to a man who provides members of the group much-needed assistance in learning Arabic, understanding some texts, and gaining access to reading materials. The two *hajia* who introduced me to the group had no problem contributing the amount, especially because they run a small business of ice and local drinks (*lemu hari*), which helps them make their monthly contributions and some occasional gifts to the instructor. In contrast, for several women who have no source of income, affording the monthly contribution may be a matter of some juggling, as is the case for a woman who "manages to save enough from the amount her husband provides for the daily expenses (*kudin kayan miya*)." Ultimately, most manage to contribute, because they "are investing in a rewarding knowledge, one that serves here and in the hereafter."

In its neighborhood, the Quartier Abidjan Makaranta is the only Islamic learning circle exclusively devoted to housewives. Even though several of its key members have dropped out since it was launched, the *makaranta* has relatively succeeded in maintaining the core of its founders. Along the way, other women have joined the walk, adding diversity to the group, especially in terms of generations and socioeconomic backgrounds. In fact, in the last few years, many younger and newlywed housewives have joined, sometimes despite their husbands' criticisms and reticence. According to the dominant discourse in Niger, under most social conditions, it falls on the husband to provide religious guidance to his wife, who might find the initiative challenging. However, this is only in theory; in practice, only a few husbands can assume this role due to their limited Islamic learning, pedagogical inexperience, and perceptions of gender roles.[4] Additionally, because religious learning represents a significant social capital and an authorizing asset, women's cultivation of it may constitute a source of tension within many households due to social ideologies that generally favor men as far as learning and education are concerned.

In any case, the Quartier Abidjan Makaranta has brought to the forefront women's interest and role in the current knowledge economy in Niger. A community-based initiative, the *makaranta* has become an important part of its members' religious and the communal lives. It demonstrates not only how women can innovate and appropriate a scholarly tradition but how the idea of the religious self can inspire the cultivation of knowledge.

Through my conversations with the two *hajia*, I realized the significance of the *makaranta* activities in their daily lives. For example, attendance to the *makaranta* is associated with a religious goal, because "a better practice of Islam" is predicated on the mastery of the knowledge of the tradition, the Qur'an, and the hadiths. They have rarely missed the sessions of the *makaranta*. I have also noticed the skills these women have acquired over time, especially in dealing with the Islamic texts, to the point that they can tutor other people. The significance of the transformation I discuss here is better understood when one considers the fact that, for many participants, the *makaranta* is their first experience of a learning community. The two *hajia* are "illiterate" (*illettrées*), as people would call them in urban lingo. They have no formal school education, neither Islamic nor secular, but have now become part of a knowledge economy that has transformed not only Muslim practices but also the modes of construction of Islamic authority in an urban context.

Overall, and on closer consideration, it must be said that the initiatives described here are not exclusive to housewives, nor to this particular neighborhood of Niamey. Across the city, similar initiatives have developed targeting youth, traders, Westernized elite, or simply working class women—in particular, the *travailleuses*.

The Majlis Ousman Dan Fodio of Niamey: Targeting the *Travailleuses*

Contrary to the Quartier Abidjan Women's Makaranta, the Majlis[5] Ousman Dan Fodio targets primarily women intellectuals (also referred to as *femmes travailleuses* or *femmes fonctionnaires*) who are employed in the state administration or in the formal economic sector. In the last two decades, this learning institution has been a dynamic center for several intellectual and devotional activities, including lectures, sermons, conferences, debates, and, most importantly, Qur'an classes for women. One of the main Islamic organizations of the country, the Association Nigérienne pour l'Appel et la Solidarité Islamique, runs the mosque. Over the years, the mosque has become a rallying point for this Islamic organization and part of the francophone elite which has embraced Islam and engages now in an active campaign that promotes Islamic norms. Not surprisingly, it rapidly became the headquarters of Muslim groups seeking to convert this elite, generally viewed as too secular and even anti-Islamic. Because of their social and political impact, women workers, male civil servants, and students have become the primary targets of Ousman Dan Fodio's activities.

According to Maiga, an instructor and key figure of the Majlis, the *travailleuses* have particularly distinguished themselves from other groups, as they have become the main participants in Islamic learning activities in Niamey. Many are not only *scolarisées* (schooled), but they hold also important executive positions in the state administration or in the modern private sector. Graduates of the state educational system, these women now turn to Islamic learning to know (*bey, faham*) their religion and follow appropriately its prescriptions. Maiga characterizes this attitude in terms of thirst for knowledge (*soif de savoir*) and practice informed by enlightening knowledge (*pratique de l'Islam dans la lumière du savoir*). As he remarks, "Today, we have a new generation that seeks to know more about Islam and which commits itself to the sacrifice this requires. They abandon the old practices of *suivisme* [blind following] to discover for and by themselves the true meaning of Islam." To quench this thirst, to use Maiga's metaphor, women "take matters in their own hands."

This is important to note because "women and youth who used to be under the tutelage of either their husband or their parents to access a higher degree of Islamic learning are now in charge of most of our initiatives." Indeed, current efforts to access higher Islamic learning in urban contexts differ from previous ones in that they do more than expose Muslims to the sites of learning. They use strategies that accommodate social categories—particularly women and youth; they also require abnegation and conviction from the individual as well as pragmatism to take advantage of the learning opportunities. Thus, more than a social responsibility of the community or the family, Islamic learning has become a religious prescription primarily lived and enacted in the individual. The focus on and provision for specific social categories have introduced particular organizational and pedagogical manners that change both the meaning of being an instructor and the attitudes of the learner in the Islamic learning institutions.

In explaining the goals, motives, and methods of Ousman Dan Fodio, Maiga resorts to the idea of a rupture from *suivisme*—a neologism created from the French word *suivre* (to follow). It became popular among proponents of Islamic reform and antimaraboutic practices who intended to distance themselves from the clerics and put an end to what they viewed as a blind following. More importantly, *suivisme* suggests a perception of the self as an autonomous and rational agent who not only could achieve a higher learning but should persist on this path. Cast primarily as a personal and individual endeavor, this epistemic project rests on the assumption that it falls on the learners, not on the cleric, to create the conditions for their own enlightenment. By breaking from *suivisme* and taking matters in their own hands, they put themselves in the position to learn directly from the source and practice appropriately. In most cases, the *makarantu* such as Ousman Dan Fodio have been created to serve this philosophy and its socioreligious agenda.

The promotion and adoption of these learning attitudes have been greatly influenced by the antimaraboutic discourse that various Muslim actors have been articulating since the early 1990s (Sounaye 2009b). Muslim actors promoting Islamic renewal (Masquelier 1999, 2009) have relentlessly pushed for a rejection of epistemic postures they found inhibiting, particularly the modes of production of knowledge that centered on the instructor (*malam*) who owned the *makaranta* and therefore was responsible for the curriculum and the management of the institution.

In contrast, the most active of the new *makarantu* resulted from collective action and a shared agenda. Unlike the classical *makarantu*, which are usually owned by their founder, the new ones are primarily communal learning circles and are understood as collective goods that are sustained through the compulsory effort and contribution of all members. As a consequence, according to Amina, a young woman who attends the Majlis classes, the *makarantu* are "initiated, supported and managed by the group." If the instructor–learner relationship is strong and reinforced, in many cases it is devoid of the master–disciple connotation that characterized Sufi learning centers and institutions.

In other words, when he criticizes *suivisme*, Maiga intends to stress the shift in learning relationships and the status of each of the two parties. In his view, renouncing *suivisme* implies a deployment of critical thinking, which centers on the learner rather than on the authoritative figure of the classical *malam* (cleric), who is not only instructor but primarily the owner of the institution in the classical *makaranta*. This way of understanding Islamic learning and its transmission assumes that people have the choice to follow, distance themselves, or simply select how they want to relate to the instructor and the institution as a whole.[6] Although Maiga assumes leadership in the *makarantu* where he teaches, he does not see himself as a *malam*, an authoritative figure who leads a group of disciples and is surrounded by a clientele. Rather, he is an *ustaz* who limits himself to writing and teaching. In fact, he is involved in several learning initiatives similar to that of the Majlis and has written a series of booklets, all in French, discussing topics such as the status of women in the Muslim context, the benefit of a pious life, and the consequences of gossiping.

What is questioned is not the relevance of learning or knowledge in Muslims' daily lives, nor the role of learning in shaping authority and personalities. On the contrary, in the current context, learning practices have acquired more dynamism, especially in terms of their organization and the strategies deployed by Muslim promoters of a pious learning. The classical modes of cultivation of Islamic learning face criticism precisely because, according to the actors I focus on here, the *malam* and the ulama social category as a whole, have not been able to adapt to the need of various social categories eager to learn and "know the scriptures of their religion," as Maiga put it. Thus, the epistemic relationship that constitutes the transmission is reinvented and redefined.

One of the consequences of these attitudes is that, in most of the *makarantu* I have observed, the instructor is not viewed as a *malam* but rather an *ustaz*, a term that signals his or her authority may not be spiritual, but only pedagogical. Obviously, we should not lose sight of the fact that the teaching–studying–learning relationship is primarily among adults, a dimension that may significantly affect the modes and the perceptions of authority within this context. In any case, calling on the responsibility of the learner has been an approach many *ustaz* have adopted and an orientation that has resulted in a new Islamic knowledge economy.

The importance of the individual in this context is emphasized when Amina remarks that the commitment to serve Islam should focus primarily on the personal intellectual development of the Muslim subject: "One should learn first." Consequently learning and helping others learn should be the focus of *taimakon adini* (serving Islam). For it is only when she is knowledgeable that the believer can achieve good practice. In that sense, *suivisme*, which implies relying primarily on the *malam*, has not only hindered the understanding (*faham*) of Islam, it has impeded the development of the religious personality of the Muslim subject. Thus, to emancipate themselves from this tutelage and become better Muslims, young men and women, Maiga says, are now committing to learning: "*Maintenant, les gens cherchent le savoir*" (People are now seeking knowledge). But perhaps more than that, they have access to conditions that make this search for knowledge possible.

Accommodating the Learner and the Mobility of Islamic Learning

The cultivation of Islamic knowledge has been a central preoccupation in West African Muslim societies, particularly in the context of reform (Kobo 2012; Loimeier 2009; Umar 2004; Brenner 2001). In many contexts, reform meant the promotion of particular interpretations and readings of foundational texts and sources. It also translated into specific practices and truth claims, best communicated through learning circles, whether formal or informal but always revolving around the meaning of paradigmatic texts and practices. The history of Islamic learning is replete with cases of communities forming and of individuals traveling to distant countries to acquire a higher learning (Willis 1979). However, the most striking aspect I see in contemporary urban Niger is how some social categories such as housewives and the *travailleuses* have devised strategies and devoted spaces for Islamic learning, often against all odds and the burden of their life conditions (Sounaye 2012; Alidou 2005). Rising up against these constraints, many women have become authoritative figures, spokespeople of Islam, and therefore major players in the current transformation of the religious landscape. As they take the mission to cultivate Islamic learning and spread the Sunna, they accommodate and satisfy what they view as the religious need of their individual lives and that of their communities.

Obviously, if seeking *beyrey* (knowledge) has acquired such popularity among urbanites, it is also because of the channels and the mode of production and circulation this commodity relies on. It appears that, for many women and young urbanites, Islamic learning is more than a cultural product; it is a commodity, a sign of distinction, and a mode of asserting one's religiosity—all of which have increased its value and the social capital of its bearer. Wearing the hijab in certain milieus in Niamey has become fashionable. Similarly, investing time, energy, and means to acquire this precious and distinctive capital has become in itself a mode of distinction, an attitude and practice that women emulate and in which they compete with one another. It is not surprising, then, that their active quest for learning leads to attitudes and practices that are strategically designed to accommodate specific categories, families, or simply individuals. Both Quartier Abidjan and Ousman Dan Fodio exemplify this process. Seeking to have an impact on the family and the society, their initiatives target women, because in her household, a woman is *uwar guida* (Hausa, literally, "mother of the household"), a metaphor that stresses her nurturing role and strategic position in the moral economy of the city. The husband is *mai gida* (Hausa, literally, "owner of the household") and for that reason responsible for the material wellbeing of the household. In contrast, the provider of the moral bread, so to speak, is the *uwar guida*, especially with regard to the offspring. Concerned that the Westernized elite is too secular, the initiatives will target the *scolarisés* (people trained in the secular public schools) and the civil servants; or, seeking to ensure that Islam receives more consideration in the future, the initiatives will focus on youth, who are "the rulers of tomorrow" (Amina).

Such attention to particular social conditions and backgrounds can also be seen in the way many young women are reinventing the modes of distribution of Islamic knowledge as they ride their motorbikes and travel across the city to tutor other women. Rahamatu is one of these new "distributors" of *beyrey* and caretakers of the newly committed learners. She acquired her motorbike in 2009 and now crisscrosses Niamey five days a week to meet women in *makarantu* or in their own houses. Her mobility has inspired many young people, especially those enrolled in the formal madrasas, to start study groups in homes or workplaces. Illustrating these changes, many faculty and staff members at Abdou Moumouni University of Niamey, one of the elite institutions of the country, contract with the *ustaz*, who come to their homes to teach their children the Qur'an and Arabic. This practice was hardly possible a few years ago, in part because of the lack of interest in such forms of knowledge and the traditional learning relationship which typically requires that the learner walk to the cleric's house or place of instruction.

When I was younger, my siblings and I walked between forty-five minutes and an hour to get to the *malam*'s (Muslim cleric) house on the outskirts of Niamey, where we would memorize the Qur'an. Today, although the *malam* still operates as an important instructor and provider of "social service" (especially during events such as weddings or funerals), in many urban areas he faces fierce competition in the business of Islamic learning, especially from the graduates of the formal Islamic learning institutions who claim better mastery of Arabic and therefore of the Islamic scriptures. The emergence of these *ustaz* has diversified the modes of production and transmission of Islamic learning, mainly by providing many families and urban dwellers greater access to Islamic learning. Moreover, to mark his difference from the *malam*, the *ustaz*, this servant of the new knowledge economy, comes to the learners with his knowledge and mastery of Arabic, a skill the previous generations of Islamic instructors rarely emphasized.

In sum, the *ustaz* have generally adapted to the constraints and opportunities of urban life by providing a flexible schedule, walking to the house of the learner, and delivering the knowledge—a system unheard of only a few years ago. Similarly, adjusting to socioeconomic and professional conditions, many learning circles now operate according to their members' daily schedules. A *makaranta* of mostly housewives, for example, would hold its sessions on weekdays and, in the case Quartier Abidjan Makaranta, in the late afternoon. A *makaranta* of mostly *travailleuses* will meet on Saturdays and Sundays. One that targets men civil servants will meet after work; and one designed for students on a campus is likely to meet at night in the main mosque of the campus or in a classroom. Obviously, these adjustments are made to accommodate the learners, but they are also instituted to meet the demands for Islamic learning among these social categories.

Youth Groups, Islamic Learning, and Relating to the Prophetic Model

I have described how group and individual initiatives create what may be called the feminization of Islamic learning. In this section, I shift to a learning circle exclusively designed for men, which, unlike the Quartier Abidjan Makaranta, is organized around a mosque I visited in 2004 and 2008, in Zinder, Niger. Even though the site is quite formal, the group itself is informal. Attendance to the study sessions is not compulsory, because the group follows no specific curriculum; no fees are paid, and no homework is expected, in part because no lecture is given. Participants are responsible for whatever they want to study, the instructor intervening only to advise or suggest reading materials. In fact, most participants bring their own booklets or the excerpts they want to study. Illia, who leads the study circle, is less an instructor than a coordinator, often playing the role of a tutor who "facilitates the understanding of the text," as he says. Usually, two tutors alternate, each leading the study group three nights and three mornings. Illia is a graduate of a secular institution, Abdou Moumouni University of Niamey, and is now a civil servant in the town; Abdallah is a graduate of the Islamic University of Medina who, after graduation, instead of returning to his hometown of Kano, accepted an offer to take up *da'wa* (call to Islam) and serve Islam (*taimakon adini*) in Zinder. After all, Kano is only a few hours away. Since then, Abdallah has become one of the leading voices of the *izala* reform in Zinder both on the radio and in the Islamic learning institutions where he is involved.

The group's nightly sessions begin after the last prayer of the day (*isha'a*), around 8:00 p.m., and its morning sessions are held immediately after the first prayer of the day (*fajr*), around 5:30 a.m. The participants are mostly young students, graduates of Abdou Moumouni University waiting for employment, traders, and civil servants. Unlike the Quartier Abidjan and the Ousman Dan Fodio groups, no specific socioprofessional category dominates here. I had my first encounter with the group while I was doing fieldwork on the emergence of *izala* in Zinder when I overheard one of my informants discussing the schedule of the group. On the night of my first visit to the group, eleven young men were scattered in the mosque, each with his *littafi* (booklet) and taking turns with Illia reviewing what they had previously studied before moving on to another section of their *littafi*. Two men, probably in their forties, who took their *littafi* from one of the shelves of the mosque, were also part of the group. Illia himself, sitting in the middle of the mosque, had a stack of books that included the collection of hadiths by Muslim, an especially popular reference in the *izala* circles. As I would discover later, most of the learners were studying hadiths, an indication that they had already memorized a substantial part of, if not the whole, Qur'an. Learning the hadiths, the accounts of the life and acts of the Prophet Muhammad, has become important because of the social and ethical agenda of the group, which is primarily to follow in the footsteps of the Prophet. Thus, by relating the Sunna, more than the Qur'an, hadiths provide illustrations and actual situations within which the Prophet put Islam to work. Reading hadiths is therefore both formative and transformative, because they model religiosity. In fact, how a Muslim should behave and act is a question that Muslims have debated since the *izala* discourse made its way into the public arena. To win the argument over this fundamental question, proponents of the *izala* discourse have used various strategies—in particular, setting up learning circles and reading groups that have now produced a well-established trend of scholarly practices.

As a social category, youth have been particularly active in these new configurations of Islamic learning institutions, both in formal and informal settings. In fact, like the women's initiatives discussed above, those of their male counterparts have created the conditions for a social, cultural, and even political valuation of Islamic learning that has changed the knowledge economy within Muslim communities. The prestige of being a young Muslim who has mastered the hadiths and can engage in any debate on Islam has become one of the drivers that motivates not only the young learners of the *izala* mosque in Zinder but many other youth who have found in reading and study circles a social space and, more important, an avenue where they can change and commit to the Sunna of the Prophet Muhammad. One of the realities of being urbanites in Niger is that, as they define a social project inspired by the Prophet Muhammad shaped by their reading and understanding of the hadiths, many organizations, formal or informal, have provided a space for learning and intellectual exercise and, more importantly, an opportunity for socialization for their young members. Many of the young students, who are generally viewed as too secular to find interest in learning the Qur'an and studying the hadiths, are now bound to a scholarly sphere that has offered an alternative to the streets and idleness. After a secular education from which many have greatly benefited, they now turn to a religious one, mainly to fit into a society that has given prestige to being Muslim and taking inspiration and models from the Sunna.

A powerful illustration of this process can be seen in the proliferation of the Clubs des Jeunes Musulmans over the last few years in Niamey and across Niger. Promoting Islam-informed life among urbanites and students of the secular schools, the clubs have become dynamic youth spaces as they take on the mission to spread the Qur'an and a Sunna lifestyle. Predominant in the secondary schools, these organizations have become key players in spreading an Islamic ethos in public schools and in the urban public sphere in general. Their main objective is fighting the lack of interest in Islam of which most young students are accused. To this aim, the clubs have developed various social practices and learning activities such as reading groups and Arabic literacy programs which have given materiality to what they refer to as *animation religieuse* (religious activism). In most of the lycées of Niamey, the same process has led to more students taking Arabic as one of their mandatory foreign languages.

By focusing on knowledge and emphasizing the need for further Islamic learning to lead an appropriate religious life, the brokers of this new knowledge economy intend to not only free themselves from *jahilci* (ignorance, lack of proper morality), as they repeatedly put it, but to set the foundations for a new society, enlightened and guided by Islamic principles. To achieve this new moral order, the cultivation of knowledge becomes indispensable. In many cases, the model is not the formal madrasa or the Qur'anic school but rather the study groups that form among colleagues, coworkers, classmates, and members of the same association. A recurrent critique of the formal madrasa, an institution that predates the current initiatives, emphasizes its failure to address the ills of the society and its inability to inculcate Islamic values to youth and therefore contribute to the moral formation of the community. Many observe that the formal madrasa produced morally handicapped Muslims who not only failed to learn the Qur'an and the hadiths but also became socially unfit and burdensome to the community (personal interview with Khalid, 2008; personal interview with Cheick Suleyman, 2001). More flexible and therefore more manageable than a formal madrasa, the learning groups and circles came to represent the forms of gathering through which housewives, students, and civil servants innovate and establish new teaching and learning practices that have inspired a new scholarly tradition. Thus, the popularity the *makaranta* has acquired could be read as a shift that is gradually transforming the modes of production, transmission, and circulation of Islamic knowledge.

Concluding Remarks

In Niger, especially in the context of Islamic reform, learning is increasingly perceived and understood as transformative. For many women and youth, Islamic learning has become a significant part of their religious practices and an essential element of their lives. That is why I contend that a new culture of learning has developed within those milieus, which, for many individuals, groups, and communities seeking knowledge, amounts to an expression of piety. At the core of the discourse of knowledge production, transmission, and circulation lies an ideal of molding Muslim subjects. This has been particularly perceptible with Islamic reform initiatives in urban areas. The current profusion of Islamic learning sites confirms such an ideal. Due to the nature of interactions in those contexts, this trend is not limited to the formal madrasa but expands over a broad domain of activities and institutions promoting Islamic learning. The profusion of learning centers and the leadership women increasingly demonstrate in this domain reveal the significance of this culture and translate the emergence of social categories that are now ready to commoditize a service they can provide.

How *neman ilimi* is invested with a socioreligious value is indicative of a new knowledge economy that lies at the intersection between a transformative project and the intent to actualize oneself as a subject fully committed to the words of God. To achieve such a degree of piety, one needs to learn. Placed in a broader historical context, obviously, the claims I highlight here are familiar to many Muslim communities that have used the appeal of scholarship and promoted the idea that learning secures good practice to establish themselves and engage the social and political realities of their times. West Africa, in general, has experienced communities of learning that have consistently articulated this discourse. Contrary to the claims of the reform discourses, this has been a constant in African Muslim societies as demonstrated by the scholarly traditions that have developed in these social contexts over centuries.

However, what the reform discourses and their initiatives also illustrate is the fact that knowledge informs and transforms; often projects of social and moral transformations rely on mechanisms, strategies, and initiatives whose aim consists essentially in altering the moral economy of the society. For such agendas, promoting a new knowledge economy has become central. What part of the tradition is conveyed? How is the tradition read, interpreted, and conveyed? What practices develop along these processes of reading, interpretation, and writing? Who leads these processes? These are questions that help us better assess the specificity of the current knowledge economy.

To draw a parallel and open the debate to a broader historical perspective, it is important to mention the colonial experience and how, within that context, the introduction of Western education has also relied on institutions, practices, and actors that have promoted the particular knowledge economy the colonial logic and agenda needed. Therefore, that these promoters of reform in Niger focus on Islamic learning should not surprise, especially when we consider that historically sociopolitical reforms have often relied on educational means (Babou 2007, 113). What is specific to the contemporary context is the involvement of new categories such as women and youth organizations and the claim that religiosity should be based on the degree of learning. It became obvious that, to grasp the significance of this religious culture, one must consider the role of Islamic learning circles in informing individual subjectivities and shaping collective moral order. In this case, an interesting move to recenter the problematic of learning and public order could be to analyze the ways in which what I call knowledge economy—the production, circulation, and transformation of Islamic knowledge—relates to other discursive platforms, in particular sermons and preaching, which also aim to disseminate and popularize religious knowledge.

NOTES

1. In most of Muslim West Africa, *hajia* is the prestigious title for women who have accomplished the hajj, the Muslim pilgrimage. It is one of the five pillars of Islam and held once a year. In countries such as Mali and Senegal, the equivalent for *hajia* is *adja*.
2. In proper Hausa, one would have said *mun samu ilimi* because of the incommensurability of knowledge, but she used the term *karu* to stress the augmentation as a material reality one can produce.
3. Izala is an Islamic reform movement that emerged in Northern Nigeria in the 1970s and spread to Niger and other countries in West Africa. Izala has systematically targeted Sufi organizations and practices it deemed unlawful (bid'a).
4. *Mata malam* (the scholar's wife) is not necessarily the *malama* (woman scholar) of the town.
5. A center comprising a mosque and several class and conference rooms.
6. Obviously, this is far from the reality in many contexts.

REFERENCES

Alidou, Ousseina. 2005. *Engaging Modernity*. Madison: University of Wisconsin Press.
Babou, Cheick A. 2007. *Fighting the Greater Jihad: Amadu Bamba and the Founding of the Muridiyya of Senegal, 1853–1913*. Athens: Ohio University Press.
Brenner, Louis. 2001. *Controlling Knowledge: Religion, Power, and Schooling in a West African Muslim Society*. Bloomington: Indiana University Press.
Cooper, Barbara N. 1997. *Marriage in Maradi: Gender and Culture in a Hausa Society in Niger, 1900–1989*. Portsmouth, NH: Heinemann.
Eickelman, Dale F.. 1992. *Knowledge and Power in Morocco*. Princeton: Princeton University Press.
Glew, Robert S. 1996. "Islamic Associations in Niger." *Islam et Sociétés au Sud du Sahara* 10: 187–204.
Kobo, Ousman. 2012. *Unveiling Modernity in Twentieth-Century West African Islamic Reforms*. Boston: Brill.
LeBlanc, Marie Nathalie. 1999. "The Production of Islamic Identities through Knowledge Claims in Bouaké, Côte d'Ivoire." *African Affairs* 98 (393): 485–508.

Loimeier, Roman. 2009. *Between Social Skills and Marketable Skills: The Politics of Islamic Education in 20th Century Zanzibar.* Leiden: Brill.

Maikorema, Zakari. 2007. "La naissance et le développement du mouvement Izala au Niger." In *Islam, Sociétés et Politique en Afrique Subsaharienne: Les exemples du Sénégal, du Niger et du Nigeria,* edited by Hassane Souley, Xavier Moyet, et al., 51–74. Paris: Indes Savantes.

———. 2009. *Islam dans l'espace nigérien: 1960–2000.* Paris: Harmattan.

Masquelier, Adeline. 1999. "Debating Muslims, Disputed Practices: Struggles for the Realization of an Alternative Moral Order in Niger." In *Civil Society and the Political Imagination in Africa,* edited by J. L. Comaroff and J. Comaroff, 219–50. Chicago: University of Chicago Press.

———. 2009. *Women and Islamic Revival in A West African Town.* Bloomington: Indiana University Press.

Meunier, Olivier. 1997. *Dynamique de l'enseignement islamique au Niger.* Paris: Karthala.

———. 1998. *Les voies de l'Islam au Niger dans le Katsina indépendant du XIXe au XXe siècle: (Maradi, pays hawsa).* Paris: Publications scientifiques du Muséum.

———. 2002. "Développement du wahhabisme au Niger: Analyse socio-historique de la diffusion du mouvement *Izala* dans la ville de Maradi." In Cahiers africains de recherche en education. "*L'éducation dans la société africaine.*" 1: 121–52.

Moulaye, Hassane. 1995. "La transmission du savoir religieux en Afrique sub-saharienne: un exemple du commentaire coranique tafsirue sub-saharie." Thesis, Université Paris IV Sorbonne.

Reveyrand-Coulon, Odile. 1993. "Les énoncés féminins de l'Islam." In *Religion et modernité politique en Afrique noire,* edited by J. F. Bayart. Paris: Karthala.

Sounaye, Abdoulaye. 2005. "Les politiques de l'Islam dans l'ère de la démocratisation de 1991 à 2002." In *L'Islam politique au sud du Sahara,* edited by M. Perez-Gomez. Paris: Karthala.

———. 2009a. "Islam, État et société: à la recherche d'une éthique publique au Niger." In *Islam, Etat et Société,* edited by René Otayek and Benjamin Soares. Paris: Karthala.

———. 2009b. "Izala au Niger: Une alternative de communauté religieuse." In *Lieux de sociabilité urbaine en Afrique,* edited by Laurent Fourchard, Odile Goerg, and Muriel Gomez-Perez. Paris: Harmattan.

———. 2011. "Go Find the Second Half of Your Faith with These Women! Women Fashioning Islam in Contemporary Niger." *Muslim World* 101 (3): 539–54.

———. 2012. "Les Clubs des Jeunes Musulmans du Niger: Un cadre de formation et un espace intergénérationnel." In *L'Afrique des générations. Entre tensions et négotiations,* edited by Muriel Gomez-Perez and Marie Nathalie LeBlanc. Paris: Karthala.

Umar, Muhammad S. 1993. "From Sufism to Anti-Sufism in Nigeria." In *Muslim Identity and Social Change in Sub-Saharan Africa,* edited by L. Brenner. Bloomington: Indiana University Press.

———. 2004. "Mass Islamic Education and the Emergence of Female Ulama in Northern Nigeria: Background, Trends, and Consequences." In *The Transmission of Learning in Islamic Africa,* edited by Scott S. Reese. Leiden: Brill.

Willis, John Ralph. 1979. *Studies in West African Islamic History,* vol. 1, *The Cultivators of Islam.* London: Frank Cass.

PLURAL POSSIBILITIES?

13.
HOW (NOT) TO READ THE QUR'AN? LOGICS OF ISLAMIC EDUCATION IN SENEGAL AND CÔTE D'IVOIRE

Robert Launay and Rudolph T. Ware III[*]

(translated from the French by Robert Launay)

⁂

THIRTY YEARS AGO, in any West African Muslim community, you could see boys (and often girls) seated in a circle, writing boards in hand, chanting texts in Arabic, usually passages from the Qur'an. The master or one of his advanced students stood in the middle of the circle, wielding a rod ready to strike the head of the unfortunate pupil who botched his recitation. The aim of the exercise was the memorization of the Qur'an; the pupil ought to be able to recite any passage of the Qur'an correctly and melodically, if not melodiously. Few children understood what they were reciting. In general, a pupil was authorized to undertake the discursive study of religion only after having been *submitted* to Qur'anic education or, as one former student put it, having been "immersed in the bath of suffering." This elementary instruction was aimed at interiorizing rather than understanding the Qur'an, in order to fashion a fit recipient worthy of carrying the Word of God. Once this condition was satisfied, it was then possible to begin to understand its meaning through the use of that necessary but suspect tool, human reason.[1]

Such practices are becoming increasingly rare throughout much of Islamic West Africa (cf. Brenner 2001; Alidou 2005). In the eyes of an increasing number of Muslims, this kind of pedagogy seems out of date, if not incoherent. How, in effect, can you justify learning a foreign but sacred language while apparently neglecting the meaning of specific words, not to mention notions of grammar? Indeed, the merits or failings of such a system of education is one of the principal

---

[*] Originally published as "Comment (ne pas) lire le Coran? Logiques de l'enseignement religieux au Sénégal et en Côte d'Ivoire," in Holder (2009).

sites whereby so-called reformist, fundamentalist, and Islamist movements challenge supposedly traditionalist practices of Islam.[2] Often such movements are analyzed from a social or political perspective, although many of their activities are in the field of education. It would be tempting to reduce their objections to traditionalist practices to ideological quarrels—that is, to clearly articulated differences of principle. However, traditionalists and reformers are separated less by what they proclaim than what literally goes without saying, by the ways in which they construe religious sense and non-sense. Their differences need to be situated at the epistemic rather than the ideological level.

Classical pedagogical practices (qualifying them as traditional implicitly adopts the modernist epistemic perspective) follow from a certain understanding of learning and reading, particularly of sacred texts. They are based on the assertion that the Qur'an is literally the word of God and, as such, perfect and infallible. In a sense, Divine speech in classical Arabic is untranslatable, because any translation depends on the translator's interpretation; as the product of human effort, it is subject to error. This is why, in the classical tradition of Islamic learning, *tafsir*, the exegesis of the Divine work, was the last discipline to be taught to students, well after the memorization of the Qur'an and the study of jurisprudence, grammar, the life of the Prophet, poetry, and rhetoric. On the other hand, modernist education begins with a mastery of the Arabic language in order to grasp the meaning of the Divine Word. The aim here is to be able to grasp the exoteric meaning of the Qur'an to enable discussion of what God commands or recommends, forbids or discourages.

In classical Islamic education, the form and attributes of the Divine Word often seem to take precedence over the literal meaning. This is obviously the case for pupils beginning their Qur'anic education, but it is also true in the transmission of knowledge in certain disciplines. *Tajwid*, the recitation of the Divine Word—specifically its correct recitation (including melody)—constitutes an act of worship, the accomplishment of a divinely ordained duty. If we follow this logic, a botched recitation is at the very least inefficacious and at worst impious. For example, on one occasion in Korhogo (Côte d'Ivoire), Launay observed a preacher fulminating against worshiper who mispronounced the words *Allahu 'akbar* as *Alla haki baru*, a local pronunciation of the *takbir* which, according to him, was an incorrect approximation. It is important to note that, throughout his sermon, the preacher never alluded to the meaning of the words, only to their pronunciation.

This faith in the efficacy of the Divine Word spoken in Arabic is not limited to the practices of daily prayer and Qur'anic recitation. For example, in the Dyula community of Korhogo, part of the funerary ritual consists of reading an entire book of over a hundred pages of praise to the Prophet on behalf of the deceased.

To accomplish the task rapidly, three or four detached pages are distributed to each literate member of the audience. When the signal is given, one might see thirty men simultaneously chanting the pages they have each been assigned, finishing the recitation in several minutes rather than several hours. Obviously, an outside observer would be unable to understand the words, but these texts are, in this context, a matter of form, and their specific meaning is, at least for this purpose, irrelevant.

Such practices, to which we can add the recitation of the profession of faith (*shahada*); the call to prayer (*'adhan*), which is the voiced symbol of Islam that is pronounced in the ear of newborn babies; or else the manufacture of talismans from Qur'anic verses, depend on a faith in the intrinsic capacity of the Divine Word to produce results through its own power (Lory 1993; Hamès 2007). The educational system of the reformists privileges reason rather than the efficacy of speech. It is the mind's understanding of the meaning of words that enables the body to perform the duties and public expressions of faith. Of course, traditionalists also engage and employ reason, but they believe above all that the Divine Word creates its own capacity to form subjects.

A whole series of pedagogical strategies are rooted in this belief, and various disciplinary practices follow from the idea that humans need to be humbled before they become receptacles fit to receive the Sacred Word. In the interviews that Rudolph Ware conducted with *talibés* and former *talibés* of Senegalese Qur'anic schools, many respondents cited *yar* as the principal feature of their spiritual experience.[3] In Wolof, the most usual meaning of this word is "to raise, to educate, education." But the primary meaning of the word *yar* is "whip, rod." In other words, when elders sought a formulation of the abstract concept of education, they chose a noun that evoked corporal discipline. It is easy to understand the link between Qur'anic education and *yar* in terms of the classic Senegambian idea that pain is virtually indispensable for the acquisition of learning and for any education worthy of the name. Qur'anic masters have a reputation for the harshness of their corporal punishment, although this is only one aspect of the emphasis on suffering and privation.

One must be humbled to attune oneself to learning, and this is the principal justification of that other very controversial characteristic of Qur'anic schooling—begging for alms, a practice that the Portuguese noted in Senegambia as early as the seventeenth century.[4] This is a codified practice common to most Muslim societies in West Africa, which is not to say that it does not also stem from material considerations. But it is primarily linked to the necessary inculcation of modesty, of self-renunciation, which is one of the major dimensions of Qur'anic education. This conception was frequently stressed in the field, as in the testimony of Amadu Basiru Jeng, a Murid *talibé* interviewed by Rudolph Ware who grew up in a rural

Muslim community (*daara*) near Touba. He explained that "it is hard to lighten oneself. . . . But making yourself lighter allows you to elevate yourself; you leave what it heavy behind." Such practices and the conceptions that underpin them are profoundly rooted in Senegalese, and more generally West African, culture and history (Ware 2004b).

Among Ware's interlocutors, many associated the hardships experienced in Qur'anic schools with two central Wolof notions: *toj xol bi*, "breaking the heart," and *defarat jikko*, "building character." This is precisely the sense of comments by Abdu Ali Sekk, a young scion of a maraboutic family in Tivaouane, as he explains this characteristic conception of Qur'anic school: "When the child reaches the age of seven, he is sent to the *daara*, because the *daara* builds character (*defar jikko*), a character [formed by] the worship of God. [In Qur'anic school,] they sweep the character clean . . . [they] clean it and purify it to make it beautiful. That is the character that they build in the *daara*, the house of the Qur'an."[5]

This image of cleaning the character is often compared to washing dishes, as if it were literally necessary to clean out a receptacle fit to hold the Sacred Word. For some, this is precisely the dimension lacking in reformist schools. In Senegal, several former *talibés*, including teaching marabouts, readily admitted that the "Arab schools" (*sic*) provided solid instruction in the Arabic language and furnished a good, if not excellent, discursive education in religious principles. For example, Ibrahima Badiane, director of a Qur'anic school in Tivaouane with more than 1,500 pupils, considers that, while "Arab" schools provide good "teaching" (*jàngle*), they do not furnish an "education" (*yar*). He remarks that *jàngle* without *yar* is like "taking a bowl and putting food inside before you wash it."[6] In numerous interviews, informants stressed the difference between *jàngle* and *yar*, two words that can logically be translated as "teaching" and "education." *Jàngle* comes from the verb *jàng*, "read, study," and implies ideas very different from *yar*. Despite differences in meaning that follow from etymological differences, the usual distinction between *jàngle* and *yar* is comparable to the distinction in Arabic between *ta'alim*, "teaching, instruction," and *tarbiyya*, "education."

Classically, education in the Muslim world was first and foremost a pedagogy based on discipline, memorization, interiorizing texts, and the imitation of physical example of the practice of faith. These are the same notions that structured the study of the Islamic sciences, even if discipline ceased to take the form of corporal punishment or begging for alms. In normal circumstances, an *ijaza*—that is, the permission to teach a given book[7]—was not conferred until the master was convinced from his disciple's behavior that the "science of jurisprudence" (*fiqh*) or the "science of self-purification" (*tasawwuf*)[8] he had studied was fully inscribed in the core of his being. Building character, disciplining the *nafs* (the inferior, carnal soul which "incited to evil") by sacred knowledge and by finding a guide to the straight and narrow path were at the heart of the preoccupations of classical Islamic Sufi thought. Divine revelation is indisputably the highest level in the hierarchy of Islamic knowledge. Reason (*'aql*) supplements but cannot replace revelation as a form of knowledge. The master is not simply responsible for teaching the text but for physically integrating it and thus permitting his disciple to incarnate it in his own turn. Only those who had been subjected to such an education and who had literally been able to incorporate the Qur'an were authorized to teach it.

The master's example was physically reproduced by his disciples, who brought their "gift of themselves" (*hadiya*) and pious service (*xidma* in Wolof, from the Arabic *khidma*) in order to earn salvation (Babou 2007, 105–6) and the acknowledgment of their master, the only keys that could open the possibilities for any knowledge they acquired. In the *Cahiers Ponty*, among the testimonials of Senegalese students in the mid-twentieth century, this paradigm of imitation is repeatedly mentioned; pupils observed the minutest details of the teacher's behavior, copying and repeating his gestures and attitudes.[9] In short, the master instructed his pupils as much by the movements of his body as by words.[10] Moreover, respect and affection for the master as the physical representative of Islam was an established concept, because it was thought that the *sérignes* could communicate their "blessing" (*baraka*) to their disciples. The veneration of agents of the Book was in the image of the Book itself, by definition the source of miracles.[11]

It must be stressed that the idea of the interiorization of the Qur'an was neither metaphorical nor symbolic. In the Qur'anic schools of West Africa, the Holy Book was incorporated in the most literal possible way, by drinking it.[12] Drinking the Qur'an was a means of understanding the power of the Qur'anic word; such physical incorporation of the word dates to the early years of Islam. In manuals for schoolteachers written in North Africa in the ninth and tenth centuries, such practices are traced to the first generations of Muslims.[13] This practice was continued in West African Qur'anic schools. Sanneh (1989, 149) relates that, among the Jakhanke of Senegambia, the child would literally lick the *basmala*,[14] while Santerre (1973, 11) states that, in the Malian town of Bandiagara, the *basmala* was normally drunk rather than licked or eaten.

This physical incorporation of the Word of God rests on faith in the power of the Divine speech which, as researchers have noted, is being supplanted by modernist interpretations that understand and teach the Qur'an in a strictly literal and exoteric way. Teaching the Qur'an in West Africa, where Maliki law predominated, followed the principle of a physical, corporal, personified, and incarnated model. This tradition seeks not only to form minds but to (re)form the movements and the members of the body. In one *Cahier Ponty*, Malick Fall cites the Maliki principle stipulating that a child should begin praying when he is seven. But the author adds that, in his natal town of Dagatch, children were actually expected to pray well before then, in order that "these things be profoundly anchored in their hearts, become familiar to their souls, and that the requisite gestures and postures become strictly habitual."[15]

This approach based on physical example and practice and personified by a master is much appreciated in the Maliki *madhhab* and indeed serves to distinguish it from the practices of other schools. Yasin Dutton (1999) has shown that Imam Malik always preferred personified practice as exemplified in *'isnad*[16] to hadith themselves as a source of *fiqh*. Although he was the first scholar to compile an authoritative collection of hadith, whenever any hadith, even one with a sound *'isnad*, departed from "current practice" (*'amal*) in Medina, he consistently preferred the latter.[17] The transmission of a lived Islam by a thousand people to another thousand people was sounder than the transmission of hadith from person to person, even when such hadith would ultimately figure in the books that constitute *fiqh* (Dutton 1999; Motzki 2002). To put it another way, in the Maliki school, Islam is not taught; it is transmitted.

It is because the meaning of the Divine Word is so important that it must be approached with great precaution to minimize the possibility of error. Traditionalist religious authority is entirely logically based on such principles. In this respect, the soundest guarantee of religious knowledge is its direct, personal, face-to-face transmission by a qualified teacher, a qualification determined in large measure by the authority of the master from whom he, in turn, obtained his knowledge. The integrity of knowledge depends on the validity of its chain of transmission—*ijaza*, *'isnad*, or *silsila*. These are, after all, the same principles that determine the reliability of a hadith, which depends of the integrity of each link in its chain of transmission (Graham 1993).

In this way, religious authority is entirely personalized, indeed personified. It is not possible to distinguish clearly between the content of knowledge and the person who possesses it. This is no doubt the reason why, when Robert Launay attempted in Korhogo to construct a hierarchy of knowledge, to determine which marabout was more knowledgeable (or at least reputed to be so) than another, he could never obtain any consensus. It was out of the question that anyone, especially a marabout, could consider himself more knowledgeable than his teacher, past or present. It was equally presumptuous, if not impious, for a marabout to pronounce judgment on the extent of the knowledge of his peers. Ordinary believers were no doubt freer to emit favorable or unfavorable judgments, but it was quickly apparent that these depended on the nature of the ties between the marabout and the informant. It became obvious that the logic of the system left no room for abstract, depersonalized, "disincarnated" knowledge.

It goes without saying that, in West Africa, Sufi brotherhoods, where the *wird* is directly transmitted from *shaykh* to *talibé*, constitute the most obvious example of this highly personalized form of religious authority. But this kind of authority and the logic that underpins it is hardly confined to Sufism. If, for over a century, Sufism has been the most important vector in Senegal for the transmission of Islam, the situation has been very different in northern Côte d'Ivoire (to cite only one example); there, where Sufi brotherhoods never played such a prominent role, religious authority in the Muslim community was just as personalized. And if today the guardians of this epistemology are often Sufis, this is perhaps because they have been able to conserve, thanks to the structures of the *turuq* (in the face of a century of epistemological contestation) a more diffuse approach.[18]

It must be stressed that classical Islamic conceptions of knowledge and religious authority are based on a logic that is not always explicit, precisely because, for its partisans, it goes more or less without saying. This approach has nothing to do with a so-called *Islam noir*; like Sufi brotherhoods, it is—or at least used to be—commonly found throughout the Muslim world.[19] If this perspective is threatened with disappearance in certain regions of West Africa, this is not because a putatively global Islam is in the process of replacing a more parochial one (if we may borrow a metaphor from another religion), much less because a supposedly "purer" Islam is in the process of replacing a "mixed" variety, guilty of the crime of "Word fetishism." Nor is it the result of a process that would suggest that a superior form of religious logic is eclipsing a "prelogical" form of Islam, last bastion of the "savage mind." Rather, we are faced with two irreconcilable regimes of truth. It is certain that we share a form of rationality with the reformists; simply reciting the Qur'an from memory can seem a somewhat meaningless exercise. We can, of course, always find explanations, if not excuses, for such practices. For example, it might be supposed that, to the extent that Africans might formerly have lacked truly educated scholars, it was nonetheless necessary for teachers whose knowledge was relatively limited to teach children the necessary rudiments of prayer and of the faith. Similarly, when paper was a precious commodity and books eminently perishable, perpetually menaced by fire or voracious insects, rote learning protected against the total eradication of knowledge, an Islamic precursor of *Fahrenheit 451*. Such explanations are not necessarily false, but in important respects they are beside the point.

The single most important epistemic difference distinguishing adherents of the classical approach from reformists is that the former are convinced of the opacity of signs, the latter of their transparency. For reformists, the Qur'an can be reduced to the meaning of its words. Whoever masters its language thus has access to the content of the book and can decipher its message. Proper religious schooling is exemplified by the madrasa if not Anglo-Arabic or Franco-Arabic schools (Launay1992, 92–98; Brenner 2001). In principle, Arabic is taught the same way as English or French; pupils, separated according to grade level, begin by learning the alphabet before studying vocabulary and grammar. Admittedly, in some madrasas, instruction is hardly different from that provided by Qur'anic schools, except that blackboards have replaced writing boards. But even such apparently trivial innovations suggest the acceptance of a change in fundamental principles. From the moment one accepts these principles, classical Qur'anic education is at best a second-rate fallback option; at worst, frankly inadequate.

From the modernist perspective, knowledge is an abstract quality that can be evaluated. It should be objectively possible to determine who knows more than whom, at least in a given subject. School examinations furnish a paradigm of how one might arrive at such judgments. From such a point of view, religious authority stems naturally from any given individual's degree of knowledge. It makes no difference how he acquires this knowledge, and even less who has transmitted it. Diplomas are conferred by institutions and not, like *ijaza*, by individuals. Moreover, all means of transmitting knowledge are valid—books, radio, television, even the internet (Starrett 1998). In reality, of course, ordinary believers are not in a position to judge objectively the degree of knowledge needed to confer religious authority. Under such circumstances, reputation becomes a fundamental asset, but it is established in a very different manner than among classically trained scholars, where it is a function of scholarly networks and their insertion in local communities. To the extent that, for reformists, knowledge is not anchored in such networks, the politics of reputation is open to more impersonal forms of creation and diffusion, notably the mass media—newspapers, radio, television, audio and video cassettes. In this way, the very media that are a source of knowledge for reformists are also a source of power. In principle, of course, their opponents can also employ such media. Audio cassettes in particular suit them relatively well, given the importance they place on oral transmission. On the other hand, access to cutting-edge technologies such as radio and television, not to mention the internet, is largely controlled by modernist elites who share the same conception of knowledge as reformists, even if they do not necessarily share their point of view. As a result, classically trained preachers tend to be excluded from such media de facto rather than de jure.

To the extent that the mass media tend to validate the abstract conception of knowledge that they convey, they privilege the diffusion of reformism in the Islamic public sphere. Moreover, such media visibility makes reformists easier for outside observers, especially journalists and academics, to notice. But if reformists gain ground in this way, this should not be taken to constitute the triumph of rationalism over obscurantism, or else one risks uncritically reproducing the reformists' discourse. Conceivably, new postmodern ways of understanding are emerging that may oblige us to realize that the very idea of the transparency of signs, of the inseparable link between signifier and signified, is not self-evident. The conviction that signs are inherently opaque can constitute an equally coherent system of thought. This hardly implies that classical Islamic scholars are really postmodernists *avant la lettre*. For such scholars, the opacity of signs is a source of anxiety rather than of celebration; for them, reformism gives rise to uncontrolled if not uncontrollable interpretations of the Word, which in this way risks desacralization and banalization.

For the time being, the public sphere is characterized by a struggle for control over education, not only between so-called traditionalists and reformists but also partisans of secular schooling. From an ideological standpoint, classical and reformist educators are in the same camp and harbor a common suspicion of all forms of secular ideology. On the other hand, there is a real epistemic rupture between practitioners of classical Islamic education on one side and reformists and secularists on the other. These two latter groups share a common vision of the form, if not the content, of knowledge. Indeed, there is no inseparable gulf between Anglo-Arabic or Franco-Arabic schools and state systems. As a result, certain countries have chosen to incorporate, or even privilege, such a style of religious learning. These similarities and differences between systems of education in West Africa have their equivalents elsewhere in the Muslim world— Indonesia, for example—and are in no way specifically African. On the other hand, the balance of power is not everywhere the same. Largely thanks to the so-called structural adjustment policies of the International Monetary Fund and the World Bank, secular schools have lost much of their luster, having to make do with increasingly insufficient means in order to educate more and more youths for largely nonexistent jobs. It is hardly astonishing, under the circumstances, that some states are now increasingly, if sometimes reluctantly, willing to make concessions to reformists and to Franco- or Anglo-Arabic schools. Secular ideology is largely the province of quasi-hereditary elites who can afford private schools for their children or, even better, schooling abroad. The vacuum left by the state, not only in the field of education but also in its attempts to include youth in the national economy, leaves room for expansion, not only for reformist but for classical Islamic education.

These two incompatible conceptions of knowledge imply different logics, not only with respect to education but above all concerning spiritual authority, with, on one hand, personal and personalized authority validated by chains of transmission, and, on the other, authority based on abstract and impersonal knowledge, but which is perfectly consistent with a star system propelled by mass media. In the recent past, it seemed that the triumph of a fully modern reformist ideology was inevitable, and its discourse on the inadequacy, if not the absurdity, of classical practices was virtually taken for granted, at least by outside observers. However, with the withdrawal of the state, personal ties—patron-client ties, of course, but also ties between classically trained marabouts and their followers—have increasingly emerged as more reliable than state institutions. Reformist trends will not, of course, vanish into thin air. But it may be that classical education finds a second wind and that the Islamic public sphere in West Africa will be confronted not only by an ideological divide but by an epistemic divide that is less obvious but runs deeper. But there is another possible outcome. Recent research reveals that teaching marabouts are experimenting with pedagogical practices pioneered by reformist educators at the same time as parents exert pressure that their children receive a religious formation and education.[20] There are certainly attempts to develop a hybrid epistemology through a combination of practices that, on one side or the other, have been contested. It remains to be seen whether such a hybrid form of Islamic education will be capable of resolving the apparent contradictions between its very different sources.

NOTES

1. Cheikh Hamidou Kane's novel, *L'aventure ambigüe* (1961), includes a striking portrait of this kind of Islamic education. For recent academic analyses, see Ware (2004a) and Ndiaye (1985).

2. All these labels are problematic, to say the least.

3. The principal sources used here are from interviews conducted in 2001–2002 with former *talibés* in the regions of Tivaouane and Touba, as well as the *Cahiers Ponty*, archived at the Institut Fondamental d'Afrique noire in Kakar, which are made up of various notebooks written by former pupils of the Ecole Normale William Ponty. Nine of these notebooks, five hundred manuscript pages of extremely rich documentation, were written by Senegalese authors who recount their experiences of Qur'anic education in the *daara* in the 1920s and 1930s.

4. See notably the writings of the Cape Verdian Francisco de Lemos Coelho, *Descripção da costa de Guiné* (1667), cited in Mbaye (1976), *L'Islam au Sénégal*, doctoral thesis, UCAS, Dakar: 238.

5. Ware, interview with Abdu Ali Sekk, Tivaouane, August 2001. The Wolof term *daara* is derived from the Arabic work *dar*, "house, home" (here *dar al Qur'an* means "the house of the Qur'an").

6. Ware, interview with Ibrahima Badiane, Tivouane, July 17, 2001. The same idea was expressed in an interview with Xaliil Lo, Ngaabu, May 28, 2002.

7. In principle, an *ijaza* is conferred by a scholar (*'alim*) who in turn holds his own *ijaza*, forming a chain that reaches back to the Companions of the Prophet and ultimately to Muhammad; indeed, Launay was shown documents in Côte d'Ivoire where the chain was extended from Muhammad to the angel *Jibril* (Gabriel) and through a series of angels all the way to God.

8. *Tasawwuf* is the Arabic term for Sufism.

9. See in particular Baba Ndiaye, "L'Islam en pays noir; l'école coranique, in *Cahier Ponty* Vii-Se-1 (Kakar: Institut Fondamental d'Afrique noire in Kakar), 36. See also the statement of D. K. in Colin (1980, 120) as well as Sanneh (1997, 124–25).

10. On this point, see the example of medieval Damascus, from Al-Yununi, *Dhayl mir'at al-zaman* (Hyderabad, 1374–1380/1954–1961, 2/57) cited in Chamberlain (1997, 29).

11. For a useful discussion of the power of the Holy Book, see Mommersteeg (1991) and Lory (1993). For a discussion of amulets, see Brenner (1985) and Hamès (1993).

12. Ware, interviews with Ibrahima Sey (Touba, May 2002) and Masamba Buso (Mbake, May 30, 2002). See also the first chapter of Ware's thesis (2004a), notably the section entitled "Initiation." See also Mamadou Ndiaye (1985, 175), who notes in this respect that, according to a questionnaire from the Institut Islamique, the only medical care given to most *talibés* was holy water (*saafara*). However, in their answers, several people suggested that *saafara* was the first therapeutic option, and not the only one. For example, Ibrahima Sey indicated that, if the *saafara* was insufficient, the children were sent to a doctor, adding nonetheless that, in most cases, the *saafara* was effective. Such recourse to *safaara* is mentioned in a number of the *Cahiers Ponty*, notably Demba Beye, "Etude coranique de Gassama" (*Cahier Ponty* VII-Se-3 [Kakar: Institut Fondamental d'Afrique noire], 32).

13. Rudolph Ware develops this notion in chapter 1 of "Knowledge, Faith and Power: A History of Qur'anic Schooling in Senegal" (2004a). For sources mentioning the ingestion of the Qur'anic text during the earliest period in Islam, see notably the works of Fu'ad Aswani (1955, 317) and Khaled (1986), the last also including the book of Muhammad b. Sahnun.

14. The *basmala* is the action of reciting *bismillah*, the opening formula of the suras of the Qur'an and an invocation generally pronounced at the beginning of any action in daily life.

15. Malick Sèye Fall, "L'Éducation traditionelle," *Cahier Ponty* XV-SE-575 (Dakar: Institut Fondamental d'Afrique noire), cited in Colin (1980, 114–15).

16. A chain of persons who relate a hadith.

17. It is moreover one of the principal characteristics of the Maliki school to consider the practices of the people of Medina (*'amal ahl al-Madina*) as a source of jurisprudence.

18. See Ware (2004a), especially the chapter "The Seriñ and the Shaikh: Teaching Tasawwuf, and Tariqa" (166–200).

19. To cite just one example, Dale Eickelman (1985), in recounting the education of a Moroccan notable in the early twentieth century, demonstrates that the memorization of the Qur'an was practiced as commonly north of the Sahara as the south. For a systematic critique of the notion of *Islam noir*, see Ware (2014).

20. Aside from the above-mentioned studies of Alidou (2005), Brenner (1985, 2001) and Ware (2004a, 2004b), see also Meunier (1997).

REFERENCES

Alidou, Ousseina. 2005. *Engaging Modernity: Muslim Women and the Politics of Agency in Postcolonial Niger*. Madison: University of Wisconsin Press.

Babou, Cheikh Anta. 2007. *Fighting the Greater Jihad: Amadu Bamba and the Founding of the Muridiyya of Senegal, 1853–1913*. Athens: Ohio University Press.

Brenner, Louis. 1985. "The Esoteric Sciences in West African Islam." In *African Healing Strategies*, edited by Brian M. du Toit and Ismail H. Abdalla, 20–28. Buffalo, NY: Trado-Medic Books.

———. 2001. *Controlling Knowledge: Religion, Power and Schooling in a West African Muslim Society*. Bloomington: Indiana University Press.

Chamberlain, Michael. 1997. "The Production of Knowledge and the Reproduction of the A'yan in Medieval Damascus." In *Madrasa: La transmission du savoir dans le monde musulman*, edited by Marc Gaborieau and Nicole Grandin, 28–62. Paris: Arguments.

Colin, Roland. 1980. *Systèmes d'éducation et mutations sociales: Le cas du Sénégal*, vol. 1. Paris: Honoré Champion.

Dutton, Yasin. 1999. *The Origins of Islamic Law: The Qur'an, the Muwatta' and Madinan 'Amal*. Richmond, UK: Curzon.

Eickelman, Dale. 1985. *Knowledge and Power in Morocco: The Education of a Twentieth-Century Notable*. Princeton, NJ: Princeton University Press.

Fu'ad Aswani, Ahmad. 1955. *Al-tarbiya fi al'Islam aw Al'ta'alim fi ray as'Qabisi*. Cairo: Dar al-kutub al-'arabiya.

Graham, William A. 1993. "Traditionalism in Islam: An Essay in Interpretation." *Journal of Interdisciplinary History* 23 (3), 495–522.

Hamès, Constant. 1993. "Entre recette magique d'Al-Bûnî et prière Islamique d'Al-Ghazâlî. Textes talismaniques d'Afrique occidentale." In *Fétiches II: Puissance des objects, charme des mots. Systèmes de pensées en Afrique noire*, edited by Albert de Surgy. No. 12: 187–223.

———, ed. 2007. *Coran et talismans. Textes et pratiques magiques en milieu musulman*. Paris: Karthala.

Holder, Gilles, ed. 2009. *L'Islam, nouvel espace public en Afrique*. Paris: Karthala.

Kane, Hamidou. 1961. *L'aventure ambigüe*. Paris: R. Julliard.

Khaled, Ahmed. 1986. *Al-Qasibi: Risala al-mufassila li-ahwal al-muta'allimin was akham al mu'allimin was al matu'allimin. Épitre détaillée sure les situations des élèves, leurs règles de conduite et celles des maîtres*. Tunis: STD.

Launay, Robert. 1992. *Beyond the Stream: Islam and Society in a West African Town*. Berkeley: University of California Press.

Lory, Pierre. 1993. "Verbe Coranique et magie en terre d'Islam." In *Fétiches II: Puissance des objects, charme des mots. Systèmes de pensées en Afrique noire*, edited by Albert de Surgy. No. 12: 173–86.

Mbaye, Ravane. 1976. "L'Islam au Sénégal." PhD. diss., Université de Dakar.

Meunier, Olivier. 1997. *Dynamique de l'enseignement islamique au Niger: Le cas de la ville de Maradi*. Paris: Harmattan.

Mommersteeg, Geert. 1991. "L'éducation coranique au Mali: Le pouvoir des mots sacrés." In *L'enseignement islamique au Mali*, edited by Bintou Sanandkoua and Louis Brenner, 45–61. Bamako, Mali: Jamana.

Motzki, Harald. 2002. *The Origins of Islamic Jurisprudence: Meccan Fiqh before the Classical Schools*. Leiden: Brill.

Ndiaye, Mamadou. 1985. *L'enseignement arabo-islamique au Sénégal*. Istanbul: OCI/IRCICA.

Sanneh, Lamin. 1989. *The Jakhanke Muslim Clerics: A Religious and Historical Study of Islam in Senegambia*. Lanham, MD: University Press of America.

———. 1997. *The Crown and the Turban: Muslims and West African Pluralism*. Boulder, CO: Westview.
Santerre, Renaus. 1973. *Pédagogie musulmane d'Afrique noire: L'école coranique peule du Cameroun*. Montreal: Presses Universitaires de Montréal.
Starrett, Gregory. 1998. *Putting Islam to Work: Education, Politics, and Religious Transformation in Egypt*. Berkeley: University of California Press.
Ware, Rudolph T. III. 2004a. "Knowledge, Faith and Power: A History of Qur'anic Schooling in Twentieth-Century Senegal." Unpublished PhD dissertation in History, University of Pennsylvania.
———. 2004b. "Njàngaan: The Daily Regime of Qur'anic Students in Twentieth-Century Senegal." *International Journal of African Historical Studies* 37 (3): 515–38.
———. 2014. *The Walking Qur'an: Islamic Education, Embodied Knowledge, and History in West Africa*. Chapel Hill: University of North Carolina Press.

CAHIERS PONTY

Wane, Amadou. "Trois ans d'école coranique." Cahier William Ponty VII-Se-2, Institut Fondamental d'Afrique Noire, Dakar, 1943–44.
Ndiaye, Baba. "L'Islam en pays noir, l'école coranique" ("L'Islam au Sénégal, l'école coranique"). Cahier William Ponty VII-Se-I [ca. 1941–44].
Gueye, Sega. "L'école coranique." Cahier William Ponty VII-Se-9, Institut Fondamental d'Afrique Noire, Dakar [ca. 1941–44].
Fall, Abdelkader. "Une école coranique que vous avez fréquentée et que vous connaissez bien." Cahier William Ponty VII-Se-6, Institut Fondamental d'Afrique Noire, Dakar [ca. 1941–44].
Fall, Cheikh. "L'école coranique." Cahier William Ponty XV-Se-6, Institut Fondamental d'Afrique Noire, Dakar, 1946–48.
Fall, Médoune. "L'école coranique." Cahier William Ponty VII-Se-8, Institut Fondamental d'Afrique Noire, Dakar [ca. 1941–44].
Diop, Abdourahmane. "Une école coranique que vous avez frequentée et que vous connaissez bien." Cahier William Ponty VII-Se-7, Institut Fondamental d'Afrique Noire, Dakar [ca. 1941–44].
Diagne, Mody. "La religion, celle de votre famille, la vôtre." Cahier William Ponty VII-Se-4, Institut Fondamental d'Afrique Noire, Dakar, 1940–41.
Beye, Demba. "Étude coranique de Gassama." Cahier William Ponty VII-Se-3, Institut Fondamental d'Afrique Noire, Dakar [ca. 1941–44].

14.
NEW MUSLIM PUBLIC FIGURES IN WEST AFRICA

*Benjamin F. Soares**

THIS CHAPTER DISCUSSES new kinds of Muslim public figures that have appeared in recent years in West Africa.[1] Although the study of Islam in Africa has developed considerably in recent years, only a few studies have sought to understand the changing role and influence of such new public figures in West Africa, who are effectively Muslim public intellectuals.[2] By Muslim public intellectual, I mean those people who communicate about Islam or as Muslims to the public or various publics in Africa and sometimes beyond. This communication by Muslim public intellectuals can be oral or written communication and might be face-to-face communication in sermons and teaching or mass-mediated via television, radio, audiocassette, video, DVD, or the internet. My definition of Muslim public intellectual is intentionally rather broad to encompass those we might characterize as "traditional" Muslim intellectuals or the ulama, who are overwhelmingly men, as well as newer Muslim intellectuals, such as secular-educated newspaper columnists, media stars, youth activists, women preachers, activists, and so forth.

Muslim public intellectuals' understandings and practice of Islam in West Africa and the kinds of social and political agendas they have sought to advance have varied considerably. Such Muslim public intellectuals in West Africa call themselves Sunnis, or less often Shia, reformists, modernists, Sufis, Salafis, Islamists, and occasionally feminists. Whereas some Muslim public intellectuals have

---

* I would like to thank Penda Mbow for first putting me in contact with Sidy Lamine Niasse. I am grateful to both her and Leonardo Villalón for various exchanges about this chapter and for making copies of some of Sidy Lamine Niasse's publications available to me before I was able to meet him. I am also grateful to audiences at Ahfad University for Women in Omdurman, the Bayreuth International Graduate School of African Studies, the Centre for Contemporary Islam at the University of Cape Town, the Netherlands Interuniversity School for Islamic Studies, Université de Toulouse II-Le Mirail, and the international conference, "Islam, Citizenship and the New Media in Pre- and Postrevolutionary Egypt," at the Netherlands-Flemish Institute in Cairo for valuable feedback.

been concerned with taking control of the state and Islamizing its institutions, particularly law and education, others have been more concerned with questions of personal piety, ethical reform, and extirpating the allegedly un-Islamic from themselves and others. Still others have focused on questions of justice, poverty, and women's rights. Several factors have facilitated the rise of these new Muslim public figures in West Africa, who have become increasingly prominent since at least the 1990s. The spread of mass education in the postcolonial period as well as transformations in forms of Islamic education and learning have opened up spaces for new kinds of religious actors such as Muslim public intellectuals. Liberalization of the media and the proliferation and spread of both old and new media technologies have also had an enormous influence on modalities of religious expression (see Hackett and Soares 2015) and on Muslim public intellectuals in particular.

If the sociological theorizing of intellectuals—for example, in the work of Shils, Mannheim, Gramsci, Foucault, and Bourdieu (for an overview, see Kurzman & Owens 2002)—has largely relied on European and North American empirical data, important work on the sociology of Muslim intellectuals (e.g., Otayek 1993; Roy 1992; Zaman 2002, 2011), changes in the public sphere in Muslim societies (Eickelman and Piscatori 1996; Eickelman and Anderson 1999; Salvatore and Eickelman 1999), and modern Muslim education (Hefner and Zaman 2007) are useful starting points for thinking historically and comparatively about Muslim public intellectuals. In drawing from that work, some of the key questions to ask about public intellectuals concern their educational trajectories, social positioning, transnational ties, affiliations, and aspirations; if and how they might be changing as a social group; and their relationship to other social and political movements, including what might be called Islamic social movements (cf. Wiktorowicz 2004).

I focus here on new kinds of Muslim public intellectuals and changing modalities of religious expression among Muslims in Senegal and Mali, neighboring countries with much in the way of shared history and culture. As some scholars have noted (e.g., Launay 1992; Soares 2007; and Otayek and Soares 2007), the study of Islam in Africa has often been reduced to the study of either Sufism or so-called Islamic reform. In much of the existing literature on Islam in Africa, there is frequently a presumed teleology whereby Muslims are moving inexorably toward purportedly more modern modalities of religious expression. It is useful to consider some examples of that literature. In a wide-ranging article on Islamic reform in sub-Saharan Africa, Roman Loimeier (2003) emphasizes the historical depth and antecedents of such reform in examples from Nigeria, Senegal, and Tanzania. This is most welcome, as is Loimeier's argument about the need to understand the various local contexts ("local frame conditions") for reform and the intellectual production of Muslim scholars in such reform in Africa. In his study of Islamic education in Zanzibar, Loimeier (2009) advances similar ideas but more specifically as they relate to education. Drawing on Louis Brenner's work on the history of madrasas in Mali (Brenner 2007), Loimeier argues that: "In the 20th century, learning has become a standardized, open, depersonalized process of sequential learning in which learning has lost its sacred and initiatic character" (2009, 162).

The considerable merits of this important comparative work aside, I do have certain reservations about some of its assumptions about Islamic reform, education, and learning. First, I want to argue that the Weberian notions of rationalization and disenchantment it shares with other commentators about Muslim societies such as Ernest Gellner (1981) and Francis Robinson (2004) are insufficient analytical tools for making sense of so-called reform in a comparative context or changing modalities of religious expression more generally. Second, and following from the first point, the assumed teleology that propels Muslim societies toward reform[3] and the end point, which is assumed to have certain identifiable characteristics such as rationalization and modernist disenchantment and to flow naturally from modern education and learning, are problematic. In this essay, I consider three prominent West African Muslim public figures: a Muslim public intellectual from Senegal; a charismatic Muslim preacher and media star from Mali; and a young woman preacher with a radio program in Mali. As I argue, it is difficult to understand these new public figures and their modalities of religious expression if one limits oneself to the Weberian analytical optics of rationalization and disenchantment and other such assumptions usually made about contemporary and modern forms of Islam, education, and learning.

In Mali and Senegal, where Muslims constitute a clear and overwhelming majority, religious messages in the public sphere have come to be centered predominantly, though not exclusively, around Islam. In a way, one might even go so far as to say that Islam has come to saturate the sphere of public discourse in postcolonial Mali and Senegal, both laïc or secular states in which the state and their leaders have long actively associated themselves with Islam and Muslim religious leaders. Since the 1980s and especially the 1990s, new kinds of Muslim religious figures in both Senegal and Mali have assumed much more prominent public roles. These specifically Muslim public figures are different from the traditionally educated ulama or leaders of Sufi orders, which have long been present and important in both countries.[4] Most of (though not all) such Muslim public figures are men, and they include authors of books, pamphlets, and newspaper articles; preachers whose sermons are broadcast on radio and television or circulate on audio, video, and DVD; those involved in Muslim educational institutions, public and private radio stations, and television; and activists and leaders of the many new Islamic associations, including Muslim women's and Muslim youth associations. The educational trajectories of the three Muslim public figures described here are quite varied. It is nevertheless striking how none of them has had any direct experience with secular state schooling. Instead, they have partaken in some of the "traditional" and "modern" Islamic educational options available to them according to their rather different personal circumstances—traditional Islamic education, including personalized shaykh–disciple relationships, the modern-style madrasa in West Africa, Saudi primary and secondary schooling in Arabic, and the Islamic university, al-Azhar in Egypt—which have helped to shape, though not determine, their subsequent careers. As I will explain, the media and new media technologies have also played key roles in the making of the careers of these three Muslim public figures.

A Cosmopolitan Public Intellectual

The first of these new Muslim public figures I would like to consider is Sidy Lamine Niasse from Senegal.[5] Sidy Lamine is a member of the Niasse family, a lineage of hereditary Muslim religious specialists from Kaolack in Senegal. He is the grandson of the noted Muslim scholar Abdoulaye Niasse (d. 1922); son of the important scholar of the Tijaniyya Sufi order, Muhammad Niasse (d. 1959); and nephew of Ibrahim Niasse (d. 1975), the famous Tijani shaykh with millions of followers in Africa from Senegal to Sudan and beyond.[6] Born in 1950, Sidy Lamine had a fairly conventional Islamic education in his hometown Kaolack. That is, he underwent a traditional Islamic education, studying from a young age to a fairly advanced level in the *daara* (Wolof) or Qur'anic school his family had long operated.[7] He subsequently taught Arabic for several years in Senegal before going in the mid-1970s to study in the Faculty of Shari'a and Law (*qanun*) at the prestigious Islamic university of al-Azhar in Egypt. In the late 1970s, after he had returned to Senegal, Sidy Lamine was arrested along with his older brother, Ahmed Khalifa, the infamous "Ayatollah of Kaolack," founder of the revolutionary Iran-inspired Senegalese Hizbullah, for radical critiques of the Senegalese government.

After release from prison, in 1984 Sidy Lamine founded *Wal Fadjri*, a French-language newspaper, even though he had no formal training in journalism or education in French, the official language of Senegal. *Wal Fadjri*, whose name is taken from the opening of the sura, *al-Fajr*, "the Dawn," in the Qur'an began as a radical, explicitly Islamic bimonthly newspaper that called for Islamic revolution. However, *Wal Fadjri* eventually appeared more frequently, and it has become one of Senegal's most respected daily newspapers and went on to become among the country's most important and influential media groups.[8] In 1997, Sidy Lamine founded a private radio station, also called Wal Fadjri, and there are now several Wal Fadjri FM stations, a publishing house, an award-winning website, and, most recently, a television station, Walf TV. Today, neither his newspaper nor other media outlets could be characterized as Islamic, let alone Islamist. In fact, today the newspaper is fairly indistinguishable from Senegal's other secular newspapers with its professional journalists and editorial staff who ostensibly operate independently of the owner. His radio and television stations carry secular as well as religious programming. In any case, I cannot enter into the details of Sidy Lamine's political activities and shifting allegiances; pan-Islamic and pan-African affinities; his ties to Iran, Libya, and Iraq (under Saddam Hussein); or conflicts with his siblings over the Niasse family's legacy in the Tijaniyya, Senegal's most important Sufi order by the number of adherents and in the country's religious field more generally.

Instead, I would like to focus on some of Sidy Lamine's specific interventions in public debate, particularly through the medium of his publications. These include five books or pamphlets, usually published simultaneously in Arabic (the written language he knows best and that of the country's ulama and Muslim religious establishment) and in French (Senegal's official language and the main language of written communication for the country's francophone elite as well as the country's press). His first pamphlet about the Islamic state was published in the 1980s, when many young African Muslims sought in the Iranian revolution a model for transforming their own societies. Like many others at the time, Sidy Lamine called explicitly for the Islamization of the state, and early issues of the newspaper featured photos of Ayatollah Khomeini and slogans about the need for revolution.[9] This was certainly in keeping with the revolutionary zeal of the period, when, as Sidy Lamine has explained, many were fascinated by the Iranian revolution and anticipated that Muslims would unite, rise up, and triumph (see Niasse 2003).

However, Sidy Lamine's more recent publications illustrate the development of his thought and trajectory over time. In his 1999 book, *Sharifu* (Niasse 2009), he invokes both Muslim scholar Abu Hamid al-Ghazali (d. 1111) and seventeenth-century French philosopher René Descartes to debunk the case of Sharifu, the five-year-old Tanzanian Muslim boy, the alleged "living miracle," who visited Senegal in May 1999. Some leading Senegalese Muslim religious leaders had helped to organize a gathering in a Dakar football stadium to which spectators flocked by the thousands to be blessed by the so-called miracle child, who had visited Benin, Côte d'Ivoire, and other African countries before traveling to Senegal. In his book, Sidy Lamine harshly criticized the religious leaders (and other members of the organizing committee) involved in Sharifu's visit to Senegal, the Senegalese government, and the media hype about this "hoax." Souleymane Bachir Diagne, a student of both Althusser and Derrida who is Senegal's most famous living scholar of Western philosophy (and now professor of philosophy in the United States), wrote the preface to Sidy Lamine's book.[10] Aside from his philosophical writings, Diagne is the author of a short popular text in French about Islam, *100 mots pour dire l'islam*, which is explicitly addressed to young francophone Muslim radicals in Senegal (see Diagne 2001).[11] That Diagne endorses Sidy Lamine's activities is an indication of the latter's change in orientation from youthful revolutionary to engaged citizen critical of his elders, including Muslim religious leaders, the government, and other citizens, who, in his view, are often entirely too credulous.

In 2004, Sidy Lamine published a pamphlet that features a color photo of former British Prime Minister Margaret Thatcher shaking hands with Crown Prince (and eventually King) Abdullah of Saudi Arabia (d. 2015) on the cover. At the time, many Senegalese thought the woman in the photo with Abdullah was Queen Elizabeth II.[12] Sidy Lamine cites a wide array of sources, including hadith and classical Islamic jurisprudence as well as such world-renowned contemporary thinkers as the Qatar-based Egyptian scholar Yusuf al-Qaradawi (quoting him from his Al Jazeera satellite television program), Sudanese Islamist Hasan al-Turabi (his book about women), and the Syrian Sunni scholar–cum–television personality Muhammad Sa'id Ramadan al-Buti (d. 2013), to refute the position of those he calls "Islamists" and "fundamentalists," who say unrelated men and women are not permitted to shake hands when greeting each other. He explains that this had recently become a subject of public debate in Senegal after a prominent leader of a Sufi order had been admonished for shaking hands with an unrelated woman (Niasse 2004, 8). As Sidy Lamine notes, all people, including men and women, regularly shake hands in Senegal and to refuse to do so can "cause discomfort" and even "create discord" between people (Niasse 2004, 29–30). When questioned about shaking a woman's hand, the leader of the Sufi order in question is reported to have remarked that he had not noticed whether the person whose hand he shook was a man or a woman, indicating, according to Sidy Lamine, "his good faith and the purity of his heart" (Niasse 2004, 30). In Sidy Lamine's way of thinking, it is licit for unrelated men and woman to shake hands as long as "there is no sexual pleasure or temptation" involved in the act (Niasse 2004, 55). Sidy Lamine concludes his pamphlet by making the argument that, by focusing so much attention on such matters as men and women shaking hands, Islamists in Senegal and elsewhere are actually diverting attention from the much more pressing and urgent matters Muslims face in the world today. One can also read this pamphlet as a spirited defense of Senegal's Sufi orders and leaders, who have come under attack from certain reformist Muslims and Islamists, who sometimes look to Saudi Arabia for inspiration. A journalist who clearly understands the power of the media, Sidy Lamine's use of Abdullah's photo on the cover of the pamphlet is both visually arresting and a bold statement of an ideological position. This pamphlet and the cover image in particular were widely discussed in Senegal, effectively becoming a major media event.

Although Sidy Lamine is uncomfortable with labels and has told me that he would not call himself a Muslim reformist,[13] the term does seem to characterize him at least in part. In addition, we can call him a rationalist and a modernist if we consider the subjects of his books, style of argumentation, and public activities. However, one should not forget that Sidy Lamine remains firmly committed to the Tijaniyya. He regularly invokes his family's long association with the Sufi order and actively participates in public gatherings of the Sufi order, where his family still plays a prominent role. He sometimes speaks publicly about the Tijaniyya, the secret, esoteric knowledge associated with Sufism, and the ties between *shaykh* and disciple.

At the same time, he is quick to emphasize that his practice of the teachings of the Tijaniyya is a personal and private matter. In some ways, Sidy Lamine seems to fit Loimeier's "patterns" of reform, in which modernizing and rationalizing impulses are in the ascendancy. As Sidy Lamine himself notes, he is a product of his times, and the way that he comports himself as one of Senegal's leading intellectuals (secular or Muslim) is rather different from his father, uncle, and grandfather, all renowned members of the ulama. They all taught in Arabic and actively sought to propagate the Tijaniyya. His father and uncle also wrote widely read and cited books and treatises about Islam and the Tijaniyya in Arabic. With his newspaper, radio stations, publications, and television station, Sidy Lamine is a cosmopolitan public intellectual who communicates with the masses as well as the country's francophone elite and the country's ulama. One might even consider Sidy Lamine a post-Islamist, one who is pragmatic and actively advocates the importance of rights and ethical behavior but is not necessarily secular in outlook or orientation (cf. Bayat 2007; Otayek and Soares 2007).

A Muslim Media Star

Many Malians today would point to Chérif Ousmane Madani Haïdara as among the most important of the country's new Muslim public figures.[14] Born in 1955 into a lineage of hereditary Muslim religious specialists closely associated with the Tijaniyya, Haïdara had a rather modest education, a fact he frequently emphasizes in his sermons, public pronouncements, and interviews. Indeed, after beginning with traditional Qur'anic education, his formal schooling was limited to only six years of study in a fee-paying private madrasa in Ségou, then Mali's second largest city. In the madrasa where Haïdara studied, he received a modern-style education in Arabic that combined learning of the Arabic language, Islamic studies, and modern subjects with the use of modern pedagogical techniques.[15] Since leaving the madrasa, Haïdara has had no other formal education. Some of his classmates from the madrasa and his other contemporaries attest to his intelligence, the wide range of his intellectual interests, and the breadth of his reading in areas related to Islam despite his limited formal education. Haïdara eventually went on to become a preacher, and, since the 1980s, he has had a reputation as an eloquent and frequently controversial orator. Interestingly, he has claimed the Egyptian preacher 'Abd al-Hamid Kishk's fiery sermons as the main inspiration for his own sermons, which have been recorded on audiocassette since the 1980s. Haïdara's fiery and often controversial sermons (see below) have garnered considerable attention, and many long painted him as a radical and an Islamist. He is also the head of one of Mali's most successful modern-style Islamic associations, Ançar Dine (Ansar al-Din in Arabic), which has many thousands of members, including a high percentage of women members, from Mali and neighboring countries, particularly Burkina Faso and Côte d'Ivoire.[16] Although Haïdara founded Ançar Dine prior to the overthrow of Moussa Traoré's regime (1968–1991), his association flourished given the changed climate with political liberalization and the greater freedom of association that followed. Haïdara's sermons on audiocassette, video, radio, and, most recently, DVD have helped to make him one of Mali's most important Muslim religious leaders and a veritable Muslim media star to whom a generation of aspiring younger Muslim figures in Mali have looked for ideas, models, and inspiration (for examples, see Soares 2007, 2010). In recent years, he launched a website (apparently defunct before being relaunched) and, like some other African Muslim religious leaders, has even joined Facebook (see below).[17]

In his sermons and public pronouncements, Haïdara frequently offers guidance and instruction on how to be a proper or authentic Muslim. In his proselytizing, or *da'wa* in Arabic, he has long been concerned with a very public Islam of personal piety and correct religious practice—a standardized way of being Muslim of regular ritual daily prayer and fasting during the month of Ramadan—and frequently denounces allegedly un-Islamic practices and behavior. If many reformist Muslims in Mali (as elsewhere) often put great emphasis on *bid'a* (Arabic) or unlawful innovation, Haïdara talks much more often about being what he considers a real, honest Muslim.

However, Haïdara's penchant for courting controversy has been a key element in the making of his career. In recorded sermons in the 1990s, he preached that Muslims could perform the ritual daily prayers (*salat*) in whatever vernacular language they speak, rather than in Arabic, as most Muslims in the world do. As one might imagine, this caused an uproar from some of Mali's leading Muslim scholars and intellectuals, who denounced him in no uncertain terms. Indeed, members of AMUPI (or the Association malienne pour l'unité et le progrès de l'Islam), the government-sponsored national Islamic organization founded in the 1980s, even arranged to have some high-profile Muslim preachers publicly castigate him. In the late 1990s, Haïdara criticized those Malian Muslims who condemn beauty pageants for their hypocrisy and talked about his own enjoyment of such pageants. In a much-discussed sermon, he used his characteristic humor to point out that all beauty contest participants in Mali had Muslim names and usually hailed from the country's most renowned centers of Islamic learning. He made this point to condemn those he called hypocrites, not the women contestants, whose beauty he praises. In his sermons in recent years, he has urged Malians—even those engaging in extramarital sex—to use condoms to prevent the spread of HIV/AIDS. He has provocatively stated that adulterous Muslims do not want to commit a second sin in addition to the sin of adultery—that is, the transmission of HIV—and should therefore use condoms to avoid doing so.

It is not surprising that the tackling of such topics, including beauty pageants, sex, adultery, HIV/AIDS, and rising drug use among youths in his sermons attracted considerable attention and generated enormous controversy.[18] Indeed, over the years and cumulatively, such controversial topics broached in his sermons have helped to make some of Haïdara's public pronouncements into media events and spectacles. Some of the sermons and the controversy surrounding them have also made them into a form of entertainment for many people.[19] However, Haïdara's message is not merely a moralizing one; it is a call for all Muslims to better themselves, their behavior, and society. He has devoted a lot of time recently to one such societal project, raising funds for and building a health center in Banconi, the poor neighborhood in Bamako where he lives. This is emblematic of how he has changed as he has aged. Today, Haïdara seems to court less controversy, and he is no longer considered an Islamist or a radical. In fact, he seems to have joined the ranks of highly respected charismatic Muslim religious leaders—indeed, even becoming a member of what we might call the country's Muslim establishment.

While not a member of any Sufi order, Haïdara is not opposed in principle to Sufi orders, as are most reformist Muslims in Mali. In fact, in his sermons and public pronouncements he has sometimes directed sharp criticism at those, including reformist Muslims (dubbed "Wahhabis" in Malian and francophone West African parlance), for failing to be true Muslims because of lax moral standards, dishonesty, and hypocrisy. However modern or contemporary the topics of Haïdara's sermons or rational his style of argumentation (cf. Schulz 2006a), his religious authority depends heavily upon his hereditary charisma as a descendant of the Prophet Muhammad. In fact, many people venerate Haïdara, the Muslim media star, much like the country's esteemed leaders of various Sufi orders and those considered living Muslim saints. Over the past decade, Haïdara has even held the annual gathering of his followers during the celebration of the *mawlid*, the birthday of the Prophet Muhammad, in a stadium in central Bamako. As most Malians note, no secular political leader could ever attract such crowds. The videos, DVDs, and photos of these *mawlid* celebrations that center on Haïdara and the adoring crowds show how he is treated like a living Muslim saint whose blessings are eagerly sought. In fact, these large gatherings are reminiscent of the "visits," or *ziyara* (Arabic), many Malian Sufi leaders and their families organize in the country's celebrated Islamic religious centers (see Soares 2005a) with the important difference that Haïdara's is held in the secular space of a stadium. It is also significant that he convenes his followers in the capital Bamako—where reformist Muslims who are well known for vigorously denouncing celebrations of the *mawlid* as *bid'a*, have their highest profile in the country.

On Haïdara's Facebook fan page, which was apparently created in 2010 and had nearly 50,000 "likes" by 2014, are many posts in which individuals exalt Haïdara. Some of his Facebook fans (who, according to their profiles, hail from Mali, Burkina Faso, Côte d'Ivoire, France, and beyond) call him a "man of God." One frequent poster on his Facebook fan page has even referred to Haïdara as the Mahdi—the divinely guided figure who is awaited at the end of the world. It is striking that many postings on Haïdara's Facebook page seem to be asking him for his blessings—that is, ostensibly for his intervention with God to improve health or to attain success. These Facebook friends seem to be treating Haïdara the way that many Malian Muslims have long treated exalted Muslim religious leaders.

Not surprisingly, it is difficult to characterize someone like Haïdara. He seems to present a creative and controversial synthesis of sometimes seemingly incommensurable positions—strict moral and ethical rectitude along with acknowledgement of the pleasure of beauty pageants and condom use for potential adulterers, and even prayer in the vernacular (though he no longer seems to advocate this, at least publicly). If Haïdara sometimes seems to play the part of the Muslim reformist or modernist, his saint-like comportment and the many Malians who treat him as a living Muslim saint suggest that he is perhaps best characterized as a saint-like modernizing Muslim of sorts—indeed, even as a celebrity with his fans both real and virtual. Although such a charismatic Muslim public figure uses the mass media and modern organizational methods, disenchantment is not useful in helping us to understand his career, fame, or success.

A Muslim Woman Preacher and Religious Specialist

The Muslim media star and celebrity Haïdara is not the only new kind of public religious figure in contemporary Mali. In fact, a whole new generation of younger Muslim religious leaders has emerged in Mali.[20] These include some involved in a new movement of young Muslims interested in Sufism who are frequently dubbed "Rasta" Sufis because of their dreadlocks (see Soares 2007, 2010, 2016). In Mali, some of these new Muslim public figures are also women.[21] Born in the late 1970s, Penda (a pseudonym) is the president of a Muslim women's association and the host of an Islamic radio program on a private radio station in one of Mali's regional urban centers. Penda was born in Saudi Arabia, where her Malian father, who comes from a lineage of Muslim religious specialists, had gone to study at the Islamic University in Medina that was founded in 1961. Penda's father was one of many students from around the world who have attended this university, which has not only sought to promote "good" Muslims but has also endeavored to "reverse processes of Westernization" (Zaman 2007, 256). The Islamic University in Medina has also been especially successful in propagating Salafi ideas, including vehement anti-Sufi views, among its students and many graduates. When Penda was in her early twenties, she left Saudi Arabia with her family to return to live in Mali. Prior to studying in Saudi Arabia, Penda's father had close personal and even kin ties to some of Mali's major Sufi leaders. In addition, Penda's mother's sister's was for many years married to one of the most prominent leaders of the Qadiriyya Sufi order in the country. Be that as it may, while in Saudi Arabia, Penda's father, like many students at the Islamic University in Medina, enthusiastically embraced a Salafi perspective.[22] He became openly critical of the way many Malians practice Islam and was strongly anti-Sufi in his views. Upon return to Mali, Penda's father maintained close ties with some of those in his Saudi network and eventually became an employee of al-Muntada al-Islami, the UK-based Saudi-funded charity that has educational and health care projects in Mali (see Benthall 2006).

After marrying one of her paternal cousins, Penda lived for some time in Bamako. Once she divorced her husband (with whom she maintains cordial relations), she moved to her father's family's hometown, where her father worked in a regional office of al-Muntada al-Islami. More educated than many Malian women, because she had attended Saudi primary and secondary schools and a teacher training college, Penda became involved in a new Muslim women's association and the burgeoning private radio sector that the liberalization of the media facilitated. She worked first as a volunteer at a private radio station and eventually came to host a regular radio program in which she gives sermons and lectures about Islam, the rights of women, the problems women face, among other topics. She is fluent in Arabic (the language in which she studied in Saudi Arabia), speaks French (the official language of Mali) with proficiency, and converses freely and preaches in several of Mali's vernacular languages.

Penda's father was a well-known but controversial figure in the regional urban center where he and Penda lived. Before his death in 2007, he and his daughter barely spoke to each other, because, as Penda explained, her father was a radical and a conservative Muslim whose views about Islam—we can gloss as Salafi—she rejected outright. In fact, she defends and asserts her rights as a Muslim woman to interpret Islam. Moreover, she is a strong and vocal advocate of women's rights. Penda has received the support of many of her father's kin, who reject her father's Salafi and specifically anti-Sufi views. She also has the support of her mother's family, including her mother's sister, whose affines are members of one of the most eminent lineages of Muslim religious specialists affiliated with the Qadiriyya in Mali.

Interestingly, the Saudi-born and -educated Penda regularly has acted as a guide for Muslims visiting her hometown who wish to visit the tombs of the celebrated Muslim saints buried there. Many Malians regularly undertake *ziyara* to the tombs of Muslim saints to pray and ask the saints for blessings and/or intercession with God. For example, the young so-called Rasta Sufis frequently organize such visits to saints' tombs in various places in Mali. When some of them have visited Penda's hometown, she has acted as their guide. She offers those going on *ziyara* instruction and guidance on how to approach the tombs and how to address their prayers and requests properly so that they might be answered. Someone like Penda who was born, raised, and educated in Saudi Arabia would no doubt have been regularly exposed to the oft-expressed Saudi opprobrium of such practices as the visiting of tombs and seeking a saint's intercession with God. Indeed, such practices are routinely denounced as *bid'a*—or unlawful innovation.

Penda also learned in her schooling, as well as in what her father sought to instill in her, that all such related "magical" practices are illicit. It is, therefore, perhaps even more remarkable that Penda has a reputation for her knowledge of the Islamic esoteric sciences (or magic by most anthropological definitions)—that is, those secret practices (*asrar* in Arabic) that remain central to what it means to be Muslim for many Malians and Senegalese.[23] Several years ago, when a leading Malian filmmaker wanted to make a documentary about Muslim religious leaders' use of the Islamic esoteric sciences in the country, Penda was the only woman he interviewed and filmed. Such Islamic "magic" is, of course, something reformist and modernist Muslims, as well as Salafis (like Penda's father) never cease to condemn as *bid'a*. But Penda seems to have no doubt that her use of the Islamic esoteric sciences are perfectly licit and seems willing to argue with anyone who might call them into question. Of course she did not learn such practices through her formal modern schooling but instead sought out such knowledge on her own from her acquaintances, including some of her kin, who are known practitioners of the Islamic esoteric sciences. Penda herself has become highly respected and much admired for her services in the Islamic esoteric sciences as well as for her views expressed on the radio and in person. Like the other two Muslim public figures, engagement with the media—in Penda's case, private radio—has been key to the making of her career. But unlike the other two charismatic figures described earlier in this essay, the Malian woman preacher with modernist views about women's rights earns some of her income from the esoteric sciences.

* * *

In closing, I would like to emphasize that I could not agree more with Roman Loimeier when he writes that one must understand change in Islamic religious practice—and Islamic reform, in particular—in context. All too often religious change and Islamic reform are assumed to come in a predetermined package from outside Africa, possibly from the Middle East, the presumed center of the Muslim world. The three public figures I have considered here—the Senegalese Muslim public intellectual, the Malian media star, and the Malian women preacher who engages in esoteric practices—only make sense when they are understood within their own contexts. But forms of modern education and learning are often assumed to be one such package that will lead to predictable outcomes. The madrasa-educated Haïdara, with his advocacy of condoms and beauty pageants in his sermons and his saint-like and celebrity comportment, seems somehow distinctively Malian. In fact, he has no equivalent in Senegal or the other West African countries I know. Even the Muslim public intellectual Sidy Lamine Niasse, with his complex global connections, can only be understood within the Senegalese context. Indeed, his career as a respected public figure is intimately related to the long and illustrious, albeit sometimes controversial, history of his family in Senegal and the complex Senegalese religious field as well as his own distinctive educational and personal trajectory from traditionally trained aspiring member of the ulama to al-Azhar–trained intellectual to Islamist revolutionary to engaged citizen. Although processes of the rationalization of religion certainly can be identified in both Senegal and Mali, it would be a mistake to misread the phenomena around such figures as disenchantment or as necessarily leading to a predetermined end point facilitated by the forms of modern Islamic education and learning they have experienced. Someone like Penda, the young woman preacher who asserts her rights as a woman and preaches against certain forms of religious conservatism, is at the same time a respected practitioner of the Islamic esoteric sciences. Such examples show how assumed teleologies are sometimes less useful than many analysts lead us to expect. Finally, these case studies demonstrate the need to move beyond some of the classical social theorists like Weber (or his interpreters) to develop new analytical tools for understanding contemporary changes in the practice of religion and in the changing modalities of religious expression in particular.

NOTES

1. This is part of a larger project on Muslim public figures in colonial and postcolonial West Africa. See Soares (2004, 2005b, 2007, 2010) and Soares and LeBlanc (2015).
2. See, for example, work on Nigeria, such as Loimeier (1997), Kane (2003), and Umar (2004).
3. "Today, the mediation of the established 'ulamâ' is increasingly becoming superfluous, a development which is going to influence their future social role and position in society considerably" (Loimeier 2003, 256–57.). Compare this with Zaman (2002), who is skeptical of predictions about the inevitable demise of the ulama. Loimeier also puts great emphasis on how the position of the individual has become much more pronounced for reformists and their discourses. Space limitations prevent me from addressing this point here.
4. The roles of Sufi orders and their leaders have differed considerably between Mali and Senegal.
5. For a short biography of Sidy Lamine Niasse, see Loimeier (2001, 403). See also Kane (2000).
6. On this branch of the Tijaniyya, see Seesemann (2011).
7. On this traditional Islamic education in Senegal and more generally in the Senegambia, see Ware (2004, 2009, 2014) and Launay and Ware (2009, and their chapter in this volume).
8. See http://www.walf.sn as well as Niasse (2003), where Niasse reports some of the newspaper's and media group's history as well as some of his personal views and biography.
9. Some of these covers of *Wal Fadjri* from the 1980s are reproduced in Mattes (1989).
10. Cf. Amselle's (2008) reading of the career and trajectory of Souleymane Bachir Diagne; cf. the riposte in Diagne (2015).
11. In a personal conversation Diagne explained that this was his target audience.
12. Some newspaper coverage of the pamphlet and controversy also reported erroneously that it was the British monarch in the photo.
13. Interviews with Sidy Lamine Niasse in 2005 and 2006.
14. The following discussion about Haïdara draws on some of my publications, though I take the analysis in different directions here. See Soares (2004, 2005a, 2005b, 2006). On Haïdara, see also Davis (2002); Schulz (2006a, 2006b); and Holder (2009, 2012).
15. On these madrasas in Mali, see Sanankoua and Brenner (1991) and Brenner (2001, 2007).
16. Ançar Dine is not to be mistaken for another Malian organization with the same name that Iyad ag Ghaly founded in 2012 in Kidal.
17. See http://www.ancardinehaidara.com/ and his fan page: http://www.facebook.com/pages/Cheick-cherif-Ousmane-madani-haidara/112837645422817, which now redirects to https://www.facebook.com/wilibali.
18. Cf. Schulz (2006b), who curiously devotes little attention to such controversial topics in Haïdara's sermons and the making of his career.
19. On religion and entertainment, see Meyer and Moors (2006); cf. Schulz (2006b).
20. I have written about some of these young Muslims in Soares (2005b, 2007, 2010, 2016).
21. See Amber Gemmeke's (2008) PhD thesis on so-called marabout women, Muslim women specialists in the Islamic esoteric sciences, in Dakar, Senegal.
22. On Nigerian students who have studied at the Islamic University of Medina, see Thurston (2013, 2015).
23. On the Islamic esoteric sciences in Mali, see Soares (2005), especially chapter 5, and Berndt (2008). See also Brenner (1985) and Hamès (2007).

REFERENCES

Amselle, Jean-Loup. 2008. *L'Occident décroché: Enquête sur les postcolonialismes.* Paris: Stock.
Bayat, Asef. 2007. *Making Islam Democratic.* Stanford, CA: Stanford University Press.
Benthall, Jonathan. 2006. "Islamic Aid in a North Malian Enclave." *Anthropology Today* 22 (4): 19–21.
Berndt, Jeremy Raphael. 2008. "Closer Than Your Jugular Vein: Muslim Intellectuals in a Malian Village, 1900 to the 1960s." PhD dissertation, Department of History, Northwestern University, Evanston, IL.
Brenner, Louis. 1985. *Réflexions sur le savoir islamique en Afrique de l'Ouest.* Talence, France: Centre d'Étude d'Afrique Noire, University of Bordeaux I.
———. 2001. *Controlling Knowledge: Religion, Power and Schooling in a West African Muslim Society.* Bloomington: Indiana University Press.
———. 2007. "The Transformation of Muslim Schooling in Mali: The Madrasa as an Institution of Social and Religious Mediation." In *Schooling Islam: The Culture and Politics of Modern Muslim Education,* edited by Robert W. Hefner and Muhammad Qasim Zaman, 199–223. Princeton, NJ: Princeton University Press.
Davis, Kimberley. 2002. "Preaching to the Converted: Charismatic Leaders, Performances and Electronic Media in Contemporary Islamic Communities." Master's thesis in sociology and anthropology, Concordia University, Montreal.
Diagne, Souleymane Bachir. 2001. *100 mots pour dire l'islam.* Paris: Maisonneuve et Larose.
———. 2013. "On the Postcolonial and the Universal?" *Rue Descartes* 2 (78): 7–18.
Eickelman, Dale F., and Jon W. Anderson, eds. 1999. *New Media in the Muslim World: The Emerging Public Sphere.* Bloomington: Indiana University Press.
Eickelman, Dale F., and James Piscatori. 1996. *Muslim Politics.* Princeton, NJ: Princeton University Press.
Gellner, Ernest. 1981. *Muslim Society.* Cambridge: Cambridge University Press.
Gemmeke, Amber Babke. 2008. *Marabout Women in Dakar: Creating Trust in a Rural Urban Space.* Berlin: Lit.
Hackett, Rosalind I. J., and Benjamin F. Soares, eds. 2015. *New Media and Religious Transformations in Africa.* Bloomington: Indiana University Press.
Hamès, Constant, ed. 2007. *Coran et talismans: Textes et pratiques magiques en milieu musulman.* Paris: Karthala.
Hefner, Robert W., and Muhammad Qasim Zaman, eds. 2007. *Schooling Islam: The Culture and Politics of Modern Muslim Education.* Princeton, NJ: Princeton University Press.
Holder, Gilles. 2009. "'Maouloud 2006,' de Bamako à Tombouctou: entre réislamisation de la nation et laïcité de l'État: la construction d'un espace public religieux au Mali. In *L'islam, nouvel espace public en Afrique,* edited by Gilles Holder, 237–89. Paris: Karthala.
———. 2012. "Chérif Ousmane Madani Haïdara et l'association islamique Ançar Dine: un réformisme malien populaire en quête d'autonomie." *Cahiers d'études africaines* 206–7 (2): 389–425.

Kane, Ousmane. 2000. "Muhammad Niasse (1881–1956)." In *La Tijâniyya*, edited by J.-L. Triaud and D. Robinson, 219–35. Paris: Karthala.
———. 2003. *Muslim Modernity in Postcolonial Nigeria*. Leiden: Brill.
Kurzman, Charles, and Lynn Owens. 2002. "The Sociology of Intellectuals." *Annual Review of Sociology* 28: 63–90.
Launay, Robert. 1992. *Beyond the Stream: Islam and Society in a West African Town*. Berkeley: University of California Press.
Launay, Robert, and Rudolph Ware. 2009. "Comment (ne pas) lire le Coran? Logiques de l'enseignement islamique au Sénégal et en Côte d'Ivoire." In *L'islam, nouvel espace public en Afrique*, edited by Gilles Holder, 127–45. Paris: Karthala.
Loimeier, Roman. 1997. *Islamic Reform and Political Change in Northern Nigeria*. Evanston, IL: Northwestern University Press.
———. 2001. *Säkularer Staat und islamische Gesellschaft in Senegal. Die Beziehungen zwischen Staat, Sufi-Bruderschaften und islamischer Reformbewegung in Senegal im 20. Jahrhundert*. Berlin Germany: Lit.
———. 2003. "Patterns and Peculiarities of Islamic Reform in Africa." *Journal of Religion in Africa* 33 (3): 237–62.
———. 2009. *Between Social Skills and Marketable Skills: The Politics of Islamic Education in 20th Century Zanzibar*. Leiden: Brill.
Mattes, Hanspeter. 1989. *Die islamistische Bewegung des Senegal zwischen Autonomie und Außenorientierung: Am Beispiel der islamistischen Presse Études islamiques und Wal Fadjri*. Hamburg: Wuqûf.
Meyer, Birgit, and Annelies Moors, eds. 2006. *Religion, Media, and the Public Sphere*. Bloomington: Indiana University Press.
Niasse, Sidy Lamine. 1999. *Sharifu. Fin de la nuit*. Dakar: Wal Fadjri.
———. 2003. *Un arabisant entre presse et pouvoir*. Dakar: Wal Fadjri.
———. 2004. *Réplique à ceux qui interdisent des poignées de main entre l'homme et la femme. Les preuves*. Dakar: Wal Fadjri.
Otayek, René. 1993. "Introduction: Des nouveaux intellectuels musulmans d'Afrique noire." In *Le radicalisme islamique au sud du Sahara: da'wa, arabisation et critique de l'Occident*, edited by René Otayek, 8–18. Paris: Karthala.
Otayek, René, and Benjamin F. Soares. 2007. "Introduction." In *Islam and Muslim Politics in Africa*, edited by Benjamin F. Soares and René Otayek, 9–44. New York: Palgrave.
Robinson, Francis. 2004. "Other-Wordly and This-Wordly Islam and the Islamic Revival." *Journal of the Royal Asiatic Society* 14 (1): 47–58.
Roy, Olivier. 1992. *The Failure of Political Islam*. Translated by C. Volk. Cambridge, MA: Harvard University Press.
Salvatore, Armando, and Dale F. Eickelman, eds. 1999. *Public Islam and the Common Good*. Leiden: Brill.
Sanankoua, Bintou, and Louis Brenner, eds. 1991. *L'ensiegnement islamique au Mali*. Bamako, Mali: Jamana.
Schulz, Dorothea E. 2006a. "Morality, Community, Publicness: Shifting Terms of Public Debate in Mali." In *Religion, Media, and the Public Sphere*, edited by Birgit Meyer and Annelies Moors, 132–51. Bloomington: Indiana University Press.
———. 2006b. "Promises of (Im)mediate Salvation: Islam, Broadcast Media, and the Remaking of Religious Experience in Mali." *American Ethnologist* 33 (2): 210–29.

Seesemann, Rüdiger. 2011. *The Divine Flood: Ibrahim Niasse and the Roots of a Twentieth Century Islamic Revival*. New York: Oxford University Press.

Soares, Benjamin F. 2004. "Islam and Public Piety in Mali." In *Public Islam and the Common Good*, edited by Armando Salvatore and Dale F. Eickelman, 205–26. Leiden: Brill.

———. 2005a. *Islam and the Prayer Economy: History and Authority in a Malian Town*. Edinburgh and Ann Arbor: Edinburgh University Press and the University of Michigan Press for the International African Institute.

———. 2005b. "Mali: Im Visier der Islamismus-Fahnder." *INAMO* 41: 16–18.

———. 2006. "Islam in Mali in the Neoliberal Era." *African Affairs* 105 (418): 77–95.

———. 2007. "Saint and Sufi in Neoliberal Mali." In *Sufism and the "Modern" in Islam*, edited by Martin van Bruinessen and Julia Howell, 76–91. London: I. B. Tauris.

———. 2010. "'Rasta' Sufis and Muslim Youth Culture in Mali." In *Being Young and Muslim*, edited by Linda Herrera and Asef Bayat, 241–57. Oxford: Oxford University Press.

———. 2016. "Malian Youth between Sufism and Satan." In *Muslim Youth and the 9/11 Generation*, edited by Adeline Masquelier and Benjamin Soares, 169–88. Albuquerque: University of New Mexico Press.

Soares, Benjamin F., and Marie Nathalie LeBlanc. 2015. "Islam, jeunesse et les trajectoires de mobilisation en Afrique de l'Ouest dans l'ère néolibérale: un regard anthropologique." In *Mobilisations collectives en Afrique: contestations, résistances et révoltes*, edited by Kadya Tall et al., 67–90. Leiden: Brill.

Thurston, Alexander. 2013. "Managing Ruptures, Telling Histories: Northern Nigerian Muslim Intellectuals and Arab Universities, 1900–2011." PhD dissertation, Department of Religious Studies, Northwestern University, Evanston, IL.

———. 2015. "Nigeria's Ahlussunnah: A Preaching Network from Kano to Medina and Back." In *Shaping Global Islamic Discourses: The Role of al-Azhar, al-Medina, and al-Mustafa*, edited by Masooda Bano and Keiko Sakurai, 93–116. Edinburgh: Edinburgh University Press.

Umar, Muhammad S. 2004. "Mass Islamic Education and Emergence of Female 'Ulama in Northern Nigeria: Background, Trends, and Consequences." In *The Transmission of Islamic Learning in Africa*, edited by Scott Reese, 99–120. Leiden: Brill.

Ware, Rudolph T. 2004. "Njàngaan: The Daily Regime of Qur'anic Students in 20th Century Senegal." *International Journal of African Historical Studies* 37 (3): 515–38.

———. 2009. "The Long Durée of Quran Schooling, Society, and State in Senegambia." In *New Perspectives on Islam in Senegal*, edited by Mamadou Diouf and Mara A. Leichtman, 21–50. New York: Palgrave.

———. 2014. *The Walking Qur'an: Islamic Education, Embodied Knowledge, and History in West Africa*. Chapel Hill: University of North Carolina Press.

Wiktorowicz, Quintan, ed. 2004. *Islamic Activism: A Social Movement Theory Approach*. Bloomington: Indiana University Press.

Zaman, Muhammad Qasim. 2002. *The Ulama in Contemporary Islam: Custodians of Change*. Princeton, NJ: Princeton University Press.

———. 2007. "Epilogue: Competing Conceptions of Religious Education." In *Schooling Islam: The Culture and Politics of Modern Muslim Education*, edited by Robert W. Hefner and Muhammad Qasim Zaman, 242–68. Princeton, NJ: Princeton University Press.

———. 2011. "The 'Ulama': Scholarly Tradition and New Public Commentary." In *Muslims and Modernity: Culture and Society since 1800. The New Cambridge History of Islam*, vol. 6, edited by Robert W. Hefner, 335–54. Cambridge: Cambridge University Press.

15.
COLLAPSED PLURALITIES: ISLAMIC EDUCATION, LEARNING, AND CREATIVITY IN NIGER

*Noah Butler**

SOME OF THE ways in which Muslims in Niger make choices about learning challenge the idioms of education they frequently invoke. As such, this chapter shifts focus away from understanding types of education only in terms of the preparations they provide—religious, moral, secular, practical, quotidian, or otherwise—and the linked outcomes they promise. Instead, it considers how the actualities of learning and anxieties about schooling challenge ideologies of education.

Scholars and Muslims alike surround Islamic learning in Africa with issues of formality and personality, such that formal, impersonal schools (whether madrasas, *écoles Franco-Arabes*, or Western-modeled secular schools) contrast with differently formalized, though more personal, traditional Qur'anic schools. Types of schools are thus separated by rhetorics of difference, which distinguish between forms of instruction, classifications of knowledge, and, ultimately, larger conceptualizations about what constitutes an Islamic education and what it does for a student both practically and in abstract terms of personhood. Nigeriens tend to juxtapose schools, explaining that they prepare Muslims in different ways for different purposes.

---

* Iterations of what became this chapter benefited from suggestions from several people. Benjamin Soares and Rüdiger Seesemann commented on an early (and very different) version during a workshop on "Islam and Muslim Youth in Africa" hosted by the Institute for the Study of Islamic Thought at Northwestern University. Later, comments from co-members of an African Studies Association panel on Islamic education in Africa helped orient revisions and additions. Conversations with Abdoulaye Sounaye clarified the complexity of Niger's educational landscape. As usual, Robert Launay's questions and points have been invaluable and much appreciated. Catherine Corliss has been helpful in important ways.

A growing focus on varieties of education in Islamic Africa contrasts types of schools. Classifying educational options and the genealogies of their development establishes a layered background (Wilks 1968; Gaffney 1994; Tamari 1996, 2002; Starrett 1998; Loimeier 2009). In the foreground, however, there are some creative and potentially new ways that Nigerien parents navigate opportunities and view their children's education: Students are going to two sorts of schools at once.

By examining students in Niger studying simultaneously in two systems, this chapter takes a novel perspective on Islamic education in West Africa. Most scholarship on Islamic education in Africa focuses on one type of school, on comparing different types of schools, or on students transitioning from one type of school to another (generally from Qur'anic school to another type). Simultaneously studying in dual systems is either a recent practice or underexplored historically and ethnographically. Regardless, it calls for increased analytical attention.

As Brenner (2001) points out, the schools and schooling instituted during French colonialism informed ideas about Qur'anic education as well as epistemes governing styles and purposes of learning (see Messick 1993). In such a climate of transformation, whether or not Muslim children would (or could) attend two schools at once would be a critical vantage point from which to reread colonial and postcolonial histories and ethnographies (see Santerre 1973).

The contemporary educational landscape in Niger has been changing since independence (and certainly was not static during and prior to colonization). New choices and reasons about how best to make them confront parents. And yet despite the diversity of options available and arguments about their respective benefits, some parents and students actively continue to blur the edges of educational options by refusing to settle for one form alone. Consequently, this chapter examines educational plurality and some of the ways choices, and the creativity informing them, collapse rather than isolate the options available.

Snakebites and Broken Ankles

Two Zarma proverbs, both kin to Emerson's warning that "foolish consistency is the hobgoblin of little minds" (Emerson 1993, 24), recall the themes of continuity and change—social, religious, economic, and otherwise—that a discussion of Islam in Niger (and West Africa) generally invokes:

> If you walk on the same path every day a snake will bite you.

And,

> If you walk on the same path every day you will fall in a hole, break your ankle, and have to hop home.

These two proverbs criticize blind continuity and point to the importance of plural options and choosing between them. Here, Hardin's (1993, 1–2) point about paths as metaphors in situations of social and educational change is instructive:

> As educational opportunities expand and household formations change, conflicts between individual aspirations and socially prescribed ideals of behavior emerge. Social mores and traditions provide both resources for and constraints on action in a world where social forms and everyday practice are continually influencing each other, and individuals find themselves choosing between what are often competing and incompatible goals. With each decision or choice, new paths take shape. Some options open to view and others become less desirable. . . . The path each society takes, as well as the final outcome, is the result of unique articulations between past orientations and choices and contingencies that individuals of a given society face on a daily basis.

The context in which the two proverbs were invoked is as significant as the metaphor of paths, both in Hardin's phrasing as well as in the proverbs themselves. Neither proverb was about Islamic education per se; both were about justifying some actions that were Islamic and others that most would say were not. A man who was simultaneously two kinds of religious specialist, a *zima*[1] and a marabout,[2] cited the proverbs to justify his complicated social footings. He did not blend the duties of one role into the other; he practiced them as entirely separate endeavors. Some consulted him because of his expertise in particular forms of Islamic animal sacrifice.[3] Others came to him for Zarma sand divination. Still others sought him out for one, then the other. He cited the two proverbs, the first seriously and the second to add some humor, to explain why people would see him for two different services, as well as in what terms he justified practices that most Muslims would consider as exo- if not non-Islamic. At once, then, his bifurcated role speaks as much to the tolerance of his Muslim neighbors as to how people perceive the benefits of keeping traditions distinct and the risks of combining them—a point that serves nicely as an analogue to discussions of Islamic education in Niger.

This is a chapter about a plurality of choices more than it is about a plurality of types of schools. Specifically, it examines how distinct educational possibilities might be disconnected from a unilineal temporal trajectory that stresses accumulations of knowledge as teleological. As such, it focuses on creativity more so than themes of hybridity, complementarity, or even competition—all of which are inherent to discussions of education in Africa but which continue to focus on singular forms of education.

Continuity and Change, Compatibility and Competition

The theme of continuity versus change is a loose analytical valence on which to chart heterogeneous processes. Notwithstanding, it is a fundamental locus of discourse and debate for many Muslims in Niger (see Masquelier 2009). Framings of continuity and change cast light on time and the ways that education shapes it.

Hamidou Kane's *Ambiguous Adventure* (1961) recounts the life and schooling of Samba Diallo (a protagonist not so loosely modeled after Kane himself) (Butler 2010). Kane's story mirrors a reality for many contemporary West African Muslims educated in so-called traditional Qur'anic schools: that these schools represent an initial phase of religious education that is later followed by entrance into various types of other schools—many, if not most, modeled on Western methods of pedagogy and curricula. Kane's narrative of colonialism, postcoloniality, education, Islam, and the growth of secularism is a well-worn touchstone. Samba Diallo begins Qur'anic school as a young boy, and then, partly due to his success there and partly due to French colonial practice to encourage secular education of boys from noble lineages, he attends the colonial school. He eventually enters the French university system and returns to Senegal, only to be considered too European in his education and outlook.

What Kane so artfully points out is that Qur'anic education is about far more than just local tradition and religious community. It instantiates a process of moral formation, signaling religious learning as much as providing it (Sanneh 1989, 1997; Launay 1992; Eickelman 1994; Hammoudi 1997; Launay and Soares 1999; Launay and Ware 2009). For Kane, educational sequentialism, the progression from Qur'anic school to colonial school, was a synecdoche of social change. Qur'anic school was not replaced by a competing form of education but rather relocated temporally, relegated to a kind of primary school, if not preschool, preceding other types of (usually Western-modeled) education.

Although the social change that Kane describes as both rooted in and stemming from the colonial period differs from the contemporary terrain of neoliberalism (Alidou 2005; Soares 2005, 2006; Gemmeke 2009; Masquelier 2009), his point about educational sequentialism remains instructive. Many of the people, old and young, I knew in Niger (especially most of the men) went to Qur'anic schools in their youth. Only a few, however, continued beyond that. For many, their Islamic educations either stopped or, if they entered madrasas or Franco-Arabe schools, changed.

The themes of continuity and change that confront each other in Kane's narrative illustrate issues of educational compatibility and competition. In Niger, as across francophone West Africa, colonialism and postcoloniality saw competing forms of education and competing ideas about the benefits of being educated in one way or another (Santerre 1973, Meunier 1997). Loimeier (2005, 404) draws attention to the scale and reach of changes: "While Islamic traditions of learning and scholarship have arguably been presented, in the past, as exclusivist and confined to small circles of scholars and their disciples, sub-Saharan Africa has been transformed, in the last thirty or forty years, in much more intensive ways than many other parts of the planet. The transformation of sub-Saharan Africa was characterized by multiple processes of modernization, urbanization, mass education, and the emergence of modern civilian societies and subsequent changes in the structures of the organization of time and space."

In such a climate, or perhaps because of it, the debates about the practical values of a Qur'anic education still inform different conceptualizations of learning (see Hefner and Zaman 2007). Brenner (2001) characterizes Qur'anic and non-Qur'anic education in terms of their respective epistemes: "esoteric" and "rational." He argues that these two categories are ideal schemas along a shifting typology of the appreciation and application of educational forms. They are epistemes about learning and education more than simply modalities of its transmission. Still, as he points out, these are not strictly analytical constructs but rather divisions that matter in real ways. A Nigerien soldier illustrated precisely this point with a discussion about education. Slamming his pistol flat on the table like a domino, he declared, "Physics shoots bullets; magic stops them." In other words, each episteme—rational and esoteric—explains very different (though in his example, very interrelated) things.

Historically and ethnographically, the difference between rational and esoteric epistemes has come to bear in three ways: (1) competition, (2) sequentialism, and (3) complementarity. As Launay's (1990) initial distinction between "pedigrees and paradigms" illustrates, what Brenner would later label as "esoteric" and "rational" epistemes often compete. Launay's categories of pedigree and paradigm distinguish between modes of religious authority and show how different perceptions of knowledge, opportunities to access it, and the articulations between knowledge and power shape perceptions of religious authority between Sufis and non-Sufis in Côte d'Ivoire.

Kane's narrative recalls the pervasiveness of educational sequentialism as a first-this-then-that pattern (i.e., Qur'anic school then other sorts of school). Other schools, certain madrasas, and most Franco-Arabe schools for example, focus on the complementarity of aspects of religious education as well as religious and nonreligious education. Yet a fourth possibility remains, one as analytically salient as ethnographically real: intentionally straddling dual systems of education at once.

A Topography of Education in Niger

There are essentially four sorts of schools in Niger: (1) Qur'anic schools, (2) madrasas, (3) Franco-Arabe schools, and (4) secular schools.[4] Qur'anic school has for centuries been a central part of the Islamic landscape in West Africa. Regionally, the methods of instruction vary little, though there are differences depending on a teacher's training, standing, school size, and the extent to which education includes labor. In its most basic form, and at the elementary level, Qur'anic school involves rote learning of the Qur'an. Sanneh (1989, 153) explains the sequence: "During their time at the Qur'an school students go through five stages.... The educational course begins with learning the letters of the Arabic alphabet. Then follows vowelling, and at this point the pupil is made to practice cursive writing in which consonants run together with the appropriate vowelling. Once this step is reached and the student can decipher individual words, he starts to commit to memory parts of the Arabic Qur'an, beginning with the shortest *surat*. Thus commence the first steps towards memorizing the Qur'an, with pauses along the way." Later, other sources such as hadith and Sunna, legal texts, poems, interpretations, and commentaries enter and are discussed and debated. Tamari's work on Qur'anic education (2002, 2008, this volume) is notable for the focus it places, ethnographically and historically, on the phases of Qur'anic education: "Throughout West Africa, two basic phases are distinguished in traditional Islamic education: the elementary phase, which usually culminates in the recitation and writing out of the Qur'an from memory; and a second phase involving study of the religious sciences, Arabic language and literature through the careful reading and commentary of recognised texts" (Tamari, 2002, 92). Her work notes not just that "advanced-level instruction had been relatively neglected" as a scholarly focus (2002, 92) but how local languages have been differently involved at the elementary and advanced levels; precise and detailed translations from Arabic to local languages are significant pedagogical components at the advanced stages (1996, 2002, 2009; Tamari and Bondarev 2013).

The learning that students undergo is about far more than strictly committing the Qur'an to memory. Fortier (1997, 2003) draws attention to the discursive practices shaping and shaped by rote instruction as well as the specific pedagogical methodologies and sequences involved. Ware (2004, 2014) and others note that internalizing in various ways knowledge of the Qur'an embodies it as divine revelation (O'Brien 1969, 1971; Sanneh 1997; Butler 2006b; Launay and Ware 2009). A student becomes, literally *and* figuratively, a more moral being.[5]

Indeed, Qur'anic school involves much more than simply a "traditional" education or instruction in the Qur'an and religious texts. It delineates an environment for the transmission and elucidation of moral frameworks (Fortier 1997, 2003). As Morgan and Armer (1988, 635) note in their comparative study of Islamic and Western education in northern Nigeria, "the experience of Islamic schooling served as a social entry point into the elaborate adult network of patron-client relations that underlay the social organization of the community. Consequently, most northern Nigerian youth today are still expected to achieve at least moderate levels of Islamic schooling." In this context, rudimentary Qur'anic school indexes more than solidarity derived from similar experiences; it indexes paths of access to networks in the short term and the potential for personal connections within a community in the long term.

The argument that Qur'anic school provides a moral education as much as an intellectual one has lost some traction in places. Some Nigerien parents consider Qur'anic school as an initial formation not as an ongoing process of the accumulation of knowledge. As a Nigerien man joked, "I memorized the Qur'an by the time I was twelve. I forgot it when I was thirteen."[6]

The second type of school in Niger is the madrasa. In contemporary Niger, the word *madrasa* can mean several things, and the usage of the term is somewhat fluid. Elsewhere in the Muslim world and depending on the context, the term is used rather narrowly to refer to schools led by reformist bodies or more broadly to denote school in general. Madrasa implies at base a school with some level of religious instruction and Arabic language training. Still, some madrasas will incorporate local languages and at times even French in order to place a premium on the clarity of communication as opposed to the rigidity of language of instruction (see Tamari 2002). Especially in the earlier stages, communication and continued comprehension in Arabic can pose challenges for some students. As Constantin quips in his discussion of Islam in East Africa, "One does not preach in the desert" (1988, 67); yet as a Nigerien dryly told me in reference to a preacher and teacher known for his exclusive use of Arabic, "He's preaching in the desert."

In West Africa, as they spread, madrasas tended to be associated with "Wahhabist" teaching (Kaba 1974, see also Launay 1992; Launay and Soares 1999). Although the term *Wahhabi* has declined in use over the past decade or so in Niger, many madrasas still do maintain ideological affiliations with more recent incarnations of reformist trends. For some time in francophone West Africa, madrasas were met with uncertainty if not political resistance. Consider the Malian national government's statement: "While the marabout is a good Muslim who leads a solitary struggle with the goal of disseminating the reading of the Qur'an, the master of the madrasa is affiliated with a highly structured expansionist sect, the actions of which go far beyond the limits of our country" (as cited in Niezen 1991, 237).

In Niger, waves of madrasas were built in rural areas, sometimes accompanied by dispensaries, and almost always fronted by placards announcing the source of funding (often but not exclusively Saudi). As Kane (2008, 169) points out though, the direct correspondence between Wahhabism and the involvement of Saudi-funded nongovernmental organizations (NGOs) has been overstated: "No matter how generous, Saudi Arabian NGOs have not been able to fund all Wahhabi-minded groups in the Muslim world. Most of them, I would argue, did not receive significant funds from Saudi Arabia for proselytization purposes." He notes that endogenous reform movements played an important role for some time, focusing efforts on religious debate as opposed to politics: "Many Wahhabi groups in Nigeria, Mali, Senegal and elsewhere emphasized the reform of religious practices but abstained from challenging ruling elites in their countries and did not seek to capture political power" (Kane 2008, 169; see also Kobo 2009, 2012). Indeed, recently across Niger, the affiliations between madrasas and reform movements have slackened; no longer is a madrasa education so consistently shorthand for reformist affiliations.

The third type of school in Niger, the Franco-Arabe school, began in the 1980s and became a popular educational alternative by the 1990s. They tend to be located in urban areas or larger towns. As the name implies, these schools blend instruction in French and Arabic. Some Franco-Arabe schools tilt more to the French side of the spectrum, with Arabic only as a language class and with little, if any, religious instruction. Others incorporate pedagogy in Arabic in various courses and involve religious instruction. Curricula tend to be broad, including geography, history, and other facets of a general education. Some schools teach geography and history, for example, as they would be taught in secular schools; in others, however, these subjects are taught from the points of view of the contributions of Islamic history and sciences. Pedagogy that situates the historic and scientific contributions of Muslims in particular and Islamic society more broadly is increasingly popular in different sorts of madrasas as well (Loimeier 1997, 2005, 2009; Brenner 2001).

Finally, the fourth type of school in Niger, secular schools, were established during colonialism and employed Western curricula and modes of pedagogy. They have changed since colonialism, however, as have the Western schools they exemplified (see Reichmuth 1993). Historically, secular education in Niger was predominantly urban, located in pronounced ways in Niamey. As Kelley (2002, 120) notes,

> Beginning in the 1930s and accelerating after World War II, the political and social influence of the evolués, or "evolved people," of Niger began to increase. They were drawn from among the small number of educated men in Niger, mostly Zarmas from lower social classes who had migrated to Niamey and other urban centers and taken up work as low-level

functionaries in the colonial bureaucracy. Over time, the evolués began to rise through the bureaucracy, vying with chiefs as the preferred intermediaries between the French colonists and the people of Niger. Then, as now, the urban-dwelling evolués viewed their uneducated brothers and sisters in the bush with distance even contempt. The evolué took to eating different foods, speaking a different language (i.e., French), and wearing different clothing. After World War II, when France initiated the long process of withdrawing from its colonial possessions, including Niger, it left the state governmental and bureaucratic apparatus in the hands of this relatively small and isolated class.

Kelley's lopsided use of the word *educated* here implies that "the small number of educated men in Niger" were those educated in the secular French colonial tradition. Despite its asymmetry, his point locates secular education within the general views of a segment of the populace at the time and the social and political climate that shaped and spread notions of secular education in a newly independent Muslim-majority country. As he suggests, for some time in urban areas, secular education outlined class distinctions.

The rural-urban split is instructive but also imprecise. Rural and urban are not mutually exclusive, everlasting social and spatial categories outside of each other's presence and influence: people move between them, and notions about what constitutes life in each change and articulate over time. Trajectories of urbanization, deurbanization, and reurbanization exist simultaneously and sequentially, driven by the intersection of a variety of causes. Seasonal circulation and labor migration also present new opportunities and complicate the distinctions between rural and urban.[7] Indeed, cities in Niger are less consistently the sites for opportunity or migration than they once were. Niezen's description of Mali parallels the present Nigerien context: "During the past two decades, students have even come to regard the sociopolitical rewards of Western education as unattainable because they can neither continue their studies nor find work" (1991, 236). The benefits of a Western education are thus in important ways often more potential than practical.

Niger has ranked last more often than not for the twenty-five-year span since the inception of the United Nations Development Programme's Human Development Index (UNDP HDI) in 1990: last for ten years in total, second to last for nine years (eight above Sierra Leone and, more recently, one above the Democratic Republic of the Congo), between two and five slots above last for six years. The latest UNDP HDI ranks Niger 188 out of the 188 counties recorded (2015, 211). Despite the challenging economic situation in Niger, access to Islamic education is now and has been for some time something that even the most cash poor and most isolated could encounter. It has been a viable option for urbanites and villagers alike. Insofar as Niamey and other urban centers offer more secular education options, they also offer a great many options for Islamic education. With structural adjustment, increased NGO involvement, and a variety of austerity measures, new forms of education are becoming increasingly prevalent and accessible, and not just in urban areas.

The four types of schools described above are more of a spectrum than a definitive classificatory typology. Many of the noteworthy developments, as is also the case elsewhere in Islamic Africa, are happening at loci of intersection and transformation—for example, how madrasas are becoming more varied and pervasive and how Franco-Arabe schools are adapting secular and religious subjects. Education and religion are shifting not just in terms of practices and opinions but, as Umar's (2001, 2009) work in northern Nigeria notes, as discursive categories. As poles of this spectrum, Qur'anic school and secular school seem to offer such contrasting styles of transmitting knowledge, teaching, and subject matter that they would, paradoxically perhaps, also seem to be the most complementary (complementary in the sense of a lack of redundancy). Yet, as the following cases demonstrate, students bookend their educations in ways that matter beyond just the nonredundancy of curricula.

Differences and similarities become particularly notable when students undergo Qur'anic education alongside another form of learning. The combination signifies what educational choices can be creatively made and how. Not just in Niger but throughout Islamic West Africa, the recrudescence of Qur'anic education along with the popularity of secular education highlight the interstices of educational forms as well as ideologies of education and learning more generally.

Collapsed Pluralities: New Liminalities?

In many ways, education involves people in process. If, at the very least, students are inevitably destined to become adults, then the process of learning has certain liminal characteristics. All forms of education involve sequence: Some things come before others (i.e., skills, texts, curricula, pedagogical methods, modes of evaluation). Yet to consider education as a process of accumulation—accumulation of knowledge, norms, mores, signaling capacities—categorizes educational options such that one modality of education accomplishes some things whereas another does others. Focusing on what categories of education offer, curricular or normative or practical, presents a limited perspective because of the link it places between knowledge and action: Amselle (1998, 151) puts it, "Those who postulate a link between knowledge and power most often bring out the distortions of meaning that would result from placing the act of knowledge in the sphere of action." Two cases help us focus more on the people who are learning rather than on the processes whereby they are taught or the philosophies that inform them.

Qur'anic School and Secular School

Recalling though contrasting the earlier discussion of *The Ambiguous Adventure*, this case is set in Niamey, a city of contrasts, as Youngsted (2004, 96) describes:

> Niamey is the capital of postcolonial Niger, the nerve center of the nation's political, administrative, commercial, and intellectual activities. Niamey is a sprawling, polycentric setting, a city of social, cultural, and visual contrast. Camels, goats, pedestrians, motorcycles, jalopies, and luxury sedans share the dusty, crowded streets. Cardboard shelters are constructed outside the walls of grand villas. The city saw a building boom in the 1970s as some of the most interesting architecture in West Africa—modern Sudanese-style buildings largely financed by the country's uranium mines—was constructed. Niamey's character is also defined by the sublime beauty of the rolling hills, gnarled acacias, and rice fields on the banks of the muddy, mighty Niger River as well as the fetid garbage heaps lining the streets of neighborhoods, all boiled and baked by the relentless Sahelian sun. When the heat is not oppressive, winds blow sand and dust in from the Sahara, blocking out the sun and carrying dreaded diseases, or rain squalls flood the city's open sewers.

Educational options are pervasive and varied in Niamey. Qur'anic training takes place in compound courtyards, single-room neighborhood schoolhouses, mosques or hangars abutting them, and larger formal schools that accommodate students across the age range and have several teachers and multiple classrooms.

Attachment to one's Qur'anic instructor is a hallmark of learning in Sufi traditions (O'Brien 1971; Launay 1992; Eickelman 1994; Sanneh 1997; Ware 2004).[8] In addition to labor, mendicancy is fairly common, especially at the early stages of a Qur'anic education. Rurally, students begging for meals or receiving them as alms (*zakat*) is expected. People feed *talibés* because they know them to be legitimate students. The almsgiving is at once an act of religious obligation and a recognition of the students' religious service. Patterns of loyalty, attachment, and labor associated with Qur'anic schooling differ in urban and rural areas.

Gripes about Qur'anic students begging in urban contexts are not uncommon in West Africa (Ware 2004, 522–23), though few Nigeriens would still couch the phenomenon as the "social plague" that Monteil (1964, 145) initially did.[9] In one Twistesque tale, a friend in Niamey explained how he refused to give food or small change to mendicant *talibés*.[10] He reasoned that there was no way to verify that they were real students and detailed several stories of rackets run by "faux marabouts" organizing what amounted to street gangs of imposter-students begging for profit. Street children would also pretend to be *talibés* in the hopes that posing as a pupil would legitimize their solicitations. An assumption is that true Qur'anic students almost always carry their tablets with them as proof. Students carefully guard their tablets, knowing that if it is lost or damaged they will be punished; in some contexts, they are expected to leave their tablets with their teacher. Among street children, a knockoff industry has appeared with older kids, who have a command of Arabic and some of the minutiae that goes into tablet decoration, producing them for sale either to tourists or to other street children to use as props when begging.

Both in rural and urban contexts, Qur'anic schooling has little if any government funding. "It's the fault of the state," is how one marabout put it, discussing the issue of begging students in Niamey. "The state gives money to the French schools but not to the Islamic schools. So the teachers send their students out to beg." As Ware (2004, 524) suggests, "The economic functioning of Qur'anic school has always rested on the narrow shoulders of children."[11]

A sixteen-year-old young man living in Niamey attends both Qur'anic school and secular school. His case draws attention to an involvement with education in religious and secular ways. His father, who is in his sixties and has two wives, is known in the neighborhood as a particularly learned man and runs a small Qur'anic school. He has taught his son the Qur'an since he was a small boy. Rarely seen without a book in hand (usually the Qur'an, though sometimes one of the thin numerology pamphlets that were popular with street-side booksellers in Niamey), the father occasionally makes amulets for people in the neighborhood without being asked to do so. As a neighbor put it, "If he makes it [an amulet] for you, you need it."

Under a tree behind his house, mud bricks outline the form of a mosque. In it the father instructs his sons and others, a group of about dozen or more young boys of varying ages, in the Qur'an. At the end of the school day, the son comes home and changes out of his school uniform of khakis and a maroon shirt and into a long white boubou. He studies at night, and, depending on the book, it is obvious whether his father or teachers at the secular school assigned the text. At exam times throughout the school year, Qur'anic study takes a pause. During the summer, the son's Qur'anic study is intense. Time, not just circadian but calendric as well, informs how he pursues his educations and how he can best do so.

Qur'anic School and École Franco-Arabe

The second case comes from Kiota, Niger. Kiota is Niger's most celebrated Sufi pilgrimage center. Since the 1970s, Kiota has been famed as a center of learning. Since the 1990s, town leadership has made significant and successful efforts to expand local educational opportunities in general and for girls in particular. For a large rural town, Kiota has an array of schools.

A local notable supervised a small Qur'anic school, one of several in town. He had hired a Tuareg scholar to teach about thirty young children, mostly boys and a handful of girls. The students learned twice a day—for several hours early in the morning and then for several hours in the evening. If time is a resource, then it is clear that by beginning and ending the day with their studies, these students were left free to do other things during the day.

Fields flank Kiota on all sides. The collective tempo of the comings and goings of people working them structure the days. The Qur'anic school in Kiota provided its pupils the time necessary to contribute agricultural or domestic labor. The interconnections between Qur'anic learning and labor are well established ethnographically and historically.[12] Yet, as it turns out, the only person working in the fields during the interval between the morning and evening sessions was the teacher. Many, if not most, of the students attended another school during the day. Categorizing this other school is problematic. Some residents referred to it as a Franco-Arabe school, which in this case is a loose interpretation, considering that the school delayed (sparse) French instruction until the upper levels and also used Zarma language in addition to Arabic. Others referred to the school as the town's madrasa. This was a tongue-in-cheek commentary by residents about how they confront reformist arguments that their town promulgates a cult of personality because it is a pilgrimage site and famed for its spiritual authorities. That people referred to the school with different terms (and in different languages) suggests that the classificatory schemas of schools are context driven. On the one hand, residents half-jokingly refer to their school as a madrasa but also as a purposeful gesture to reclaim the term *madrasa* itself. On the other hand, they acknowledge readily that their school is unique for the area and successful at educating many boys and girls broadly but religiously, and as such represents a new sort of Muslim pedagogy for the area.

Pluralities

The two cases described above call attention to the geometries of education in Niger. The differences between urban and rural settings, Niamey and Kiota, are significant. In both contexts parents send children to dual schools, collapsing the pluralities of educational options available. The possibilities to bookend education are not limited to urban areas. Rather, collapsing the pluralities of education is also about time and how different sorts of education involve it.

Historically, Qur'anic school has left workable hours of the day open for students to labor. The students in both Niamey and Kiota did not work, and so these open hours left their parents time to send them to other schools. This is not to say that the connections between work and Qur'anic education are fading, only that in some contexts they are being rethought.

The Qur'anic school in Kiota was not the only one there, and many of the others did involve day and evening labor. Ware's discussion of the "changing perceptions of time and labor regimes of students" (2004, 515) helps here. As he suggests, the correspondence between labor and farming has been overstated because farming is not a year-round activity. The cases in Niger support this observation, but also call attention to nonagricultural "labor regimes." In rural areas, when farming or gardening are not active, students perform other sorts of labor—they do not, as it were, receive any seasonal downtime. Agricultural labor in urban areas is rarely an option.

In most traditions of Qur'anic schooling in West Africa, labor demonstrates loyalty to one's sheikh or marabout and is generally framed as a form of spiritual submission (*tarbiya*). So going to a different school instead of working introduces significant questions about spiritual dedication as shown through labor and whether a laborless Qur'anic education is perceived as a complete one. In turn, Qur'anic school in West Africa is continuing as a historical form but is changing in articulation with new sets of expectations and structural pressures but also due to parents' decisions (Masquelier 1999; Alidou 2005).

Nor is social position insignificant. Prior to French colonial attention to Qur'anic education, nobles benefited from a labor force drawn from servile groups (slaves and captives, *banniya* and *tam*, respectively). With the abolishment of slavery by the French (in 1898) followed by tolerance of Qur'anic education, servile groups potentially became sources of labor for marabouts instead of for nobles (Stoller 1981, 767; see also de Sardan 1984, 27; Mauxion 2012).[13] From the colonial period onward, then, the capacity to provide labor, rather than putatively immobile class or caste status, theoretically secured access to education (Marty 1931, 190; Tamari 1996; Hanretta 2009; Hall 2011). As de Sardan (1984) argues, this had significant ramifications for labor extraction.

Parents have faced new burdens recently. Sending a child to two schools potentially increases parents' financial obligations for tuition at the very least. There is a core difference between sorts of schools in terms of tuition. Madrasas, Franco-Arabe schools, and secular schools bill outright, though in various formats and in different amounts. By contrast, the families of the Qur'anic students are frequently enmeshed in gift economies, offering ongoing and fluid recompense to the marabout in addition to any labor that the student might provide (see Butler 2006a).

Different places were characterized by different combinations. The students in Niamey bookended secular school with Qur'anic school. The students in Kiota bookended a progressive Franco-Arabe madrasa with Qur'anic school. In both instances, Qur'anic school was the common denominator. These combinations speak to the distribution of processes of collapsing education plurality, not simply as a geographic trend or a recipe involving religious and nonreligious schools. In part, this is due to the free time that Qur'anic school provides—now, instead of labor, it is bookending other sorts of learning. Collapsing the pluralities of education is not exclusively determined by the palette of options per se (of which there are more in Niamey, of course) but simply by the fact that there are options.

Conclusion

This chapter has loosely invoked the imagery of bookends. Like the distinct educational forms discussed, bookends provide support but do not come into contact with each other. Nigerien Muslims apprehend new practices of combining education by keeping learning discrete and its modalities separate—and, in doing so, signaling how such separation prevents the sorts of ready-made hybridity that would otherwise be implied.

Indeed, new sorts of strategies are at play, not just new forms of schools and new perceptions of what constitutes religious education. Practically, the fact that Muslim students are attending two different schools at the same time risks analytically privileging complementarity, the notion that each school is in a sense providing what the other cannot. Each school does precisely this, of course, but not *just* this. The sorts of descriptive terms frequently invoked in contrasting different sorts of schools can project a split caricature: The impersonal, formal, rational, Western-style madrasa/écoles Franco-Arabe/secular school variously confront the personal, esoteric, informal, traditional Qur'anic school. Naturally such a split poses problems because the chorus of potential analytical adjectives risks obscuring the ways in which Muslims navigate them.

Although the examples in this chapter do speak to themes of connection, complementarity should not exhaust the ways these examples can be understood. Understanding creativity contributes to discussions about contemporary Islamic education in West Africa in ways that agency, the history of change, and historicity of groups and movements alone cannot. It is essential to ask not just *what* religious education signals but *how*.

Questions of what education means and how it might fit into or further divide social categories remain salient; such questions have also spurred ways of understanding the relevance of education aside from its mere practicality. More and diverse educational opportunities continue to become available to and embedded in the lives of Muslims in West Africa. These are cast in terms of conceptualizations and discourses as well as everyday practices. As such, the extent to which education itself becomes indexical of Islam matters in ways beyond allegory.

The choices that parents, and sometimes children, make about education combine personal and impersonal, more or less religious, more or less practical, moral and amoral, or any number of the splits that map onto the contrasts and comparisons of the varieties of Islamic education in West Africa. But these choices are not just about ordering options—after all, the different educational options are not puzzle pieces: Nigerien Muslims hold varying perceptions about different forms of education; discussing the extent to which forms of education do or do not tend to fit well together limits the discussion to themes of categorization and not action. How people assimilate their educational options can also be communicative. Sending a child to two schools at once is about engaging (and sometimes ignoring) the complicated perceptions that others have about religious education.

Islamic education is a signifier that, in the case of Niger, collapses somewhat the distinction between being and becoming educated. In this sense, the simultaneous pluralities of education confront previously separate, even antagonistic, lines of criticism—of Qur'anic school as being anachronistic and out of step with the times or of madrasas or Franco-Arabe schools as being amoral if not foreign.

Regardless of the type of education and the style of transmission of knowledge, some didactic content as well as some forms of learning come before others. And yet the cases presented in this chapter contradict educational sequentialism and ideological exclusivity. Going to two schools at once might risk being read as a sort of hedging of bets in an economic climate framed by continued uncertainty. This may be part of a set of motivations, though far from the only motivation. Delimiting Islamic education in terms of the potentiality of its outcome takes a rather limited view of education as strictly preparatory and morally proprietary. Qur'anic education signals a particular type of religious learning, a madrasa education quite another, and a Franco-Arabe or secular education another still. Going to two schools at once in Niger indicates that learning is becoming a process as much instantiated as pursued.

NOTES

1. A *zima* is, for lack of a better term, a Zarma ritual specialist. Stoller (1989, 1995) has written extensively on Zarma spirit possession (see also Vidal 1990). Stoller points out that Zarma possession is not outside of the influence of Islamic idioms. In the context of Hausa, Masquelier (1996, 1999, 2001, 2008, 2009) highlights such ontological flux and flow in great detail, noting articulations between so-called traditional religion and Islamic practice and debate.

2. *Marabout* is a blanket term referring to various Islamic holy persons and religious specialists. It can be a loaded term because of a long history of indiscriminate colonial usage. Still, it is prevalent in colloquial usage in Niger in multiple contexts. Geertz (1968, 43) describes the etymology: "'Marabout' is a French rendering of the Arabic *Murabit*, which in turn derives from a root meaning to tie, bind, fasten, attach, hitch, moor. A 'Murabit' is thus a man tied,

bound, fastened to God, like a camel to a post, a ship to a pier, a prisoner to a wall; or, more appropriately, as *ribat*, another derivative, means a fortified sanctuary, a place of marabouts, like a monk to a monastery."

3. He was considered an expert in white chickens, which are basic sacrificial offerings because of their symbolic value and their price. They are the most inexpensive animal to sacrifice and therefore common.

4. See Meunier (1997) for an overview of the Islamic educational landscape in Niger. Reichmuth's (1993) work in Nigeria draws helpful contrasts in terms of different sorts of educations and their connections to larger issues of religious community. Loimeier's (2005) and Tamari's (1996, 2009; Tamari and Bondarev 2013) work discusses issues of language and instruction elsewhere in Africa.

5. Rote learning is not the only form of the embodiment of knowledge. Labor as a demonstration of faith embodies knowledge through action. Another method in Niger is to drink Qur'anic verses and thus literally embody them without having committed them to memory. Marabouts will sometimes prepare particular verses for consumption by particular students. Outside of an educational context, clients often receive or request Qur'anic verses from their marabouts, which are sometimes manipulated in esoteric ways to be rendered more effective. Verses are written on wooden tablets, washed off into a bowl, and usually fortified with litanies said over the bowl, before being given to the student or client to drink.

6. Having memorized the Qur'an by age twelve seems precocious; the norm is around fourteen or fifteen.

7. *L'exode*, seasonal or temporary rural-to-urban migration within Niger or internationally, whether to the coast (generally Benin, Togo, Ghana, and Côte d'Ivoire) or recently north to Algeria and Libya or Europe, was and is popular among younger Nigerien laborers and traders. Jean Rouch's film *Les Maîtres Fous* (1954–1955) focuses on the spiritual practices of a group of Nigerien migrants to Accra. Similarly, his film *Jaguar* (1954, re-edited 1967) highlights the economic agility of Nigerien traders, as too does Stoller's reprise of *Jaguar* (1999) as well as his more recent work on Nigerien traders in New York (2002). Levtzion notes that rural-urban movements fall against the backdrop of a long history of Islamic urbanization and interconnection between cities: "In Islam," he writes, "migration to the town was considered meritorious because it is in the urban milieu that one can fully practice the Muslim way of life. Also, the mobility of the trader stands in stark contrast to the stability of the peasants" (Levtzion 1979, 13). The Nigerien context in general and the history of the *exode* there in particular demonstrates multidirectional flows of people and ideas. Ferme's (1994) work on Islam in Sierra Leone details pathways of movement, flows of ideas, and religious synthesis outside urban areas.

8. Discussions of attachment and dependency recur in scholarship on Sufism in West Africa. These citations are of course partial, meant to show a variety of modes of attachment and expectations of students.

9. Monteil (1964, 145) writes: "The little mendicants, sent by their marabouts, are considered a social plague in the cities. Often in the country the custom is to send the young Qur'anic school students begging for their food" (my translation).

10. *Talibé* is another one of the problematic terms in the discourse about Islam in francophone West Africa. It is a French variant of the Arabic *talib*; there are local language synonyms as well (i.e., *talibizay* in Zarma). Despite its being a frenchified variant, the term *talibé*, extends beyond French-speaking Nigeriens.

11. There are possibilities for analyzing the significance of labor in Qur'anic education beyond the economic. Meillassoux, Rey, and Terray—the trio of the structural-Marxists

writing on kinship as a mode of labor extraction in West Africa—by way of their competing interpretations, highlight the complexity involved in connecting issues of age, labor, and even at times idioms of fictive kinship or fosterage. They underscore the importance of youth labor historically in agrarian West Africa. As Hart (1985, 259) notes: "Debate hinged on the powers of elders over young men in West African societies. Meillassoux thought it came from their superior knowledge; Rey found a mechanism akin to class extraction of surplus labor; while Terray insisted on a functionalist interpretation of kinship as a production organization." Returning to their debate raises new questions that can be adapted to examining how to analyze or even theorize labor among Qur'anic students—labor that at the very least would be an extension of their familial obligations as opposed to a drastic shift from them. Moreover, labor often tends to have a spiritual component in Tijani and Mouride rhetorics (see O'Brien 1971, 28–33, 56–57, 85–100, on the Mouride concept of *njebbel*, submission in part through work as a demonstration of faith). Labor is a form of submission and struggle, and so as much a moral and spiritual activity (*tarbiya*) as a productive and economic one (see Ware 2014). In Niger, this line of theological reasoning is not without its detractors; some Tijanis, for example, view the practice as anachronistic and child labor. Their opponents argue that such reasoning is inherently singular and wedded to the wage-labor hallmarks of an increasingly monetized neoliberal economy. The debate highlights that labor in the context of Qur'anic education matters in more than economic ways.

12. See Ware (2004, 2014) for a summary of the literature on labor and Qur'anic schooling. The intersection of labor and learning is a topic that occupies much social scientific scholarship on Qur'anic education in West Africa.

13. See Hanretta (2009) for discussion of the rhetoric of the French abolition of slavery versus the reality of the continued forms of servility.

REFERENCES

Alidou, Ousseina. 2005. *Engaging Modernity: Muslim Women and the Politics of Agency in Postcolonial Niger*. Madison: University of Wisconsin Press.

Amselle, Jean-Loup. 1998. *Mestizo Logics: Anthropology of Identity in Africa and Elsewhere*. Translated by Claudia Royal. Stanford, CA: Stanford University Press.

Brenner, Louis. 2001. *Controlling Knowledge*. Bloomington: Indiana University Press.

Butler, Noah. 2006a. "Costs of Knowledge: Some Economic Underpinnings of Spiritual Relations in Islam in Niger." *Research in Economic Anthropology* 24: 309–28.

———. 2006b. "The Materialization of Magic: Islamic Talisman in West Africa." In *Studies in Witchcraft, Magic, War and Peace in Africa: Nineteenth and Twentieth Centuries*, edited by Beatrice Nicolini, 263–76. Lewiston, NY: Mellen.

———. 2010. "Cheikh Hamidou Kane." In *The Encyclopedia of African Thought*, edited by F. Abiola Irele and Biodun Jeyifo, vol. 2, 28–30. New York: Oxford University Press.

Constantin, François. 1988. "Charisma and the Crisis of Power in East Africa." In *Charisma and Brotherhood in African Islam*, edited by Donal B. Cruise O'Brien and Christian Coulon, 67–90. Oxford: Clarendon.

de Sardan, Olivier. 1984. *Les sociétés Songhay-Zarma*. Paris: Karthala.
Eickelman, Dale. 1994. *Knowledge and Power in Morocco: The Education of a Twentieth-Century Notable*. Princeton: Princeton University Press.
Emerson, Ralph Waldo. 1993 [1841]. *Self Reliance and Other Essays*. Mineola, NY: Dover.
Ferme, Mariane. 1994. "What 'Alhaji Airplane' Saw in Mecca, and What Happened When He Came Home: Ritual Transformation in a Mende Community (Sierra Leone)." In *Syncretism/Anti-Syncretism: The Politics of Religious Synthesis*, edited by Charles Stewart and Rosalind Shaw, 27–44. London: Routledge.
Fortier, Corrine. 2003. "'Une pédagogie coranique': modes de transmission des saviors islamiques (Mauritanie)." *Cahiers d'études africaines* 43: 235–60.
———. 1997. "Mémorisation et audition: l'enseignement coranique chez les Maures de Mauritanie." *Islam et sociétés au sud du Sahara* 11: 85-105.
Gaffney, Patrick. 1994. *The Prophet's Pulpit: Islamic Preaching in Contemporary Egypt*. Berkeley: University of California Press.
Geertz, Clifford. 1968. *Islam Observed: Religious Development in Morocco and Indonesia*. Chicago: University of Chicago Press.
Gemmeke, Amber. 2009. "Marabout Women in Dakar: Creating Authority in Islamic Knowledge." *Africa* 79: 129–47.
Hall, Bruce. 2011. *A History of Race in Muslim West Africa, 1600–1960*. New York: Cambridge University Press.
Hammoudi, Abdellah. 1997. *Master and Disciple: The Cultural Foundations of Moroccan Authoritarianism*. Chicago: University of Chicago Press.
Hanretta, Sean. 2009. *Islam and Social Change in French West Africa*. Cambridge: Cambridge University Press.
Hardin, Kris. 1993. *The Aesthetics of Action: Continuity and Change in a West African Town*. Washington, DC: Smithsonian Institution Press.
Hart, Keith. 1985. "The Social Anthropology of West Africa." *Annual Review of Anthropology* 14: 243–72.
Hefner, Robert, and Muhammad Qasim Zaman, eds. 2007. *Schooling Islam: The Culture and Politics of Modern Muslim Education*. Princeton, NJ: Princeton University Press.
Kaba, Lansine. 1974. *The Wahhabiyya; Islamic Reform and Politics in French West Africa*. Evanston, IL: Northwestern University Press.
Kane, Cheikh Hamidou. 1961. *L'aventure ambigüe*. Paris: R. Julliard.
Kane, Ousmane. 2008. "Islamism: What Is New, What Is Not? Lessons from West Africa." *African Journal of International Affairs* 11: 157–87.
Kelley, Thomas. 2002. "Squeezing Parakeets into Pigeonholes: The Effects of Globalization and State Legal Reform in Niger on Indigenous Zarma Law." *NYU Journal of International Law and Politics* 34: 101–70.
Kobo, Ousman. 2009. "The Development of Wahhabi Reforms in Ghana and Burkina Faso, 1960–1990: Elective Affinities between Western-Educated Muslims and Islamic Scholars." *Comparative Studies in Society and History* 51:502–32.
———. 2012. *Unveiling Modernity in Twentieth-Century West African Islamic Reforms*. Boston: Brill.
Launay, Robert. 1990. "Pedigrees and Paradigms: Scholarly Credentials among the Dyula of the Northern Ivory Coast." In *Muslim Travelers: Pilgrimages, Migration, and the*

Religious Imagination, edited by Dale F. Eickelman and James Piscatori, 175–99. Berkeley: University of California Press.

———. 1992. *Beyond the Stream: Islam and Society in a West African Town*. Berkeley: University of California Press.

Launay, Robert, and Benjamin Soares. 1999. "The Formation of an 'Islamic Sphere' in French Colonial West Africa." *Economy and Society* 28: 497–519.

Launay, Robert, and Rudolph Ware. 2009. "Comment (ne pas) lire le Coran? Logiques de l'enseignement religieux au Sénégal et en Côte d'Ivoire." In *L'Islam, nouvel espace public en Afrique*, edited by Gilles Holder, 127–45. Paris: Karthala.

Levtzion, Nehemiah. 1979. "Toward a Comparative Study of Islamization." In *Conversion to Islam*, edited by Nehemiah Levtzion, 1–23. New York: Holmes and Meier.

Loimeier, Roman. 1997. *Islamic Reform and Political Change in Northern Nigeria*. Evanston: Northwestern University Press.

———. 2005. "Translating the Qur'ān in Sub-Saharan Africa: Dynamics and Disputes." *Journal of Religion in Africa* 35: 403–23.

———. 2009. *Between Social Skills and Marketable Skills: The Politics of Education in 20th Century Zanzibar*. Boston: Brill.

Marty, Paul. 1931. *Islam et les tribus dans la colonie du Niger*. Paris: Librairie Orientaliste Paul Geuthner.

Masquelier, Adeline. 1996. "Identity, Alterity, and Ambiguity in a Nigerien Community: Competing Definitions of 'True' Islam." In *Postcolonial Identities in Africa*, edited by Richard Werbner, 222–44. London: Zed.

———. 1999. "Debating Muslims, Disputed Practices: Struggles for the Realization of an Alternative Moral Order in Niger." In *Civil Society and the Political Imagination in Africa: Critical Perspectives*, edited by John L. Comaroff and Jean Comaroff, 219–50. Chicago: University of Chicago Press.

———. 2001. *"Prayer Has Spoiled Everything": Possession, Power, and Identity in an Islamic Town of Niger*. Durham, NC: Duke University Press.

———. 2008. "When Spirits Start Veiling: The Case of the Veiled She-Devil in a Muslim Town of Niger." *Africa Today* 54: 39–64.

———. 2009. *Women and Islamic Revival in a West African Town*. Bloomington: Indiana University Press.

Mauxion, Aurélien. 2012. *Democracy Building: Local Elections and Governance in Northern Mali*. Unpublished PhD diss., Department of Anthropology, Northwestern University.

Meunier, Olivier. 1997. *Dynamiques de l'enseignement islamique au Niger*. Paris: Harmattan.

Messick, Brinkley. 1993. *The Calligraphic State: Textual Domination and History in a Muslim Society*. Berkeley: University of California Press.

Monteil, Vincent. 1964. *L'islam noir*. Paris: Editions du Seuil.

Morgan, William and Armer, Michael. 1988. "Islamic and Western Education in a West African Society: A Cohort-Comparison Analysis." *American Sociological Review* 53: 634–39.

Niezen, Ronald. 1991. "Hot Literacy in Cold Societies: A Comparative Study of the Sacred Value of Writing." *Comparative Studies in Society and History* 33: 225–54.

O'Brien, Donal Cruise. 1969. "Le talibé mouride: étude d'un cas de dépendance sociale." *Cahier d'études Africaines* 9: 502–7.

———. 1971. *The Mourides of Senegal: The Political and Economic Organization of an Islamic Brotherhood*. London: Oxford University Press.
Reichmuth, Stefan. 1993. "Islamic Learning and Its Interaction with "Western" Education in Ilorin, Nigeria." *Muslim Identity and Social Change in Sub-Saharan Africa*, edited by Louis Brenner, 179–97. Bloomington: Indiana University Press.
Sanneh, Lamin. 1989. *The Jahanke Muslim Clerics: A Religious and Historical Study of Islam in Senegambia*. Lanham, MD and London: University Press of America.
———. 1997. *The Crown and the Turban: Muslims and West African Pluralism*. Boulder, CO: Westview.
Santerre, Renaud. 1973. *Pédagogie musulmane d'Afrique Noire: l'école coranique peule du Cameroun*. Montréal: Presses de l'Université de Montréal.
Soares, Benjamin. 2005. *Islam and the Prayer Economy: History and Authority in a Malian Town*. Ann Arbor: University of Michigan Press.
———. 2006b. "Islam in Mali in the Neoliberal Era." *African Affairs* 105: 77–95.
Starrett, Gregory. 1998. *Putting Islam to Work: Education, Politics, and Religious Transformation in Egypt*. Berkeley: University of California Press.
Stoller, Paul. 1981. "Social Interaction and the Management of Songhay Sociopolitical Change." *Africa* 52: 765–80.
———. 1989. *Fusion of the Worlds: An Ethnography of Possession among the Songhay of Niger*. Chicago: University of Chicago Press.
———. 1995. *Embodying Colonial Memories: Spirit Possession, Power, and the Hauka in West Africa*. New York: Routledge.
Tamari, Tal. 1996. "L'exégèse coranique (*tafsir*) en milieu mandingue." *Islam et sociétés au sud de Sahara* 10: 43–80.
———. 2002. "Islamic Higher Education in West Africa: Some Examples from Mali." In *Yearbook of the Sociology of Islam*, vol. 4, *Africa*, edited by Thomas Bierschenk and Georg Stauth, 91–128. Münster: LIT.
———. 2008. "L'enseignement islamique traditionnel de niveau avancé: cursus, pédagogie, implications culturelles et perspectives comparatives." *Mande Studies* 8: 39–62.
———. 2009. "The Role of National Languages in Mali's Modernising Islamic Schools (Madrasa)." In *Languages and Education in Africa: A Comparative and Transdisciplinary Analysis*, edited by Birgit Brock-Utne and Ingse Skattum, 163–74. Oxford: Symposium.
Tamari, Tal, and Dmitry Bondarev. 2013. "Introduction and Annotated Bibliography ('Qur'anic Exegesis in African Languages')." *Journal of Qur'anic Studies* 15: 1–55.
Umar, Muhammad Sani. 2001. "Education and Islamic Trends in Northern Nigeria: 1970s–1990s." *Africa Today* 48: 127–50.
———. 2009. "Islam and the Public Sphere in Africa: Overcoming the Dichotomies." Working paper, Institute for the Study of Islamic Thought in Africa, Northwestern University.
United Nations Development Programme. 2015. *Human Development Report*. New York: UNDP.
Vidal, Laurent. 1990. *Rituels de possession dans le Sahel: exemples Peul et Zarma du Niger*. Paris: Harmattan.
Ware, Rudolph. 2004. "Njàngaan: The Daily Regime of Qur'anic Students in Twentieth-Century Senegal." *International Journal of African Historical Studies* 37: 515–38.

———. 2014. *The Walking Qur'an: Islamic Education, Embodied Knowledge, and History in West Africa*. Chapel Hill: University of North Carolina Press.

Wilks, Ivor. 1968. "Islamic Learning in the Western Sudan." In *Literacy in Traditional Societies*, edited by Jack Goody, 161–97. Cambridge: Cambridge University Press.

Youngstedt, Scott. 2004. "Creating Modernities through Conversation Groups: The Everyday World of Hausa Migrants in Niamey, Niger." *African Studies Review* 47: 91–118.

CONTRIBUTORS

Ousseina Alidou is Professor of Linguistics and African Cultural Studies and teaches in the Department of African, Middle Eastern and South Asian Languages and Literatures at Rutgers University. She is author of *Engaging Modernity: Muslim Women and the Politics of Agency in Postcolonial Niger* (University of Wisconsin Press 2005) and *Muslim Women in Postcolonial Kenya: Representation, Leadership and Social Change* (University of Wisconsin Press 2013).

Cheikh Anta Babou is Associate Professor of History at the University of Pennsylvania in Philadelphia. He is author of *Fighting the Greater Jihad: Ahmadu Bamba and the Founding the Muridiyya of Senegal, 1853–1913* (Ohio University Press 2007).

Liazzat J. K. Bonate is Assistant Professor at the Centre for African Studies at the Eduardo Mondlane University, Maputo, Mozambique. She has previously taught at the Seoul National University. She specializes in African history and Islam in Africa and has published on the history of Islam, Sufism, gender, Islamic education, and liberation struggle in Mozambique.

Noah Butler is a Lecturer in anthropology at Loyola University. His research explores social relations of knowledge, forms of exchange, and modes of authority in Islam in Niger.

Corinne Fortier is a researcher at the Centre National de la Recherche Scientifiaque (CNRS) in Paris and a member of the Laboratory of Social Anthropology (Collège de France). She was awarded the bronze medal of CNRS in 2005. Her anthropological research investigates questions of body, gender, filiation, and transmission of Islamic knowledge in Sunni Islam and in Muslim societies, especially in Mauritania.

Robert Launay is Professor of Anthropology at Northwestern University. He is author of *Traders without Trade: Responses to Change in Two Dyula Communities* (Cambridge University Press 1982) and *Beyond the Stream: Islam and Society in a West African Town* (University of California Press 1992).

Ashley E. Leinweber is Assistant Professor of Political Science at Missouri State University. Her research focuses on the political engagement of the Muslim minority of the Democratic Republic of the Congo and has been published in *Review of African Political Economy* (March 2013) and *Cahiers d'Etudes Africaines* (June 2012), among others.

Roman Loimeier is Professor in Social and Cultural Anthropology at the University of Göttingen. He has authored a number of books on Muslim societies in Africa, such as *Muslim Societies in Africa: A Historical Anthropology* (Indiana University Press 2013) and *Between Social Skills and Marketable Skills: The Politics of Islamic Education in 20th Century Zanzibar* (Brill 2009).

Rüdiger Seesemann is Heisenberg Professor of Islamic Studies at the University of Bayreuth (Germany). Specializing in the study of Islam in sub-Saharan Africa, he has authored several articles and two monographs, *Ahmadu Bamba und die Entstehung der Muridiyya* (Klaus Schwarz 1993) and *The Divine Flood: Ibrahim*

Niasse (1900–1975) and the Roots of a Twentieth-Century Sufi Revival (Oxford University Press 2011). Seesemann serves as co-editor of the book series Islam in Africa (Brill Academic Publishers).

Benjamin F. Soares is Senior Researcher at the African Studies Centre at Leiden University and Professor of Anthropology at the University of Amsterdam. He recently co-edited *New Media and Religious Transformations in Africa* (Indiana University Press 2015) and *Muslim Youth and the 9/11 Generation* (University of New Mexico Press 2016).

Abdoulaye Sounaye is Research Fellow at the Zentrum Moderner Orient, Berlin. He works on Salafism in urban Niger.

Tal Tamari is Senior Researcher at the Centre National de la Recherche Scientifique, Paris. She has conducted extensive research in Mali, Guinea, and The Gambia on Islamic scholarship and education.

Alex Thurston is Visiting Assistant Professor of African Studies at Georgetown University. His book *Salafism in Nigeria; Islam, Preaching and Politics* (Cambridge University Press) is forthcoming in 2016.

Muhammad Sani Umar is Professor in the Department of History at Ahmadu Bello University, Zaria, Nigeria. He is author of *Islam and Colonialism: Intellectual Responses of Muslims of Northern Nigeria to British Colonial Rule* (Brill 2005).

Rudolph T. Ware III is Associate Professor of History at the University of Michigan, and the founder and director of the IKHLAS research initiative for the study of Islamic Knowledge, Histories and Languages, Arts and Sciences. He is author of *The Walking Qur'an: Islamic Education, Embodied Knowledge, and History in West Africa* (University of North Carolina Press 2014).

INDEX

'Abd Allah b. Hisham, 42
'Abduh, Muhammad, 212
Abdullah b. Fodio, 83
Abdullah bin Abdulaziz Al Saud, 273–74
Abubacar Musa Ismael "Mangira," 106
Abu Madyan, Shu'ayb, 228n11
African Muslim Agency, 112
Aga Khan Foundation, 204–7, 210
agricultural labor, 35–36, 50–51, 161, 297–98
Ahl al-Sunna, 107, 109, 112
Ahmad, Awad Mohammed, 131
Ahmadu Bello, 127–29, 131–32, 133–34
al-Akhdari, 'Abd ar-Rahman, 41, 65
al-A'lam, Yusuf, 43
al-Alawi, Sayyid 'Umar b. Ahmad b. Sumayt, 105
al-Alawi, Sharif Muhammad, 97
'Alawiyya, 138, 214–17, 220–21, 226–27, 228n18, 228n22
Alfa Bokar Karabenta, 42
Algeria, 6, 180
al-Ghaythī, Sa'īd b. Rashīd, 143
Alidou, Ousseina, 22, 237
Almoravids, 54–55n6, 62
alphabet, Arabic: *abajada* alphabet, 37–38; *abatasha*, 37–38
al-Amawīand, Burhān b. 'Abd al-'Azīz, 142
Ambiguous Adventure (Kane), 5, 47, 288, 295
'Ameir, 'Amīr 'Alī, 143, 146
Amselle, Jean-Loup, 294
amulets, 10, 42, 98, 216, 296
Ançar Dine, 275
Angoche (Mozambique), 21, 95, 108–9, 114–15
Ansar al-Sunna, 107
Arabic: and the al-Azhar school network, 178–79, 181, 184–87; and book study in West Africa, 42–46; and clash of competing education systems, 6–9; and combined education systems, 11; and competing knowledge systems in Kenya, 219, 220; and decolonization of education systems, 17–20; and elementary Qur'anic study, 37–38; and Falke's influence on education, 81; and Franco-Arabic schools, 19–20, 23, 104, 184–85, 262, 263, 285, 288–89, 290–92, 294, 296–97, 299–300; and

Hadhrami tradition in Kenya, 215, 217, 223–24; and higher education in Kenya, 229n37, 230n47; and the integrated madrasa curriculum, 196, 201, 204, 206, 208; and Islamic education in Mali, 54n1; and Islamic education in Northern Nigeria, 120, 121–25, 126–30, 130–33, 134, 137; and Islamic education in Senegal and Côte d'Ivoire, 255–56, 258–59; and Islamic education in Zanzibar, 138–40, 142, 146–47; and Islamic poetry, 52; and *makarantu* of Niger, 234–35, 239–40; and *marabout* term, 300n2; and mobility of Islamic learning, 246; and Muslim public figures in West Africa, 271–72, 274–75, 277–79; prosody, 66; and Qur'anic schools of Angoche, 96, 97–99, 100, 105–6, 108–11, 114; and Qur'anic schools of Mauritania, 61–62, 66–67, 69, 70, 71, 76nn15–16; and styles of Islamic education in West Africa, 29–30, 31, 53, 54–55n6; and *talib* term, 301n10; and transitions to advanced studies, 40; and youth study groups, 249. *See also* alphabet, Arabic
Arabic Literature of Africa (Hunwick), 81
Arif, Aida, 131
Armer, Michael, 291
arranged marriages, 198–200
al-'Ashmawi, 'Abd al-Bari, 41
'Ashura' (Tenth Muharram), 36
'Asim, Muhammad b., 42
associations, Islamic: Association de Développement Communitaire pour les Mamas Musulmanes, 161; Association des Ulamas Musulmans Algeriens, 180; Association malienne pour l'unité et le progrès de l'Islam (AMUPI), 275–76; Association Nigérienne pour l'Appel et la Solidarité Islamique, 242; Bureau Islamique pour la Défense des Droits Humaines, 161; Centre Sociale pour le Développement Communitaire, Mapendo, Maendeleo, and Dawati, 161; Club des Jeunes Musulmans, 239, 248; Collectif des Associations des Femmes Musulmanes Pour le Développement du Maniema, 160; Communauté Islamique en République Démocratique du Congo (COMICO),

158, 159–61, 164, 166; Conseil National des Droits de l'homme en Islam, 161; Conselho Islâmico de Moçambique (Islamic Council of Mozambique), 106; Dawa'tu Islamiyya, 161; Indian Comunidade Mahimetana, 96; Islamic Congress of Mozambique, 96, 107, 109; Islamic Council, 96, 107, 109, 112, 114; Jumiatu Islamiyya, 161; Union Culturelle Musulmane, 180–81, 185; Union des Femmes Musulmanes du Congo, 160; Union des Mamas Musulmanes pour le Développement et Droits Humaines, 161; World Islamic Call Society, 186

astrology, 10, 36, 110

al-Azhar University: and the al-Azhar school network, 173–74, 189–90, 192n34; and background of African education systems, 4; and changing Islamic education in Kenya, 212; and combined education systems, 9; and hybrid education systems, 16; and Islamic education in Northern Nigeria, 123, 129; and Islamic education in the Muridiyya, 174–81; and Islamic education in Zanzibar, 138; and Islamic modernism, 183–89; and Muslim public figures in West Africa, 271, 280; and Qur'anic schools of Angoche, 107; and Shaykh Murtalla, 181–83

Babou, Cheikh Anta, 22
al-Badawi, 'Abd al-Rahman b. Ahmad (Sharif Khitamy), 67, 219, 228n12
Bakari, Mohamad, 219, 225
Bā Kathīr, 'Abdallāh, 138
Bakht er Ruda, 129
Bakr, Sayyid Habib, 106
Bamana people and language, 44, 54–55n6
Bamba, Amadu, 177, 181–82, 189, 192n27
Bang, Ann K., 176, 214
Bangladesh, 17
al-Banna, Hasan, 212
baraka (blessing): and the al-Azhar school network, 174, 181, 184; and book study in West Africa, 43; and economics of Islamic education, 51, 52–53; and elementary Qur'anic study, 36; and Falke's influence on education, 89; and Islamic education in Senegal and Côte d'Ivoire, 259; and Muslim public figures in West Africa, 277, 279; and Qur'anic schools of Mauritania, 71; and recognition of educational achievements, 47; and transitions to advanced studies, 41

al-Barawi, 'Issa bin Ahmad al-Ngaziji, 104
al-Barawi, Umar Uways bin Muhammad, 104
Barelwis, 107
basmalah, 259
al-Baydh, 'Abdallah b. Sa'id, 221–22
al-Baydh, Muhammad b. Sa'id, 214, 221, 222–26, 223, 225–26, 226–27, 228n12
al-Baydh, Mu'taman, 226
al-Baydh, Sa'id b. Salim, 221, 222–23
al-Baydh, Sharif Muhammad, 222, 230n46
Bedouins, 62
Belgium. See colonialism, Belgian
Bella people and language, 31
Ben Badis, Muhammad, 180
Bible, 7, 76n17, 198
bid'a (innovation): and the al-Azhar school network, 183; and combined education systems, 10; and competing knowledge systems in Kenya, 220–21; and Islamic education in Northern Nigeria, 129; and *izala* reform, 251n3; and Muslim public figures in West Africa, 277, 279; and Qur'anic schools of Angoche, 106
Binji, Haliru, 129
Bi Swafiya. See Muhashamy-Said, Bi Swafiya
blackboards: and the al-Azhar school network, 179, 184; and combined education systems, 9, 11; compared with writing boards, 3–5; and decolonization of education systems, 18, 20; and diffusion of education technology, 23n3; and elementary Qur'anic study, 38; and hybrid education systems, 16; and Islamic education in Senegal and Côte d'Ivoire, 262; and Qur'anic schools of Angoche, 53, 101, 109, 114; and styles of Islamic education in West Africa, 30; and theoretical consideration for study, 1–3; and Westernization of Qur'anic schools, 53
blacksmiths, 62
Bonate, Liazzat, 21
Bourdieu, Pierre, 12
Boutros-Ghali, Boutros, 130
Boyle, Patrick M., 152, 154
Bozo people and language, 38, 40
Brenner, Louis: on epistemes of education systems, 286, 289; on individualized nature of instruction, 30; on paradigmatic shift in Islamic education, 173; on reform of Islamic education, 8, 10; on success of madrasas, 2, 270
Brigaglia, Andrea, 88
Britain. See colonialism, British

Buissert, Auguste, 153–54
al-Bukhari, Muhammad, 42, 104
Burkina Faso, 31–32, 275, 277
Burundi, 224
al-Busiri, Muhammad, 43
Buso, Mbakke, 177, 191n17
al-Buti, Muhammad Saʻid Ramadan, 273
Butler, Noah, 23

Cahiers Ponty, 259–60
Cameroon, 4
castes, 62
Catholic Church: and clash of competing education systems, 7–8; and the integrated madrasa curriculum, 197; and Islamic education in the DRC, 149–50, 150–52, 152–55, 155–56, 156–57, 159, 160, 162, 165, 166; monopoly on colonial education, 12, 22; Office of Catholic Education, 153; and Qurʼanic schools of Angoche, 107, 114; and the Regime do Indigenato of Mozambique, 99–104. *See also* Christianity and Christian schools
le Cercle des Travailleurs Musulmans de Maradi, 239
certifications: in Côte d'Ivoire, 18–19; and discipline in Islamic education, 258; and Falke's influence on education, 87, 89; and the integrated madrasa curriculum, 200; and Islamic education in Senegal and Côte d'Ivoire, 260, 262, 264n7; and Islamic education in the Muridiyya, 175; and Qurʼanic schools of Mauritania, 72–73
Chamberlain, Michael, 3
child betrothal, 196–200
Chistiyya, 107
Christianity and Christian schools: and clash of competing education systems, 7; and competing knowledge systems in Kenya, 218; and the integrated madrasa curriculum, 196–98, 204, 208; and Islamic education in the DRC, 151, 153, 155–56, 167; in Kenya, 213; and missionary education, 15; and Qurʼanic schools of Angoche, 102–3; and significance of blackboards in education, 5. *See also* Catholic Church; schools
clerical lineages, 12–14, 87
collective duties, 65–66
colonialism, Belgian: and background of African education systems, 1–2; and Catholic monopoly on education, 12; and clash of competing education systems, 7, 9; and decolonization of education systems, 17; and education in Democratic Republic of Congo, 149, 150–52, 152–55; and hybrid education systems, 16; and Islamic education in the DRC, 159, 166; and Qurʼanic schools of Angoche, 102
colonialism, British: and background of African education systems, 1–2; and changing Islamic education in Kenya, 212; and clash of competing education systems, 6–9; and combined education systems, 12, 14; and competing knowledge systems in Kenya, 218; and Falke's influence on education, 80; and hybrid education systems, 16–17, 21–22; Indirect Rule, 120, 121; and the integrated madrasa curriculum, 195, 196–97, 200, 204; and Islamic education in Northern Nigeria, 119–20, 121–25, 125–26, 126–30, 131–32, 133–34; and Islamic education in Zanzibar, 137, 138–40, 142–44, 146, 147n2; and language of elementary education, 23n8; Native Authorities, 121; and Qurʼanic schools of Angoche, 96, 99; and racial distinctions, 229n29
colonialism, French: and the al-Azhar school network, 173, 174–77, 178–81, 185–87, 189; and background of African education systems, 2; and clash of competing education systems, 6–9; and combined education systems, 11; and decolonization of education systems, 17–20; and disciplinary practices in education, 47–48; and Falke's influence on education, 80; and Islamic education in the DRC, 154; and Islamic education in Niger, 286, 288, 291–93, 296–98; and language use in colonial education, 14–15; and *marabout* term, 300n2; and Muslim public figures in West Africa, 272–73; and Qurʼanic schools of Angoche, 99–101, 103–4; and secular education, 12; and styles of Islamic education in West Africa, 55n6
colonialism, Portuguese: Acto Colonial, 99; *assimilados*, 100–102, 114; and background of African education systems, 1–2; Carta Orgânica do Império Colonial Portugues, 99–100; and Catholic monopoly on education, 12; and clash of competing education systems, 7–9; and decolonization of education systems, 17; disparagement of Islamic education, 21; Estado, Novo, 101; and hybrid education systems, 16; and the integrated madrasa curriculum, 197; and Islamic education in the DRC, 151; and Islamic education in Senegal and Côte d'Ivoire, 257; Islão Negro,

103; Native Assistance Code, 100; Native Labor Code, 99; Overseas Administrative Reform, 100; Portaria do Assimilado, 100; and Qur'anic schools of Angoche, 95–96, 96–99, 99–104, 105–6, 107, 109, 112, 114; Reforma Administrativa Ultramarina, 99–100, 103; Regime do Indigenato, 99–104, 110, 114
Comaroff, Jean, 2
Comaroff, John, 2
Comité Provinciale Feminine, 160
Committee on Higher Muslim Education, 128
Communauté Islamique en République Démocratique du Congo (COMICO), 158, 159–61, 164, 166
Comunidade Mahometana, 108–9
Concordat agreements, 102, 151, 153
Congo, Democratic Republic of: background of Muslim public schools, 149–50; and Catholic mission schools, 22; history of education in, 150–55; and hybrid education institutions, 161–65; Muslim community of, 155–61; Zairianization process, 156–57. *See also* Kasongo; Kindu; Kinshasa; Kisangani; Maniema
Congo Free State, 150
conversion, religious: and book study in West Africa, 45; and consequences of colonial rule, 14, 15–16; and Hadhrami tradition in Kenya, 222; and the integrated madrasa curriculum, 197–98; and Islamic education in the DRC, 153, 155–56, 165, 166; and Islamic education in Northern Nigeria, 128; and the Majlis Ousman Dan Fodio, 242; and Qur'anic schools of Angoche, 102
corporeality, 21, 79, 81–83, 86–89
Côte d'Ivoire: and the al-Azhar school network, 185; and chains of transmission, 264n7; and clash of competing education systems, 6; and classical Islamic education, 256; and decolonization of education systems, 17–18, 20; and hybrid education systems, 22; and Islamic education in Niger, 289; and labor migration, 301n7; and *lo* societies, 12; and Muslim public figures in West Africa, 272, 275, 277; and recognition of educational achievements, 46–47; and Sufi brotherhoods, 261. *See also* Korhogo
Coutinho, João de Azevedo, 97, 98
curricula: and the al-Azhar school network, 183, 186–87; book study (classical), 41–46; canonical texts in West Africa, 88; and changing Islamic education in Kenya, 212–13; *diāna* syllabus, 144; grammar, 42, 65, 66, 255; and the integrated madrasa curriculum, 195–96, 201–10; and Islamic education in Niger, 292; and styles of Islamic education in West Africa, 31; and Suware's influence, 56n23; and Westernization of Qur'anic schools, 53. *See also* education, classical Islamic; education, colonial; memorization; recitation; schools

Daaru ālim Ul-khabīr (Senegal), 184, 192n27
Dakar (Senegal), 179, 180
Dallal, Ahmed, 133
da'wa (proselytizing), 207–8, 275
De Herdt, Tom, 166
demographic trends, 159–61, 213
Deobandis, 105
dhikr, 100, 105–6, 111, 147, 176, 228n18
Dia (Mali): and book study in West Africa, 42, 45–46, 56n23; and economics of Islamic education, 49–52; and elementary Qur'anic study, 38–39; and growth of Islamic education, 54n4; and recognition of educational achievements, 46–48; research collection in, 29; and school types in West Africa, 31–34; and styles of Islamic education in West Africa, 54n6; and transitions to advanced studies, 39–41
Diagne, Souleymane Bachir, 272–73
Diakhaba (Mali): and book study in West Africa, 42; and economics of Islamic education, 49–50; and elementary Qur'anic study, 36, 38; and school schedules, 34–35; and school types in West Africa, 32–33; and styles of Islamic education in West Africa, 29; and transitions to advanced studies, 40
Diakhanke, 56n23
Diarra, Yakouba, 47
Diop, Elhaj Ibrahima, 179
Diouf, Abdou, 182, 191nn21–22
divination, 10, 98, 110, 287
Diwan sittat ash-shucara, 43
al-Djazuli, Muhammad, 43, 65
Djenné (Mali): and book study in West Africa, 42, 45, 56n23; and disciplinary practices in education, 48; and economics of Islamic education, 50–52; and growth of Islamic education, 54n4; and recognition of educational achievements, 46; and school schedules, 34–36; and school types in West Africa, 31–32; and styles of Islamic education in West Africa, 29, 54n6; and transitions to advanced studies, 40–41

Index | 313

dual education systems, 286–87. *See also* hybrid schools and education
Dubai, 108
Dutton, Yasin, 260
Dyula, 6, 256

economy, 18, 47–53, 49–53
education, classical Islamic: advanced study, 39–41, 130; and blackboards vs. writing boards, 1–3, 4; *chuo* tradition, 201–2; and clash of education systems, 5–6; classical pedagogy, 256; and corporal punishment, 48, 64, 74; corporate dimension of, 21, 82–83, 86–89; corpus, 21, 79, 81, 82–83, 83–86, 86–89; in Côte d'Ivoire, 20; discipline in, 47–49, 258; diversity in, 30, 74; dual education systems, 286–87; and educational pluralism, 13–15; and hybrid education systems, 9–11; hybrid schools and education, 17, 19–20, 22, 108, 161–65, 264; and Islamic education in Senegal and Côte d'Ivoire, 256, 258–59, 261–64; itinerant schools and teachers, 50–53, 80, 87, 89; *mahāzra*, 66; mobility of Islamic learning, 244–46; pace of teaching, 68–69; peer learning, 13; pupil/master relationship, 13, 89, 110, 243, 259
education, colonial: and blackboards vs. writing boards, 1–3, 3–4; and clash of education systems, 5–9; dual education systems, 286–87; and educational pluralism, 11–16; and hybrid education systems, 9–11; hybrid schools and education, 17, 19–20, 22, 108, 161–65, 264; indigenization, 121; "Reform of Teaching in Belgian Congo" (report), 154
education, elementary: and the al-Azhar school network, 179, 185, 187–88, 192n33; and book study in West Africa, 46; and clash of competing education systems, 7; and Falke's influence, 79; and Islamic education in Niger, 290; and Islamic education in Senegal and Côte d'Ivoire, 255; and Qur'anic schools of Angoche, 53, 96, 99; and Qur'anic schools of Mauritania, 61–62; and Qur'anic schools of West Africa, 36–39; and school types in West Africa, 33; and styles of Islamic education in West Africa, 29, 31; and Westernization of Qur'anic schools, 53
education, higher. *See* universities, Islamic
education, hybrid, 17, 19–20, 22, 108, 161–65, 264
education, prophetic model of, 247–49
education, secular: and the al-Azhar school network, 180–81, 187, 192n33; and background of African education systems, 1–2; and "book-ending" schooling, 298, 299–300; and changing Islamic education in Kenya, 212–13; and clash of competing education systems, 7–8; and combined education systems, 11; and competing knowledge systems in Kenya, 218–20; and decolonization of education systems, 18–20; and French colonial system, 12; and tradition in Kenya, 225–26; and the integrated madrasa curriculum, 195, 198, 201–5, 205–6, 208–10; and Islamic education in the DRC, 150–51, 152–55, 154, 157, 160, 167; and Islamic education in Niger, 288, 290, 292–94, 295–96, 298; and Islamic education in Northern Nigeria, 128; and Islamic education in Senegal and Côte d'Ivoire, 263; in Kenya, 213; and the Majlis Ousman Dan Fodio, 241–42; and *makarantu* of Niger, 239; and Muslim public figures in West Africa, 23, 268, 270–71, 272, 274, 277; and Qur'anic schools of Angoche, 101, 107; and "Westernization" concerns, 245; and youth study groups, 247–48
Educational Reform Decree, 103
educational sequentialism, 300
education gaps, 18
education reforms, 152–55, 212–13
Egypt: and the al-Azhar school network, 184–86; and book study in West Africa, 41–44; and changing Islamic education in Kenya, 212; and clash of competing education systems, 9; and competing knowledge systems in Kenya, 218–20; and disciplinary education regime, 4; and export of Islamic teachers, 22; and hybrid education systems, 16–17; and the integrated madrasa curriculum, 208; and Islamic education in Northern Nigeria, 120, 121–25, 126, 128, 130–33; and Islamic education in Zanzibar, 138; and Muslim public figures in West Africa, 271, 273, 275; and Qur'anic schools of Angoche, 96, 103, 106–7
Eickelman, Dale F., 3, 13, 17, 105–6
Ekoti language, 96, 109
elite education, 14–15
Eljah Mahmud Ba, 179–80, 183
El-Tibawi, 176
El Zein, Abdul Hamid M., 215, 228n12
Enes, António, 101
English language education, 204, 206
esoteric modes of education: and the al-Azhar school network, 173–74, 176, 189; and combined education systems, 10; and economics of Islamic education, 51; and Islamic educa-

tion in Niger, 289, 299; and Islamic education in Northern Nigeria, 134; and Muslim public figures in West Africa, 274, 279–80; and Qur'anic schools of Angoche, 97, 106, 111; and rote learning, 301n5; and school types in West Africa, 34. *See also* Sufism

Estatuto Missionário (1940), 102

Faisal bin Abdulaziz Al Saud, 131, 134
Falke, Umar, 21, 79–89
Fall, Ibra, 177
Fall, Malick, 259–60
Al-Fallah movement, 185
fard kifayah, 208
al-Farsy, Abdallah Saleh, 138, 142–43, 146, 219–20, 225
fasting, 65
the Fatiha (*fātiḥa*), 37, 40, 68, 75
Fatima binti Zacariya, 97
al-Fazazi, 'Abd ar-Rahman b. Yakhlaftan, 43
femmes travailleuses, 241–42
fiqh (jurisprudence): and the al-Azhar school network, 176, 183, 186–87; and book study in West Africa, 41–42; and clerical lineages, 14; and Falke's influence on education, 79, 83; and Hadrami tradition in Kenya, 216, 223; and higher education in Kenya, 230n47; and Islamic education in Senegal and Côte d'Ivoire, 258, 260; and Islamic education in Zanzibar, 138; and Qur'anic schools of Angoche, 110; and Qur'anic schools of Mauritania, 63, 65; and school types in West Africa, 32. *See also* Maliki jurisprudence
Fortier, Corinne, 21, 290
Foucault, Michel, 4, 10, 11
France. *See* colonialism, French
Franck, Louis, 151–52
Freitag, Ulrike, 216, 224, 228nn21–23
French language, 20
Fulbe people and language: and the Arabic alphabet, 55n12; and book study in West Africa, 44; and economics of Islamic education, 50–51; and elementary Qur'anic study, 38–39; and Falke's influence on education, 79; and Qur'anic schools of Angoche, 119; and recruitment of students, 31; and school schedules, 34, 35; and styles of Islamic education in West Africa, 54–55n6; and transitions to advanced studies, 39–40
fundamentalism, 214, 256, 273
funeral rites, 105, 256–57

The Gambia, 21, 34
Geertz, Clifford, 300n2
Gellner, Ernest, 270
gender roles. *See* women and Islamic education
al-Ghazali, Abu Hamid, 190n10, 272
Gidado, Muhammad, 126
Girouard, Percy, 122
gnosis, 173–74
Goans, 197
Golding, Robert, 152–53
Gramsci, Antonio, 140
griots, 62
Guinea, 21, 32. *See also* Kankan; Touba (Guinea)
Guinea Bissau, 32, 42
Gumi, Abubakar, 129, 131, 133, 183

habitus, 12, 16
al-Habshi, 'Ali b. Muhammad, 216–17, 221–22
hadith (traditions of the Prophet): and the al-Azhar school network, 176, 186; and book study in West Africa, 42; and clerical lineages, 14; and Falke's influence on education, 86; and the integrated madrasa curriculum, 205; and Islamic education in Kenya, 223, 230n47; and Islamic education in Niger, 290; and Islamic education in Senegal and Côte d'Ivoire, 260; and *makarantu* of Niger, 238–39, 239–41; and Muslim public figures in West Africa, 273; and Qur'anic schools of Angoche, 104, 105, 110; and Qur'anic schools of Mauritania, 65, 70, 71, 75; and styles of Islamic education in West Africa, 54–55n6; and youth study groups, 247–49
Hadhramaut, 22, 214, 216
Hadrami tradition: and Islamic education in Kenya, 214–17, 219–21, 223–26, 226–27; and Islamic education in Zanzibar, 138; and religious texts, 228n8
ḥāfiẓ, 71
Hafkin, Nancy J., 97
Haïdara, Chérif Ousmane Madani, 274–77, 280
hajias, 234–35, 236, 239–41, 251n1
Hakim, Selim, 132
Hakima, Ahmad Abu, 131
al-Halabi, Ahmad b. 'Abd al-Hayy, 43
halaqa, 216–17
Hall, Bruce, 83–84
Hallaq, Wael B., 86
al-Hamadhani, Abu l-Fadl, 43
Ḥamāhullah, 'Abd-Allah wuld Ḥajj, 66
Hardin, Kris, 287

al-Hariri, Abu Muhammad al-Qasim, 43–44, 46
Harrison, Christopher, 6
Hart, Keith, 301–2n11
Ḥassāniyya, 61, 62, 64, 66, 71, 73
Hausa people and language: and Falke's influence on education, 80, 84; and Islamic education in Northern Nigeria, 119, 120, 122, 123, 125; and *makarantu* of Niger, 234–35, 238; and mobility of Islamic learning, 245; and Zarma rituals, 300n1. See also Nigeria, Northern
Hendry, William, 140–42
al-Ḥibshī, ʿAlī b. Muḥammad, 138
hijab, 245
Ḥimīd, Rajab, 142
HIV/AIDS, 276
Hodgson, M., 86
Hollingsworth, Lawrence William, 143
Hunwick, John, 81, 132

ʿibāda (religious devotion), 65
Ibn Abu Bakr, Muhammad Maʿarouf bin Shaykh Ahmad, 104
Ibn ʿAshir, 65
Ibn Khaldun, 42
Ibn Saḥnūn, 63–64, 69
Ibrahim, Kashim, 128
ʿĪdāʿ al-nusūkh (Abdullah b. Fodio), 83
ʿId al-adha, 35–36
ʿId al-fitr, 35–36, 147
identity cards, 99–100
al-Idrīsī, Aḥmad b. Abī Bakr al-Fāsī, 80
ijāza (certificate of transmission), 72–73, 175, 264n7
ijtihad, 85
Illia, Malam, 247
illiteracy, 99, 184–85, 236, 241
Ilorin (Nigeria), 9
Indonesia, 17
initiation, 12–13, 38, 63, 79, 98, 176, 179, 201
Integrated Madrasa Project, 204–5
interfaith dialogue, 208
International Monetary Fund, 263
internet access, 213
Iran, 272
Iraq, 132, 272
al-Islami, al-Muntada, 278
Islamic Congress of Mozambique, 96, 107, 109
Islamic Council, 96, 107, 109, 112, 114
Islamic Development Bank, 107, 112
Islamism, 256, 268, 272, 273. See also reformism
Islam noir, 3, 103, 176, 261

Ismailis, 207, 218
Issa, Ali Sultan, 146
itinerant schools and teachers, 50–53, 80, 87, 89
Ittifaq, 110
izala, 129, 183, 239, 247–48, 251n3. See also reformism

Jaabikundaa (Mali), 32
Jakhanke, 259
Jamal al-Layl, Salih, 215, 216
Jamal al-Layl family, 214, 215–16
Jardim de Vilhena, Ernesto, 97, 98
Jeng, Amadu Basiru, 257–58
Jordan, 132
Jumbe, Aboud, 146

Kaʿb b. Zuhayr, 43
Kalun, 70
Kamalu ʿd-Din, 9
Kane, Cheikh Hamidou, 5, 47, 287–89, 292
Kane, Ousmane, 134
Kankan (Guinea), 34, 35, 40, 41, 47, 53
Kanuri scholars, 119
Karume, Abeid Amani, 145–46, 147
Kasongo (DRC), 156, 159, 161, 164
Katsina College, 124, 127
Kelley, Thomas, 292–93
Kenya: background of Islamic culture in, 212–14; and competing knowledge systems, 218–21; and education networks in Africa, 22; and Hadrami tradition, 214–17, 219–21, 223–26, 226–27; and the integrated madrasa curriculum, 195–96, 198, 200–201, 201–8, 210; and Islamic traditionalism, 221–26, 226–27
Kenya Institute of Education, 205, 208
Khalifa, Ahmed, 271
Khalil b. Ishaq al-Jundi, 42, 65–66, 73, 76n16
khatib, 97–98
Khitamy, Sharif (ʿAbd al-Rahman b. Ahmad al-Badawi), 67, 219, 228n12
Khoja Ismaʿili, 218
Khomeini, Ruhollah, 207, 272
Kimbanguist churches, 157, 159. See also Christianity and Christian schools
Kindu (DRC), 159–61, 162, 164, 166
Kinshasa (DRC), 158, 159, 164
Kiota (Niger), 296–97, 297–98
Kisangani (DRC), 159, 161, 164–65
Kishk, ʿAbd al-Hamid, 275
Kiswahili language: and competing knowledge systems in Kenya, 219–20; and Hadrami tra-

dition in Kenya, 215, 217, 223; and the integrated madrasa curriculum, 198, 201, 205–6; and Qur'anic schools of Angoche, 96–98, 111, 114
Korhogo (Côte d'Ivoire), 6, 10, 12, 23n9, 256, 260
Koti (Mozambique), 96
Kuwait, 131

Lagos (Nigeria), 9
laïcité, 7–8
al-Lamṭi, 65
language issues in education, 8, 43
Latin, 140
Launay, Robert, 22, 260, 289
Laye, Camara, 6
al-Layl, Ḥasan b. al-Shaykh Jamal, 142–43
Leinweber, Ashley, 22
Leopold II, King of Belgium, 150–51, 159
Levtzion, Nehemiah, 301n7
Libya, 129, 272
Lienhardt, Peter, 215
literacy, 15, 96–99, 114, 201, 249
Lo, Abd Rahmane, 177, 192n27
Lo, Serigne Mbakke Soxna, 177
local languages, 29–30, 53
Loimeier, Roman: on British colonial education, 8–9; on reform of Islamic education, 269–70, 274, 280, 281n3, 289
Lugard, Frederick, 121, 122, 124
Lupi, Eduardo do Couto, 97, 98

al-Maʻamirī, Bibi Samīra, 143–44, 146
madrasas: and the al-Azhar school network, 177–78, 178–81, 184; and background of African education systems, 2; and book study in West Africa, 42; and changing Islamic education in Kenya, 212; and competing knowledge systems in Kenya, 218–20; East African Madrasa Programme, 209; East African Madrasa Resource Centers, 196; and economics of Islamic education, 52–53; and elementary Qur'anic study, 36, 38; and Hadhrami tradition in Kenya, 222–26, 227; and Indian Ocean Sufi networks, 21; and the integrated madrasa curriculum, 195–96, 201–10; and Islamic education in the DRC, 164; and Islamic education in Niger, 285, 288–89, 290, 291–92, 294, 297, 298, 299–300; and Islamic education in Senegal and Côte d'Ivoire, 262; and Islamic education in Zanzibar, 138–40; and learning trends in Niger, 250; Madrasat al-Ghanna' al-Islamiyya, 223–26, 226–27; Madrasat al-Nur, 222–23; Madrasat Bā Kathīr, 138; Markaz al-Islamiyya, 109, 110; and mobility of Islamic learning, 246; Mombasa Madrasa Resource Center, 195; and Muslim public figures in West Africa, 270–71, 274–75, 280; and Qur'anic schools of Angoche, 96, 98–99, 102–3, 104, 107–14, 116; and Qur'anic schools of Mauritania, 62; and school schedules, 34; and school types in West Africa, 32–33; and transitions to advanced studies, 40–41; and travel restrictions on education, 190n6; and Wahhabi influence, 230n46; and youth study groups, 249. See also education, classical Islamic
magic, 279, 289. See also amulets; esoteric modes of education
al-Mahalli, Djalal ad-Din, 44
al-Mahdi, Sadiq, 134
majlis, 31, 32–35, 49, 51, 53, 54n5, 55n6, 241–44. See also education, classical Islamic
makarantu, 234–36, 236–39, 239–44, 244–46, 247–49, 249–51
Al-Maktum Foundation, 108
Malawi, 224
Mali: and book study, 41–46; and clash of competing education systems, 8; classical education in, 21, 23; and combined education systems, 10; and economic conditions, 49–53; and elementary Qur'anic study, 36–39; growth of madrasas, 2; and perceptions of traditional Islamic education, 47–49; and recognition of educational achievements, 46–47; and school curricula, 43–44; school schedules and holidays, 34–36; school types and teacher recruitment, 31–34; and sedentary vs. itinerant teachers, 31–32, 52; and styles of Islamic education in West Africa, 29, 53; and teacher earnings, 49; and teaching methods, 53; and traits of traditional Islamic education, 29–31; and transitions to advanced studies, 39–41. See also Dia; Diakhaba; Djenné; Jaabikundaa; San; Segou; Timbuktu
Malik, Muhammad b., 42
Malik b. Anas, 42, 260
Maliki jurisprudence: and book study in West Africa, 42, 44; and disciplinary practices in education, 48; and elementary Qur'anic study, 36; and Falke's influence on education, 79; and Islamic education in Senegal and Côte d'Ivoire, 259–60; and Qur'anic schools of Mauritania, 61–62, 65, 66, 70, 76n4; and school types in West Africa, 32–33; signifi-

cance of Medina in, 260, 265n17. *See also fiqh* (jurisprudence)
mallams, 126, 244. *See also* ulama
Mambrui (Kenya), 214, 221–26
Manding people and language, 29, 38–39, 45, 47, 53, 54n6, 55n12, 56n23. *See also* Dyula
Maniema (DRC), 159–61, 163–65
Manuel of Portugal, 97
al-Manufi, 'Ali, 41
marabouts: and the al-Azhar school network, 182; and begging, 295–96, 301n9; and combined education systems, 10; definition of term, 300–301n2; and economics of Islamic education, 51; and Islamic education in Niger, 287, 291, 295–96, 298; and Islamic education in Senegal and Côte d'Ivoire, 258, 260, 264; and the Majlis Ousman Dan Fodio, 243; and Qur'anic schools of Mauritania, 62–63, 65–66, 68, 70–71, 74; and rote learning, 301n5; and styles of Islamic education in West Africa, 54n6. *See also* Sufism; ulama
Maradi (Niger), 239
mā'rifa, 173
market for education, 18–20
Martin, Bradford G., 214
Marty, Paul, 177
al-Mashhūr, Abd al-Raḥmān b. Muḥammad, 138
al-Mashhūr, 'Alawī b. 'Abd al-Raḥmān, 138
Masquelier, Adeline, 237
Massano de Amorim, Pedro Francisco, 97
matrilineal kinship, 97, 100
Mauritania: and the al-Azhar school network, 181, 186; and book study in West Africa, 43; classical education in, 21; masters and forms of knowledge, 61–66; pedagogical techniques, 66–69; transmission and types of texts, 69–75
mawlid celebrations: and book study in West Africa, 43; and Hadhrami tradition in Kenya, 215–17; and Islamic education in Zanzibar, 147; and Mambrui, 222; and models of education in Kenya, 220–21; and Muslim public figures in West Africa, 276–77; and Qur'anic schools of Angoche, 106, 111; and school schedules, 36; spread of, 228n18
al-Mawsu'a al-Yusufiyya, 225
al-Mazru'i, Shaykh al-Amin b. 'Ali, 218–19, 220
Mbake Bawol (Senegal), 174
Mbakke, Abdu Lahad, 185
Mbakke, Anta, 177
Mbakke, Bashiir, 181
Mbakke, Buso, 174–75

Mbakke, Cheikh, 177
Mbakke, Falilu, 177, 184
Mbakke, Kajoor, 175
Mbakke, Khadim, 177–78
Mbakke, Momar Anta Sali, 174–75
Mbakke, Murtalla: and the al-Azhar school network, 174, 178, 181–83, 184–86, 188–89; and al-Azhar University, 22; and religious authority issues, 191n17; and Senegalese politics, 191n22
Mbakke, Mustafa, 177, 182, 190n6, 191n17
Mbakke, Mustafa Ceytu, 190n6
Mbakke, Same, 177, 190n6
Mbakke, Serigne Maam Moor, 188–89, 192n34
Mbow, Penda, 268n
Mecca, 126, 177, 179, 190n6
mederses. See madrasas
media figures and technologies: Chérif Ousmane Madani Haïdara, 274–77; and Islamic practices in West Africa, 268–71; newspapers, 271–72; Penda, 277–80; radio, 271–72; Sidy Lamine Niasse, 271–74; social media, 277
Medina, 260
Medina, Islamic University of, 105–7, 131, 177, 247, 278
Meillassoux, Claude, 301–2n11
memorization: and book study in West Africa, 46; and disciplinary practices in education, 49; and elementary Qur'anic study, 36–37, 39; and the integrated madrasa curriculum, 201; and Islamic education in Niger, 291; and Islamic education in Senegal and Côte d'Ivoire, 258; and *makarantu* of Niger, 240; and Qur'anic schools of Mauritania, 68–69, 71, 75; and styles of Islamic education in West Africa, 29; and transitions to advanced studies, 40, 41. *See also* curricula
Meunier, Olivier, 237
mḥāẓar, 66
Ministry of Education (DRC), 162
Ministry of Education (Northern Nigeria), 121, 123, 132
Ministry of Education (Zanzibar), 145–47
Ministry of Interior (Zanzibar), 145
mission civilizatrice, 101
Mitchell, Timothy, 2, 4, 16
Mkelle, Burhan, 143
mobility of Islamic learning, 244–46
Mobutu Sese Seko, 156–58
modernization: and the al-Azhar Institute, 183–89; and combined education systems, 9–10;

and competing knowledge systems in Kenya, 218, 221; and Islamic education in Northern Nigeria, 132, 134; and Islamic education in Senegal and Côte d'Ivoire, 262; and Islamic education in Zanzibar, 139; and Muslim public figures in West Africa, 268; and styles of Islamic education in West Africa, 30
Monteiro, Fernando Amaro, 104
Moorish society. See Ḥassāniyya
moral education, 82, 152, 291
Morgan, William, 291
Morocco, 186
Mossi people and language, 31
Mourides. See Muridiyya
Mousinho de Albuquerque, Joachim Augusto, 97, 101
Moyo, Hassan Nassor, 146
Mozambique: background of Islamic education in, 95–96; Islamic education before "effective occupation," 96–99; Madrasas in contemporary Angoche City, 107–14; Nacala region, 103; and recent education trends, 114–15; and the Regime do Indigenato, 99–104; Sufis and Wahhabis in, 104–7. See also Angoche; Koti; Nampula; Parapatu
mu'āmala (social duties), 65
Muhammad, Aminuddin, 114
Muhammad b. Abdullah, 86–87
Muhammad b. Adjurrum, 42
Muhammad b. 'Asim, 42
Muhashamy-Said, Bi Swafiya, 22, 195–96, 196–201, 201–10
Mujabo, Momade Sayyid, 105
al-Mundhirī, Muḥammad, 142
Muridiyya, 173–74, 174–78, 181–83, 184–86, 189–90, 301–2n11. See also Sufism
Muslim Academy (Zanzibar), 144, 146, 147
Muslim World League, 131, 186
mwalimus: and the integrated madrasa curriculum, 195; and Islamic education in Zanzibar, 137, 140, 142–46, 147nn3–4; and madrasas of Angoche City, 108–14; and Portuguese colonialism, 98; and Qur'anic schools of Angoche, 105. See also ulama
mysticism (taṣawwuf), 65, 175, 216, 223, 258, 265n8
Nābigha al Ghallāwī, 63
Nacala region (Mozambique), 103
Nagima, 97
Nampula (Mozambique), 95–96, 102, 104
Nana Asma'u, 14

al-Nasser, Gamal 'Abd, 131, 135, 184
neman ilimi (seeking knowledge), 238, 250
Neves, F. A. da Silva, 98, 111
Ngome, Charles, 196
Niamey (Niger): and Islamic education in Niger, 292, 294, 295–96, 297–99; and makarantu of Niger, 22, 234–36, 236–37, 239–41, 241–42; and mobility of Islamic learning, 245–49
Niasse, Abdoulaye, 271
Niasse, Ibrahim, 80, 185, 271
Niasse, Muhammad, 271
Niasse, Sidy Lamine, 268n, 271–74, 280
Niezen, Ronald, 293
Niger: and "bookending" schooling, 23, 294, 297–99, 299–300; classical education in, 23; context of Islamic education in, 236–39; continuity and change of education in, 288–94; contrasting education systems in, 294–99; and izala reform, 251n3; and labor migration, 301n7; and makarantu, 22, 234–36, 236–37, 239–41, 241–42; and marabout term, 300n2; and mobility of Islamic learning, 244–46; plurality of education options, 285–87; and Qur'anic schools of Mauritania, 65; and role of labor in Qur'anic education, 297–99, 302n11; and rote learning, 301n5; and youth study groups, 247–49, 249–51. See also Kiota; Maradi; Niamey
Nigeria, Northern: and Arab outreach, 130–33; background of education in, 119–20; and British Indirect Rule, 120, 121–25; and clash of competing education systems, 7, 9; Department of Education, 123; and Falke's influence on education, 88; First Republic, 132; importation of Islamic teachers, 21–22; Nigerian agency during colonial rule, 125–30; Northern People's Congress, 127–28; Northern Provinces Law School, 9, 124, 126; Protectorate of, 121–22, 138–39; and women in clerical lineages, 14. See also Hausa people and language; Ilorin; Lagos
njebbel (submission through work), 301–2n11

O'Brien, Donal B. Cruise, 176
oral transmission, 42, 68–69, 72–73, 74–75. See also memorization; recitation
Orientale province (DRC), 164, 165
Pakistan, 132
pan-Islamism, 6, 102, 131, 134, 178, 272
Parapatu (Mozambique), 95
payments to teachers, 52, 56n28, 111, 240

Penda (media figure), 278-79, 280
piety movements, 17. *See also* reformism
pilgrimages *(ḥajj)*: and the al-Azhar school network, 177, 179; and Islamic education in the DRC, 158; and Islamic education in Niger, 251n1, 296-97; and Islamic education in Northern Nigeria, 119, 126, 128-29, 130, 134; and Qur'anic schools of Mauritania, 65
Pinto Correia, Armando, 99, 102-3
Piscatori, James, 17, 105-6
poetry: and clerical lineages, 14; and competing knowledge systems in Kenya, 220; and educational pluralism, 30; and Islamic education in Senegal and Côte d'Ivoire, 256; and Qur'anic schools of Angoche, 97, 111; and Qur'anic schools of Mauritania, 65, 66-67; and women in Islamic education, 43
Portugal. *See* colonialism, Portuguese
Pouwels, Randall L., 216, 227n7
prayer *(salat)*: and the al-Azhar school network, 179; and book study in West Africa, 41-42, 43; and Falke's influence on education, 82, 86; and Hadhrami tradition in Kenya, 224; and the integrated madrasa curriculum, 201, 206; and Islamic education in Senegal and Côte d'Ivoire, 256-57, 259-60, 261; and *makarantu* of Niger, 235, 237, 239-40; and Muslim public figures in West Africa, 275, 277; and pupil/master relationship, 13; and Qur'anic schools of Angoche, 110-11; and Qur'anic schools of Mauritania, 62, 64-66, 70-71, 73, 75; and school schedules, 34; and Senegalese politics, 191n21; and youth study groups, 247
primary schools. *See* education, elementary
private schools, 18-19, 110, 138
pronunciation, 33, 70. *See also* recitation
proselytization, 112
Protectorate of Northern Nigeria, 121-22, 138-39
Protestants, 153, 157, 166
purification *(ṭahāra)*, 65, 181, 258

qāḍī (qāḍī), 147
Qadiriyya: and Islamic education in the DRC, 155; and Islamic education in Zanzibar, 138; and Muslim public figures in West Africa, 278-79; and Qur'anic schools of Angoche, 100, 104, 107, 110. *See also* Sufism
Qalun, 55n14
al-Qaradawi, Yusuf, 273
al-Qayrawani, 'Abd Allah b. Abi Zayd, 41-42, 65-66, 69

Quartier Abidjan Makaranta, 239-41, 245-46, 247
al-Qurtubi, Yahya, 41

race, 7, 103, 106-7, 201, 218, 229n29
Ramadan and 'Id al-fitr, 34-36, 40, 65, 147, 156
rationalism, 173, 262-63, 274, 289
reading, 38-39, 53, 68-69
recitation: and elementary Qur'anic study, 36-37, 39; and examinations, 15; and Falke, 79; and higher education in Kenya, 230n47; and the integrated madrasa curriculum, 201; and Islamic education in Senegal and Côte d'Ivoire, 255-57; and Qur'anic schools of Mauritania, 63, 67, 68-69, 69-71; and styles of Islamic education in West Africa, 29; and transitions to advanced studies, 40, 41; variants of recitation systems, 55n14. *See also* curricula
reformism: and competing knowledge systems in Kenya, 221; and Islamic education in Niger, 292, 297; and Islamic education in Senegal and Côte d'Ivoire, 256, 257, 261-62, 263-64; and Islamic radicalism, 120; and mobility of Islamic learning, 244-45; and Muslim public figures in West Africa, 268-70, 273-74, 275-77, 276-77, 279, 280, 281n3; re-Islamization, 250. *See also* Islamism; piety movements; Salafism; Wahhabis
Reichmuth, Stefan, 114
repetition, 69
République Démocratique du Congo Ministère du Plan, 168n7
Reveil Islamique (Islamic awakening), 180-81
Ribat al-Riyadh, 138, 217, 218
Risāla (al-Qayrawānī), 41-42, 65-66
Riyadh mosque-college, 215-17, 218, 222-23, 229n24
Robinson, Francis, 270
Romero, Patricia W., 215-16
rote learning, 261, 290, 301n5. *See also* memorization
Rouch, Jean, 301n7

saint worship, 216, 279
Salafism, 106, 178, 268, 279. *See also* reformism
Salih, 'Aydarus b. Habib, 222
Salih, Habib, 215, 216, 219, 222, 227
Ṣāliḥ, Sharif Aḥmad b., 80
Salih b. 'Alawi, 214
San (Mali), 31, 34
sanin adini (knowing Islam), 238

Sanneh, Lamin, 47, 259, 290
Santé, Ami, 160–61
Santerre, Renaud, 4, 29–30
Sanusi, Muhammad as-, 41
Saudi Arabia: and the al-Azhar school network, 179; and competing knowledge systems in Kenya, 219; and Islamic education in the DRC, 158; and Islamic education in Niger, 292; and Islamic education in Northern Nigeria, 131, 132; and Islamic education in Zanzibar, 147; and Muslim public figures in West Africa, 273, 278; and Qur'anic schools of Angoche, 106
Sawi, Ahmad as-, 44
schools: accreditation of schools, 18–19, 152; Ahmadu Bello University, 132; Anglo-Arabic schools, 263; Arab Boys School, 196; *arbita*, 216–17, 224, 226, 228n21; "bookending" schooling, 23, 294, 297–99, 299–300; Chuo Cha Kiislamu (School of Islam), 146; *daara tarbiyya* (working schools), 175–76, 182; Department of Arabic and Islamic Studies, University of Ibadan, 132; diplomas, 46, 262; and disciplinary practices in education, 48; fees, 11, 49, 162, 179, 185–86, 202, 242, 274; Franco-Arabic schools, 19–20, 185, 263, 290, 292, 294, 296–97, 298, 299; Fulfulde medium schools, 35, 39; Gordon College, 123–24, 126; Hamza bin Rashid secondary school, 108; Institut Hodari, 165; Integrated Islamic Nursery, 203; Katsina College, 124, 127; mission schools, 1–2, 7–8, 12, 14–15, 17; Mombasa Institute of Muslim Education, 219; Muslim Academy (Zanzibar), 144, 146, 147; night classes, 34–35, 64, 246–47, 296; primary schools, 163, 164; private schools, 18–19, 110, 138; public, 161–65; and recruitment of students, 31; Riyadh mosque-college, 215–17, 218, 222–23, 229n24; schedules of, 16, 30, 34–36, 38–39, 49, 55n10, 240, 246, 247; School for Arabic Studies, 9, 124, 126, 128, 129, 131; school types in West Africa, 33; "school wars," 152–55, 154–55; secondary schools, 163; Sir Bin Ali Primary School, 196; Teacher Training College, 143; Vorabia school, 179; Waterval Islamic Institute, 109–10, 112, 114. *See also* madrasas; state schools; universities, Islamic
Seeseman, Rüdiger, 22
Segou (Mali): and book study in West Africa, 42–45; and disciplinary practices in education, 49; and economics of Islamic education, 50, 52, 53; and elementary Qur'anic study, 36; and Muslim public figures in West Africa, 274; and recognition of educational achievements, 47; and school types in West Africa, 31–32, 34; and styles of Islamic education in West Africa, 29; and transitions to advanced studies, 40
Senegal: and the al-Azhar school network, 22, 173; and discipline in Islamic education, 257–59; and Islamic education in Senegal and Côte d'Ivoire, 261; Islamic madrasas in, 178–81; and Muslim public figures in West Africa, 23, 270, 280; and school types in West Africa, 32; Sengalese Hizbullah, 271; and sources on Qur'anic education, 264n3. *See also* Daaru ālim Ul-khabīr; Dakar; Mbake Bawol; Muridiyya; Touba (Senegal)
Services for Centralization and Coordination of Information (SCCIM), 104, 106
servile groups, 298
Shadhuliyya, 44, 100, 104, 110, 228n11. *See also* Sufism
Shagari, Shehu, 127
shahada (profession of faith), 257
sharia, 112, 125, 271
Shariff, Uthman, 145
Shia, 207, 213, 268. *See also* Ismailis
al-Shingīṭī, Sharīf Aḥmad b. Muḥammad al-Amīn, 80
Sīdī'Abdallah, 70–71
as-Sijilmāsī, SīdīAhmad al-ḥabīb al-Lamṭī, 71
silsilas (spiritual genealogies), 72, 81–82, 88–89, 105, 260
Siyaan, Njote, 182
Soares, Benjamin, 22–23, 106
Sokoto Caliphate, 14, 121, 127–28, 132
Somalia, 224
Songhay people and language, 40, 44, 54–55n6
Soninke, 38, 39, 44
Sounaye, Abdoulaye, 22
Sousa, Hortênsio Estevão de, 103
Starrett, Gregory, 17
state schools: and clash of competing education systems, 8; and competing knowledge systems in Kenya, 218; and decolonization of education systems, 17–20; and disciplinary practices in education, 47–48; and economics of Islamic education, 51; and elementary Qur'anic study, 36; incorporation of Islamic education, 22; and Islamic education in the DRC, 150, 152, 154, 157, 164; and Islamic educa-

tion in Northern Nigeria, 129; and Islamic education in Zanzibar, 144; and Muslim public figures in West Africa, 271; and postcolonial African education, 11; and Qur'anic schools of Angoche, 107–8; and school schedules, 34–35; and school types in West Africa, 32; and styles of Islamic education in West Africa, 30; and Westernization of Qur'anic schools, 53
stereotypes, 21
Stewart, Charles, 83–84
Stoller, Paul, 300n1, 301n7
structural adjustment, 2, 161–62, 263
Subbanu-l-Muslimīn, 9–10, 129, 183, 239, 247–48, 251n3. *See also* reformism
submission in Islam, 13, 255, 298, 301–2n11
Sudan: and the al-Azhar school network, 179; and book study in West Africa, 44; and clash of competing education systems, 9; and competing knowledge systems in Kenya, 219; and export of Islamic teachers, 21–22; and Islamic education in Niger, 295; and Islamic education in Northern Nigeria, 119–20, 121–25, 126, 128–30, 131–32, 133–34; and Islamic education in Zanzibar, 147; and Muslim public figures in West Africa, 271, 273; and Qur'anic schools of Angoche, 96, 107, 108; and school types in West Africa, 32
Sufism: and the al-Azhar school network, 173–74, 175–78, 180, 183, 189; Araic term for, 265n8; association of Qur'anic schools, 13; and book study in West Africa, 44; and chains of transmission, 228n11; changing roles of Sufi leaders, 281n4; Chistiyya, 107; and combined education systems, 10; and competing knowledge systems in Kenya, 220; and decolonization of education systems, 21; *dhikr*, 100, 105–6, 111, 147, 176, 228n18; and Falke's influence on education, 80–81, 82–83, 84, 86–87; and Hadhrami tradition in Kenya, 214–15, 225; and higher education in Kenya, 230n47; and Islamic education in the DRC, 155, 166; and Islamic education in Niger, 289, 295, 296; and Islamic education in Northern Nigeria, 129, 134; and Islamic education in Senegal and Côte d'Ivoire, 259, 261; and Islamic education in Zanzibar, 138, 147; Ittifaq, 110; and *izala* reform, 251n3; Madaniyya, 110; and the Majlis Ousman Dan Fodio, 243; and *makarantu* of Niger, 239; and Muslim public figures in West Africa, 268–70, 271–74, 276–79; Nizamiyya, 127; and Qur'anic schools of Angoche, 100–101, 102, 104–7, 107–12, 114; and Qur'anic schools of Korhogo, 23n9; "Rasta" Sufis, 278; and religious texts, 228n8; Shadhuliyya, 44, 100, 104, 110, 228n11; *tariqa*, 83, 100, 105, 107, 109–11, 214; *tasawuff*, 65, 175, 216, 223, 258, 265n8; Uwaysiyya, 104; Yashrutiyya, 104, 110. *See also* Muridiyya; Qadiriyya; Tijaniyya
suivisme, 242–44
*sukuti*s, 105
Sultan Bello Mosque, 128
Sumayṭ, Aḥmad b., 138, 142
Sunna, 248
Sunni Islam, 62, 206–7, 213, 268
suras: and book study in West Africa, 46; and elementary Qur'anic study, 37–38; and Islamic education in Niger, 290; and Muslim public figures in West Africa, 271; and Qur'anic schools of Angoche, 110; and Qur'anic schools of Mauritania, 63–64, 68–69, 69–70, 75; and transitions to advanced studies, 40
Suware, al-Hadj Salim, 56n23
as-Suyuti, Djalal ad-Din, 44
Swafiya, Bi. *See* Muhashamy-Said, Bi Swafiya
Swahili people and language, 229n29; and competing knowledge systems in Kenya, 217, 219; and the integrated madrasa curriculum, 195, 196, 201, 204, 206; and Islamic education in Zanzibar, 139; and Qur'anic schools of Angoche, 95, 97, 99, 104, 114; Swahili Arabs, 155–56, 159; Swahili Islam, 221
Sy, Elhaj Malick, 180
Sylla, Khadim, 190n9

tafsir (Qur'anic exegesis): and the al-Azhar school network, 176, 186; and book study in West Africa, 44–45, 56n23; and clerical lineages, 14; and combined education systems, 9; and Falke's influence on education, 83, 86; and Hadhrami tradition in Kenya, 223; and higher education in Kenya, 230n47; and Islamic education in Senegal and Côte d'Ivoire, 256; and Qur'anic schools of Mauritania, 65; and styles of Islamic education in West Africa, 54–55n6, 54n6; and transitions to advanced studies, 40
Ṭāhir b. AbūBakr al-Amawī, 142
al-Tahtawi, Rifaʿa, 212
tajwīd (chanting), 71, 76n13, 186
takfiriyyun, 225
Tal, Ahmad b. al-Hadj 'Umar, 43, 133

talibés (students), 257–58, 261, 264n3, 265n12, 295, 301n10
Tamari, Tal, 21, 31, 290
al-Tanwājīwī, Sīdī'Abdallah wuld Abū Bakr, 70
Tanzania, 103, 196, 224, 226, 269, 272
taqlid (imitation), 10, 72, 85
tarbiyya (mentoring), 82, 175–76, 258, 298
tawhid (theology), 14, 41–46, 108, 186, 205, 223, 230n47
teachers' unions, 162
technology of education, 23, 23n3
Terray, Emmanuel, 301–2n11
Thurston, Alex, 21
al-Tijani, Ahmad, 86–87
Tijaniyya, 79–81, 86, 88–89, 173, 271, 274, 302n11. *See also* Sufism
Timbuktu (Mali): and book study in West Africa, 42–43; and clash of competing education systems, 8; and disciplinary practices in education, 47–48; and economics of Islamic education, 49, 51–52; and elementary Qur'anic study, 36–38; and school schedules, 34–35; and school types in West Africa, 31, 32; and styles of Islamic education in West Africa, 29, 55n6; and transitions to advanced studies, 40
Tippo Tip, 155, 159
Titeca, Kristof, 166
Torah study, 76n14
Touba (Guinea): and disciplinary practices in education, 47; and economics of Islamic education, 50, 52; and growth of Islamic education, 54n5; and recognition of educational achievements, 46; and school schedules, 34, 36; and school types in West Africa, 32–33; and styles of Islamic education in West Africa, 29, 54n6; and transitions to advanced studies, 39, 41
Touba (Senegal): and the al-Azhar school network, 177, 181, 183–85, 190; and Islamic education in Senegal and Côte d'Ivoire, 258; and Senegalese politics, 191n21; and sources on Qur'anic education, 264n3
Toure, Cheikh, 180, 183–85
Toure, Hady, 180
traditionalism, 221–26, 225, 256, 257, 260
transmission of knowledge: 'Alawi teachings on, 228n11; and combined education systems, 10; continuity in oral transmission, 72–73; and Falke's influence on education, 82, 89; and *ijaza*, 264n7; and Islamic education in Senegal and Côte d'Ivoire, 260–61, 263; in Mauritania, 69–75; and Qur'anic schools of Angoche, 100, 105; and Qur'anic schools of Mauritania, 72, 74–75; writing vs. oral, 74–75
Trarza region (Mauritania), 66
Triaud, Jean-Louis, 6
trilingual education, 204
Trimingham, John Spencer, 216, 227n7
Tuareg people and language, 31, 79, 119, 296–97
tuition, 11, 298. *See also* payments to teachers
al-Tunisi, Muhammad, 44
al-Turabi, Hasan, 273
tutoring, 74, 81, 235, 241, 246–47
Tuubaa (Senegal). *See* Touba (Senegal)

Uganda, 224
ulama: and the al-Azhar school network, 176, 180; and clash of competing education systems, 6; and competing knowledge systems in Kenya, 219–21; and Falke's influence on education, 86; and Hadhrami tradition in Kenya, 224, 226–27; and hybrid education systems, 17; and Islamic education in Zanzibar, 137, 142; and the Majlis Ousman Dan Fodio, 244; and Muslim public figures in West Africa, 268, 270, 272, 274, 280, 281n3
Umar, Muhammad Sani, 21, 88
United Arab Emirates, 108
United Arab Republic, 129
United Nations: United Nations Development Programme Human Development Index (UNDP HDI), 293; United Nations Educational, Scientific and Cultural Organisation (UNESCO), 156, 188; United Nations Organization Mission in the Democratic Republic of the Congo (MONUC), 160
universities, Islamic: Abdou Moumouni University (Niger), 246, 247; Ahmadu Bello University (Nigeria), 132; Islamic Universities of Algeria, 107; Islamic University of Medina, 105–7, 131, 177, 247, 278; Islamic University of Ndaam, 189; Jamiyat al-Dawa al-Islamiyya (Libya), 107; al-Merkaz (Sudan), 107; University of Bamako (Mali), 32; University of Jordan, 131. *See also* schools
Urdjuzat al-wildan, 41
Usman dan Fodio, 14, 83, 128, 133, 241–43, 245, 247
ustaz, 244, 246
Villalón, Leonardo, 268n
Vischer, Hanns, 126
vyou tradition, 202–3

Wade, Abdoulaye, 191n21
Wahhabis: and competing knowledge systems in Kenya, 219; and Hadhrami tradition in Kenya, 223; and higher education in Kenya, 230n46; and Islamic education in Niger, 291–92; and Islamic education in Zanzibar, 147; and Muslim public figures in West Africa, 276; and Qur'anic schools of Angoche, 104–7, 112; and school types in West Africa, 33; and *takfir* practice, 225. *See also* reformism
Wal Fadjri, 271–72
waqf (endowments), 87, 147, 186, 189, 238
Ware, Rudolph, 3, 22, 257–58, 290, 296
waungwana, 215
Weber, Max, 10, 11, 270
West Africa, 12, 44–45, 268–80
Wilks, Ivor, 46, 56n23
Wolof people and language, 55n12, 175, 177, 258
women and Islamic education: and the al-Azhar school network, 184, 187–88; female teachers, 62; feminism, 268; gender roles, 245–46; hijab, 245; and the integrated madrasa curriculum, 195, 196–99, 209; and Islamic education in the DRC, 152, 160–61; and Islamic education in Niger, 22, 234–35, 236–37, 239–41, 241–44, 245–46, 248, 249–50, 251n1, 296–97; and *makarantu* of Niger, 234–35, 236, 239–41, 251n1; and Muslim public figures in West Africa, 268, 277–80; and piety movements, 17; and Qur'anic schools of Angoche, 97, 111; and Qur'anic schools of Mauritania, 66; and school types in West Africa, 33–34; tutoring, 74; women as Sufi leaders, 110. *See also* Muhashamy-Said, Bi Swafiya
World Bank, 162–63, 263
World War II, 142, 150, 154, 197
writing boards: compared with blackboards, 3–5; and decolonization of education systems, 18, 20; and elementary Qur'anic study, 37, 38–39; and hybrid education systems, 16; and Islamic education in Niger, 295–96; and Islamic education in Senegal and Côte d'Ivoire, 255, 262; and Qur'anic schools of Angoche, 98; and Qur'anic schools of Mauritania, 61–63, 64–65, 67–68, 68–69, 74; and rote learning, 301n5; and theoretical consideration for study, 1–3. *See also* education, classical Islamic
wuld al-Aqil, Aḥmad, 63

Yadālī, Muḥammad, 70
Yashrutiyya, 104, 110
Yates, A., 75
Yattara, Almamy Malik, 48, 50
Yemen, 22, 131
Yoruba, 9
Young, Crawford, 154, 155–56
Youngstedt, Scott, 295
youth groups, 247–49
Yusufiyya, 13

Zahrān, Aḥmad, 143
zakat (religious tax), 65, 295
Zaman, Muhammad Qasim, 281n3
Zanzibar: and the al-Azhar school network, 176; and clash of competing education systems, 6, 8–9; and competing knowledge systems in Kenya, 219; Department of Education, 139, 144, 147n3; and East African Muslim networks, 213; and Hadhrami tradition in Kenya, 214, 221; and hybridization of education system, 16, 22; and the integrated madrasa curriculum, 196, 208; Islamic education in, 137–47, 147n3; and Islamic education in Northern Nigeria, 120, 131; and Muslim public figures in West Africa, 270; and Qur'anic schools of Angoche, 96–97, 105; racial distinctions in, 229n29; Revolutionary Government, 137; Zanzibar National Archives, 137
Zarma people and language, 286–87, 292, 297, 300n1, 301n10
ziyara, 106, 277, 279

www.ingramcontent.com/pod-product-compliance
Lightning Source LLC
Chambersburg PA
CBHW030334240426
43661CB00052B/1627